Elvis™

Elvis Presley
aus dem CinemaScope-Film
THMUS HINTER GITTE
Foto MGM

Elvis™

A CELEBRATION

IMAGES OF ELVIS PRESLEY® FROM THE ELVIS PRESLEY ARCHIVE AT GRACELAND®

MIKE EVANS

This edition published in 2007

The Ivy Press
The Old Candlmakers
West Street, Lewes
East Sussex BN7 2NZ, UK
www.ivy-group.co.uk

Creative Director: Peter Bridgewater
Publisher: Sophie Collins
Editorial Director: Steve Luck
Design: Clare Barber
Editor: Stephanie Horner

Printed and bound in China

Contents

[1935–1977]

"Elvis is the greatest cultural force in the 20th century. He introduced the beat to everything, music, language, clothes, it's a whole new social revolution." – *Leonard Bernstein*

OK, so that was going too far. The man who conducted the New York Philharmonic and composed the music for *West Side Story* should have known better. Elvis simply didn't "introduce the beat to everything," but he was the first to acknowledge the roots of his music in blues, gospel, hillbilly and all the other rhythmically based popular music that America had created through the first half of the 20th century.

Likewise, the jive-talk language and sharp clothes that were adopted by Elvis and other early rock'n'rollers—and soon taken up by the newly identified generation of "teenagers"— weren't invented overnight, but had their basis in the bebop slang and zoot-suit fashions of big city jazz musicians in the 1940s.

Having said that, Bernstein was right about Elvis being an incalculable cultural force. It's hard now to appreciate the total impact Elvis had on what we loosely call popular culture, that melting pot of music, art, literature, attitudes, and manners that found its most vital catalyst and dynamo for change in the America of the last century. And, like Louis Armstrong, Jackson Pollock, Scott Fitzgerald, cowboy movies, and boogie woogie, Elvis and his music were uniquely American; it just wouldn't have happened, couldn't have happened, anywhere else.

In that media-driven century that has so recently come to a close, the century of the photograph, motion pictures, and television as well as records and radio, image was all important. The visual record of people and events that burned onto the mass consciousness was more potent than newsprint, more memorable even than the intimate voices of radio pioneers who gave us history as it happened over the airwaves. When his music exploded on an unsuspecting world in the early weeks of 1956, the first impression most people got of Elvis Presley, other than the almost hypnotic atmosphere of "Heartbreak Hotel," were the black-and-white photographs of the "Hillbilly Cat" in action. And in many ways the still camera, creating innumerable images frozen for all time, was the medium that defined Elvis as icon throughout the rest of his life.

From the image that for millions was the first glimpse of Elvis, mouth open, legs apart (which appeared waist up on his debut album)—it was clear that here was something different. Was he playing that guitar, or making love to it? Those pants looked like they were going to split at any moment! Was he singing, or shouting, was this a musical performance or some act of defiant celebration? Actually it was both—when that picture swiftly found its way around the world, the lines were drawn. Things were never going to be the same again.

The early television appearances, beamed coast to coast across a stunned-into-silence America, certainly upset a lot of adult folk, and got the kids on their toes, but these were mere flickering box-in-the-corner images compared to the real thing. Curiously the combination of the records themselves and an increasing flood of photographs was far more potent propaganda for the rock'n'roll revolution.

RCA Records soon caught on to this. Every new signing to the label would have the obligatory picture session for publicity purposes, but from the start they sensed that this kid from Tennessee looked different. The first time he hit their studios in New York City there was a photoshoot that revealed the strange beauty of the guy, looking into that big black microphone like a million females would want him to look at them. From Arkansas to Australia, bedroom walls were soon covered with that look. Wallpaper manufacturers, along with big band crooners, righteous preachers, teachers, and parents, held up their hands in horror.

Compared to TV, still in its infancy, the movies were a different matter. Here was a chance for the mass of people, in and outside the US, to see him move for the first time. But his first movie, *Love Me Tender*, was in truth something of an anticlimax as far as seeing the real Elvis was concerned. He played his part convincingly, and brought tears to the eyes of fans when he died at the end, but it was a never-ending chronicle of photographs that recorded the phenomenon that was barnstorming across America in the wildest series of live performances ever seen in the history of show business.

On stage, backstage, on trains, in hotel rooms, signing autographs, eating in diners, meeting the press, sitting exhausted with just his thoughts; we see more of the true Elvis in moments captured by photographers, photojournalists, and fans than in all his Hollywood output played end to end. Possibly the most memorable visual set-piece in any of his movies, the title song sequence in *Jailhouse Rock*, was only truly rendered an icon in the still images that were subsequently reproduced forever after.

Even during the mid-Sixties, the so-called “movie years” of Elvis’ career, when his professional activity was restricted to the relative privacy of recording and film studios, the photographers’ zoom lenses and flashguns were omnipresent, reporting Elvis’ every move possible, public or private. Elvis’ private life was in danger of becoming public property by virtue of his absolute fame.

Launched via the by-then all-powerful medium of television, Elvis' celebrated comeback to live performance in the late Sixties heralded a new image, and one that was to be the closest to an unofficial Elvis Presley brand identity in an age of brand identities. Purists and esthetes may not like the fact, but—like Chaplin's bowler hat and cane, and the Beatles' mop top haircuts—the much-caricatured stereotype of white rhinestoned jumpsuit with high collar and cape, wrap-around sunglasses and big sideburns, is without doubt the most popular symbol of Elvis in common currency. This was the Elvis of the cartoonists, and of the thousands of Elvis impersonators who appeared before and after his death. It was an image sustained by a couple of highly charged film documentaries following Elvis in live concert performances, and again in a mountain of photography.

The great Duke Ellington once said music is like a flower: you can't appreciate its beauty by dissecting it; the whole is greater than the sum of its parts. The same can be said of Elvis' contribution to contemporary culture. He was singer, musician, entertainer, actor, but much more than all these put together. The value of everything he did, particularly the records that provided a soundtrack to a period of unprecedented change, is enhanced when seen in the context of the society and lives he touched so fundamentally—and it's in the photographic record that this becomes most apparent; the image of Elvis is universally familiar. It was an image that became one of the cultural hallmarks of the 20th century, the epic saga of his life, from small town Mississippi to the neon-lit Las Vegas of hoofers, high rollers, and Hollywood stars, made real forever in a million photographs.

The pictures reproduced in the pages that follow are just some of them ...

Prologue

CHILD & TEENAGER

[1935–1955]

← 1941 **TUPELO** In striped pants and suspenders, six-year-old Elvis stands in front of the modest rented house the Presleys had moved into at 510½ Maple Street, Tupelo Mississippi, toward the end of 1940.

1941

c 1937

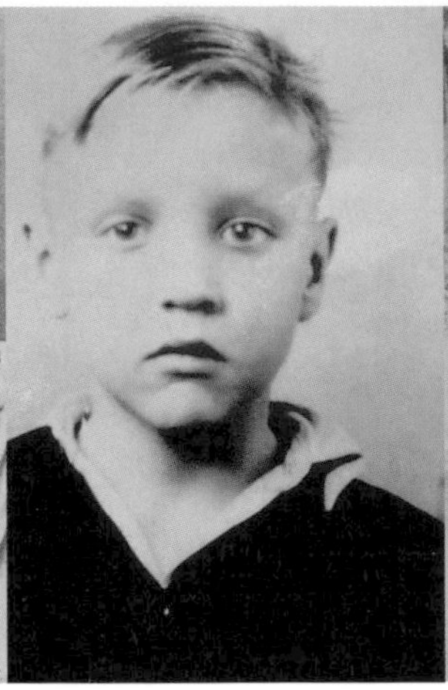

c 1941

c 1950

1935-1955

Tupelo, Mississippi, was deep in sharecropper country back in the 1930s. The land was impoverished, and most of the people were too—Vernon and Gladys Presley were no exception.

The first picture many of us see of the young Elvis, born January 8, 1935, shows him posed between his parents when he was aged just two, all of them staring at the photographer like folks did then, when they didn't get their picture taken too often.

Throughout his childhood Elvis would hear music all around, particularly from the dozens of radio stations that beamed country, gospel, and blues to the local communities. Sometimes, on their Philco Radio Phonograph, the family would tune in to syndicated stations from far afield, either big-name shows networked coast-to-coast or music programs with a regional coverage. The most famous of these in the South were Nashville's Grand Ole Opry and the Shreveport-based Louisiana Hayride.

Despite giving the impression of being a shy youngster, Elvis opened up when it came to performing music, whether entertaining school friends with impromptu guitar sessions during lunchbreaks or appearing at a talent show; all of which would be recalled years later, with varying degrees of accuracy, by those privileged by fate to be there.

1950

1954

1955

Elvis was 13 years old when his parents, after a restless time in various homes in Tupelo, decided to move to the big city. Memphis, 90 miles northwest of Tupelo, sprawls across the southwest corner of Tennessee where the stateline touches Mississippi in the south and Arkansas across the mighty river to the west. With its black blues and white country music, and gospel songs that were common to both communities, Memphis was rich with music for anyone with the ears to listen, and the teenage Elvis was all ears.

He was all eyes too, and soon noticed the way the music-makers dressed, the Western swing players in their wild floral shirts like hipcat cowboys, the bluesmen sharp as knives in zoot suits straight from Lansky's clothes store, on the corner of Second Street and Beale.

The neon-night honky tonk heaven that was Beale Street with its bars and juke joints was long a landmark in the city's historic place as a catalyst in the evolution of blues, and it soon became a magnet for the adolescent kid who still stared at that camera, be-jeaned legs apart holding a toy gun, sitting on the sidewalk with an early girlfriend, or looking ultra-cool in some flash new duds between two highschool buddies.

And very soon, it seemed like the cameras would never go away.

1937

⊕ **c1937 ELVIS AT TWO, AND PARENTS** Gladys Love Smith, born on April 25, 1912, had married Vernon Elvis Presley (four years her junior, born April 10, 1916) on June 17, 1933. Eighteen months later, just before dawn on January 8, 1935, in the small two-room house on Old Saltillo Road, East Tupelo, built by Vernon with the help of his father and brother, she gave birth to twin boys: Jesse Garon and Elvis Aaron. Delivered by Dr. William R. Hunt, Jesse Garon was stillborn at 4.00 AM, to be buried the following day in the Priceville Cemetery on the outskirts of town. The second of the twins, Elvis Aaron, was born 35 minutes later.

⊕ **1941 ELVIS AND PARENTS** The picture with Vernon and Gladys outside their clapboard house on Maple Street, East Tupelo, was taken, along with the one on page 14, around the time Elvis was starting grade school in the fall of 1941, attending the 700 pupil East Tupolo Consolidated School on Lake Street.

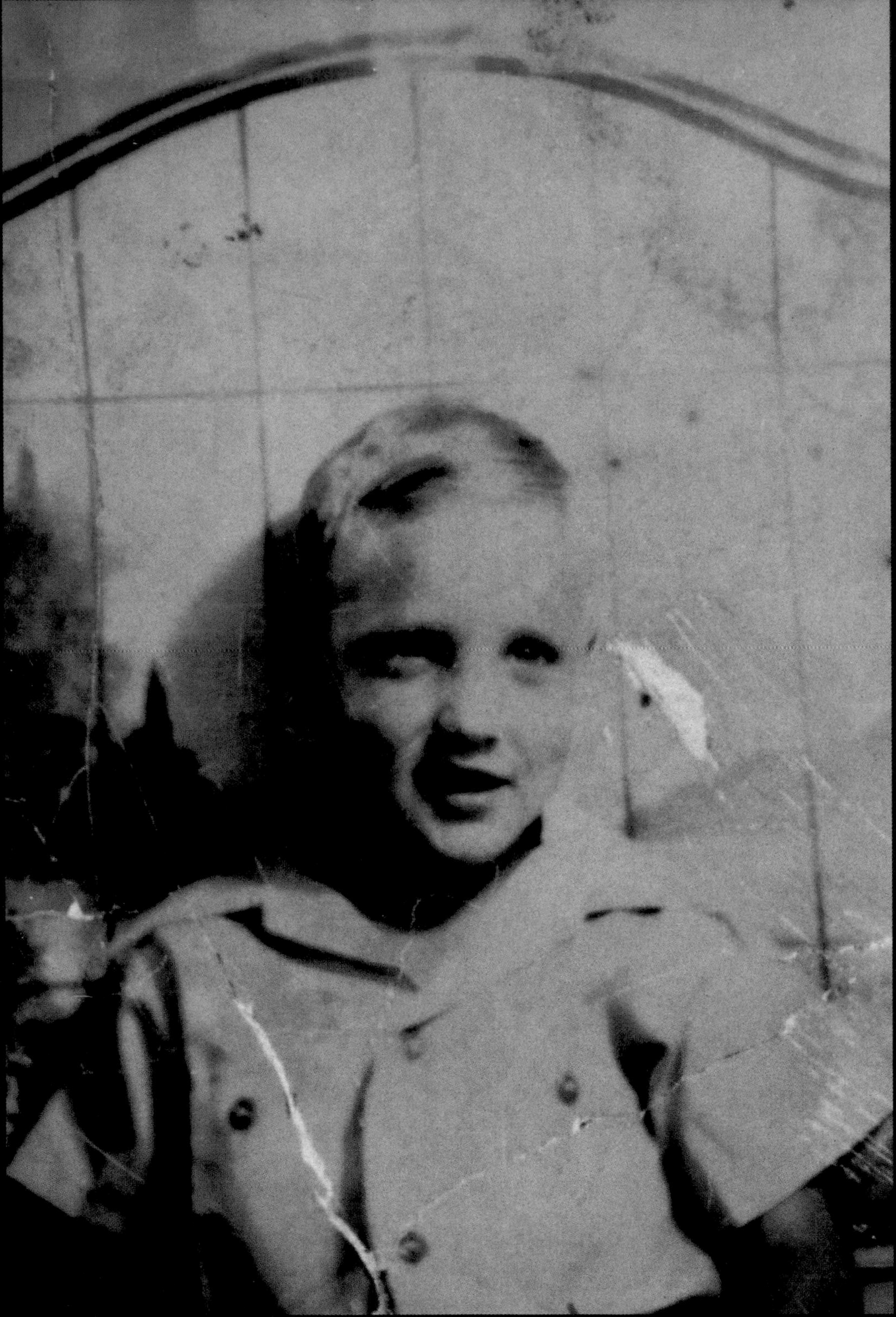

1940 ELVIS AT FIVE It was a turbulent time for the Presleys' fortunes. Vernon was released from a short jail sentence after a minor offence involving–with two others–an alleged forged $4 cheque in payment for a hog. The rest of the year saw the family struggling financially while he got back on his feet, no easy thing during the aftermath of the Depression and then the early years of World War II. By the time the young Elvis entered grade school in 1941, his father was more or less regularly in work, though in an itinerant capacity, taking jobs as far afield as Alabama. It wasn't until they moved from Tupelo to Memphis, Tennessee in 1948 that life seemed relatively settled.

c1941 CHILDHOOD Elvis' mother was, if anything, overprotective of her young son, perhaps because his twin brother had not survived. "My mama never let me out of her sight. I couldn't go down to the creek with the other kids. Sometimes when I was little, I used to run off. Mama would whip me, and I thought she didn't love me."

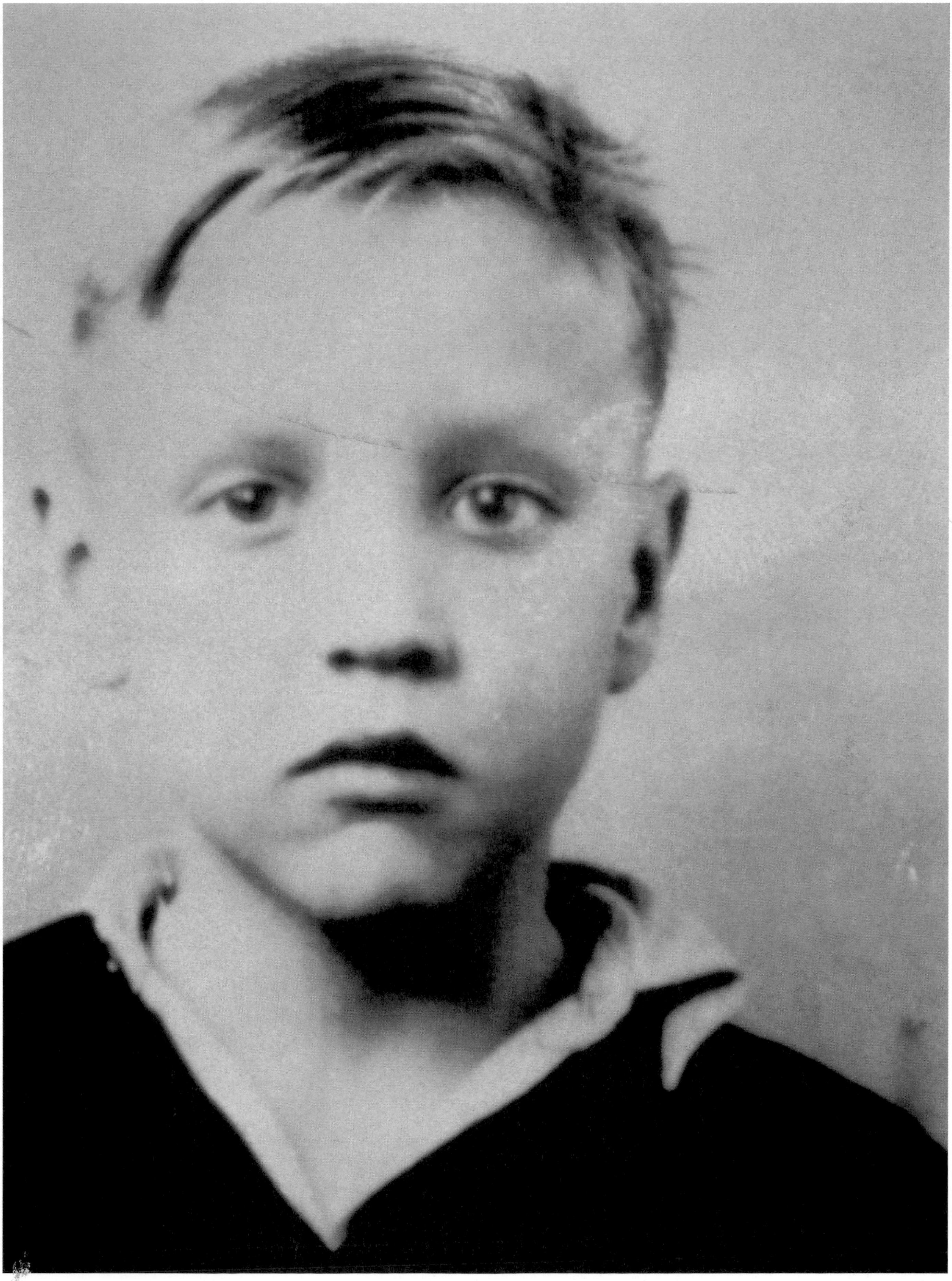

1945

c1945 TUPELO The fact that the young Elvis was increasingly fascinated by music was first evident for sure when he made what was his very first public performance, age ten, on the Children's Day at the annual Mississippi–Alabama Fair and Dairy Show, held at the Fairgrounds in downtown Tupelo. It was October 3, 1945, and Elvis took part in a children's talent contest. Years later he recalled that he came fifth, but that was really of no account to him. He remembered clearly that he had had to stand on a chair to reach the microphone, and that his rendition of the ballad "Old Shep" went down well. Most importantly, it was his first appearance in front of an audience.

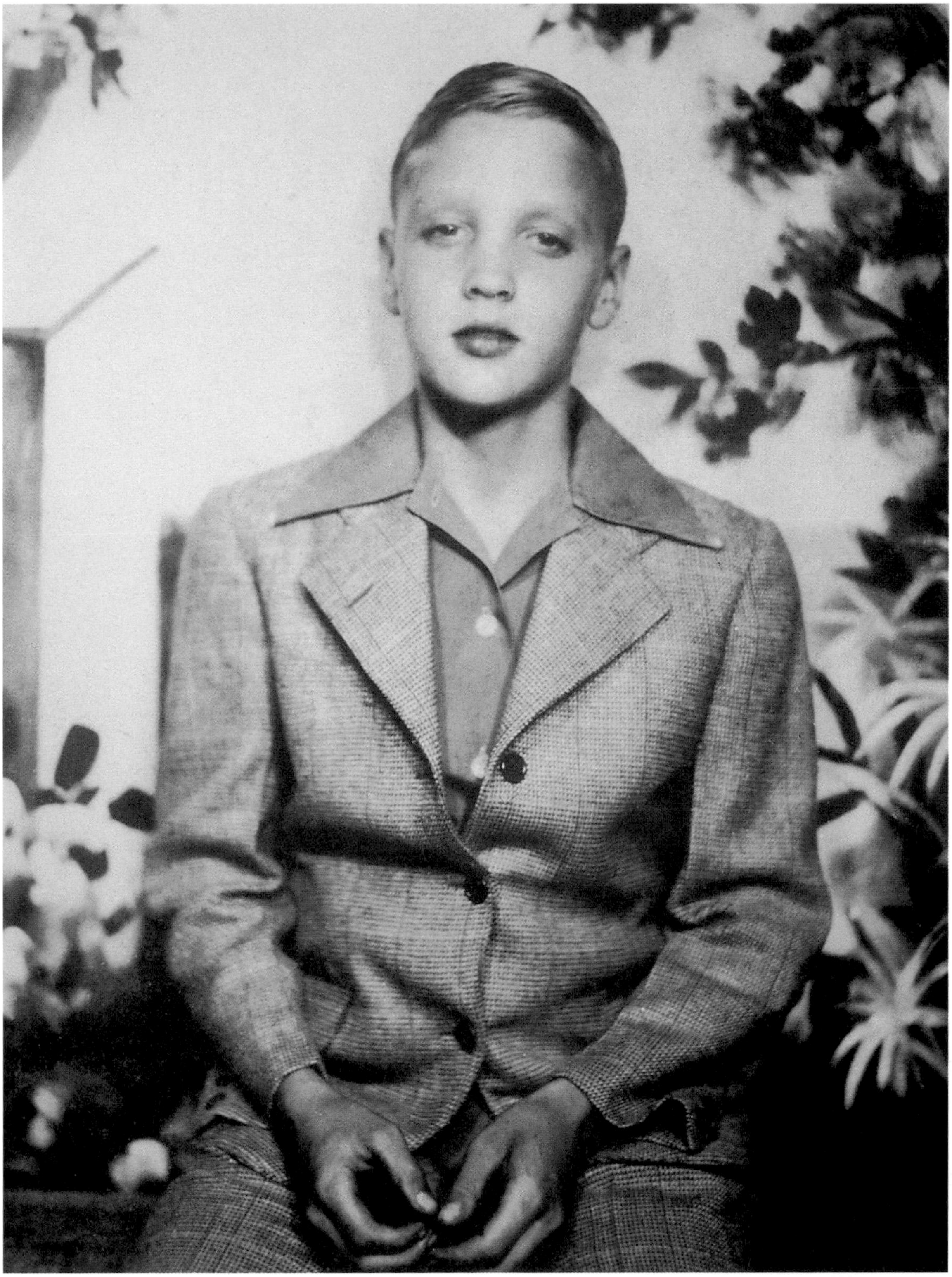

1946 GUITAR MAN Soon after his appearance at the Fair talent contest, just as significantly, Elvis was to get his first guitar. He recalled later on that the reason he sang unaccompanied at the Fair was because he didn't have a guitar at that point, and his mother subsequently bought him one for his eleventh birthday the following January. He had expressed the wish for a bicycle (or a rifle depending on the source), but his mother opted for the guitar–perhaps because she thought it safer, and certainly it was less expensive. Whatever, he was soon absorbing the music and picking up hints by listening to the performers on the Grand Ole Opry radio show, and the local radio "amateur hour" WELO Jamboree.

1946

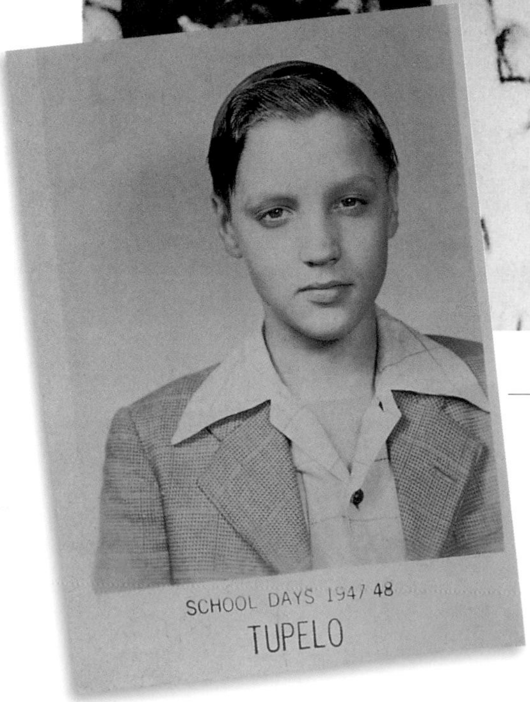

1947 SCHOOL PORTRAIT A school portrait, on the back of which was written: "Elvis Presley 1947–1948 Tupelo, Miss. Tupelo School." It was in his seventh grade year at Milam that Elvis first began taking a guitar to school, strumming for classmates during lunchtimes, and voicing an interest in gospel music and the Grand Ole Opry radio broadcasts.

1947 MILAM JUNIOR HIGH The sixth grade class at Milam Junior High School, at the end of the 1946–47 school year; Elvis *(far right, second row from top)* appears to be the only pupil wearing overalls. He started at Milam in the fall of 1946, a couple of months after the Presleys had moved–yet again–from East Tupelo to the center of town.

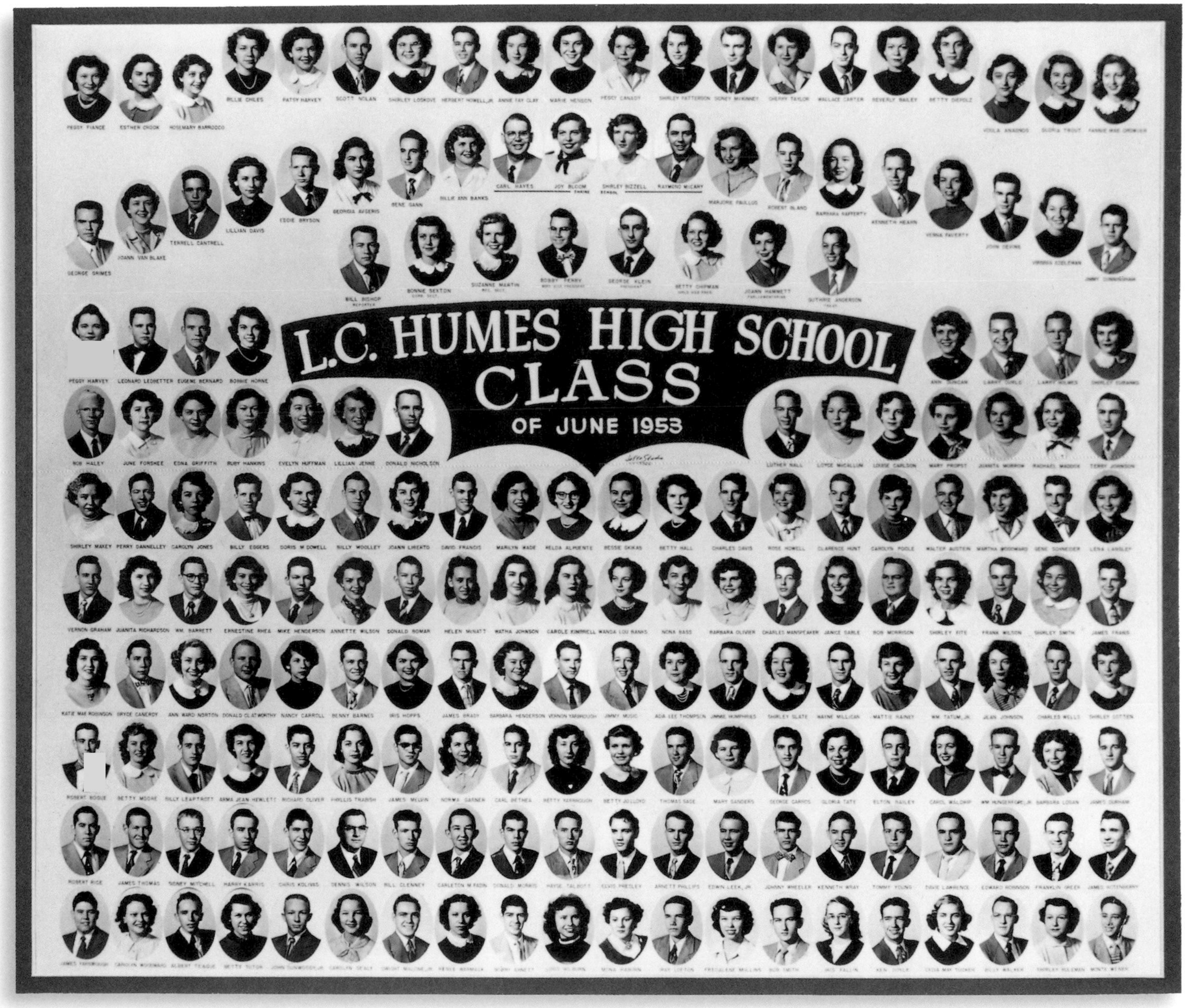

1953 CLASS OF '53 The L. C. Humes High School Class of June 1953, where Elvis' picture can be found in the center of the second row up from the bottom, 11th from the left. Elvis, having entered the school after the family moved to Memphis in November 1948, graduated on June 3, 1953. On April 9, he had performed at the school's annual Minstrel Show–billed as "Guitarist–Elvis Prestly"–singing Theresa Brewer's "Till I Waltz Again With You." He later recalled "When I came on stage I heard people kind of rumbling and whispering and so forth, 'cause nobody knew I even sang. It was amazing how popular I became after that."

1950

➔ **c1950 MEMPHIS SIDEWALK** Elvis sits on a Memphis sidewalk with one of his first regular girlfriends, Betty Anne McMahan, who lived in the same apartment house, the much sought-after public housing project Lauderdale Courts. The Presleys had moved to 185 Winchester, Apartment 328 in the Courts in September 1949. The family had initially migrated to Memphis in November 1948, first settling in Washington Street then moving to Poplar Avenue near the Courts. In an interview years later Elvis recalled how they had moved with all their belongings on top of their '37 Plymouth: "We were broke, man, broke, and we left Tupelo overnight . . . we just headed for Memphis. Things had to be better."

c1950 ROTC CADET Most American high schools in the 1950s had a branch of the Reserve Officers Training Corps attached, a voluntary cadet force that Elvis joined in 1950, when he was in the tenth grade. Years later, when he had become rich and famous, Elvis was to donate new uniforms to his old school's ROTC drill team.

1950 EARLY TEENS Posing with a toy gun outside Lauderdale Courts, the young Elvis is dressed in turned-up jeans and sports-style jacket and starting to look like the real teenager. In fact before the 1950s there were just children, juveniles and then adults; the whole concept of "teenagers" simply hadn't been invented.

1950

1950s

c1951 THE COURTS Another shot taken outside Lauderdale Courts: this time Elvis sports a flowered shirt. He was obviously already developing a dress-consciousness that would become more and more pronounced as he grew into his late teens and started playing music in front of audiences–especially female ones–around Memphis.

c1953–54 THE IMAGE By his late teens Elvis was beginning to look like the rock'n'roll stereotype that he himself created almost single-handedly. Within a year (*see overleaf*) his image had changed from that of a serious-looking adolescent. The sideburns had grown, a quiff had developed, and the hair was slicked back. He was ready to rock.

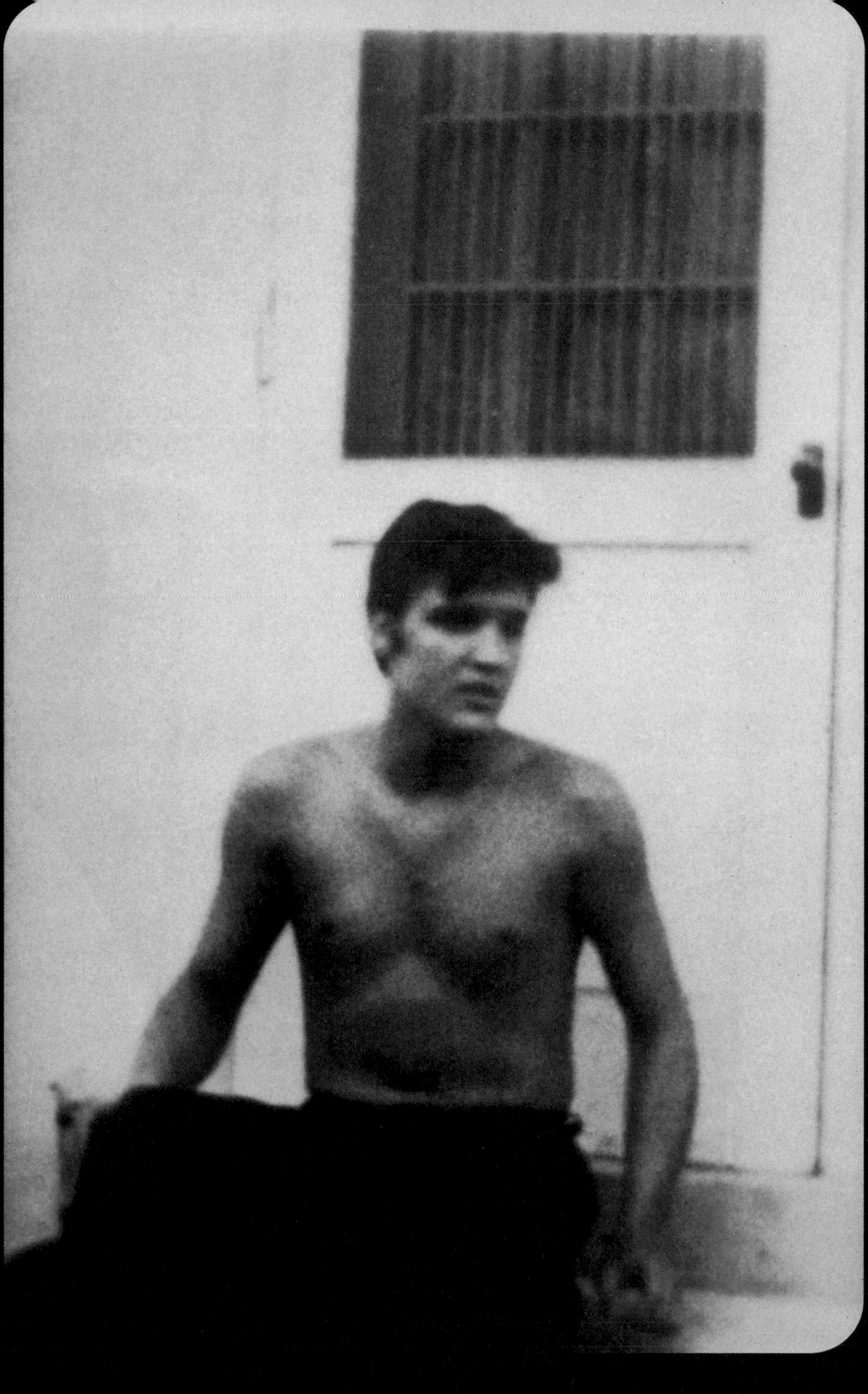

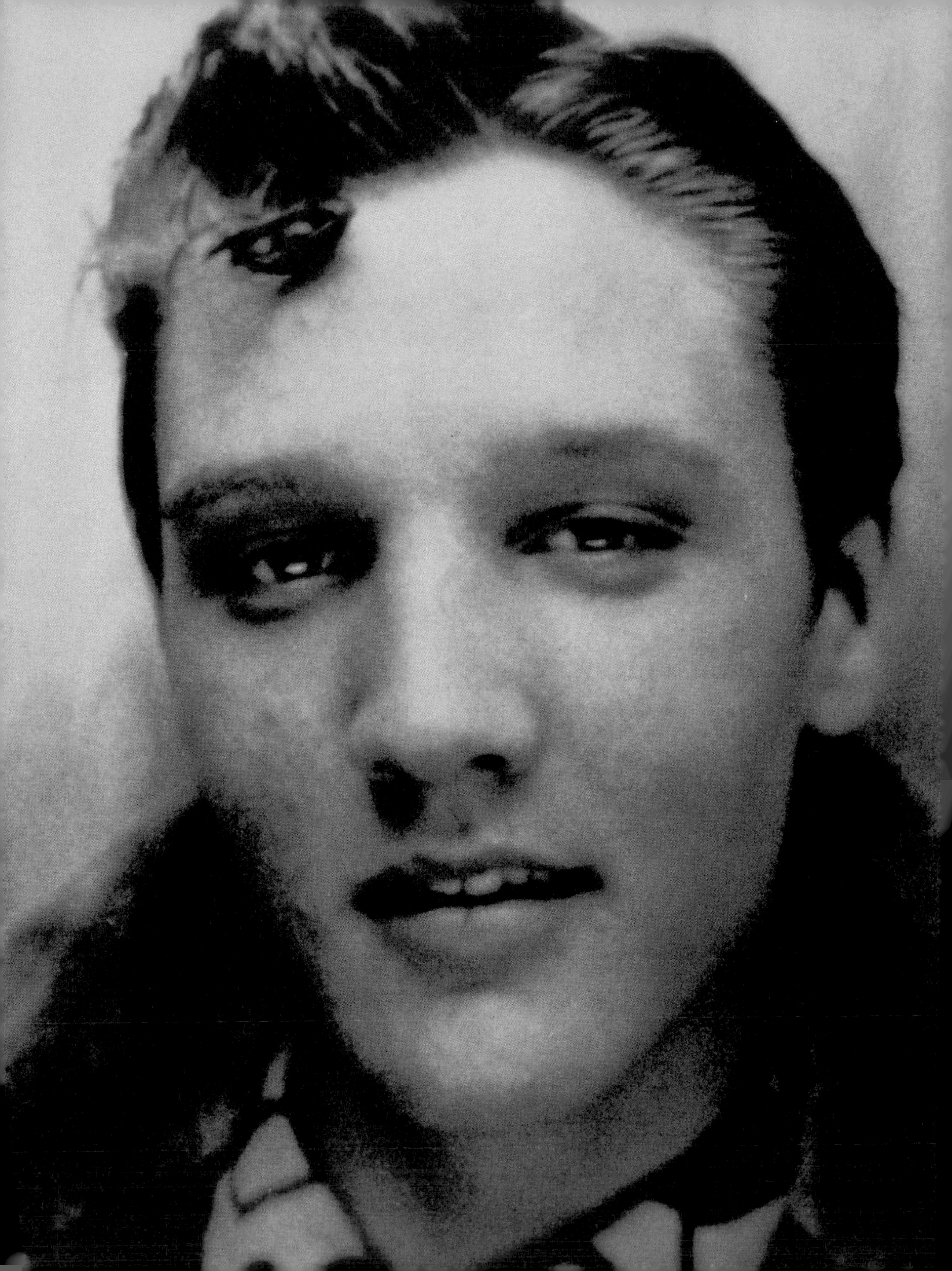

1951 SIXTEEN Just 16 and looking cool with aviator-style fur collar and hair greased, Elvis was developing a look, a way of dressing. It was a hybrid of styles picked up from movie star magazines, flash country singers, and the high-rolling rhythm and blues singers who worked the clubs downtown on Beale Street.

c1953 TEENAGER When the news media in the early Fifties coined the word teenager to describe the growing army of young people with a spending power new to their age group, Elvis' appearance at the time typified what they had in mind–a generation of kids with their own ideas about hair, clothes, and image.

1953

➔ **c1953 ROCKER** Elvis as young rocker. The picture was taken around the time Elvis left high school in 1953. It was used a year or so later as a very early publicity shot when he started releasing records on the Sun label, and playing professionally with Scotty Moore and Bill Black in clubs and dancehalls around the Memphis area.

1953
FAIR
AMUSEMEN

1953 PARDNERS Two cool cowpokes: Elvis and his cousin Gene Smith–who also lived in the city–dressed for the West at the Mid South Fair in Memphis, September 1953. The two spent a lot of leisure time together in their late teen years, and also worked together briefly at the Precision Tool Company in Memphis.

1954 BUDDIES One year later on, and life is changing fast. By now a budding rock'n'roll singer, and dressed for the part, Elvis poses with Buzzy Forbess (*left*) and Farley Guy, outside Lauderdale Courts, where all three teenagers were neighbors. With a fourth Court resident, Paul Dougher, they had been almost inseparable for the past three or four years–playing football, going to the movies, and even venturing down Main Street, which was just three blocks from the Courts, to where it met with the bright lights of Beale. The picture is believed to have been taken after Elvis returned from one of his earliest appearances on the Louisiana Hayride.

1954

1953 **PHOTO BOOTHS** As with any teenager n the early 1950s there were the inevitable sepia-inted pictures from coin-in-the-slot photo booths—he curtain draped in the background was always a giveaway—and in such pictures that we see of Elvis t is increasingly apparent that this kid had a kind of look. His hair was greased back and quiffed now, his shirt collar usually upturned, jackets casually smart, his smile a knowing grin on this one, a moody half-sneer on that one. It was 1953, and 2,000 miles west in Burbank, California, Marlon Brando was shooting *The Wild One.* The world was changing fast, and Elvis was going to be part of the change in a big, big way.

1953

1955

1955 HIGH SCHOOL PROM Hey good lookin'. With girlfriend Dixie Locke, about to go to the South Side High School Prom, May 6. Also in the picture is Elvis' cousin Gene Smith and his girlfriend Bessie Wolverton. Dixie was a regular date of Elvis' from early in 1954; they went to the movies, went to church together, baby-sat for Dixie's cousins and often just stayed home watching TV together. Their relationship finally came to an end not long after the High School Prom, as Elvis' life became more and more consumed with his musical career at the expense of most else, and his circle of friends broadened from just neighborhood and ex-school buddies to local music and media folk.

1955 HIGH SCHOOL PROM Whoa' there, man, keep that camera steady! The amateur snapper managed to cut off the top and bottom of Elvis as he prepared for the Prom, but we can still dig that cool tuxedo, neat necktie, and one of those crazy shoes. Soon, at every high school hop in the land, they'd be bopping to Elvis' own brand of jive music.

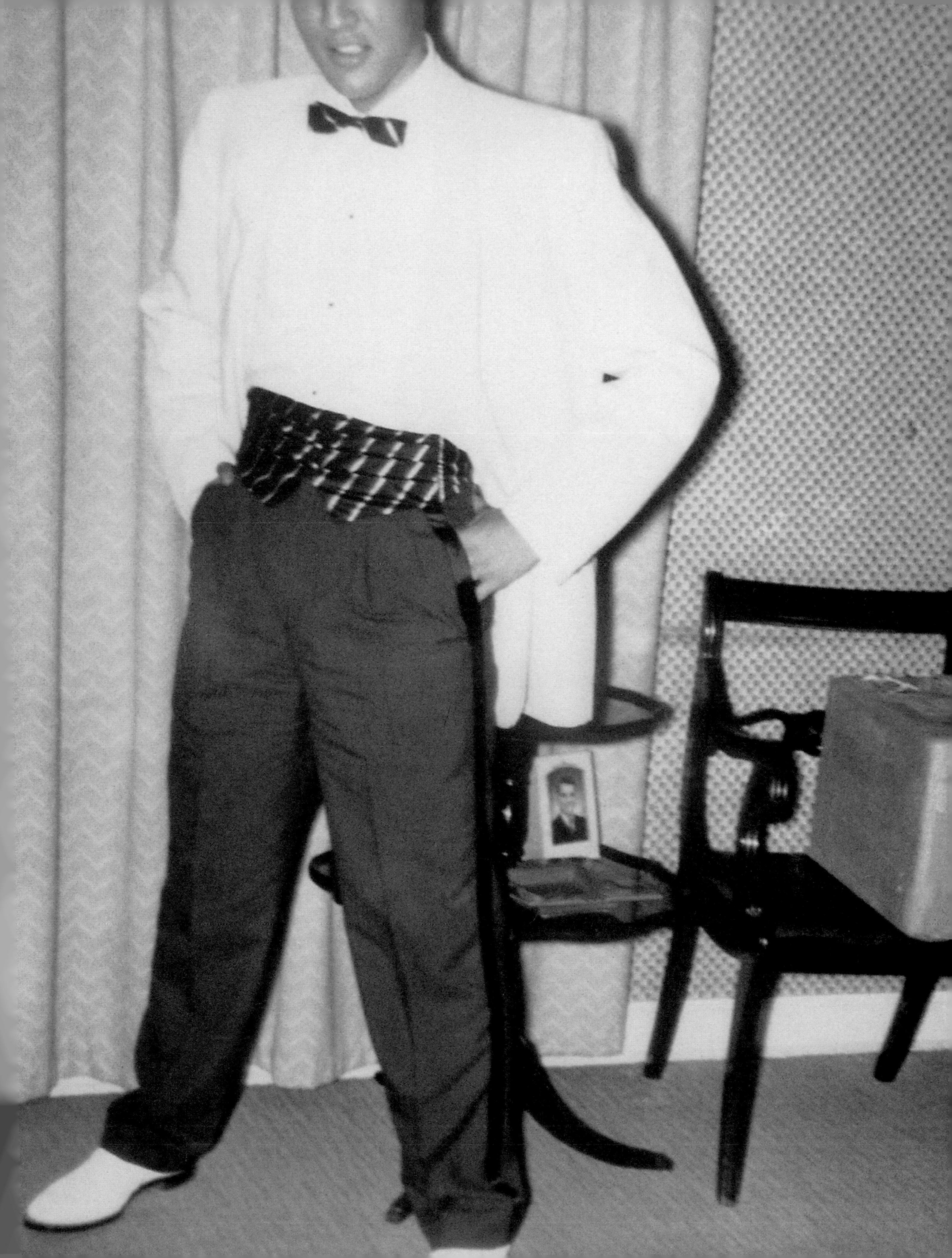

Elvis, Scotty & Bill

THE SUN YEARS

[1954–1956]

1955 **TAMPA, FLORIDA** A publicity photograph, taken backstage at a package show that Elvis was appearing on at the Fort Homer Hesterly Armory in Tampa, Florida on July 31, 1955.

January 1955

October 1955

August 1955

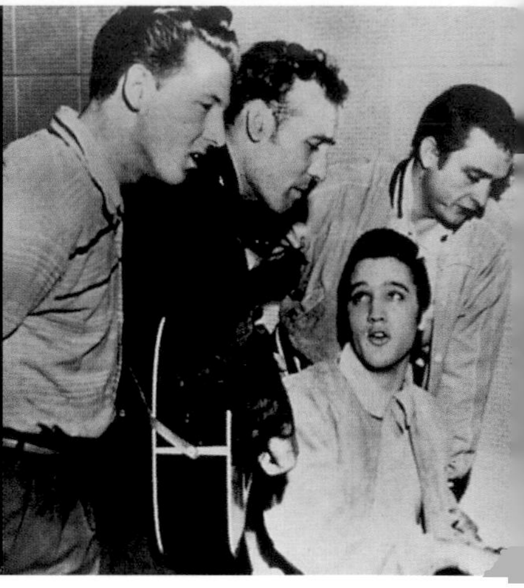

December 1956

Memphis

1954–1956

was hot, real hot, in the summer of 1953, and when Elvis walked into Sam Phillips' Memphis Recording Service, history was in the making. He was 18, and seemed so nervous that Phillips found it hard to believe that he had ever sung in public in his life. The studio at 706 Union Avenue doubled as the home of Sun Records, which was an almost 100% blues label at that time. The studio also functioned as a "walk in" facility, and the young Elvis did just that, to make an $8 acetate dub of his own singing voice. He made a second acetate the following January, but it was June before Phillips called him back to try Elvis out on various songs that might prove commercial, with none proving quite right.

Eventually, early in July, Phillips got a local guitarist, Scotty Moore, and bass player Bill Black, to play on a trial session with the singer. Moore and Black played in a Memphis outfit called the Starlite Wranglers, and after a run-through with Elvis they went into the studio. Against Phillips' preconception of what to expect (he told Moore that the youngster was a ballad singer) the most sensational take, in a session that up till then had the three just busking this idea and that to little avail, was "That's All Right," a number by blues singer Arthur "Big Boy" Crudup. In that moment, rock'n'roll was truly born.

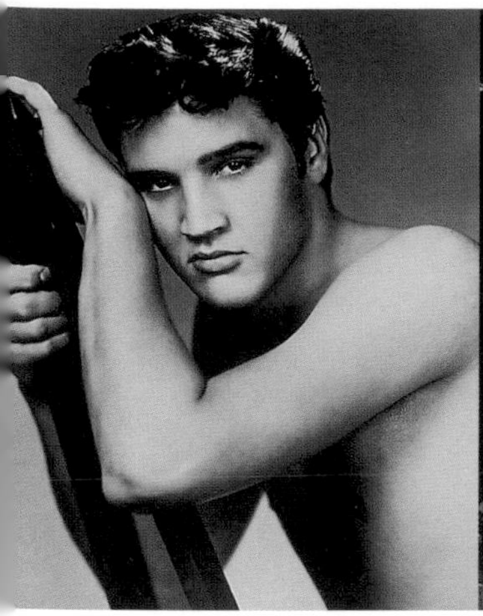

Summer 1955

July 1955

1955

It wasn't until the summer of 1954 that Elvis eventually teamed up with Scotty and Bill (and subsequently D. J. Fontana on drums) and started—debuting from the Bon Air club in Memphis on July 17—to barnstorm across the South like the twisting tornadoes that caused such mayhem over Tennessee, Arkansas, Texas, and Mississippi.

Via the pioneering records masterminded by Sam Phillips and the hugely popular Louisiana Hayride radio show, something wild was being let loose here, something nobody could control. It wasn't just about the music. For white kids from Phoenix, Arizona to Clarksdale, Mississippi, it was a true liberation, while for their parents Elvis and his music was something inexplicable, even something downright dangerous.

The timing couldn't have been more perfect. Young people across the Western world, and particularly in the United States, had surplus money to spend for the first time, and a liberty and identity as never before. The media even gave them a new name, and for the politicians and pundits it stood for a new social class: teenagers. Elvis, at 19, was one of them.

Elvis, Scotty, and Bill, as they were labeled on the bright yellow Sun 45s, conquered all in an 18-month campaign of a new kind of cool that took no prisoners.

1954

1954 SUN STUDIO Sam Phillips founded his Sun Studio and record label at 706 Union Avenue, Memphis, in 1950, specializing in black rhythm and blues players of the caliber of B. B. King, Junior Parker and Howlin' Wolf. There was also the little "record yourself" facility on which the young Elvis recorded his first acetate–"My Happiness" and "That's When Your Heartaches Begin"–as a present for his mother. Sam was also recording local country-style musicians who caught his imagination, and among them were Bill Black and Scotty Moore, whom he teamed up with Elvis. *Below*, Elvis, with Bill and Scotty at Sun Studio, and Sam Phillips in the control booth.

1954 SUN SINGLES Seven-inch 45 rpm singles by Elvis on the Sun label–of which he made only five, released between July 1954 and August 1955–with their distinctive yellow labels and sleeves, now change hands among collectors for phenomenal prices. Even rarer, and therefore more collectible, are the 78 rpm shellac discs that were released at the same time.

1954 ELVIS, SCOTTY, AND BILL A very early publicity shot with Scotty and Bill sporting some wild cowboy shirts. They were still the Starlite Wranglers–a country swing outfit, hence the shirts–when Elvis teamed up with them at the Bon Air Club. Indeed the "western" association stuck with Elvis, in this first explosion of popularity, being billed sensationally as the "Hillbilly Cat."

1955 ELVIS SIGNS New Year's Day, and Elvis signs on the dotted line, a management deal with the local Memphis radio DJ Bob Neal, seen on the right with Sam Phillips *(left)*. Neal nurtured Elvis through his early days on the road, only to be eclipsed by the altogether more strident–and commercially inspired–Tom Parker.

RCA
VICTOR

1955 RCA STUDIOS, NEW YORK From the first series of publicity shots made by RCA after signing Elvis in November for an unprecedented $40,000. Elvis was about to record in the label's studios in Nashville and New York, with the addition of session players (while retaining Scotty Moore, Bill Black, and D. J. Fontana), plus vocal group The Jordanaires, adding a new dimension to what were truly seminal recordings of the rock'n'roll era.

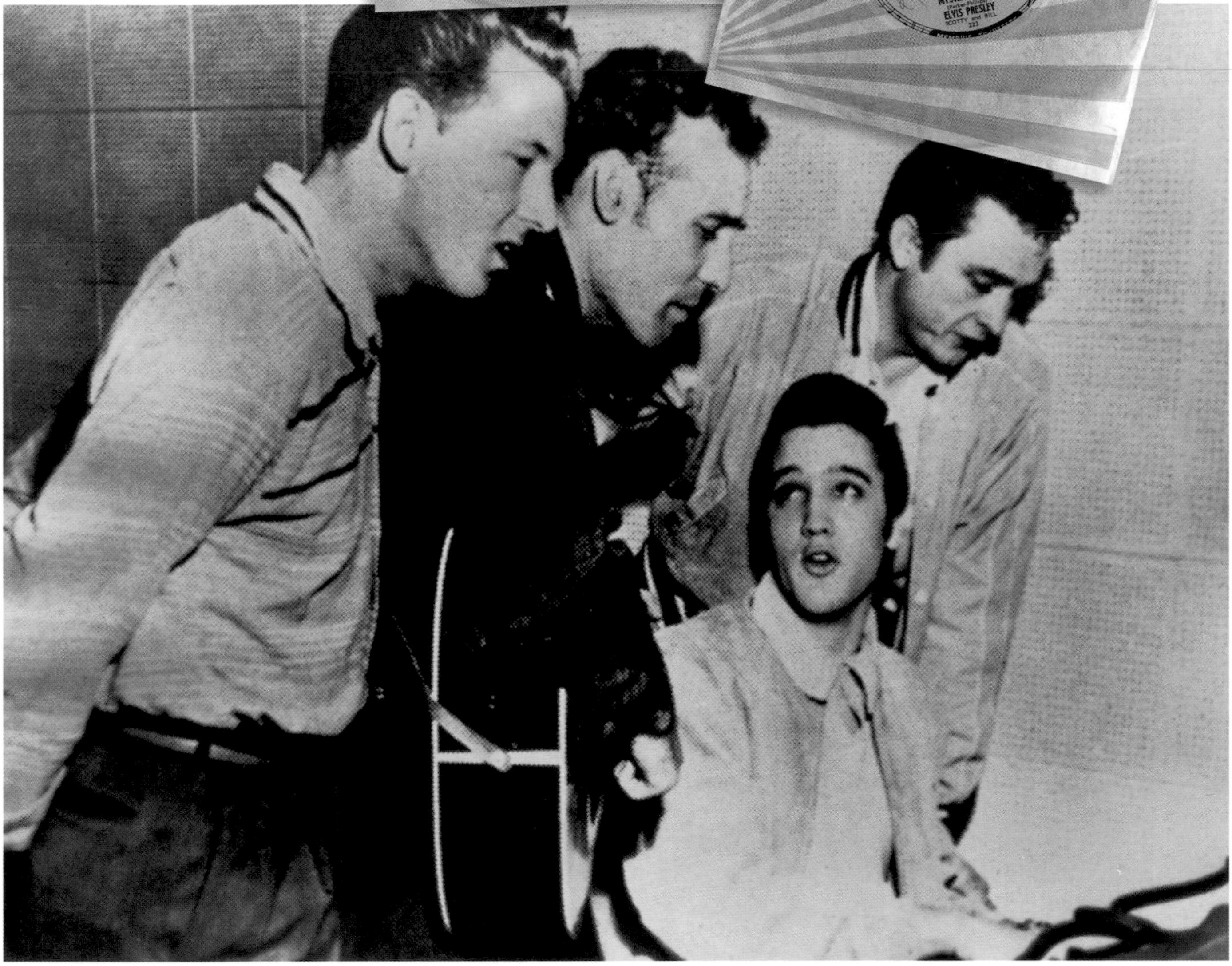

1956 MILLION-DOLLAR QUARTET Still with Sun Records in Memphis were Sam Phillips' other great discoveries, including (*from left to right*) "the killer" Jerry Lee Lewis, "Blue Suede Shoes" originator Carl Perkins, and country legend-to-be Johnny Cash. All three participated in a sensational "ad lib" session with Elvis, which was never intended for release, and was later to become known as the "Million-Dollar Quartet." Elvis stopped by his old recording studio in December, and jammed country, gospel, and rock with Perkins and Lewis, while Johnny Cash never actually appeared in the subsequent tapings, which circulated for years as bootlegs before being officially released on CD.

1956

1955

1955 TAMPA A backstage publicity shot taken during the Andy Griffith package show when it visited Tampa, Florida, in July 1955. Griffith, who headlined the showcase of stars from the Grand Ole Opry, was a hit comedian in a "hill billy" vein. Elvis, Scotty, and Bill, the posters for the show proclaimed, were added "By Popular Demand."

1955 BACKSTAGE, MEMPHIS Elvis poses backstage with local radio DJ "Texas Bill" Strength at the 8th annual Country Music Jamboree promoted by Bob Neal, at the Overton Park Shell amphitheater in Memphis. Other names on the bill, which attracted an audience of over 4,000, included Webb Pierce, Sonny James, and Johnny Cash–plus Elvis.

1955 MEMPHIS Elvis backstage at the Overton Park concert *(opposite)*, and *(above)* on stage at Ellis Auditorium, Memphis, in a show on February 6, 1955, which was compered by the local WHBQ disc jockey Dewey Phillips (no relation to Sam Phillips). Phillips was actually the first DJ to play an Elvis record on the air, "That's All Right" in 1954. At Overton Park Elvis is seen playing the Martin D-28 guitar which he bought in July 1955; the instrument was conspicuous for its custom-made tooled leather cover–bearing Elvis' name–which as well as being an attractive design, was also conceived to protect the back of the guitar from being scratched by Elvis' belt buckle.

1955

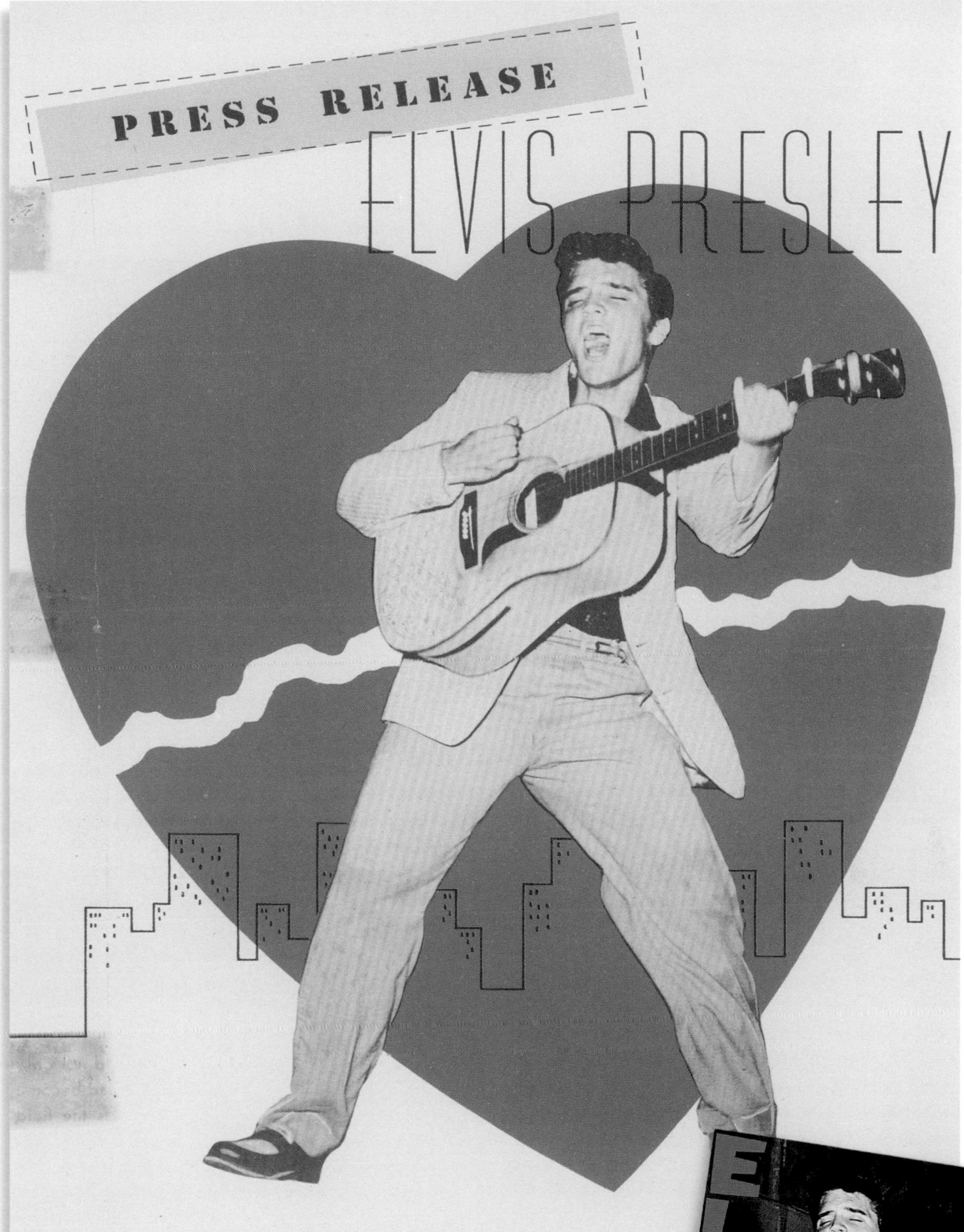

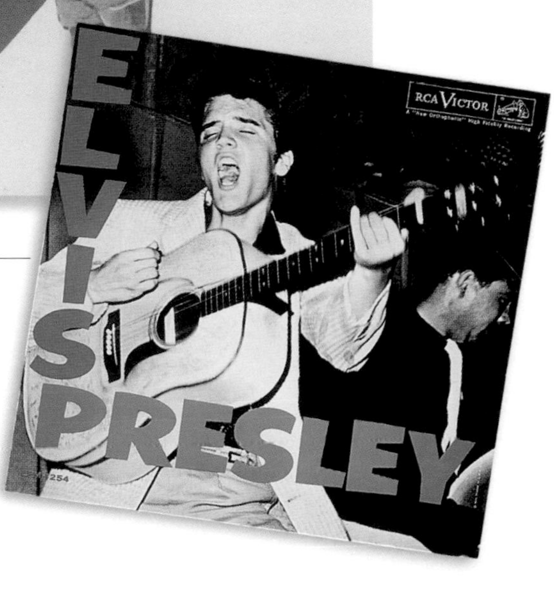

1955 TAMPA, FLORIDA This sensational image of Elvis, taken at the Fort Homer Hetserly Armory in Tampa, Florida, became an icon worldwide when it was used on the cover of his debut album. The picture seemed to accurately portray the mood of the rapidly emerging "teen" age-group. The LP marked the end of the period when Elvis was still touring only regionally with Scotty, Bill, and D. J. Fontana. Indeed the picture was taken on one such date, and the album included tracks from the early Sun Studio sessions, as well as material that was recorded at RCA Records' studios in both Nashville and New York.

1956 LOUISIANA HAYRIDE The Louisiana Hayride was a long-standing radio show that beamed western and country-flavored music across the rural South, and it became a crucial showcase for Elvis' unique sound. The main competitor to the Nashville-based Grand Ole Opry, the Hayride was carried by 190 local stations in 13 states, and, when in November 1954 Elvis signed a one-year contract for 52 Saturday night appearances, it was a major step forward. The pictures above were actually taken during Elvis' last ever performance on the Hayride, a guest appearance that took place in December 1956, long after his regular dates.

1956

1955 THE HAYRIDE Elvis' regular radio stints on the Hayride were particularly important as they led to his also being featured on most of the Hayride live package shows that toured the South. The Hayride deal was fixed while he was still with his original manager Bob Neal, and it was via the Hayride that he met Colonel Tom Parker.

1955 ANDY GRIFFITH SHOW Listen to "Blue Moon of Kentucky" with that slapped bass from Bill Black driving things crazy . . . The Bill Monroe original had been a country standard since 1946, but this was cowboy music with a swivel. Shot during their frenetic Tampa, Florida, debut on the Andy Griffith package show on July 31, 1955.

1955

Andy Griffith Show Slated At Peabody

Andy Griffith, who made his reputation on recordings of such numbers as "What It Was — Was Football" and "Make Yourself Comfortable" is coming to Daytona Beach next weekend.

His show, which will also include several country and Western entertainers, is booked for two

ANDY GRIFFITH

ELVIS PRESLEY

performances, at 7:30 and 9:30 p. m. Saturday at Peabody Auditorium.

Elvis Presley, young singer from the Louisiana Hayride Show, will be one of the personalities in the show. Presley, a singer who combines country music with bop, has made a name for himself with such records as "That's All Right Mama," "Blue Moon of Kentucky," "I Don't Care If The Sun Don't Shine" and "Good Rockin' Tonight." He'll be accompanied by Scotty Moore, on the guitar, and Bill Black, bass.

A group of Grand Ole Opry artists will include Ferlin Huskey, Simon Ceum, and Marty Robbins. Tommy Collins, of Hollywood, and Glenn Reeves are also scheduled to perform.

As a special attraction on the program there'll be Jimmie Rodgers Snow, son of the famous Hank Snow, and his Tennessee Playboys.

Griffith, star of the show, made his name in television on the show, "No Time For Sergeants," and will have a starring role in the production when it opens on Broadway in September.

COMING
Thursday and Friday
July 28 and 29—8:15
NEW
BASEBALL STADIUM
IN PERSON
THE ANDY GRIFFITH SHOW
saw him in U.S. Steel Hour T.V. production "No Time For Sergeants"
NOW SEE HIM IN PERSON
★ ★ ★
PLUS STARS OF
GRAND OLE OPRY
★ FERLIN HUSKEY
with His Hush Puppies and SIMON CRUM
★ ★ ★
★ MARTY ROBBINS
with JIMMY FARMER
★ ★ ★
SPECIAL ADDED ATTRACTIONS
★ TOMMY COLLINS
★ ★ ★
★ GLENN REEVES
JIMMY
★RODGERS SNOW
and His Tennessee Playboys
EXTRA — EXTRA
By Popular Demand
★ ELVIS PRESLEY
with SCOTTY & BILL
★ ★ ★
Don't You Dare Miss It
Tickets on sale at both Dixie Music Stores and all McDuff Hdwe. Stores. Gen. adm. advance—only $1.00.

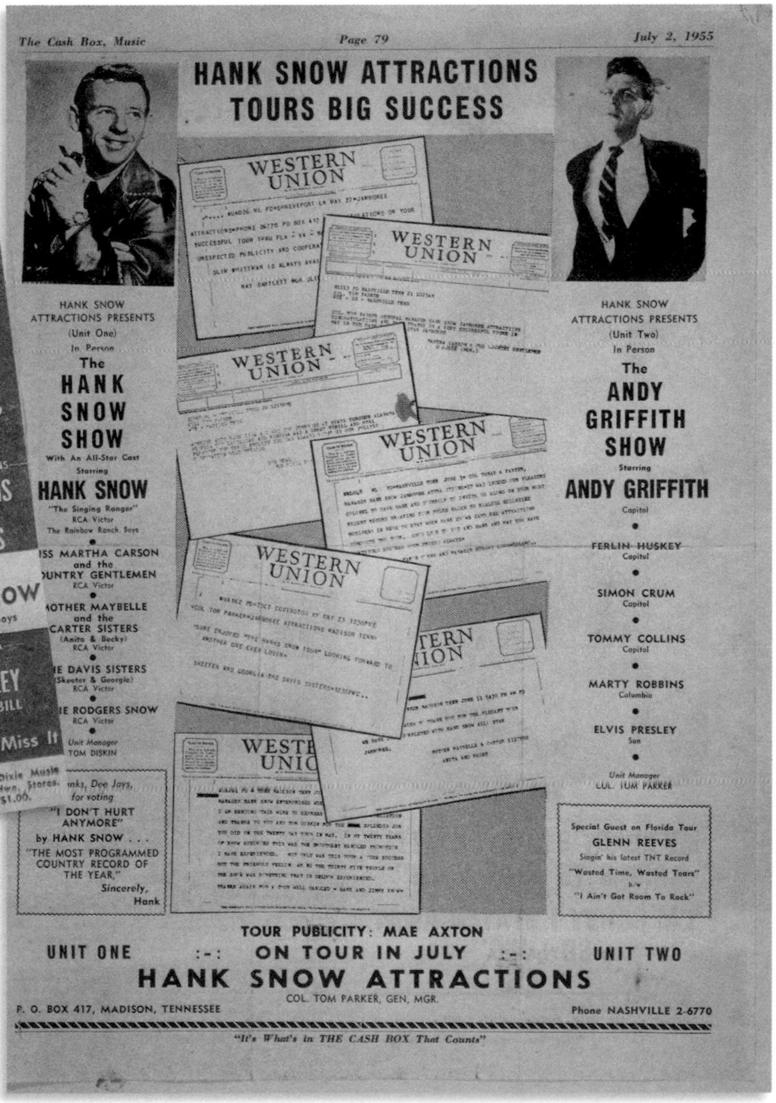

The Cash Box, Music | Page 79 | July 2, 1955

HANK SNOW ATTRACTIONS TOURS BIG SUCCESS

WESTERN UNION

HANK SNOW ATTRACTIONS PRESENTS
(Unit One)
In Person
The HANK SNOW SHOW
With An All-Star Cast
Starring
HANK SNOW
"The Singing Ranger"
RCA Victor
The Rainbow Ranch Boys
•
ISS MARTHA CARSON and the OUNTRY GENTLEMEN
RCA Victor
•
OTHER MAYBELLE and the CARTER SISTERS
(Anita & Becky)
RCA Victor
•
E DAVIS SISTERS
(Skeeter & Georgie)
RCA Victor
•
IE RODGERS SNOW
RCA Victor
•
Unit Manager
TOM DISKIN

...nks, Dee Jays, for voting
"I DON'T HURT ANYMORE"
by HANK SNOW . . .
"THE MOST PROGRAMMED COUNTRY RECORD OF THE YEAR."
Sincerely,
Hank

HANK SNOW ATTRACTIONS PRESENTS
(Unit Two)
In Person
The ANDY GRIFFITH SHOW
Starring
ANDY GRIFFITH
Capitol
•
FERLIN HUSKEY
Capitol
•
SIMON CRUM
Capitol
•
TOMMY COLLINS
Capitol
•
MARTY ROBBINS
Columbia
•
ELVIS PRESLEY
Sun
•
Unit Manager
COL. TOM PARKER

Special Guest on Florida Tour
GLENN REEVES
Singin' his latest TNT Record
"Wasted Time, Wasted Tears"
b/w
"I Ain't Got Room To Rock"

TOUR PUBLICITY: MAE AXTON
UNIT ONE :-: ON TOUR IN JULY :-: UNIT TWO
HANK SNOW ATTRACTIONS
COL. TOM PARKER, GEN. MGR.
P. O. BOX 417, MADISON, TENNESSEE
Phone NASHVILLE 2-6770
"It's What's in THE CASH BOX That Counts"

1954–55 THE PRESS Right from the start of his career, Elvis was aware of the power of the press. Even in the earliest days, every local gig around Memphis and the mid-South would mean a few column inches here, a photograph there. In addition there was the paid-for advertising that promoters and venues had to book into papers to publicize their upcoming attractions. Elvis was way down the bottom on many of these bills, below established country stars, but not for long. Later of course it was national publicity via the music trade press, then–as Elvis became newsworthy generally–the regular media. By the end of 1956, Elvis Presley was so famous he was headline news worldwide.

1955

➔ **1955 CONTACT** The level of Elvis' contact with his audience was unprecedented, and no matter how remote he would inevitably become due to superstardom, his stage shows always managed to retain that bond.

➔➔ **1955 PRESLEY FANS** These sweet southern girls (*following pages*), like all mid-teens, were experiencing something new in their lives. This wasn't something Mom would understand when she remembered her own flowering youth; this was different from anything that had gone before.

1955 BACKSTAGE, During those riotous gigs of 1955, Elvis' fan base mushroomed. First of all the backstage encounters, signing autographs and chatting, were casual friendly affairs. But soon, as the hysteria increased, the fans were mobbing him rather than meeting him. More and more Elvis found himself escorted, by local police, security men–and later his own personnel–from hotel to bandroom to stage, and vice versa back to hotel room, with a diminishing contact that he clearly regretted.

1955 TAMPA The venue of Fort Homer Hesterly Armory in Tampa, Florida where Elvis played on July 31, might sound unusual but was typical insofar as no venues were really typical at this time. Dance halls, sports stadia, theaters, cinemas, rodeo arenas, municipal auditoriums–as his popularity grew, the only thing the places he played had in common was that they simply got bigger. The first thing a local promoter had to think about when contemplating booking a show with Elvis on the bill was how to cope with the capacity crowds he was attracting.

1955

1955 CLEVELAND Backstage with fans during an event-filled trip to Cleveland, Ohio, in October 1955. On Wednesday 19, Elvis guested on a Grand Ole Opry-style show headed by Roy Acuff and Kitty Wells. Then on Thursday, an afternoon gig at Brooklyn High School in the city–also starring Bill Haley, Pat Boone, and the Four Lads–is filmed for a proposed minidocumentary to be released to movie theaters. It never appeared. Later that evening, a near-riotous appearance by Elvis ensued when, after breaking his guitar strings, he smashed the instrument on the stage. The subsequent outburst of crowd hysteria was only just controlled by police, who had to escort Elvis from the hall.

1955 BILL HALEY A backstage shot (October 20, 1955) at the Brooklyn High School Auditorium, Cleveland, Ohio, with the first (albeit short-lived) king of rock'n'roll, Bill Haley, whose crown was stolen by Elvis very soon after this photo was taken. Haley and his "Comets" (originally called the Saddlemen) came from the same country-swing tradition as Elvis' musicians. Like his young rival, Haley also looked to black rhythm and blues for much of his material. But at 10 years older than Elvis, despite worldwide smashes like "Rock Around the Clock," "Shake Rattle and Roll," and "See You Later, Alligator," once the kid from Memphis raised the sex-appeal stakes there was no contest.

1955

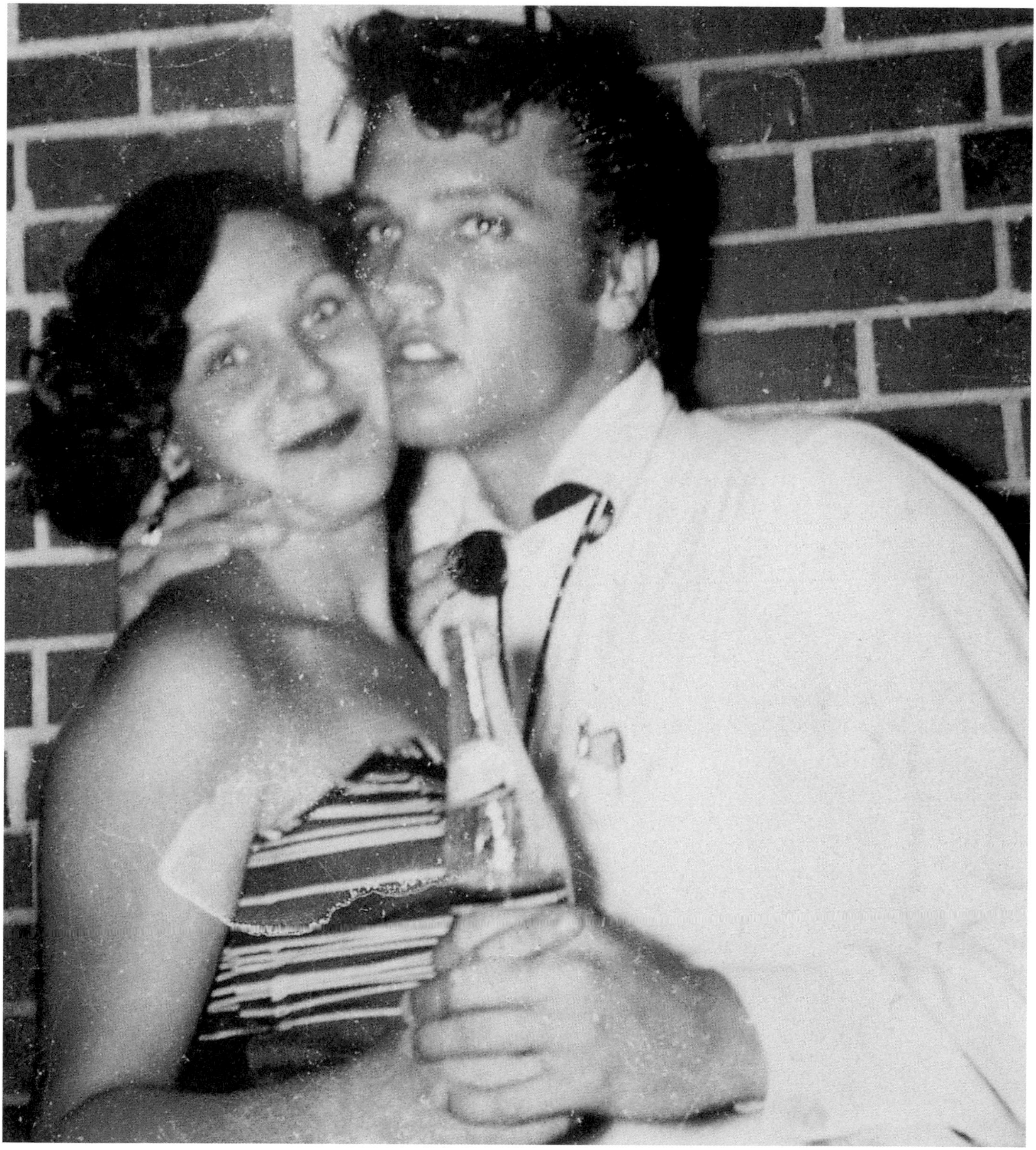

1955 MAE BOREN AXTON The sequined cowgirl is unknown, but the lady on the right is Mae Boren Axton, who worked as publicist on the Florida leg of Elvis' 1955 dates. She went on to cowrite "Heartbreak Hotel" with Tommy Durden, which transpired to be a milestone in popular music as the launchpad for Elvis Presley worldwide.

1955 JACKSONVILLE, FLORIDA All that was written on the back of this photograph was "Jacksonville Ball Park, Hope you'll remember me," but the gig itself was a milestone in Elvis' career. It was May 13, and the much-publicized occasion when rioting fans actually chased him into his dressing room, tearing off his clothes and shoes.

1955

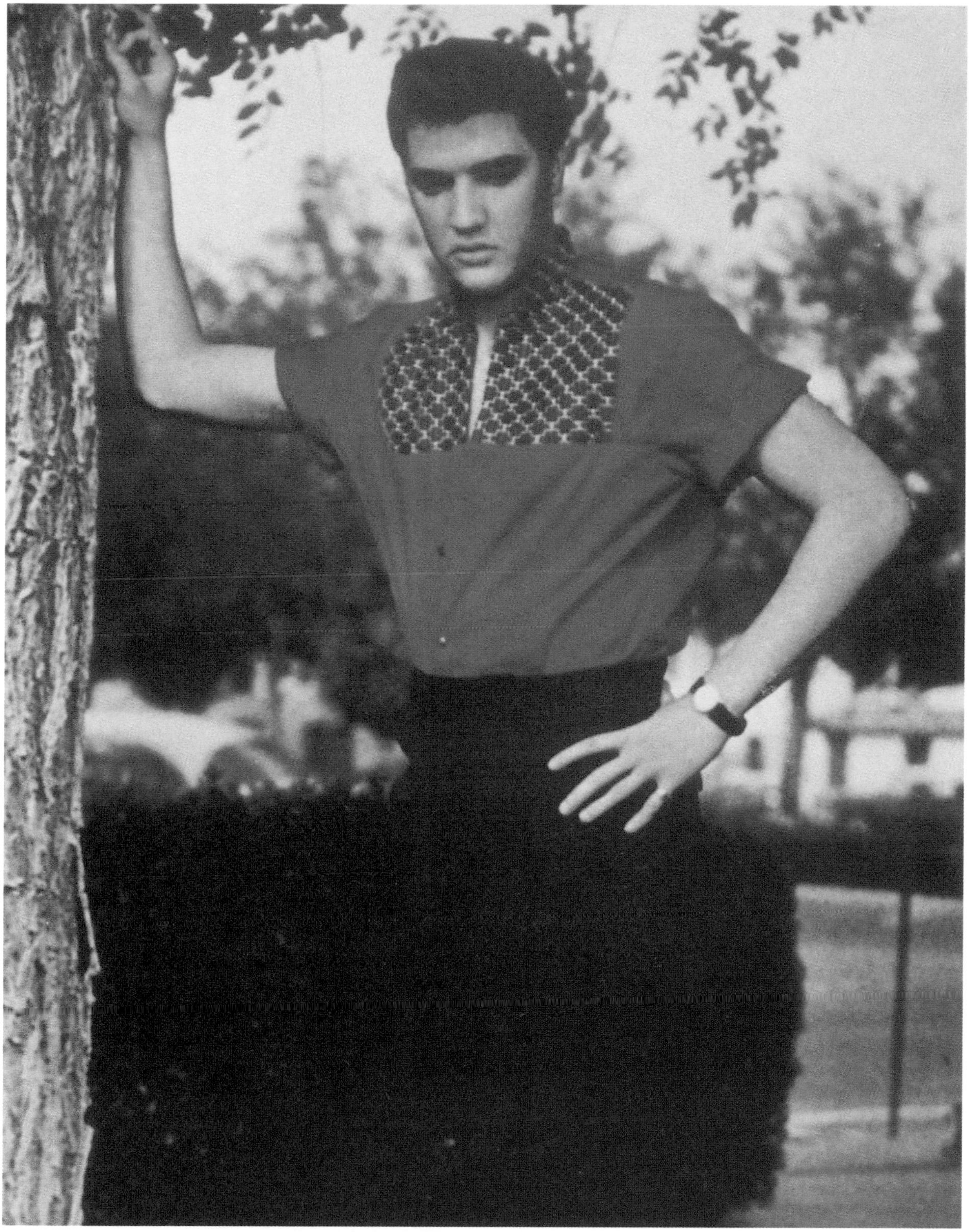

1955 MEMPHIS William Speer was a Memphis-based photographer, who in 1955 captured a smouldering Elvis in a series of portraits that, if nothing else would, guaranteed his early status as a new kind of sex symbol. The studio-lit photographs looked more like the pinup pictures of Hollywood movie stars than a local rock'n'roller.

1955 MEMPHIS There weren't that many color shots of Elvis back in 1955, and this one by an unknown photographer was used as publicity material by Colonel Tom Parker, who became the singer's manager in the lattter half of that year. Parker had promoted some of the Louisiana Hayride and other package shows the Presley trio had appeared on, and gradually assumed the management role initially performed (in a less high-powered capacity) first by Scotty Moore and then radio DJ Bob Neal. Parker was a showman, in the fairground sense, and his skill at negotiating in Elvis' favor made him a yardstick by which showbiz managers were subsequently measured.

Shake, Rattle & Roll

SUPERSTARDOM

[1956–1957]

1956 LAS VEGAS By the middle of 1956 Elvis was truly a superstar, feted by fans and celebrities alike. Among the many famous faces who visited him backstage during his first-ever Las Vegas season was Liberace. Elvis reciprocated (left) when the pianist entertainer played the Riviera Hotel in Las Vegas in November '56.

April 1956 *October 1956* *May 1956*

1956

Released in January in 1956. "Heartbreak Hotel" was much more than just another pop music record. Rock'n'roll was still in its infancy, and its main characteristic, be it by Bill Haley, Little Richard or the "Hillbilly Cat" from Memphis, was as dance music to bop the blues away. Yet the disc that triggered the seismic musical and social changes about to happen wasn't some up-tempo jive side at all. Quite the opposite, it was dark, sinister in its brooding melancholy, the new-to-the-ear "echo chamber" sound taking a whole generation down to the end of Lonely Street—and they'd never never come back. But it did smack of the blues, with the simple but insistent guitar break and Floyd Cramer's evocative piano being more "down home" than any previous pop single by a white artist—indeed, many on first hearing it on the radio imagined it was a black singer, making Elvis' teen-appeal even more controversial, especially in the still-segregated South.

But that was only the start of it. Through the following 11 months of that year he had no less than 10 singles, nine EPs, and two albums released by RCA. The statistics were staggering; after "Heartbreak Hotel" went to number one in the US (and in many other territories worldwide) his debut LP was RCA Records' first to sell over a million copies. As well

July 1956

c.1956

September 1956

as both sides of "Hound Dog"/"Don't Be Cruel" topping the charts, plus "I Want You, I Need You, I Love You," and "Love Me Tender" hitting the number three and number one spots respectively, 4-track Extended Players also regularly made the US singles charts. In August 1956, RCA took the unprecedented step of releasing seven singles on the same day, six of which were culled from his debut album of a few months earlier.

Elvis' ascendance through 1956 was due in no small part to Colonel Tom Parker, who had taken over complete management responsibilities in October 1955. After a period of what could only be described as an uneven relationship with Elvis' previous representative Bob Neal, a local radio DJ and promoter who himself had taken over a more informal management role performed by Elvis' guitarist Scotty Moore.

Elvis Presley rocketed to fame so quickly that by the end of the summer he was making his first movie, *Love Me Tender*, in which his confessed ambition to be a "serious" actor was frustrated by the studio's insistence on including musical items that had no real bearing on an otherwise straightforward dramatic plot. But the movie, inevitably, was a huge hit, and confirmed, by the end of the year, Elvis' position as the undisputed King of Rock'n'Roll.

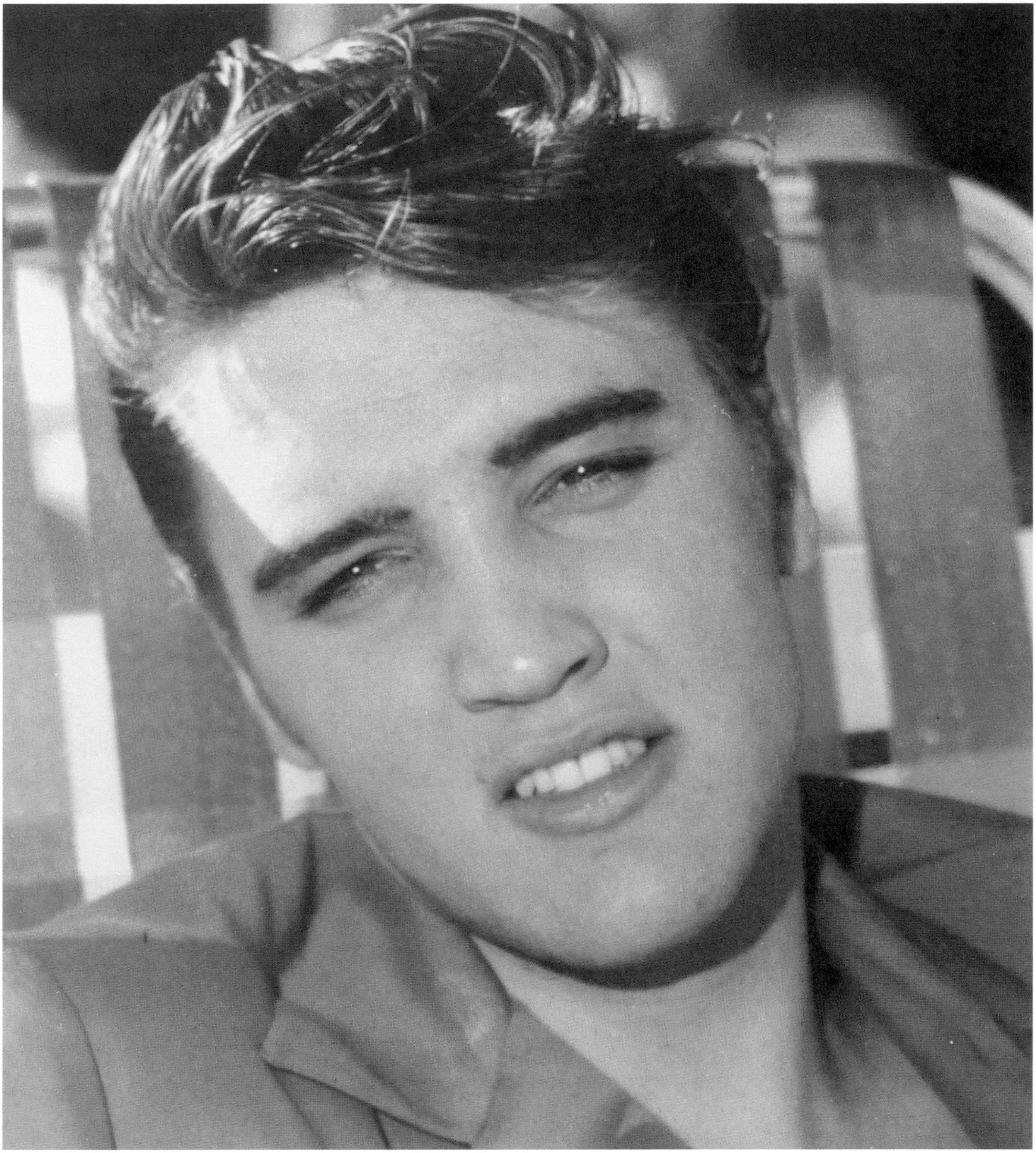

1956 HEARTTHROB It was the era of a new kind of teenagers' hero, represented primarily by smouldering screen actors like Marlon Brando and James Dean who, in their own off-screen persona and–especially in the case of Dean–in the parts they played, were able to identify more directly with the new youthful audiences, and vice versa. But it was Elvis who was the first to bring this kind of image to the role of pop singer, and the potent combination of stunning looks and the equally captivating music meant he simply couldn't miss as the prime idol for a new generation. It heralded the new phenomenon of early rock'n'roll as popular music aimed almost exclusively at teenagers.

1956

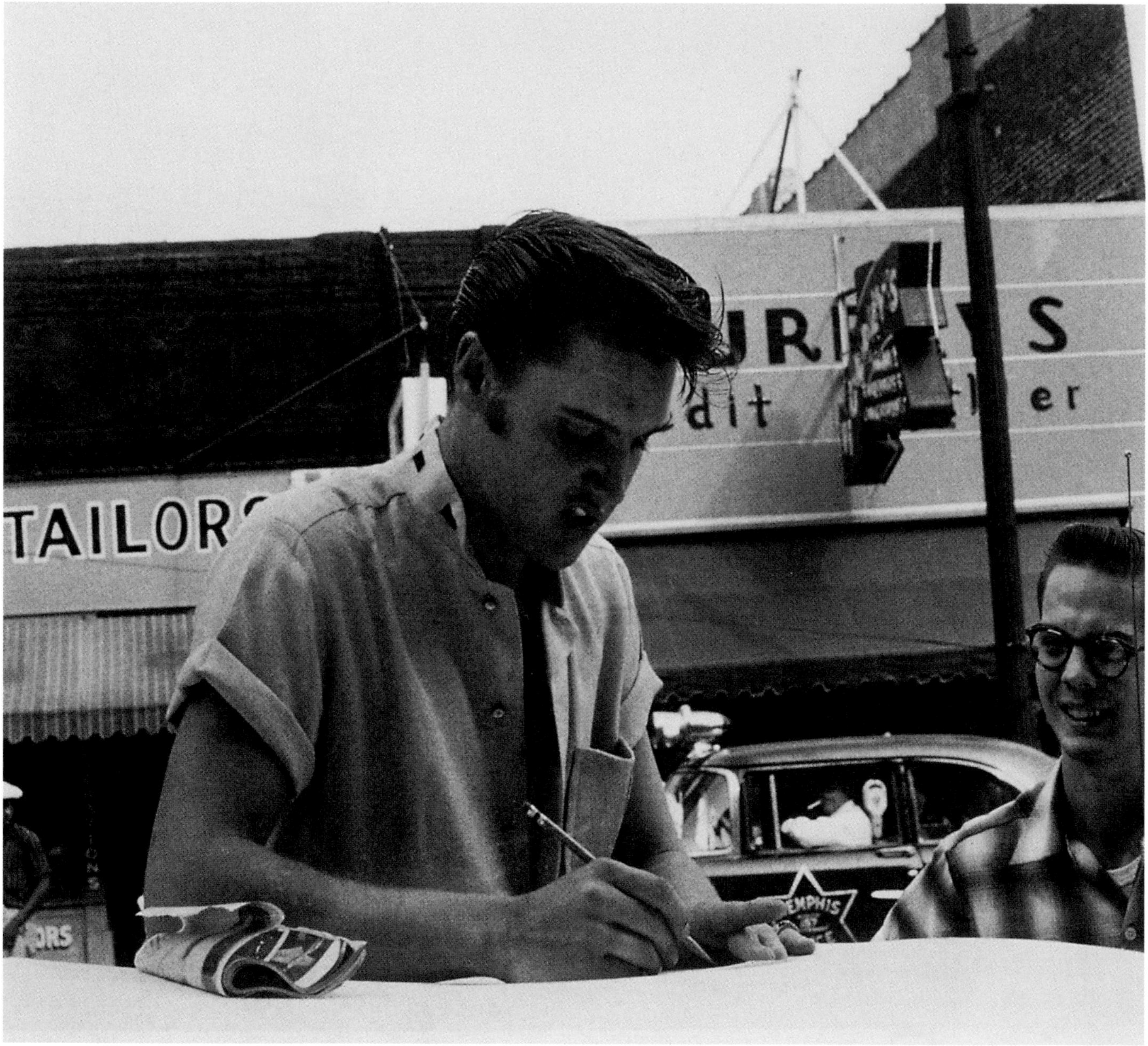

1956 LOCAL HERO Always happy to oblige, Elvis signs an autograph while out and about in the streets of downtown Memphis in the summer of '56. Despite increasing pressure brought about by fans, fame, and fortune, he endeavored to move around his home town as freely as circumstance would allow. Even at the height of the first wave of Elvis fan-mania in the mid-Fifties, he would ride out to favorite restaurants and hamburger joints, and even go to the movies. Later, when things got just a little too hectic, he started sending out for his food (though making the occasional "secret" foray into an all-night diner) and would rent an entire movie theater for after-hours showings with his friends.

1956

↑ **1956 AUDUBON DRIVE** In March 1956 Elvis purchased a new house for himself and his parents in a comfortable suburb of Memphis, at 1034 Audubon Drive. Throughout the spring decorating and furnishing the house was completed, and this shot of Elvis relaxing outside was taken in July. Although it was a seemingly extravagant gesture for someone who had only been at the top for a matter of months, the purchase nevertheless created a convention for young rock'n'roll stars in the US and elsewhere, who almost invariably signaled their success, however short-lived, by buying a house for their folks. In less than a year the Presleys, meanwhile, had moved to Graceland

1956

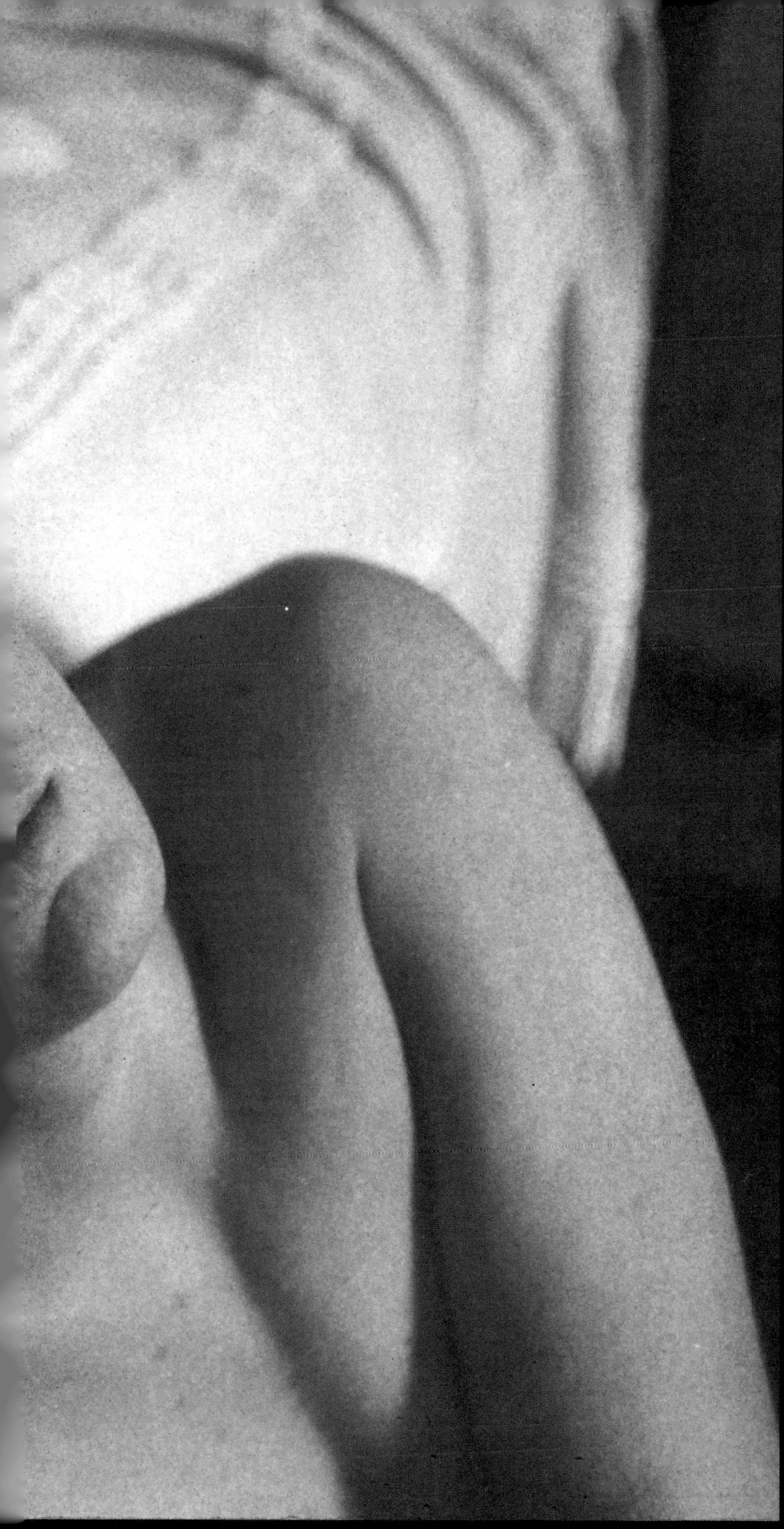

1956

➔ **1956 AUDUBON DRIVE** The face that appeared in a million bedrooms. Elvis reclines against his own bed at Audubon Drive, while all over the country, and increasingly the world, his image on photographs and posters covered fans' walls, was reproduced on bedside lamps, vanity sets, bedspreads, even pajamas.

1956

1956 ON THE ROAD Spurred on by no less than 11 guest appearances on network TV shows through 1956, which were the only chance the whole of the United States had of seeing the phenomenon of Elvis Presley in action, the live stage shows got wilder and wilder. The work schedule for Elvis, plus the musicians, the Jordanaires and the road crew, was simply frantic. In the first two months of the year Elvis performed over 30 live dates, some of them involving double or even triple appearances at a venue on the same day, in addition to four TV-shows in the "Dorsey Brothers' Stage Show" and five days in the recording studio.

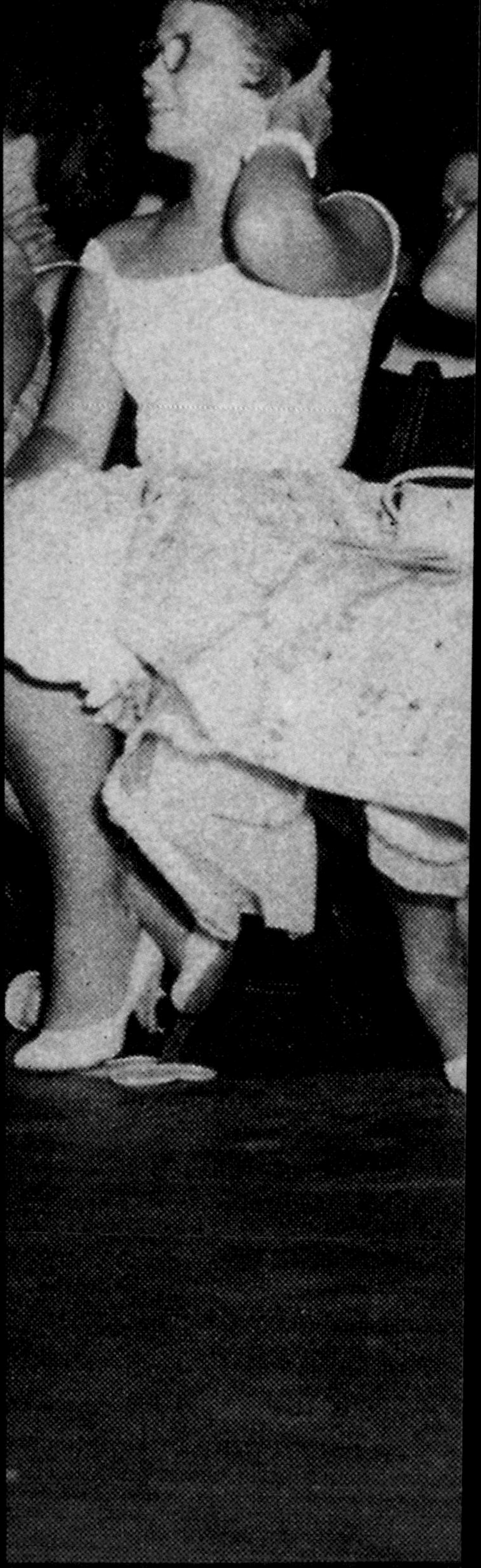

1956 ELVIS MANIA Theaters across the United States of America had never seen anything like it. Previous generations of young people had their idols who they reacted to demonstrably; the bobby soxers had jived in the aisles for jazz stars like Benny Goodman and Harry James in the Big Band era, the fans swooned as Frank Sinatra crooned, and audiences literally wept for the "Cry Guy" Johnnie Ray, but the reaction to Elvis was altogether different again. Like Elvis' vocal delivery and his stage movements, the impact he had on the audience was something that could only be described as physical.

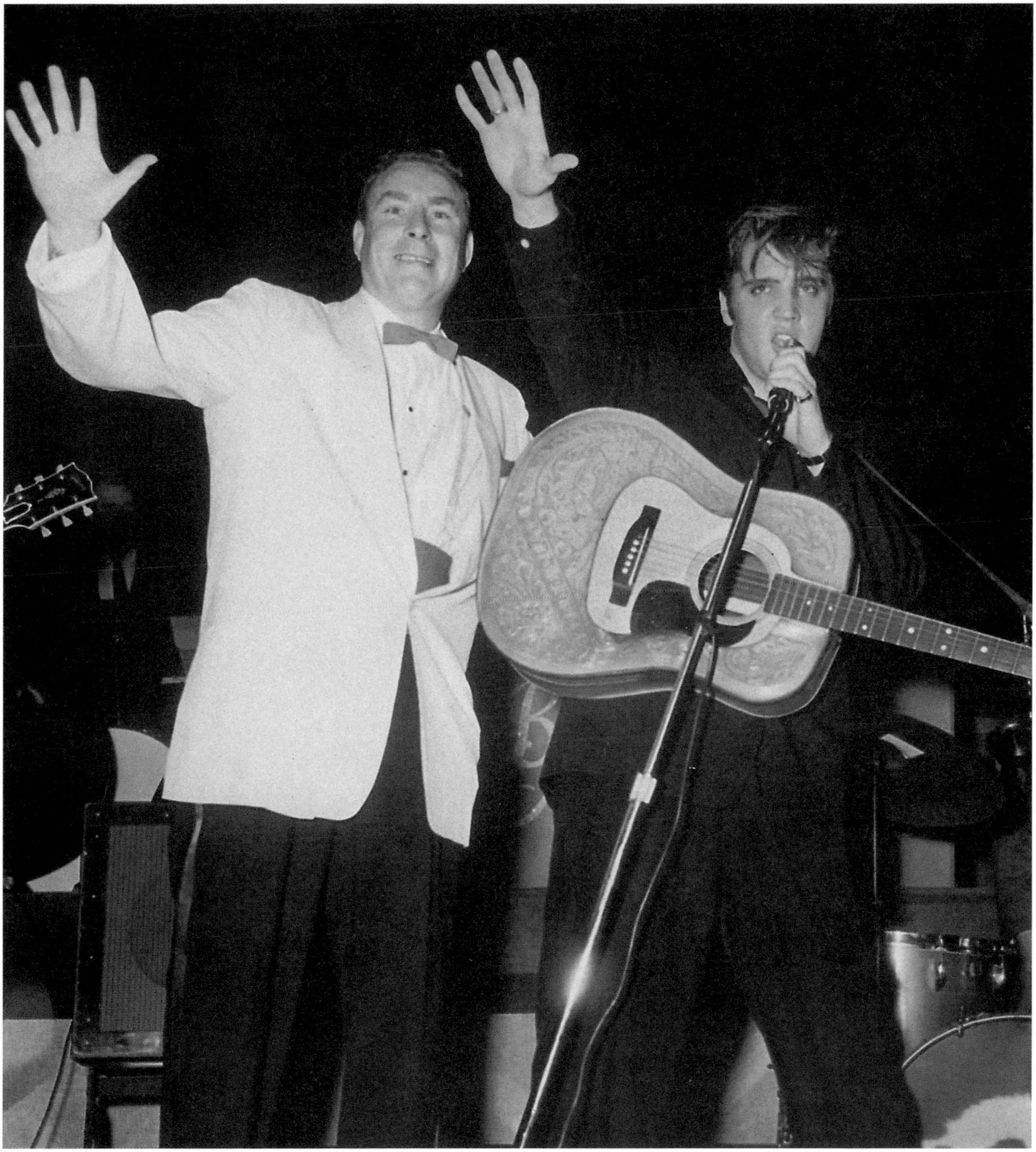

◀ **1956 DALLAS, TEXAS** A concert at the Cotton Bowl in Dallas in October 1956 grosses nearly $30,000, an amazing sum at the time, with an audience of over 25,000 screaming fans. Elvis' drummer, D. J. Fontana, later described the spectacle of the thousands of flashbulbs in the darkened arena—"It looked like war out there."

▲ ▶ **1956 ON STAGE** Elvis' whole persona—the way he swung a guitar, the way he swung his legs, and of course the way he swung his hips (*here and overleaf*)—along with the hairstyle, the scowl, and every detail of his image—became a template for the thousands of white male rock'n'roll performers who would follow in the wake of his success.

1956

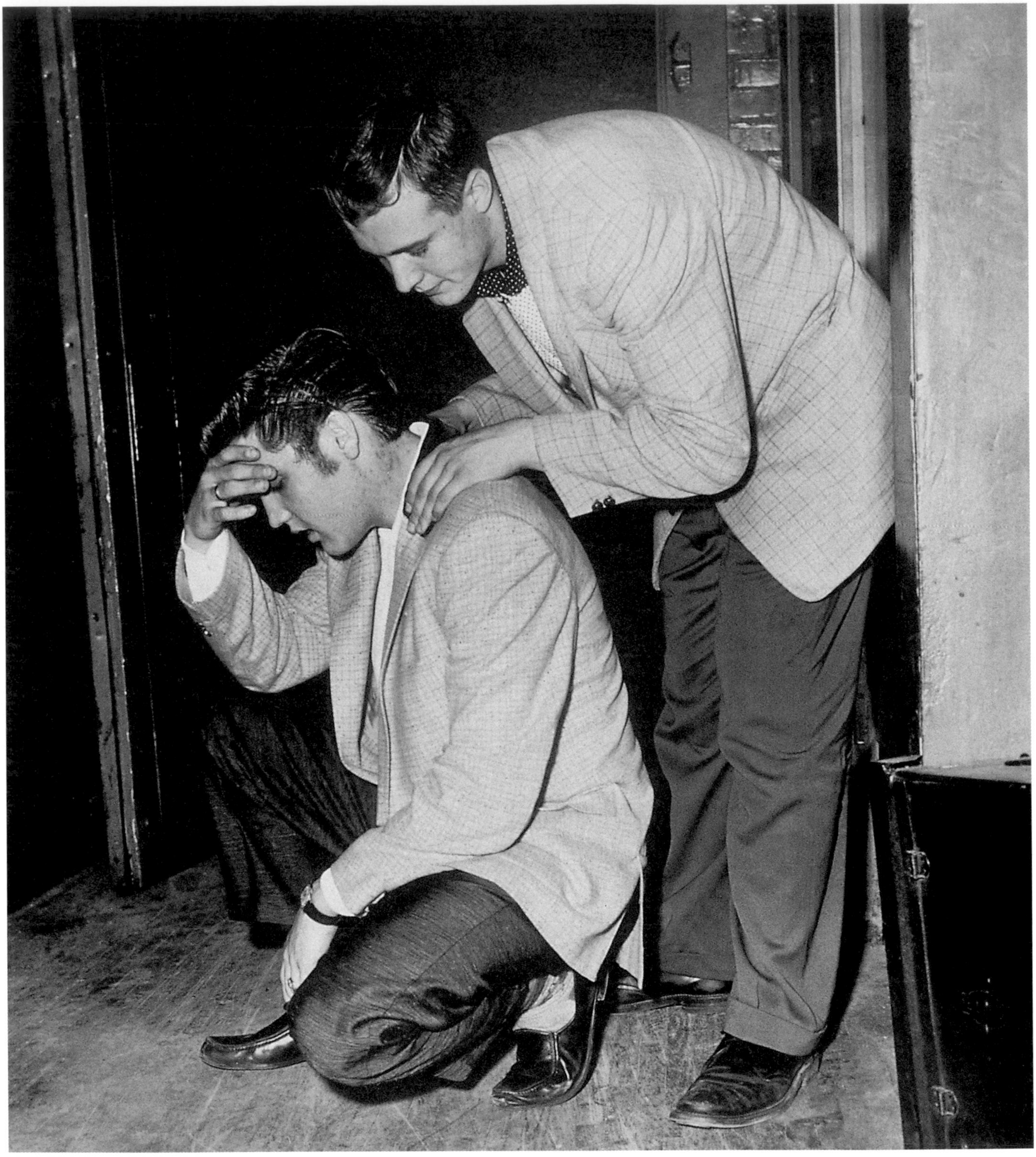

1956

➊ 1956 **ST. PAUL, MINNESOTA** The stage shows and their frequency could be, physically, extremely exhausting. Elvis is seen here backstage at an afternoon show at the Auditorium in the Minnesota state capital of St. Paul, on May13–the concert was followed by another one in the evening in the twin-city of Minneapolis.

➋ 1956 **BACKSTAGE, LAS VEGAS** Fans besiege Elvis when he agrees to sign autographs during his two-week engagement at the Venus Room of the New Frontier Hotel in Las Vegas. It wouldn't be long before this kind of intimacy with his enthusiastic followers would be deemed virtually impossible, for their safety as well as his.

PRESLEY
RCA Victor Artist
ELVIS
Autographs
VENUS ROOM
PRESLEY

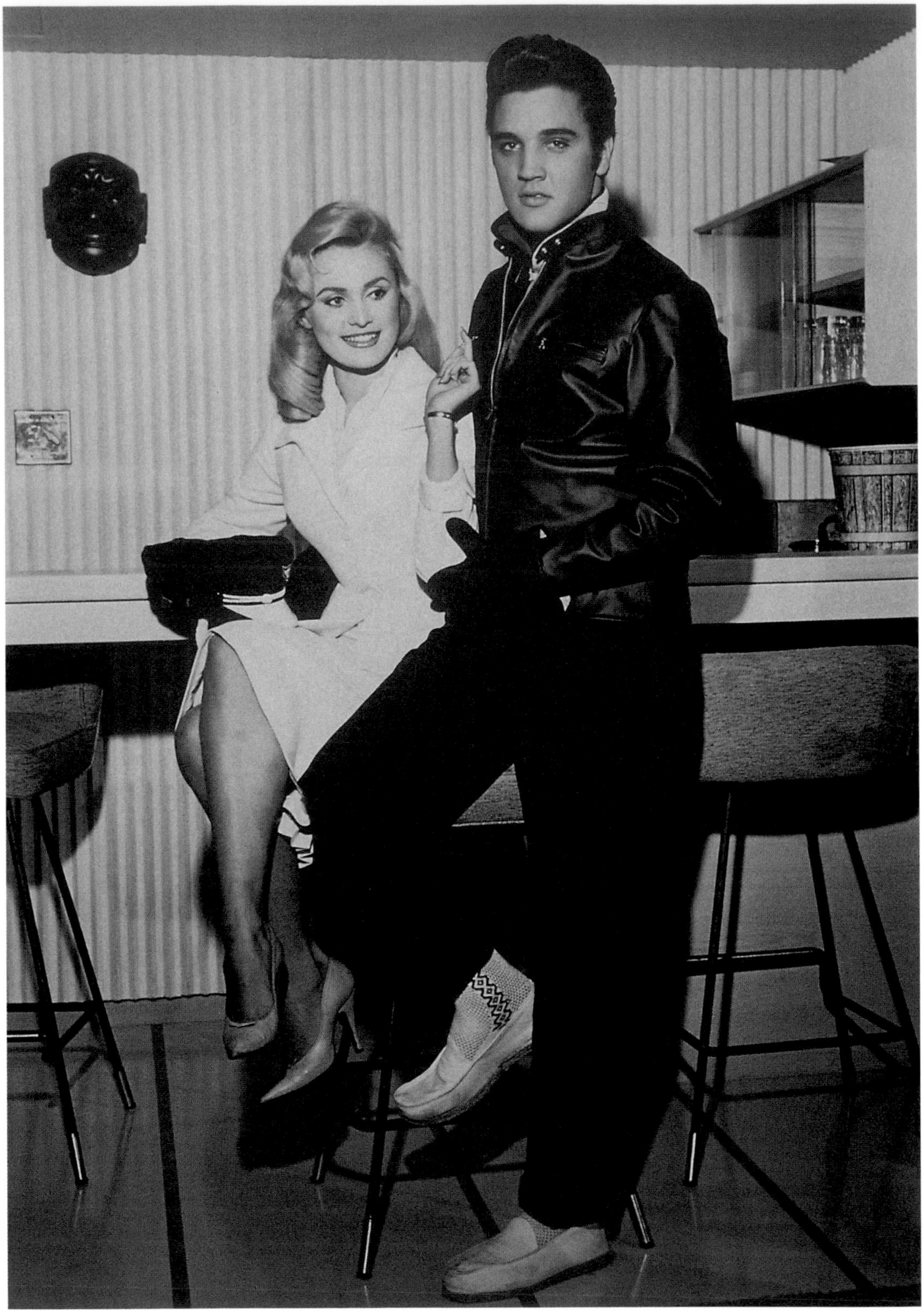

⬆ 1957 LAS VEGAS One of a series of pictures of Elvis with Hannerl Melcher, a Las Vegas showgirl and Miss Austria 1957, who spent Christmas of that year with him at Graceland. Elvis can be seen wearing a leather jacket as some of the photographs were of him and the same companion sitting astride a motorcycle.

➡ 1956 MEMPHIS This photo, taken in Memphis, shows Elvis with yet another admiring female fan. Although during this period Elvis enjoyed a lot of female company, he was yet to settle into a long-term relationship and therefore could clearly be considered just about the most eligible bachelor on the planet!

1956

EP

1956 RCA, NASHVILLE A Nashville recording session on April 14, 1956, which produced Elvis' second single for RCA, "I Want You, I Need You, I Love You." Next to Elvis is vocalist Gordon Stoker, whose gospel-based group the Jordanaires were soon to join him for recording, television and concert dates on a regular basis.

1956

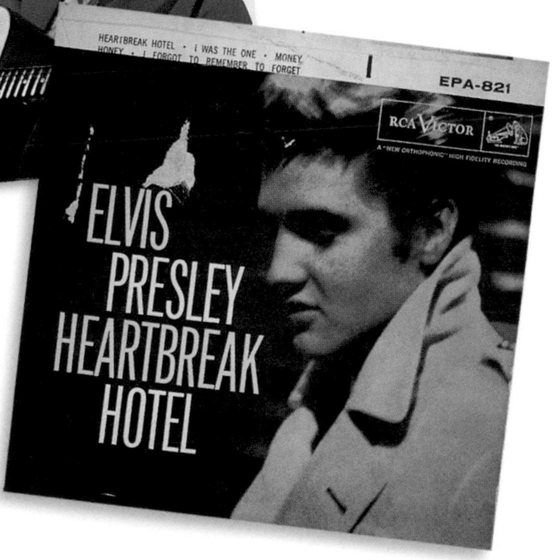

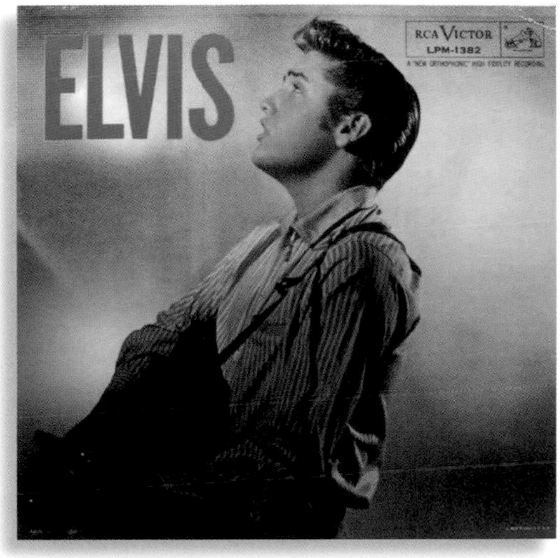

1956 RECORD BLITZ By the end of 1956, Elvis had released two albums, the second (above) being entitled simply Elvis. It featured, like his debut LP, a mixture of ballads and hard-hitting rockers–the latter including no less than three numbers which were covers of singles by Little Richard. RCA was still able to mine the back catalog it had inherited from Sun Records for material, hence on the October-released EP "Any Way You Want Me" (*left*), apart from the title track the other three songs had all originally been singles on Sun.

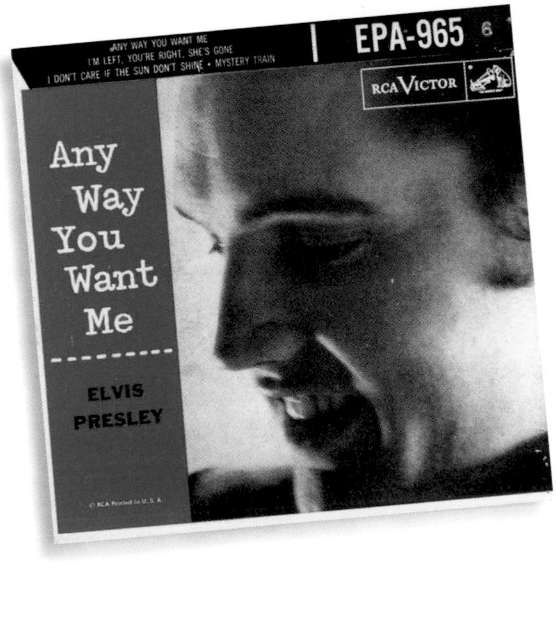

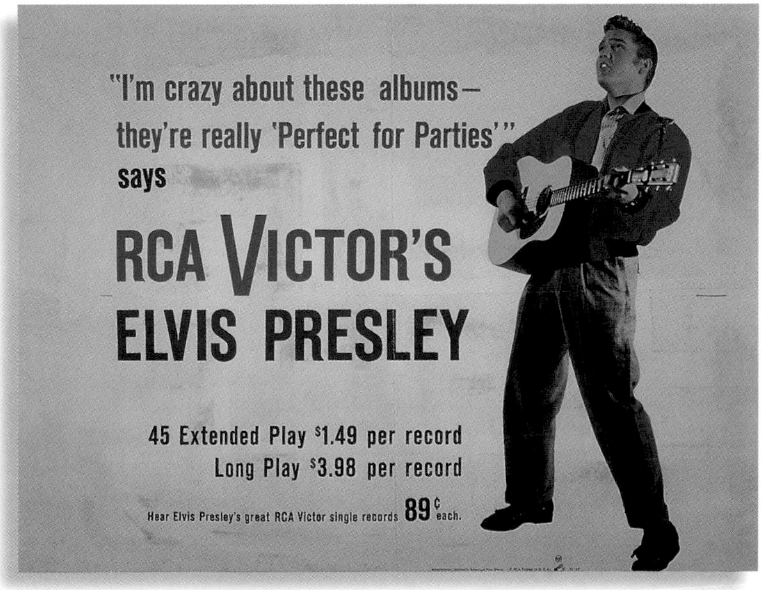

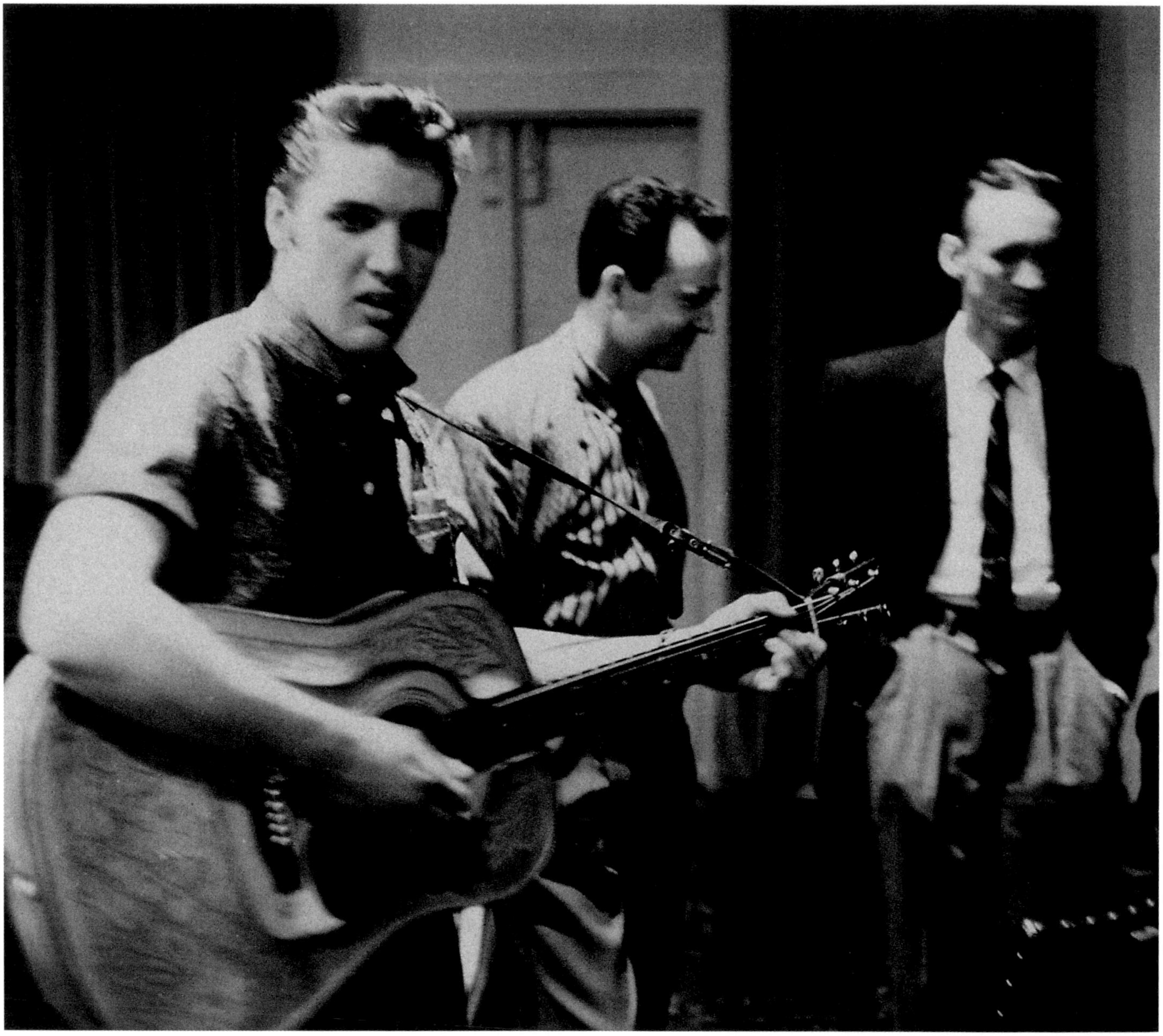

1956

1956 RCA, NASHVILLE More photographs, among over a hundred shot, from the "I Want, I Need You, I Love You" session. Above, Elvis tunes up with vocalists Gordon Stoker and Brock Speer in the background. On this session Stoker wasn't with his group the Jordanaires. He and the brothers Ben and Brock Speer making up the backing vocals trio. Opposite, Elvis is flanked by Ben Speer and (on his right) the legendary Nashville guitarist Chet Atkins. Atkins was more than just a guitar session player, being an early regular on the Grand Ole Opry, and talent scout for RCA Records from 1952, in which company he rose to the position of vice president before leaving in 1979. He died in 2001.

1956

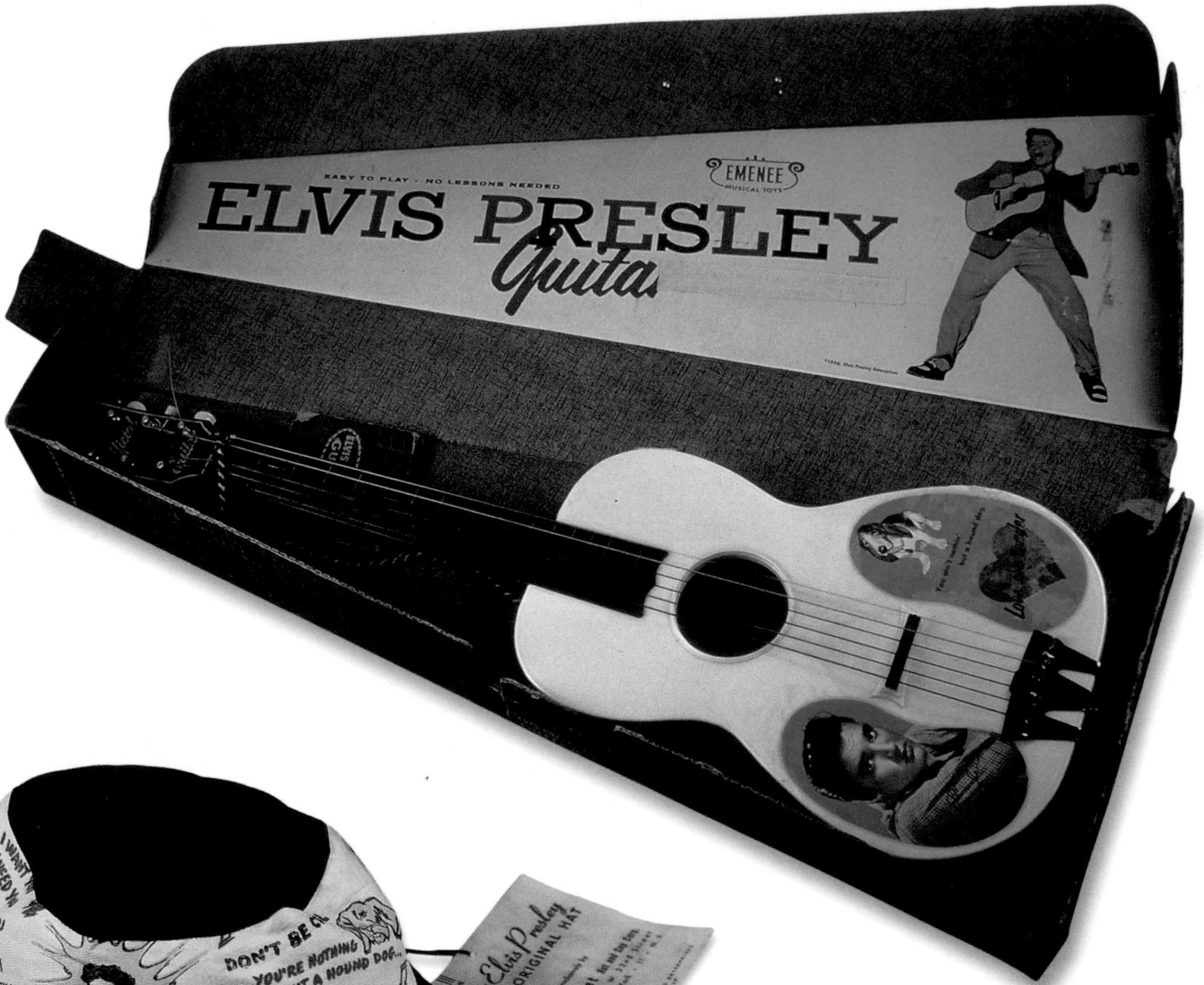

1956 MERCHANDISE Buttons (*right*) were just one of many merchandised products bearing Elvis' name and image that would start to appear in 1956. Everything from clothes to cosmetics, toys (like the plastic guitar above) to neckties–all aimed at teenagers–fueled a multimillion-dollar industry over the next two years, and continued thereafter. Not until the Beatles burst onto the American scene eight years later did any pop or movie star generate anything like the amount of spin-off merchandising that Elvis was associated with. In fact in the long term, Elvis material has far outstripped any other, being marketed in virtually every country in the world for more than 40 years.

In Person
ELVIS PRESLEY

1956 NEW FRONTIER HOTEL On May 23, 1956, Elvis made a debut that was to have a resonance in years to come, in a Las Vegas hotel showroom–his natural habitat later in his career. He played two weeks at the Venus Room in the New Frontier Hotel as "extra added attraction" to Freddy Martin's big band and comedian Shecky Greene.

1956 TRADING CARDS Some of the pictures taken next to the New Frontier pool were to appear on a set of fan trading cards. Trading cards, which were originally marketed in packets of bubble gum, are an American institution; they had long been a craze for sports fans, and the Elvis series launched in 1956 pioneered their use of rock'n'roll stars.

1956 ELVIS CONTRACT The Colonel, quickly anticipating the value of Elvis, went to the trouble of having a highly personalized document for his live appearances. Likewise, part of the deal increasingly involved Elvis being prominently displayed in all manner of promotional material, such as the table flyers *(center)* at the New Frontier.

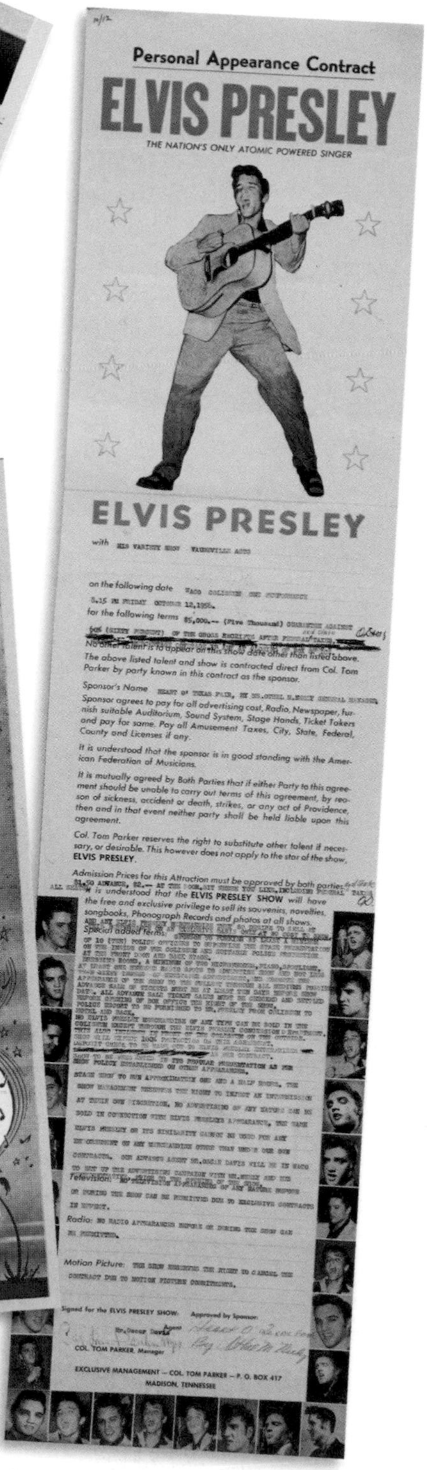

1956

1956

➲ 1956 **NEW FRONTIER HOTEL** The Las Vegas dates represented a new frontier for Elvis in more ways than just name. It was his first move into the seemingly more sophisticated, and certainly financially better-off, world of middle-class, middle-aged cabaret audiences, as opposed to the teen-dominated crowds that packed his tour concerts. And right from the start, he loved it. Although nervous about the reaction he was getting on the first few dates, Elvis went on record as taking to Las Vegas in big way. He felt relaxed there, as pictures taken around the hotel pool suggest.

"Best Wishes
Elvis Presley

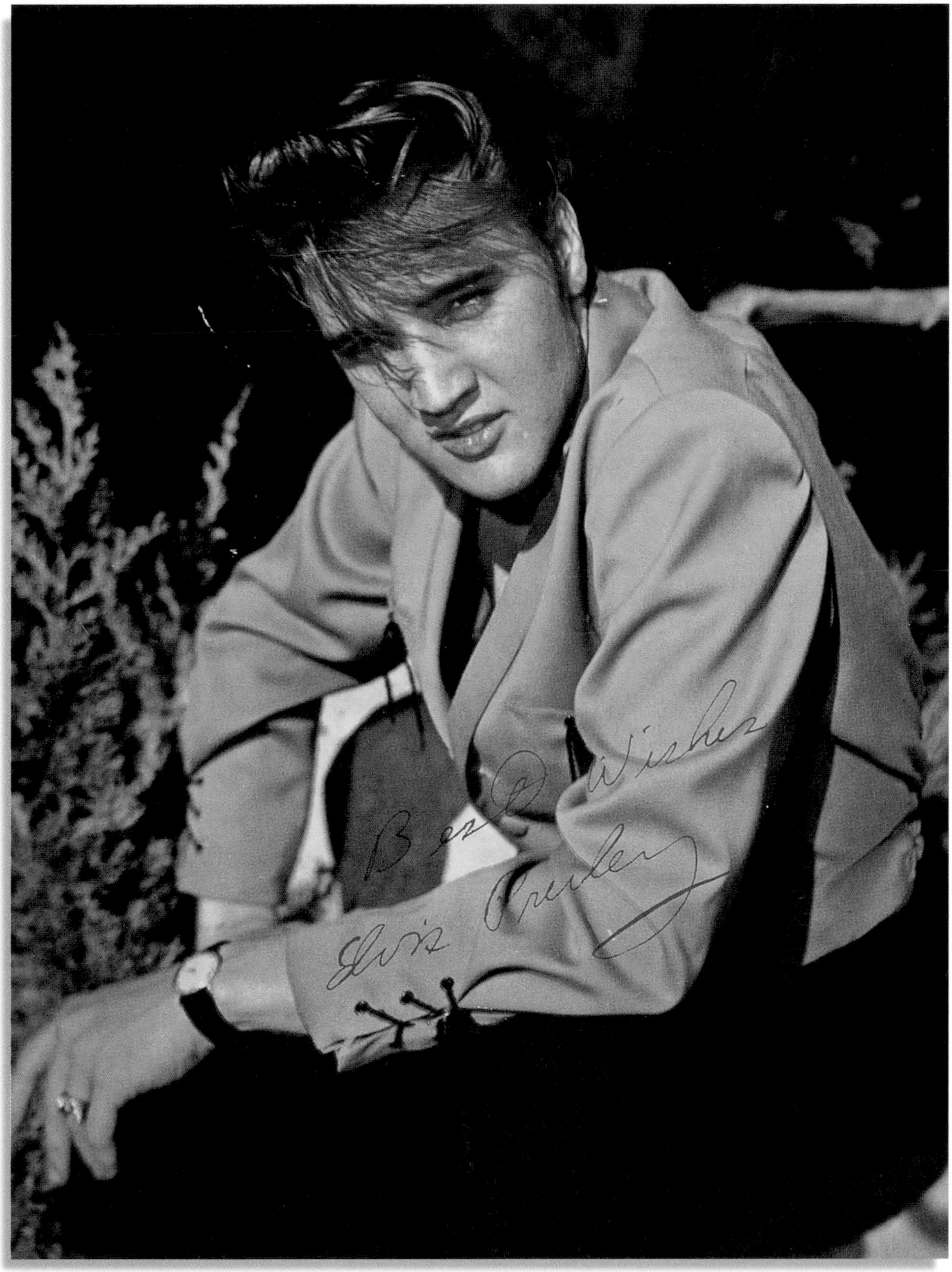

1956 AUTOGRAPHED PHOTOGRAPHS In addition to the trading cards, some of the pictures taken next to the New Frontier pool were to appear on fan photographs, inscribed with a facsimile of Elvis' autograph. In an era when most photography was in black-and-white, these more expensive colour pictures were particularly spectacular.

1956

1956 NATALIE WOOD A small-time Hollywood-based actor Nick Adams became a close friend of Elvis after Elvis' first work in the movie capital on the feature *Love Me Tender*. Adams was to later introduce Elvis to the young star actress Natalie Wood, who at that time was currently basking in her success as James Dean's co-star in the hit "juvenile delinquent" movie *Rebel Without a Cause*, in which Adams had also appeared playing a minor role. During Halloween night in 1956, Natalie Wood arrived in Memphis for a brief, three-day visit. These pictures show the two young stars clowning around at the WHBQ radio station.

1956 BACKSTAGE, MEMPHIS On September 29, 1956, Elvis and his friend Nick Adams were riding around Memphis on his Harley. They visited the Mid-South Fair, mingled in the crowd, Elvis signed some autographs, and they watched the show "Stars Over Dixie"—with Elvis appearing briefly on stage with headliner Dennis Day.

1956

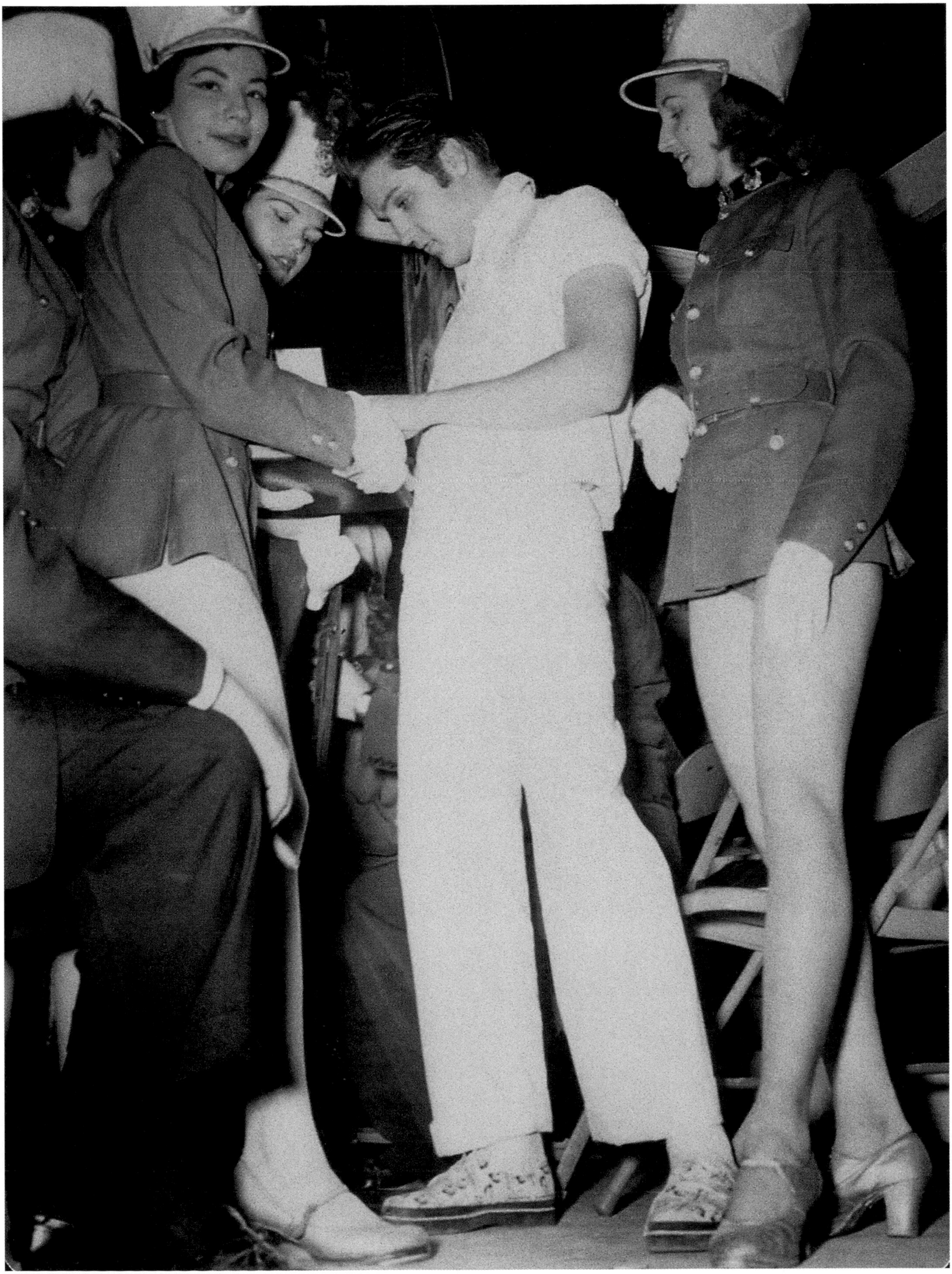

1956

1956 HOLLYWOOD One of the earliest examples of product merchandise, Elvis is presented with a sport shoe that features his name in the design. It was presented to him by the merchandiser Hank Saperstein. The Colonel had signed a lucrative deal with Saperstein in July 1956 in which they (he and Elvis) would receive $35,000 dollars against 45% of licensing fees and royalties, and which gave the merchandiser exclusive rights to exploit the image of Elvis Presley in just about everything–from bracelets to bedroom slippers. The presentation with Saperstein took place during the shooting of *Love Me Tender*.

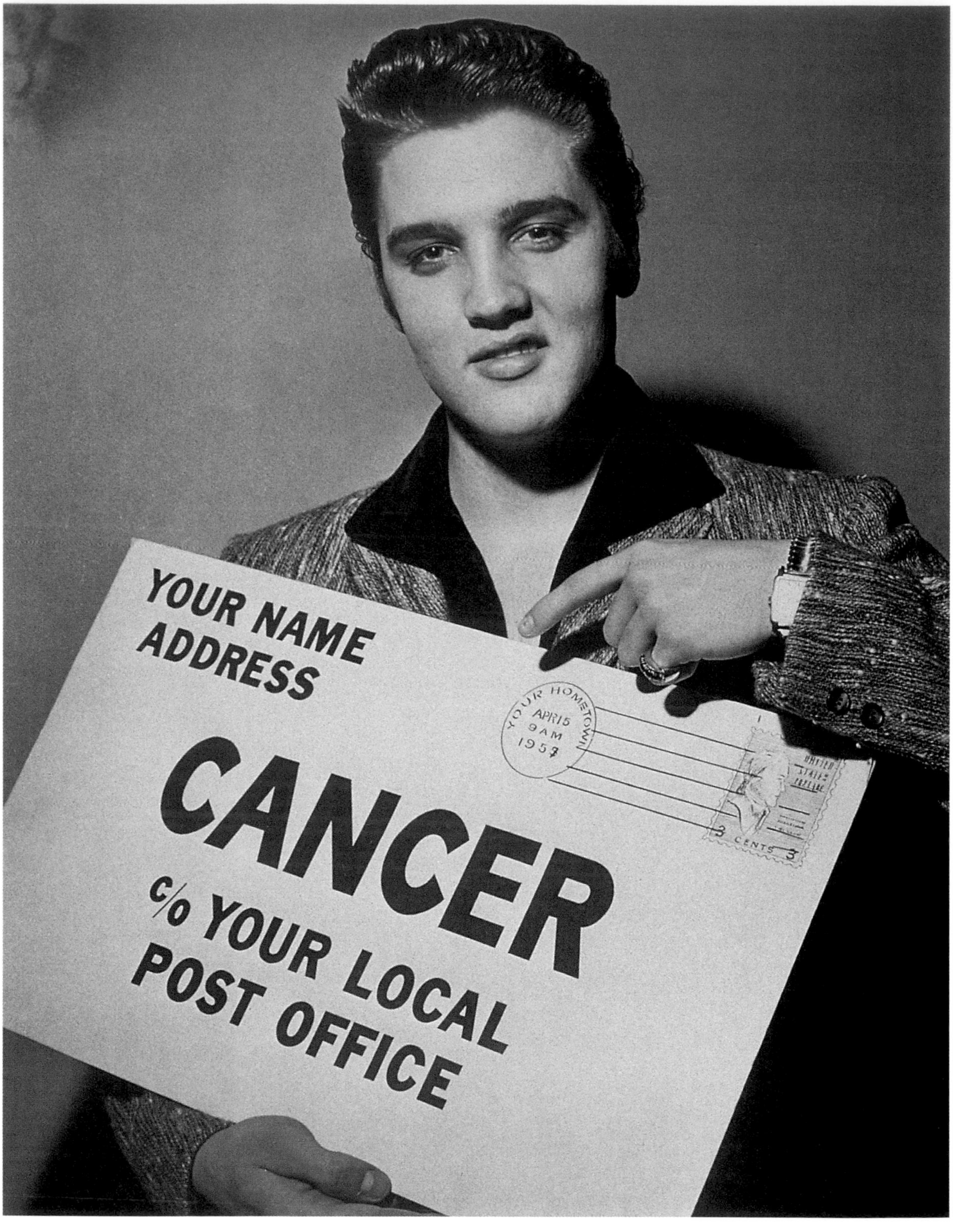

1956 CHARITY Toward the end of 1956 Elvis was noticeably more and more concerned with a number of charitable causes. One big nationwide charity venture was the annual March of Dimes, and in November Elvis publicly urged everyone to contribute as much as they could to the 1957 March in a specially prepared promotional announcement. Various other benevolent causes with which Elvis identified himself during this period included a local Memphis charity for the blind, the twice-annual Goodwill Revue (a fund-raising event organized by the WDIA radio station), and a Christmas drive to raise donations of toys for underprivileged children that was sponsored by the US Marines.

1956

JOIN
MARCH
OF
DIMES

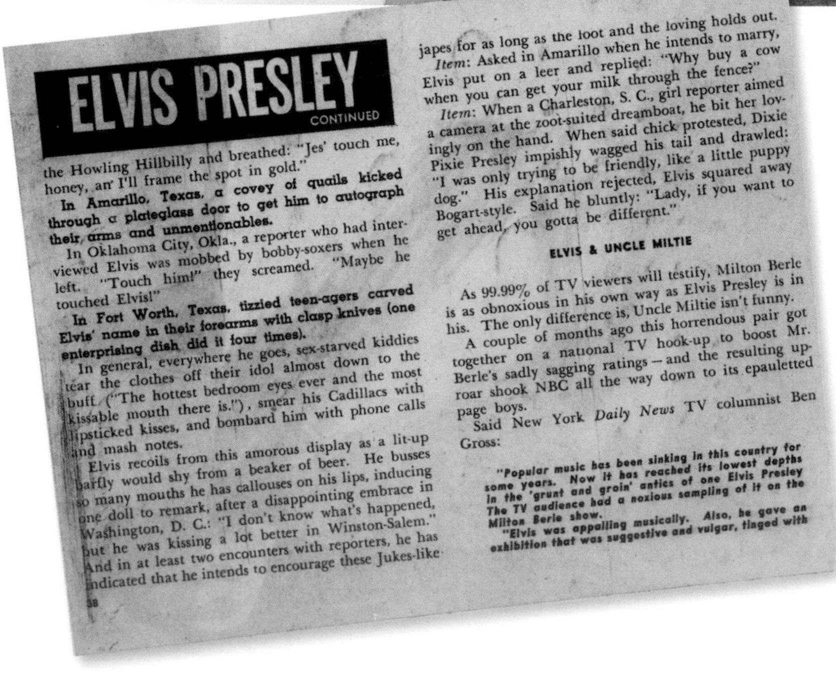

ELVIS PRESLEY
CONTINUED

the Howling Hillbilly and breathed: "Jes' touch me, honey, an' I'll frame the spot in gold."

In Amarillo, Texas, a covey of quails kicked through a plateglass door to get him to autograph their arms and unmentionables.

In Oklahoma City, Okla., a reporter who had interviewed Elvis was mobbed by bobby-soxers when he left. "Touch him!" they screamed. "Maybe he touched Elvis!"

In Fort Worth, Texas, tizzied teen-agers carved Elvis' name in their forearms with clasp knives (one enterprising dish did it four times).

In general, everywhere he goes, sex-starved kiddies tear the clothes off their idol almost down to the buff ("The hottest bedroom eyes ever and the most kissable mouth there is!"), smear his Cadillacs with lipsticked kisses, and bombard him with phone calls and mash notes.

Elvis recoils from this amorous display as a lit-up barfly would shy from a beaker of beer. He busses so many mouths he has callouses on his lips, inducing one doll to remark, after a disappointing embrace in Washington, D. C.: "I don't know what's happened, but he was kissing a lot better in Winston-Salem." And in at least two encounters with reporters, he has indicated that he intends to encourage these Jukes-like japes for as long as the loot and the loving holds out.

Item: Asked in Amarillo when he intends to marry, Elvis put on a leer and replied: "Why buy a cow when you can get your milk through the fence?"

Item: When a Charleston, S. C., girl reporter aimed a camera at the zoot-suited dreamboat, he bit her lovingly on the hand. When said chick protested, Dixie Pixie Presley impishly wagged his tail and drawled: "I was only trying to be friendly, like a little puppy dog." His explanation rejected, Elvis squared away Bogart-style. Said he bluntly: "Lady, if you want to get ahead, you gotta be different."

ELVIS & UNCLE MILTIE

As 99.99% of TV viewers will testify, Milton Berle is as obnoxious in his own way as Elvis Presley is in his. The only difference is, Uncle Miltie isn't funny.

A couple of months ago this horrendous pair got together on a national TV hook-up to boost Mr. Berle's sadly sagging ratings – and the resulting uproar shook NBC all the way down to its epauletted page boys.

Said New York *Daily News* TV columnist Ben Gross:

"Popular music has been sinking in this country for some years. Now it has reached its lowest depths in the 'grunt and groin' antics of one Elvis Presley The TV audience had a noxious sampling of it on the Milton Berle show.

"Elvis was appalling musically. Also, he gave an exhibition that was suggestive and vulgar, tinged with

38

1956 AUDUBON DRIVE Summer 1956, and Vernon and Gladys sit with Elvis in their new home at Audubon Drive. Throughout his life Elvis shared his home with his family, the Graceland mansion housing not just his wife and child but his parents, grandmother, and eventually his aunt Delta, as well various staff and other people.

1956 PRESS CUTTING An early example of "serious" journalism covering the Elvis Presley phenomenon, a highly critical piece from a mid-1956 edition of the much-respected *Life* magazine. As well as knocking just about every aspect of Elvis' music, stage act, and mannerisms–and the TV networks that chose to have him on their shows–it managed to refer to him not just as "the Pelvis," but the "Howling Hillbilly" and "Dixie Pixie Presley."

1956 BUREAU Never averse to a commercial tie-in, these pictures show Elvis in a proposed product endorsement. He poses by a fashionable piece of furniture, a bureau (chest of drawers) in the "contemporary" style of the day, in a promotional shoot for Hungerford Furniture. The sales people at the furniture company subsequently decided that Elvis' appeal was far more likely to be toward teenagers rather than their parents who probably bought the furniture for the home. For this reason the ad was eventually scrapped.

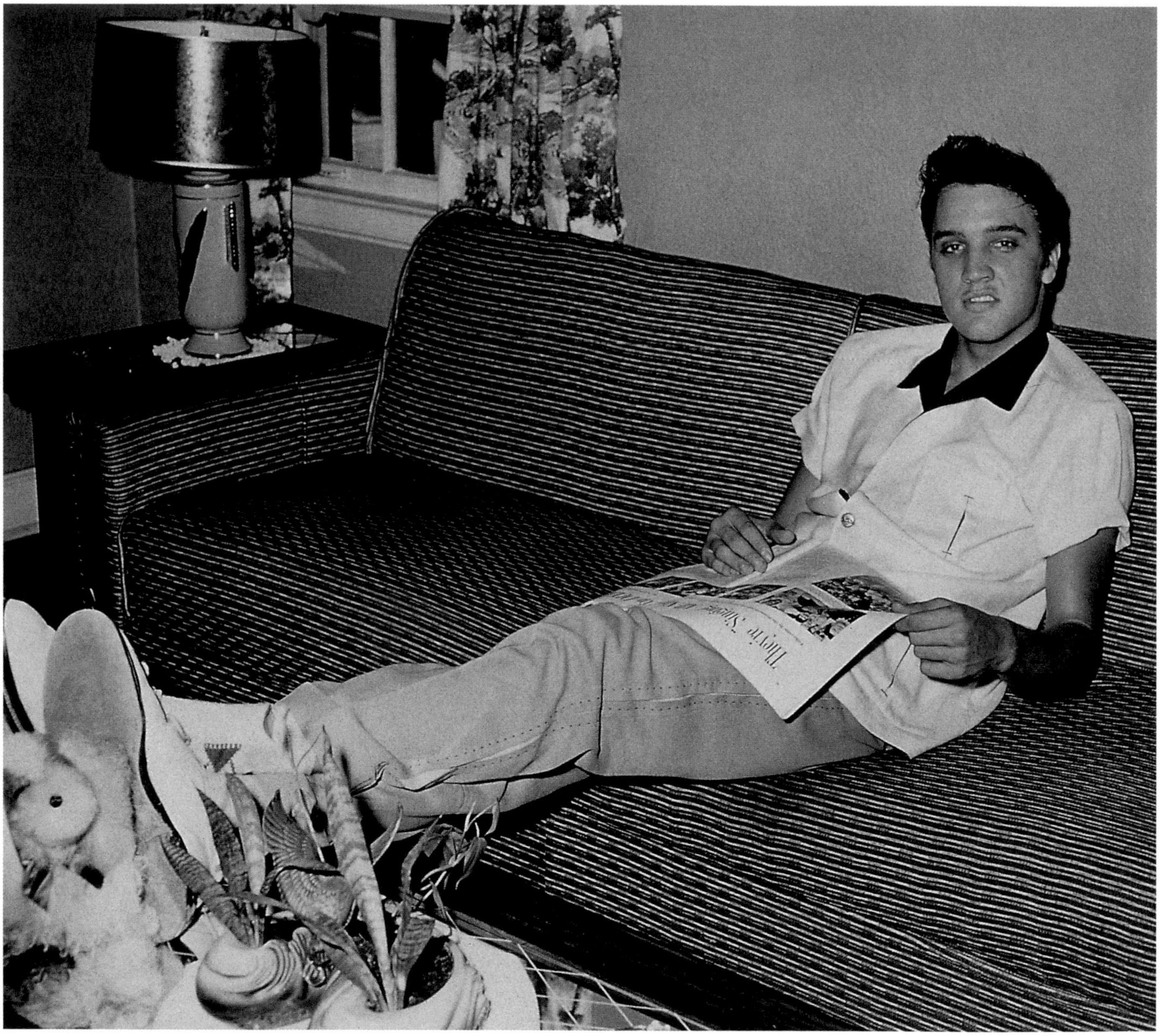

⬆ ➡ **1956 RELAXING** Elvis "relaxes" at home for a photo-shoot, and *(opposite)* examines a copy of a pop music fan magazine called *Dig,* which announces "four pages of Elvis" on its cover. One of the big commercial by-products of the rock'n'roll revolution was a publishing explosion of magazines specifically aimed at the newly emergent market of teenagers. The spending power of young people in America and elsewhere was greater than ever before, and along with fashion, music, and movies catering for the juvenile sector came reading matter covering, promoting, and advertising those same consumer areas. The fan magazine, dominated by pictures of the stars, led the field in this respect.

1956

4 Pages of
ELVIS PRESLEY

1956

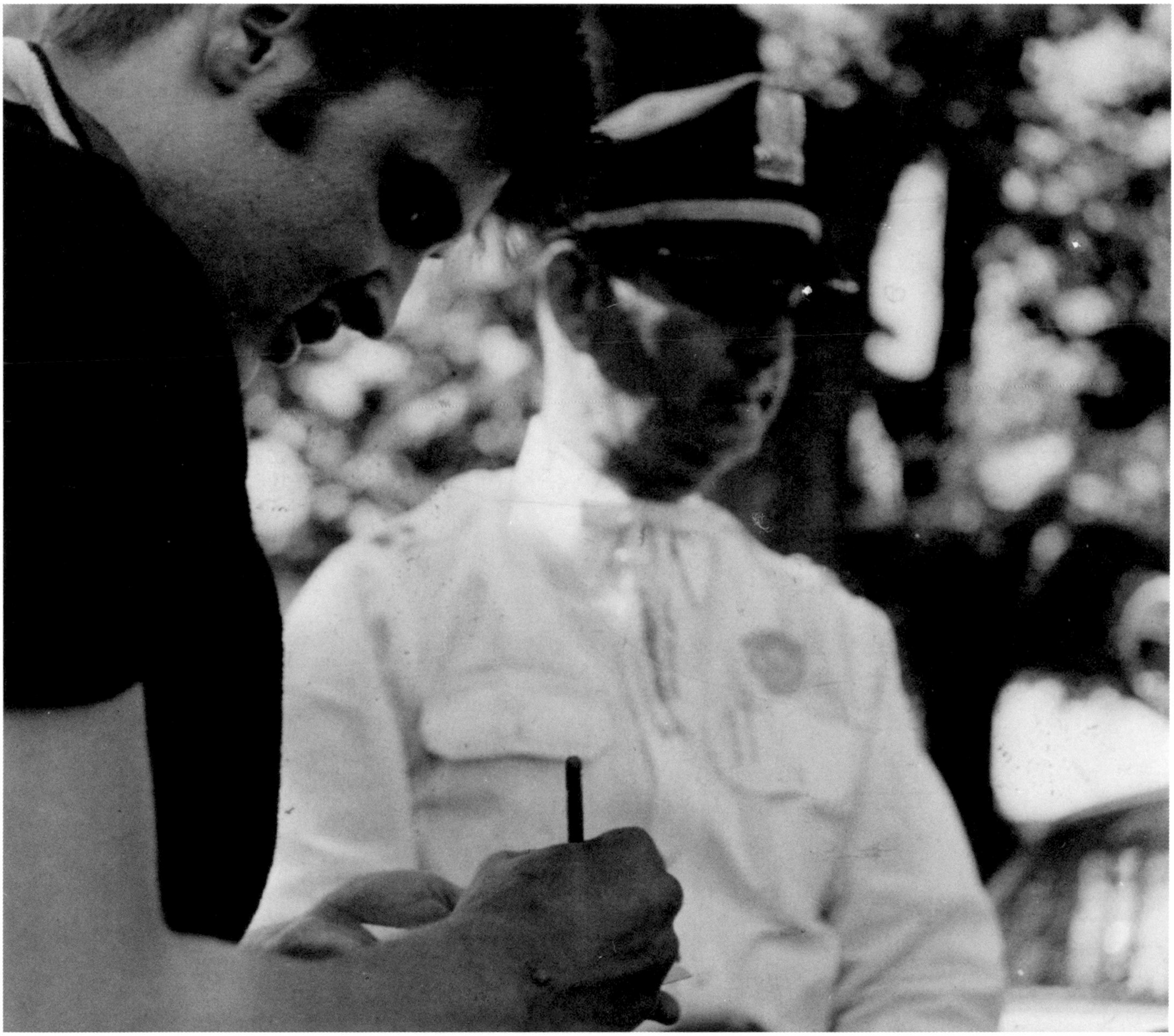

1956 MEMPHIS Despite the fact that it was becoming increasingly difficult for Elvis to move around in public without attracting attention–and usually the attention of large crowds–he still made a habit of driving around the Memphis area in one of his increasingly numerous cars. He clearly had an amiable relationship with the local police; the officer above is a captain, Fred Woodward, who knew Elvis and had personally escorted him as security. Despite the "teenage rebel" image surrounding early rock'n'roll, Elvis always had a respect for officers of the law, to the extent that later in his career he made a hobby of collecting as many honorary police badges and deputizations as possible.

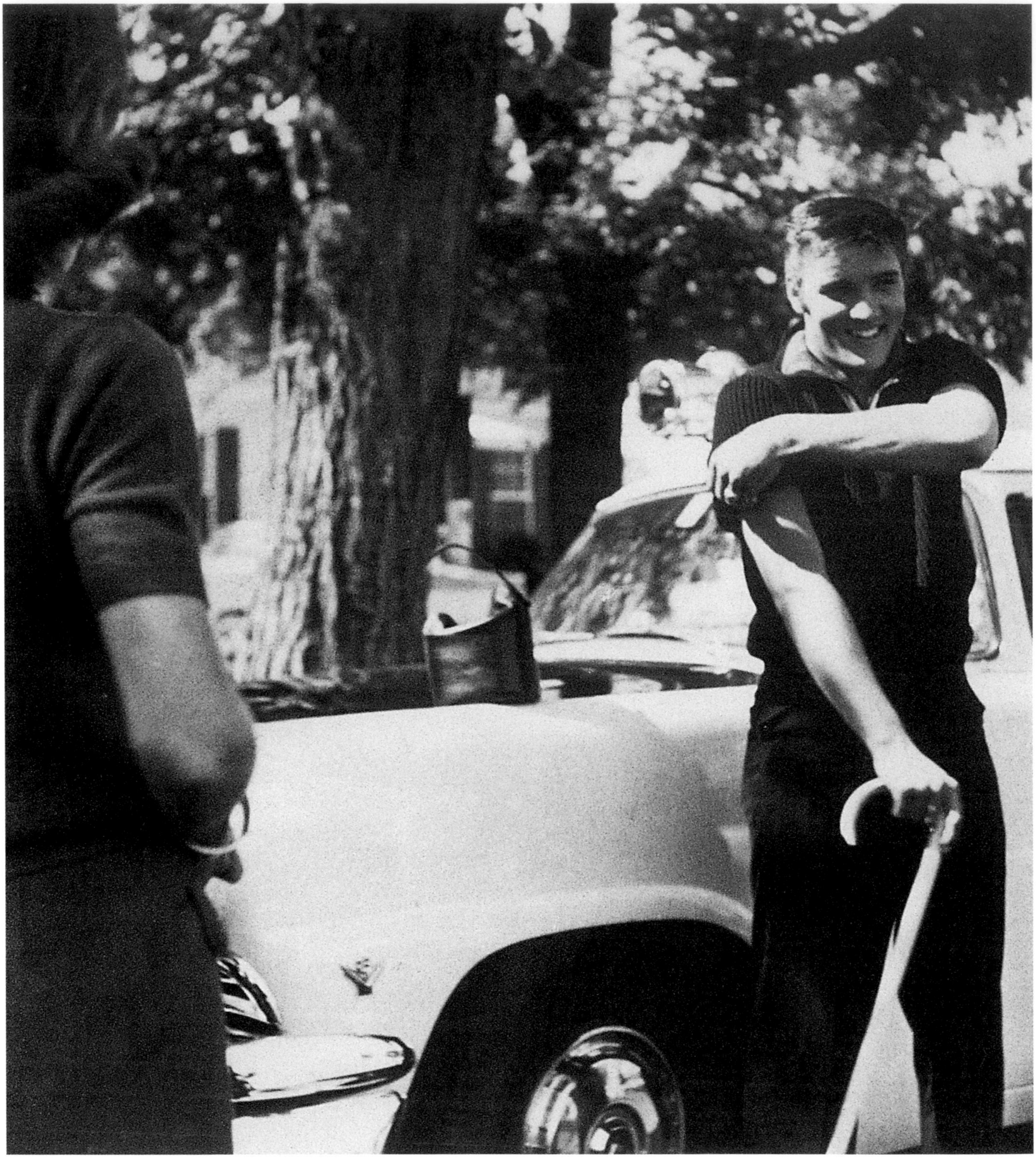

1956

1956 MEMPHIS Here, Elvis had just been talking to the police captain (*see previous page*) in a Memphis street, and right away the passing fans saw an opportunity not to be missed, to meet and greet their idol. This was in the days when he could at least still move around Memphis with some freedom. It was all to change soon.

1956 MEMPHIS Another cop, this time is it an autograph or a ticket? Elvis' flashy cars were highly conspicuous on the streets of Memphis, even though it was during that period of the mid-Fifties when the streets of America were full of spectacular fins-and-chrome monuments to the art of automobile design.

Royal
MODERN METHOD STORE
205
LOEWS

← **1956 MEMPHIS** The *de rigueur* status symbol, especially with the young, in mid-Fifties America was the most ostentatious car possible, and that usually meant the biggest, and that usually meant a Cadillac. Elvis very quickly became famous for his spectacular collection of Cadillacs.

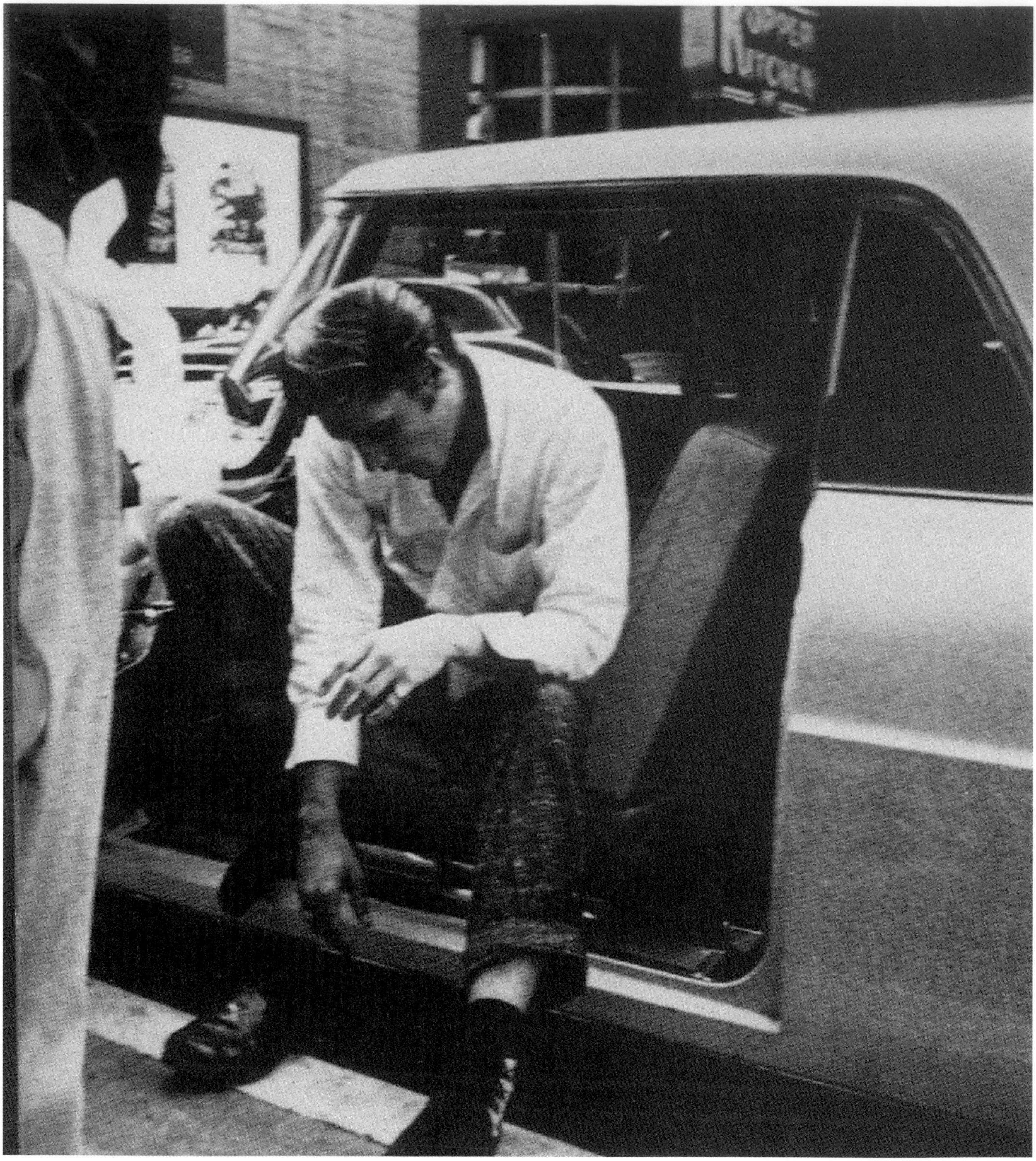

1956 FLORIDA At the beginning of August 1956, Elvis played a series of dates in Florida. On August 2, he had driven from Memphis to Miami in a brand new lavender Continental Premier *(above)* which he had traded in his 1954 yellow Cadillac for the previous week. By the end of the week, he was to trade this in for an even plusher white Continental Mark II, the Premier's bodywork already defaced with fan graffiti. Elvis referred to the increasing nuisance of his more exuberant fans scratching their names on his cars when he famously commented, "Sure they tear off my clothes, they scratch their initials on my cars, they phone my hotel all night... when they stop, I'll start to worry."

1956

1956 MEMPHIS Here, Elvis is captured while attending to one of his cars. He had a rapidly growing fleet of automobiles, prominent among which were the Cadillacs; Elvis was famous for giving these away as gifts, as well as owning them himself. As the number of automobiles increased, problem. A modest carport at the Audubon Drive home soon became too small, and when the family moved into Graceland in 1957, a much more accommodating facility was arranged. Visitors to Graceland today can see the cream of the car fleet in the specially built automobile museum across the

1956 MEMPHIS Along with his passion for expensive cars, Elvis' other consuming interest was in big, fast motorcycles, particularly the US-manufactured Harley-Davidsons. Here he is shown sporting a cap that took its inspiration from the Marlon Brando character in *The Wild One*, a movie that epitomized

1956 MOTORCYCLES Elvis astride another Harley. Elvis was getting a lot of negative press in one way and another, and this "juvenile delinquent" image of bikes didn't help, but, as RCA assured the Colonel, it all helped in selling records. Motorcycles were a symbol of youthful rebellion and many concerned adults feared the effect they had on young people—indeed *The Wild One* was actually banned in the UK until 1967. And bikers in general came in for some unsavory press during the 1960s with the association of any young leather-clad motorcyclist with California's notorious Hell's Angels. Elvis (*left*) sits on a Harley outside the house at Audubon Drive, and *(above)* poses with the biker's obligatory leather jacket.

1956

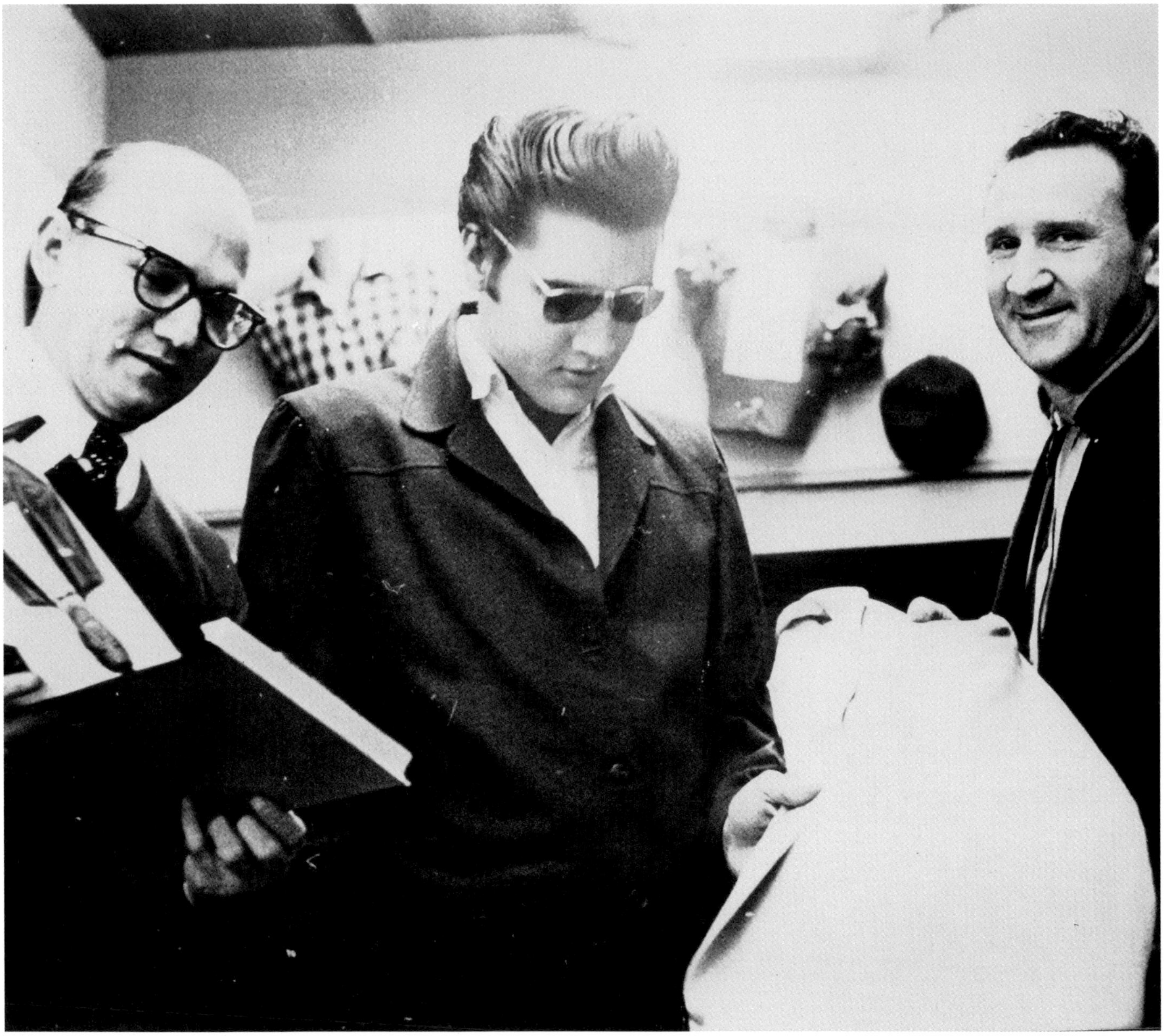

⬆ **c1956/1957 MEMPHIS** Elvis was a loyal customer of Lansky Brothers men's clothing store on Beale Street, in Memphis, for many years. Here, casually dressed and relaxed on home territory, he admires a jacket in the store, attended by Guy Lansky on the left (holding a book of fabric samples) and Bernard Lansky on the right.

1956

RHAPSODY
IN BLUE

1956 ED SULLIVAN SHOW The Ed Sullivan show (which was also officially known as "The Toast of the Town,") was the most prestigious variety program on television at the time. Here Elvis investigates behind the camera during rehearsals for his first Ed Sullivan appearance on September 9, which was actually hosted by the actor Charles Laughton, after host Sullivan had been involved in a car accident just prior to the show. The program–on which Elvis performed "Don't Be Cruel," "Love Me Tender," "Ready Teddy," and two versions of "Hound Dog"–was broadcast live, and was to attract an incredible 80% of the total American TV viewing public.

1956 ED SULLIVAN SHOW A bemused looking Elvis is caught off camera awaiting his second appearance on the Ed Sullivan show. At a press conference before the show he answered questions about his influence on teenagers: "My Bible tells me that what he sows he will also reap, and if I'm sowing evil and wickedness it will catch up with me."

➔ 1956 ED SULLIVAN SHOW Elvis on his second appearance on the Ed Sullivan show on October 28, in full throttle with the Jordanaires, who had by now assumed a regular role as his backing vocal group.

← 1956 BUTTON BADGE This novelty button utilized the then-new technique in which alternate images were visible when it was moved slightly, creating an illusion of Elvis gyrating just like on stage!

↑ 1956 ED SULLIVAN SHOW The somewhat conservative host was known to have only booked Elvis onto his show after Sullivan's rivals–the Dorseys, Milton Berle, and Steve Allen–had upped their ratings when Elvis appeared on their programs. Here on his return date in October 1956, Elvis chats to Ed Sullivan with the Colonel.

1956

1956

1956 LOVE ME TENDER A drama set in the aftermath of the Civil War, Elvis' debut movie was to have been originally titled *The Reno Brothers*, from the novel of the same name by Maurice Geraghty. However, to cash in on Elvis' unprecedented popularity as a recording star, the title was changed to *Love Me Tender*, after one of the songs featured in the film. The song, which was actually a reworking of an old Civil War ballad "Aura Lee," made it to the top of the singles chart. The movie opened nationally in the United States—and thereafter worldwide—on November 21, 1956, amid great ballyhoo, and reached Number 2 in *Variety* magazine's weekly list of top-grossing films.

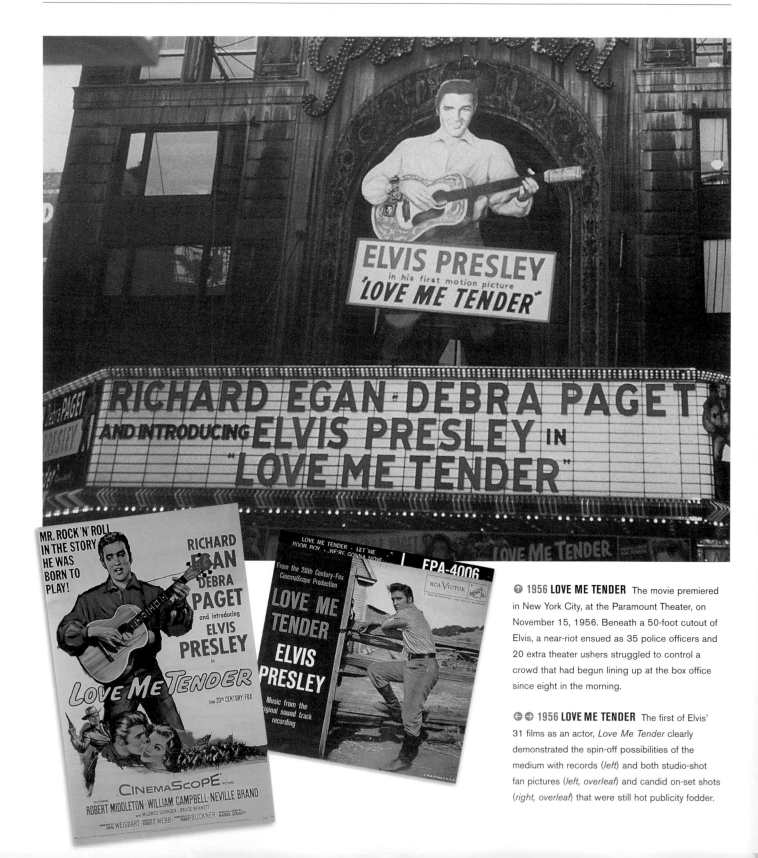

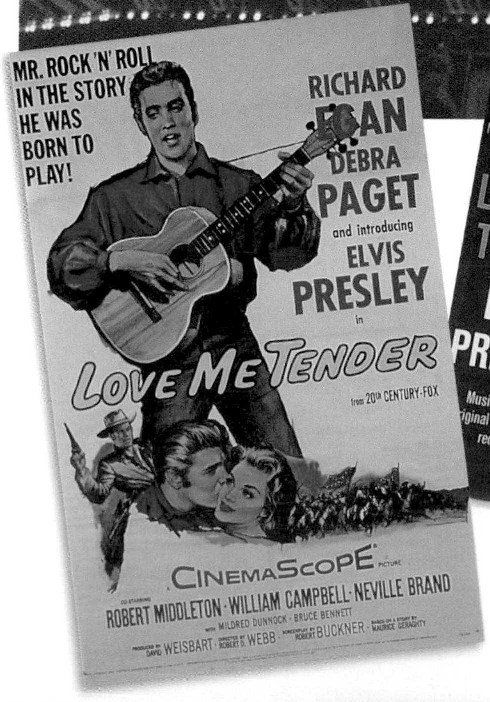

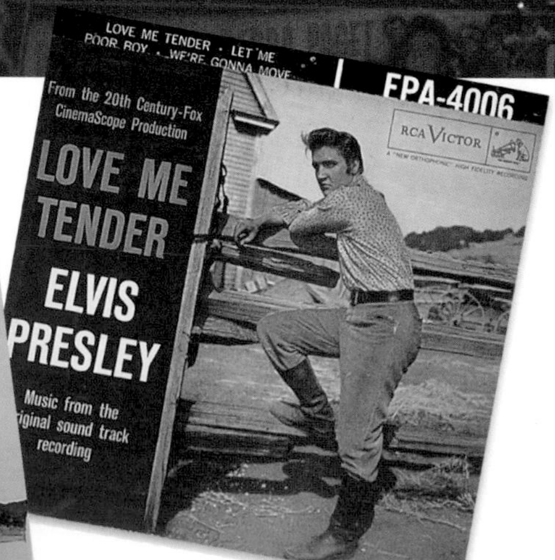

1956 LOVE ME TENDER The movie premiered in New York City, at the Paramount Theater, on November 15, 1956. Beneath a 50-foot cutout of Elvis, a near-riot ensued as 35 police officers and 20 extra theater ushers struggled to control a crowd that had begun lining up at the box office since eight in the morning.

1956 LOVE ME TENDER The first of Elvis' 31 films as an actor, *Love Me Tender* clearly demonstrated the spin-off possibilities of the medium with records (*left*) and both studio-shot fan pictures (*left, overleaf*) and candid on-set shots (*right, overleaf*) that were still hot publicity fodder.

Sincerely
Elvis Presley
Elvis Presley

↑ **1956 LOVE ME TENDER** On the outdoor set with the Colonel and Elvis' cousin Gene Smith. Produced by David Weisbart, who went on to produce three other Elvis film vehicles–*Flaming Star* (1960), *Follow That Dream* (1962), and *Kid Galahad* (1962)–it was the only film performance by Elvis for which he did not receive top billing, that honor going to leading man Richard Egan.

←→ **1956 LOVE ME TENDER** Elvis poses with costar Mildred Dunnock *(left)* who played Clint Reno's mother in the film. A solid Hollywood character actress, Dunnock specialized in motherly roles, and other major films she appeared in included *Viva Zapata*, *The Jazz Singer,* and, the same year as *Love Me Tender*, *Baby Doll,* for which she was an Academy Award nominee. On the outdoor set *(right)* with female lead Debra Paget and Elvis is the Colonel's wife Marie.

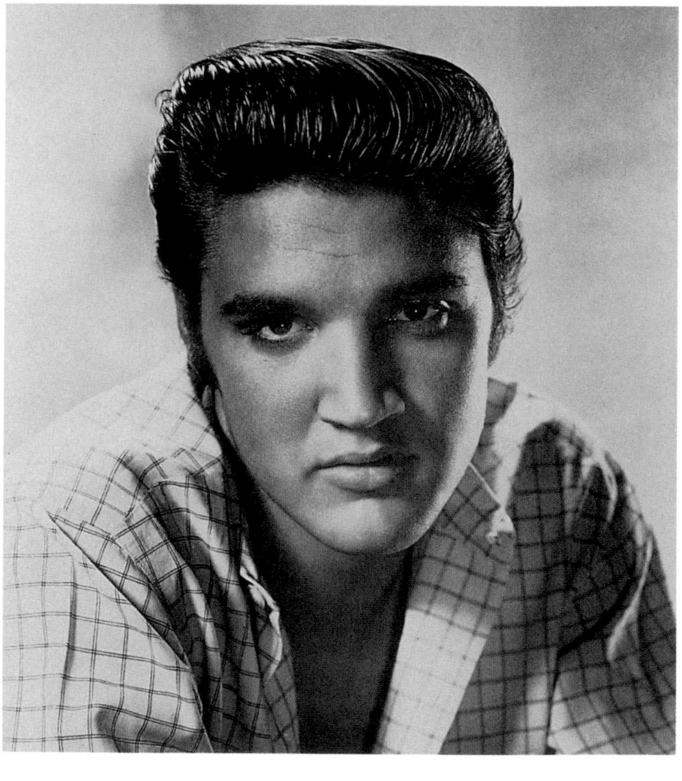

1956 PORTRAITS In what was a seemingly unlikely choice for his first movie, in *Love Me Tender* Elvis was cast in the part of Clint Reno, a role for which Hollywood stars Robert Wagner and Jeffrey Hunter had both been initially considered. The film, which was made in black-and-white in the then-new Cinemascope wide-screen process, ended with Elvis (as Clint Reno) dying, and uttering the last words "Everything's gonna be all right." It was a scene which brought his mother, Gladys, to tears when she first viewed a screening of the movie. Later in his prolific movie career Elvis went on to make two more dramatic Westerns with little or no music involved, *Flaming Star* and *Charro!*

1956

1956 PORTRAITS *Love Me Tender* was the first opportunity Elvis' fans (or his critics for that matter) outside the United States–and by the end of 1956 he was truly an international phenomenon–had of seeing the famous Elvis hips and legs in action. So even though it was basically a drama, the musical items somewhat artificially added for commercial reasons, the film proved an important stage in the promotion of Elvis' image worldwide. And with it came the posed portraits (here and previous pages) promulgated by the film studio which were a promotional element of every big Hollywood movie, in which the star often appeared in costume but obviously in a photo studio.

1956

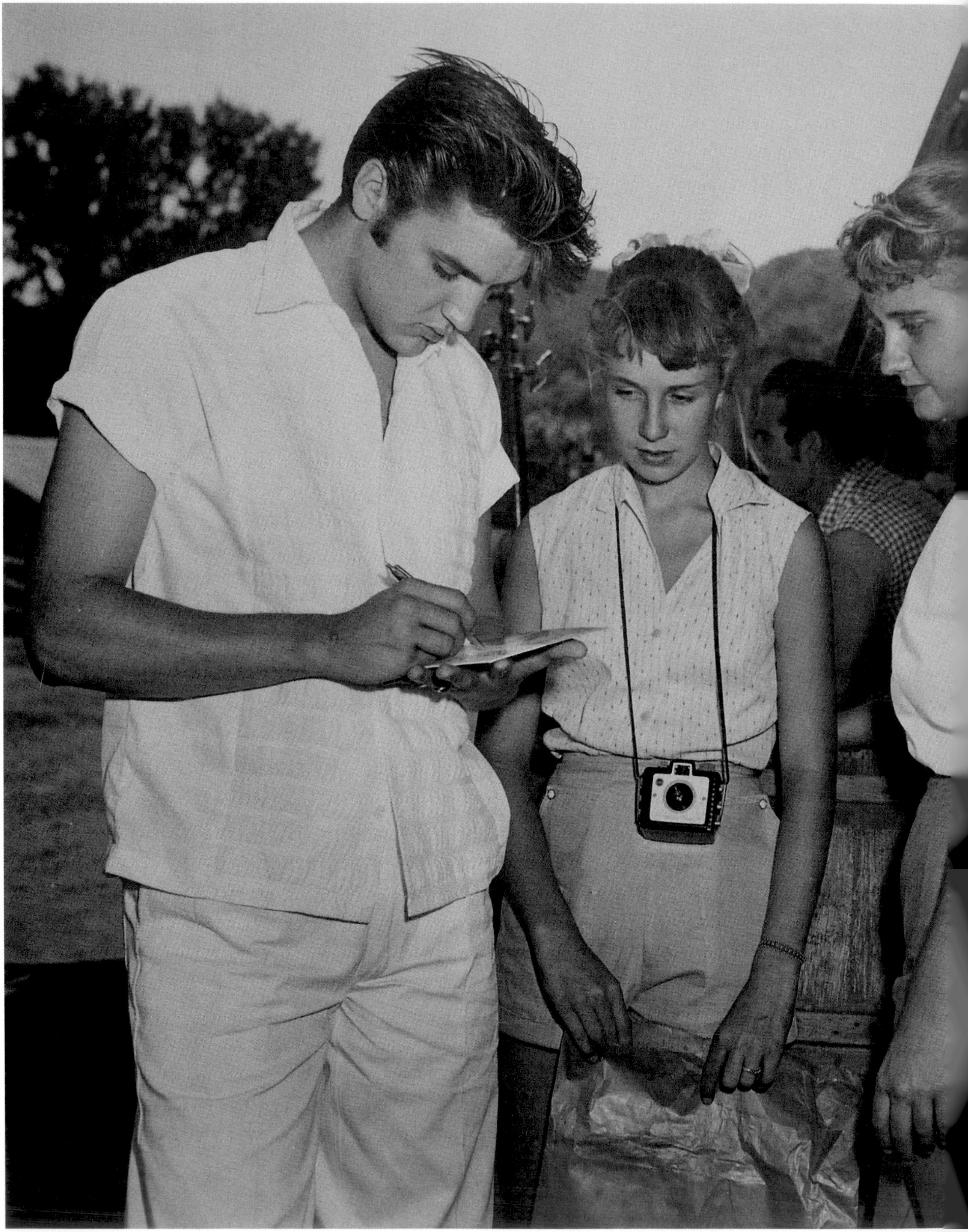

1956

1956 LOVE ME TENDER Elvis signs autographs for fans who were allowed on to the set. Filming started on August 22, 1956, with the exterior shots being done in the San Fernando Valley near Los Angeles and the interiors at the Twentieth Century-Fox studios in Hollywood. The souvenir plaques *(above)*, although referring to the movie's title, actually used pictures taken in the poolside shoot outside the New Frontier Hotel in Las Vegas.

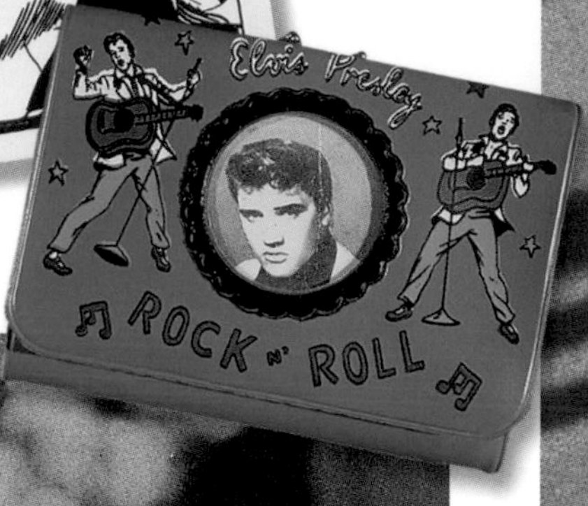

1956 MERCHANDISE The graphic images of Elvis were usually based, though often not well drawn, on familiar photographs. Those on the change purse and wallet above were clearly taken from the shots used on his debut album, while the line drawing is a version of one of the "poolside" poses at the New Frontier Hotel in Las Vegas.

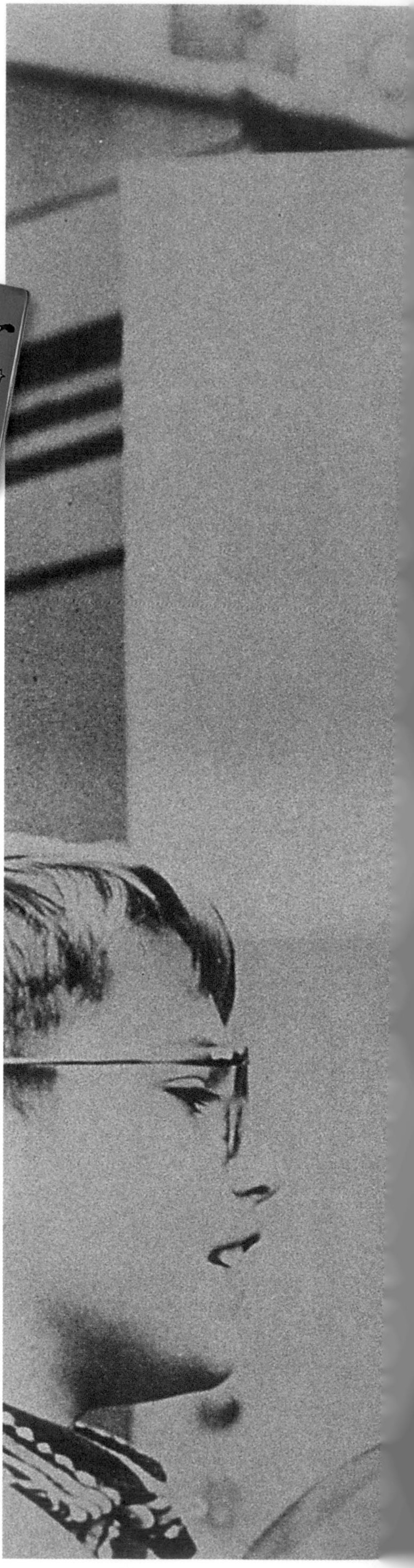

1956

1956 AUTOGRAPHS Another young fan (*opposite*), lucky enough to be allowed onto the *Love Me Tender* set during shooting, gets to meet Elvis, relaxed in shirtsleeves, between takes. Everywhere he went, whether a Memphis street (*above*), a New York hotel lounge, or a California beach, it was open season for the autograph hunter.

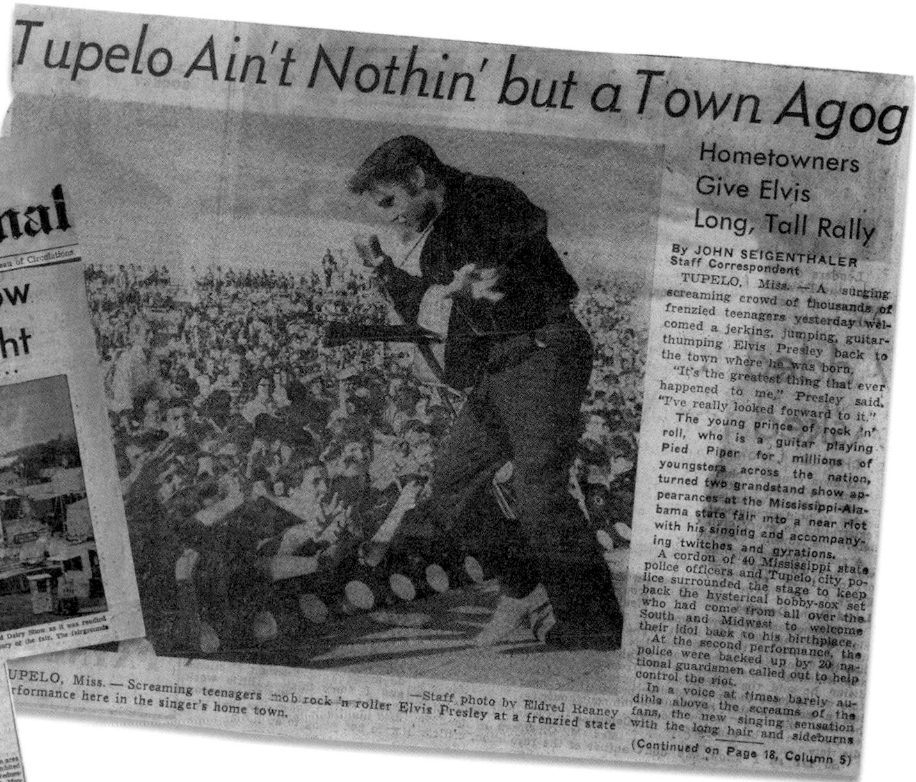

Tupelo Ain't Nothin' but a Town Agog

Hometowners Give Elvis Long, Tall Rally

By JOHN SEIGENTHALER
Staff Correspondent

TUPELO, Miss. — A surging screaming crowd of thousands of frenzied teenagers yesterday welcomed a jerking, jumping, guitar-thumping Elvis Presley back to the town where he was born.

"It's the greatest thing that ever happened to me," Presley said. "I've really looked forward to it."

The young prince of rock 'n' roll, who is a guitar playing Pied Piper for millions of youngsters across the nation, turned two grandstand show appearances at the Mississippi-Alabama state fair into a near riot with his singing and accompanying twitches and gyrations.

A cordon of 40 Mississippi state police officers and Tupelo city police surrounded the stage to keep back the hysterical bobby-sox set who had come from all over the South and Midwest to welcome their idol back to his birthplace.

At the second performance, the police were backed up by 20 national guardsmen called out to help control the riot.

In a voice at times barely audible above the screams of the fans, the new singing sensation with the long hair and sideburns

(Continued on Page 18, Column 5)

TUPELO, Miss. — Screaming teenagers mob rock 'n roller Elvis Presley at a frenzied state performance here in the singer's home town. —Staff photo by Eldred Reaney

Tupelo Daily Journal

Tupelo, Mississippi, Tuesday Morning, September 25, 1956.

Gates Open For Fair's 49th Show

Grand Ole Opry Appears Tonight

The Welcome Mat Is Out For Presley Homecoming

Elvis Traffic Brings Ban On Main Parking

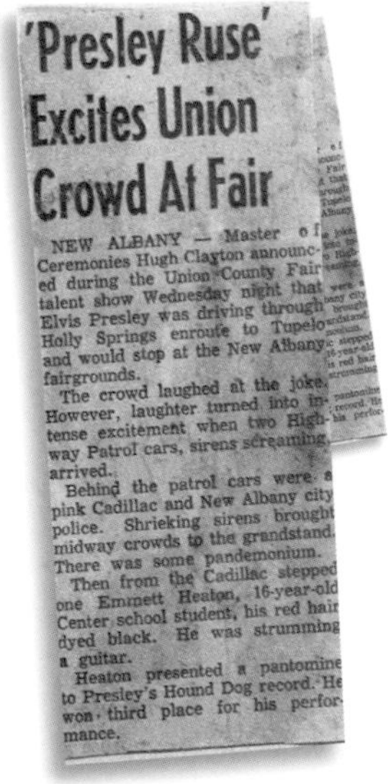

'Presley Ruse' Excites Union Crowd At Fair

NEW ALBANY — Master of Ceremonies Hugh Clayton announced during the Union County Fair talent show Wednesday night that Elvis Presley was driving through Holly Springs enroute to Tupelo and would stop at the New Albany fairgrounds.

The crowd laughed at the joke. However, laughter turned into intense excitement when two Highway Patrol cars, sirens screaming, arrived.

Behind the patrol cars were a pink Cadillac and New Albany city police. Shrieking sirens brought midway crowds to the grandstand. There was some pandemonium.

Then from the Cadillac stepped one Emmett Heaton, 16-year-old Center school student, his red hair dyed black. He was strumming a guitar.

Heaton presented a pantomine to Presley's Hound Dog record. He won third place for his performance.

That Man's Their Boy--Elvis, That Is

—Staff photo by Eldred Reaney

TUPELO, Miss—"He likes to eat hearty," Mrs. Vernon Presley tells reporters at a press conference for her son, Elvis. Presley's father, right, added that Elvis "hasn't got too big for his britches yet."

1956 TUPELO HOMECOMING September 26, 1956 saw a triumphant Elvis Presley return to his hometown of Tupelo, Mississippi, to make a sensational open-air appearance at the annual Mississippi-Alabama State Fair and Dairy Show. Memorable images of the concert were captured not only in photographs, but also in an item filmed for Fox Movietone News. This was back in the days when movie houses showed newsreels between feature films. These remain some of the most potent images of Elvis on stage. The local newspapers' treatment of the "local boy made good" say it all. He was given a real hero's return, and the pictures of Elvis with Gladys and Vernon reinforced the home-boy image.

1956

1956

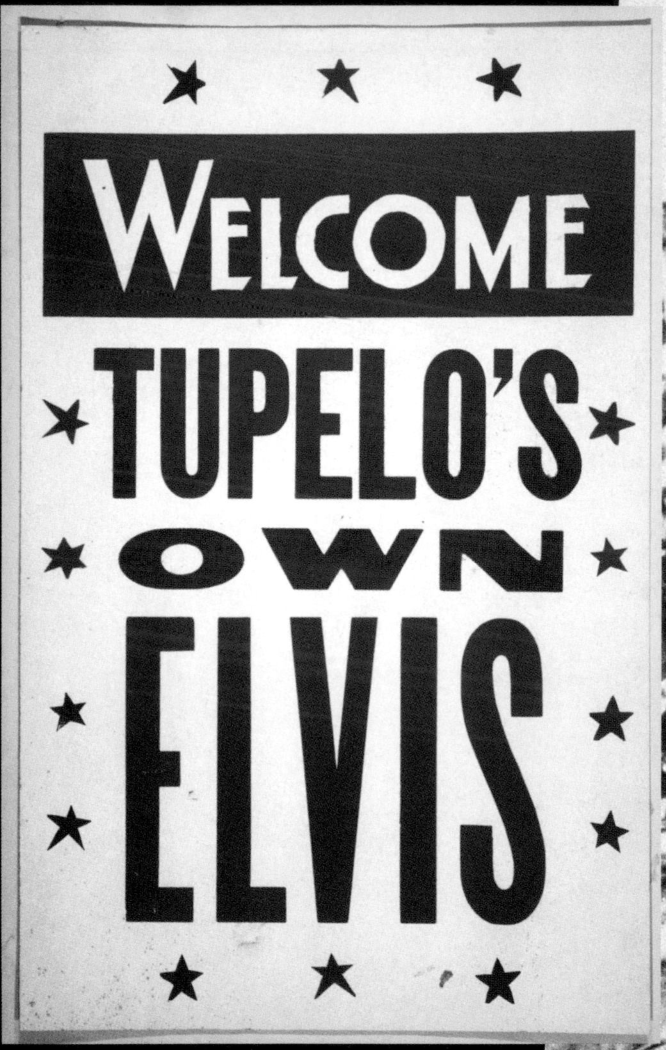

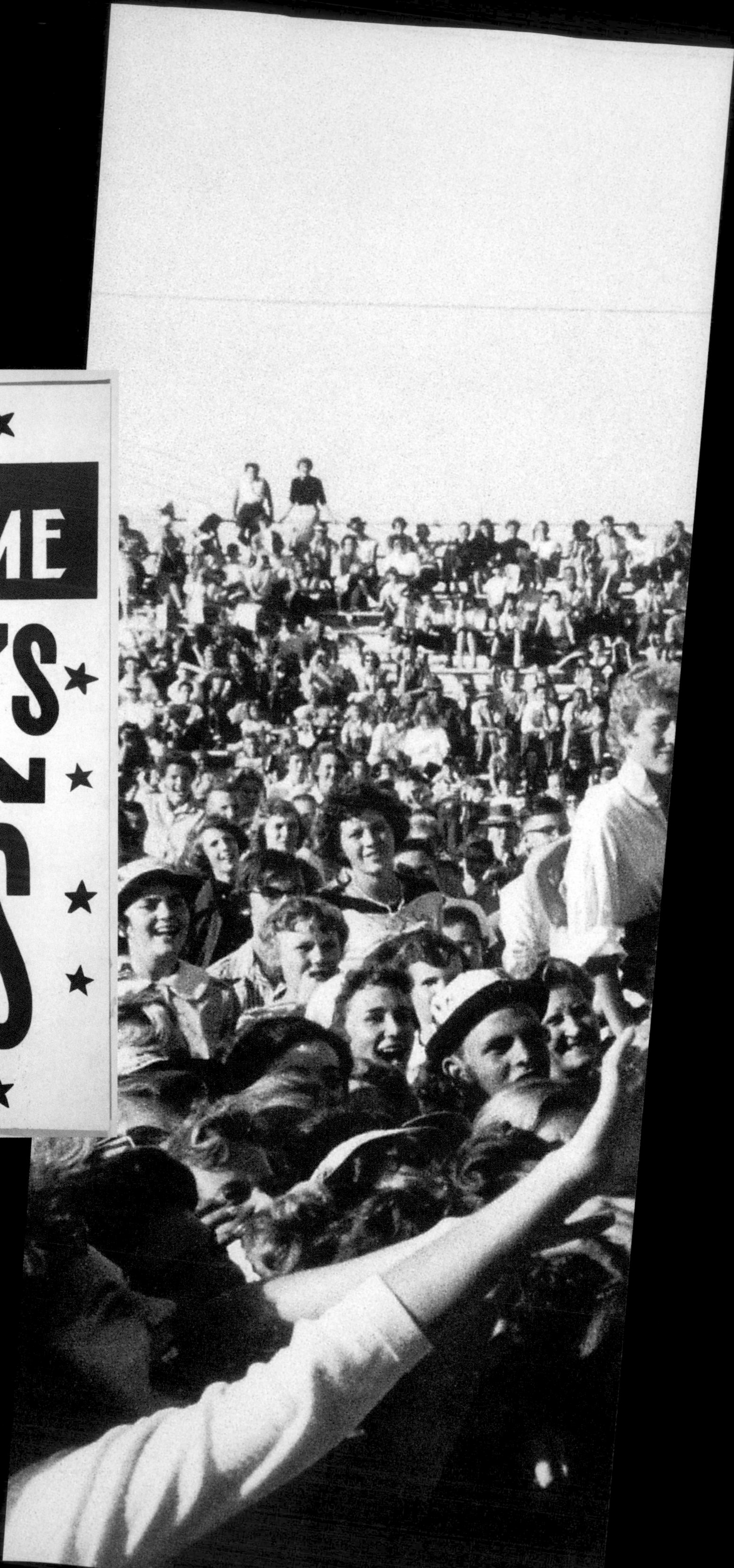

1956 **TUPELO** The fans' outstretched arms signify the absolute adoration that Elvis commanded at his live appearances in the Fifties. The Tupelo homecoming was a triumph, for the town as well as for Elvis, and his performance with Scotty, Bill, D. J., and the Jordanaires was acclaimed by close Elvis watchers as one of the most sensational he had ever given, and indeed in retrospect one of the most memorable of his entire career.

All Shook Up

THE KING OF ROCK'N'ROLL

[1957–1958]

1957 LOS ANGELES Elvis, arms outstretched and flanked by The Jordanaires and Scotty Moore, at a concert at the Pan Pacific Auditorium, Los Angeles, in September 1957.

September 1957

March 1957

September 1957

1957-1958

Colonel Tom Parker was determined to consolidate Elvis' hold on the public imagination after the unprecedented media onslaught that had dominated 1956. This he succeeded in doing through a number of shrewd moves that involved the dovetailing of Elvis' activity in the fields of recording, live appearances, and movies. The once-billed "Memphis Flash" was now truly the King of Rock'n'Roll, and wasn't going to abdicate the crown in the way that his inevitable detractors had predicted.

While *Love Me Tender* was still packing in the audiences worldwide, Elvis began work on his second Hollywood movie in January 1957, *Loving You.* This time the movie was shot in color, and unlike his debut picture it had a solid musical basis to the plot.

Meanwhile, on the live appearances front, he continued touring America, which was in the grip of an unprecedented fan mania that far outstripped any afforded previous idols like Frank Sinatra or Johnny Ray, and made his only appearances outside the US when he played dates in Canada. Inevitably, the concerts got wilder and wilder. And, despite his never setting foot in most of them, he was now a superstar in nearly every country in the world. There was even a black market demand for his discs in the Soviet Union, where his records were officially banned.

February 1957

February 1957

February 1957

And of course it was the discs which were still the backbone of his success. Rock classic followed rock classic, with singles like "All Shook Up," "Teddy Bear," "Loving You," "Jailhouse Rock," "Don't," "One Night," and "King Creole" following each other into the charts in swift succession. The last was the title track to Elvis' fourth movie, which he completed in the early months of 1958, his third picture being one that provided one of the great rock'n'roll visual icons of all time, the title number sequence in *Jailhouse Rock.*

Another of the many images of Elvis that became a true icon from this period was when he wore the celebrated gold lamé suit. It was created for him by Nudie Cohen of Hollywood, who was famous for designing flamboyant outfits for country music stars, and although it proved impractical, it was as much a part of Elvis' visual persona at the time as were the ubiquitous white jumpsuits in the Seventies.

It was a significant time in his personal life too. In the spring of 1957 he bought the Graceland mansion, out on Highway 51 in the southern suburbs of Memphis, for himself, his parents, and his grandmother to live in. Then, at the end of that same year, he received his draft notice, which saw him inducted into the United States Army on March 24, 1958.

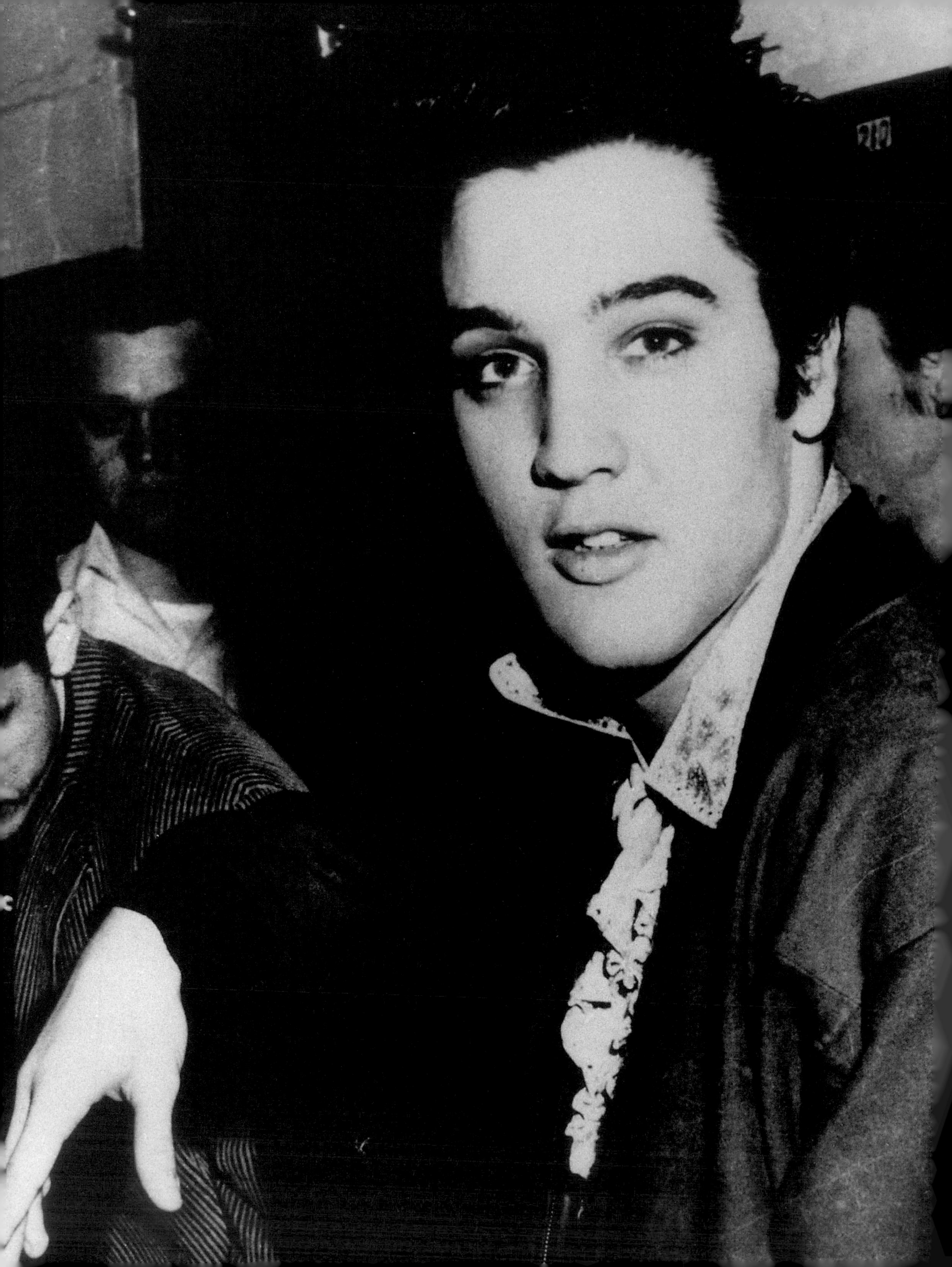

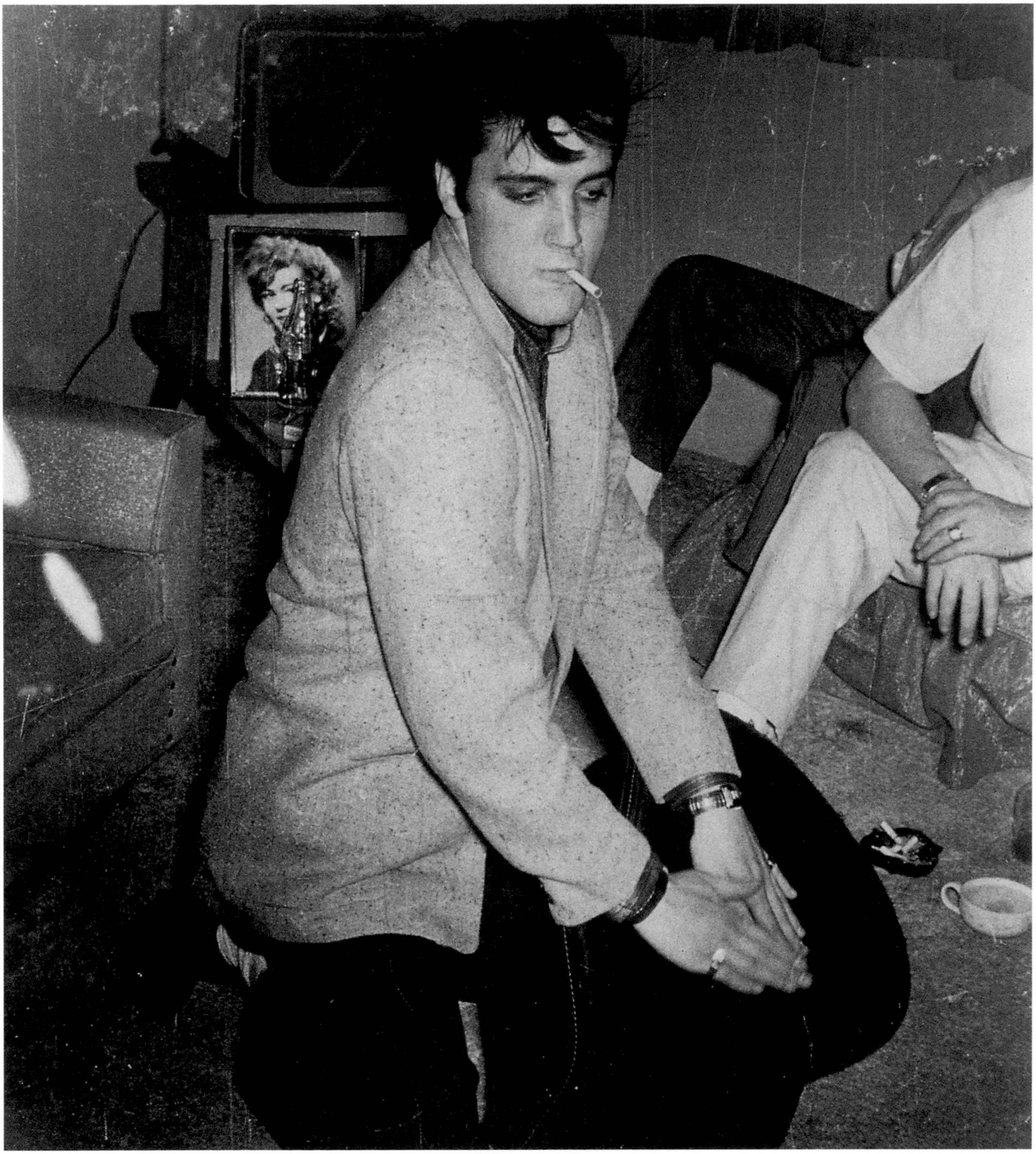

1957 **CANADA** Elvis backstage during the brief Canadian concert visit he made in the spring of 1957, which was followed later in the year by a single concert in Vancouver. Despite many offers of engagements worldwide, particularly from Europe, Elvis never performed outside the US mainland apart from dates in Hawaii and Canada.

1957 **JAM SESSION** Elvis takes part in an impromptu "jam session" in the poolroom at Graceland, using a guitar case in place of a set of bongo drums. Sessions like this often took place in dressing rooms on the road, when Elvis and his entourage found that there was more time spent waiting around backstage than actually working.

1957

1957

1957 BACKSTAGE, TUPELO In September Elvis returned to the Fairgrounds in Tupelo, where he had appeared triumphantly at his "homecoming" date the year before. He obviously thought a lot of the town of his birth, and took an active interest in the social concerns there. This engagement was actually a benefit concert organized to raise funds for an Elvis Presley Youth Recreation Center that was being planned for the city. He performed to a crowd of 12,000, and is pictured here backstage–wearing the top half of his celebrated gold lamé suit–with members of his backing group, the Jordanaires (in the checked jackets) and the now inevitable security men.

ELVIS SINGS!

STADIUM EDITION

Oregon Journal

Section 1 PORTLAND, ORE., MON., SEPT. 2, 1957 PRICE 5c

Presley First Began Singing As Youngster

Heartbreak Hotel First Top Record

Presley Creates Real Jam Session

Elvis Good 'Business'

Teenagers Took Elvis Off Truck

Rock Music 'Snappy'

Singer's Stardom Meteoric

Ticket Sales Boomed Rapidly

Tempo Pulled From Disc Jockey

Singer Subject of Debate

GOLDEN TOUCH is what Elvis Presley has in entertainment's field…

School Bells Ring for Some Here

WEDNESDAY OPENING IS

Indian Troops Ring Portuguese

1957 GOLD SUIT Alongside promotions of Elvis' image such as the record store display above, in Bayonne, New Jersey, another big publicity item was the famous gold suit, which had cost $2,500, and eventually appeared on the sleeve of the 1959 album *50,000,000 Elvis Fans Can't Be Wrong*. However, it didn't last long as a complete stage outfit. Elvis only wore both jacket and trousers a few times on live dates, the first at the International Amphitheater in Chicago on March 28, 1957. Although the suit was popular with audiences, Elvis soon discovered that the trousers in particular were hot and uncomfortable. Subsequently, Elvis was seen in just the jacket with black pants (*see following pages*).

⬆ **1957 TUPELO** The open-air Fairgrounds arena in Tupelo provided a sensational setting for Elvis' increasingly dynamic stage act. His much-publicized gyrations on the up-tempo rock'n'roll numbers were tempered by the occasional slower ballad, for at least one of which he accompanied himself seated at the piano.

➡ **1957 TUPELO** Security became an ever-increasing problem at Elvis' live appearances, not just for himself and his personal entourage but even more so for the local law enforcment agencies. Not only did police have to provide protection for Elvis, they also had to keep order and try to avoid injuries among near-riotous crowds of fans as well.

1957

1957 PRESS CONFERENCE Elvis at one of the frequent press conferences that were held while he was on tour. These on-the-road confrontations with the local–and often the national–media, served two purposes. They helped keep Elvis' name constantly in the news, and enabled him to answer personally the more hysterical criticisms, such as those accusing his "lewd" stage act of being a bad influence on the nation's youth. As the Colonel was heard to comment more than once, "any publicity is good publicity," but he did like Elvis to have the opportunity to put the record straight, and establish an "offstage" image of a clean-living, all-American boy.

1957 OTTAWA In the spring of 1957 Elvis made a couple of rare appearances outside the United States, when he visited Canada. This picture was taken March 3, backstage at the Ottawa Auditorium between two performances in the Canadian capital. He had appeared in Toronto the day before, and was to perform in Vancouver later in the year.

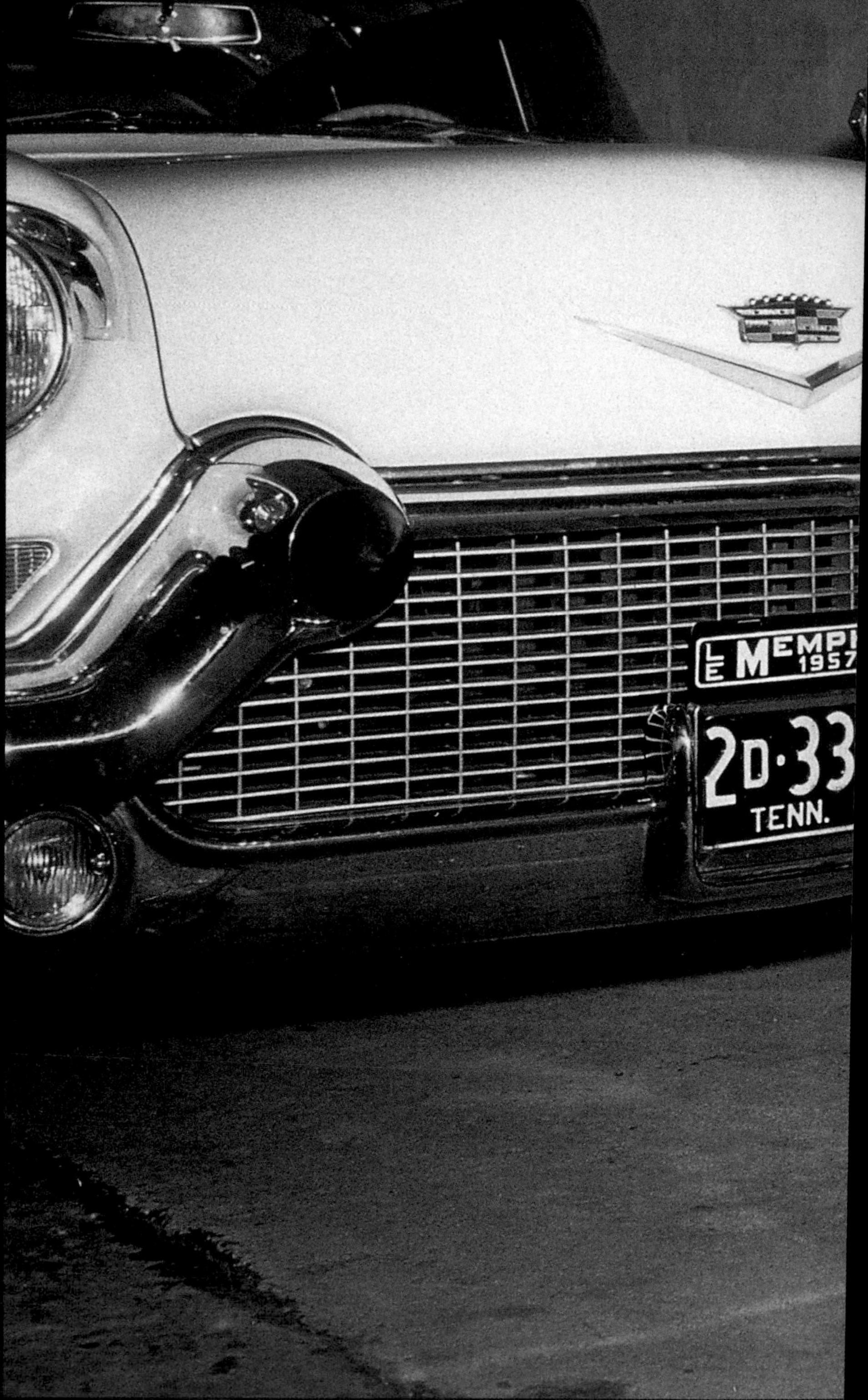

➔ 1957 **AUDUBON DRIVE** It's March and Elvis, having just returned from Hollywood where he has been filming his second feature movie *Loving You*, poses for a photograph by one of his Cadillacs in the carport at Audubon Drive. His collection of cars is getting bigger, but it's not only the carport that is becoming insufficient for his and the family's needs. The Presleys needed more privacy as Elvis' more demonstrative fan following started to become a problem, and as soon as he got back from the West Coast he began shopping around for a new, and more secluded, home.

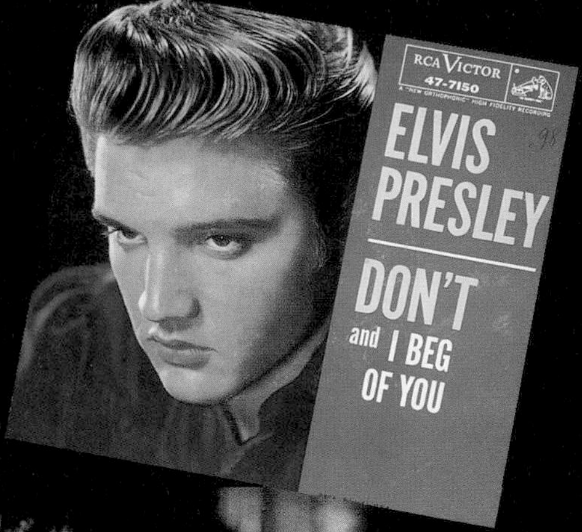

1957 ON TOUR The rigors of life on tour were sometimes reflected in candid pictures of Elvis caught by the camera in moments of reflection. He was to famously describe how the sudden impact of ultra-fame hit him: "Everything happened so blame fast I don't know where I was yesterday and I don't know where I'll be tomorrow."

1957 HOUND DOG Following his July 1956 appearance on the Steve Allen TV show, on which the host thought up the idea of him singing his hit "Hound Dog" to a real live canine on screen, Elvis adopted the idea in a variety of publicity opportunities, and the Colonel made toy dogs a merchandise item up to the end of Elvis' career.

1957 RECORDS *Top*, some of Elvis' biggest hits. *Elvis' Christmas Album*, featuring carols and seasonal songs, came out in October 1957 and hit number one in the *Billboard* album charts. Then in the following March *Elvis' Golden Records* made the number three spot. And the singles kept coming, "Don't" topping the chart in January 1958.

1957 HOUND DOGS The single "Hound Dog," with its flipside "Don't Be Cruel" was, in the summer of 1956, one of Elvis' biggest-ever hits. Originally a song that the songwriting team of Leiber and Stoller had written for the lady blues shouter "Big Mama" Thornton, it was the perfect example of Elvis taking a rhythm and blues number and making it his own. He achieved this not by aping the original, or–as in the case of many other white pop singers–by watering down its dynamism, instead Elvis' version was often even tougher than its fiery inspiration. From then on the hound dogs appeared at events such as press conferences (*above*) as part of Elvis' constant public relations image.

1957

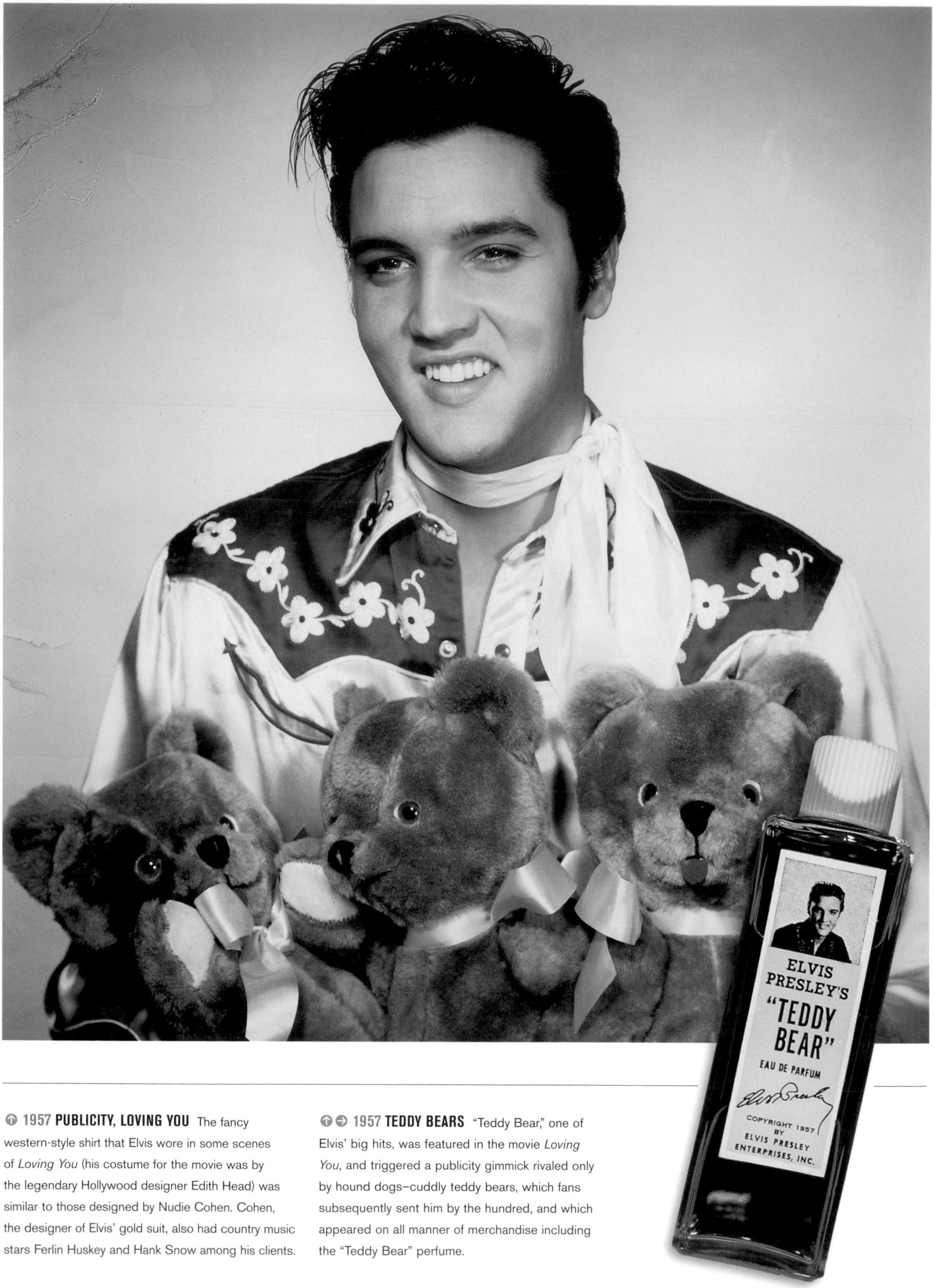

1957 PUBLICITY, LOVING YOU The fancy western-style shirt that Elvis wore in some scenes of *Loving You* (his costume for the movie was by the legendary Hollywood designer Edith Head) was similar to those designed by Nudie Cohen. Cohen, the designer of Elvis' gold suit, also had country music stars Ferlin Huskey and Hank Snow among his clients.

1957 TEDDY BEARS "Teddy Bear," one of Elvis' big hits, was featured in the movie *Loving You*, and triggered a publicity gimmick rivaled only by hound dogs–cuddly teddy bears, which fans subsequently sent him by the hundred, and which appeared on all manner of merchandise including the "Teddy Bear" perfume.

1957

↑ → **1957 LOVING YOU** On the set of his second feature film, *Loving You*, Elvis relaxes and takes the opportunity to investigate the workings of a movie camera *(above)* while awaiting the next take. Except for some location farm scenes, the movie was shot entirely on the Paramount studio lot, between late January and March 1957.

1957

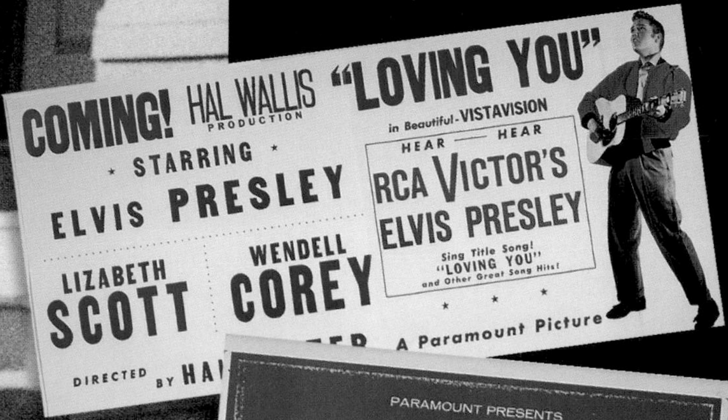
COMING!
HAL WALLIS
PRODUCTION
"LOVING YOU"
in Beautiful-VISTAVISION
STARRING
ELVIS PRESLEY
LIZABETH SCOTT
WENDELL COREY
HEAR — HEAR
RCA VICTOR'S
ELVIS PRESLEY
Sing Title Song!
"LOVING YOU"
and Other Great Song Hits!
A Paramount Picture

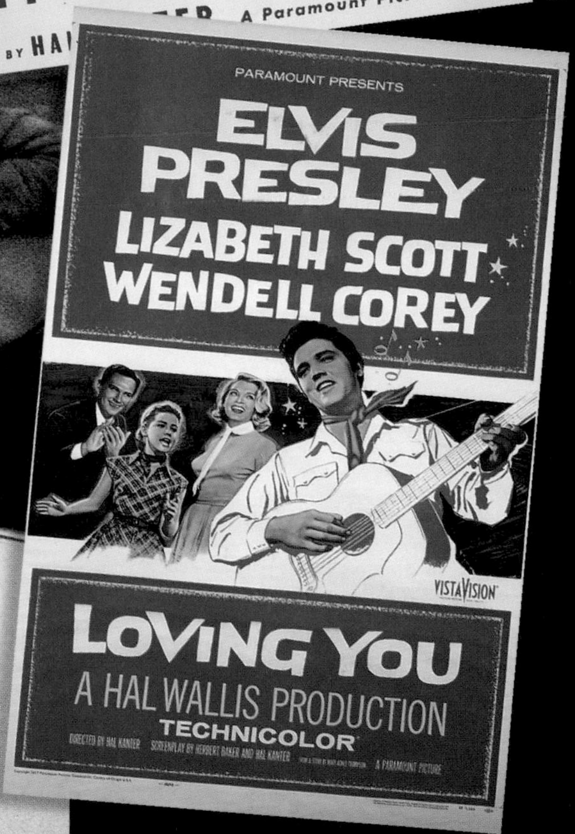
PARAMOUNT PRESENTS
ELVIS PRESLEY
LIZABETH SCOTT
WENDELL COREY
VISTAVISION
LOVING YOU
A HAL WALLIS PRODUCTION
TECHNICOLOR

1957 LOVING YOU Unlike that in his debut movie, Elvis' second movie role was far more in character. He plays a country singer, Deke Rivers (born Jimmy Tompkins) whose path to fame is strewn with fist fights and amorous clinches. This photograph, shot during the movie's production, shows Elvis and costar Lizabeth Scott in a Chrysler Imperial that was used in the film. It was one of Lizabeth Scott's last movies, the sultry blonde having made her name mainly in B movies through the 1940s and early 1950s.

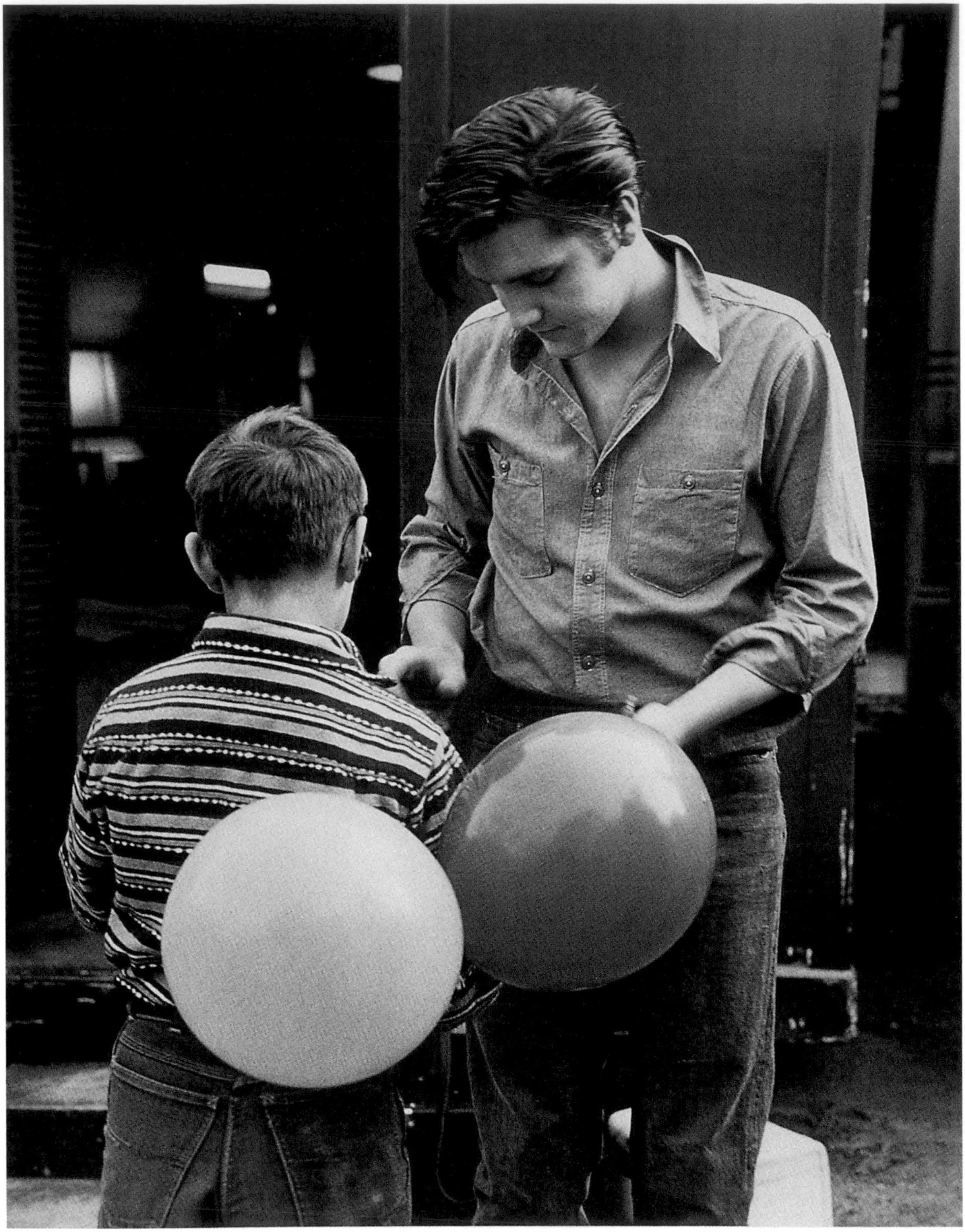

1957

↑ **1957 LOVING YOU** One of a number of casual shots of Elvis wandering around the *Loving You* set. The jeans he is wearing in this photograph, and in the picture at right, were actually from the studio wardrobe department. They were part of the on-screen costume of the character Elvis played in the movie, Deke Rivers.

→ **1957 PARAMOUNT STUDIOS** While cycling around the Paramount studio lot–the bike was presented to him during production of *Loving You*–Elvis encounters the inevitable group of fans, and uses the small boy's head as a rest on which to sign the obligatory autograph. Gladys and Vernon Presley visited the shoot, appearing as extras in one scene.

1957

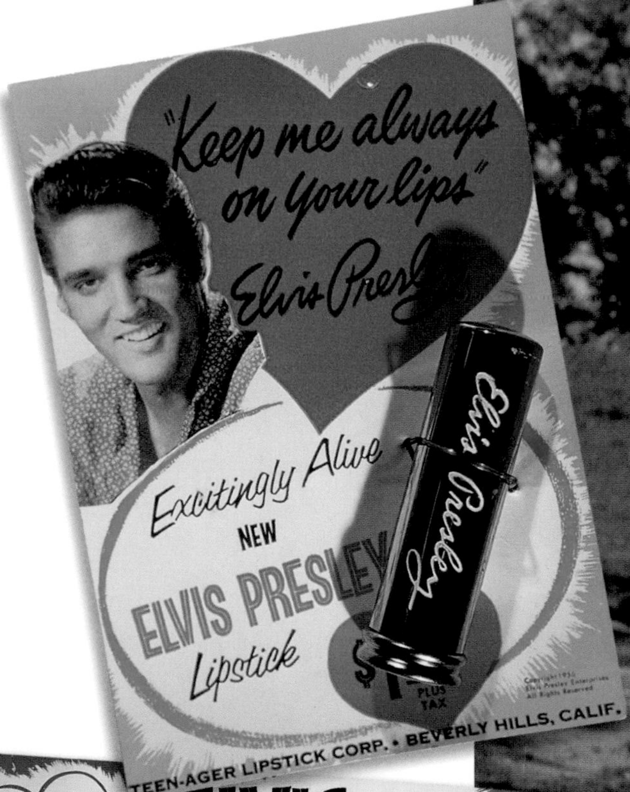

"Keep me always on your lips"
Elvis Presley
Excitingly Alive
NEW
ELVIS PRESLEY
Lipstick
PLUS TAX
TEEN-AGER LIPSTICK CORP. • BEVERLY HILLS, CALIF.

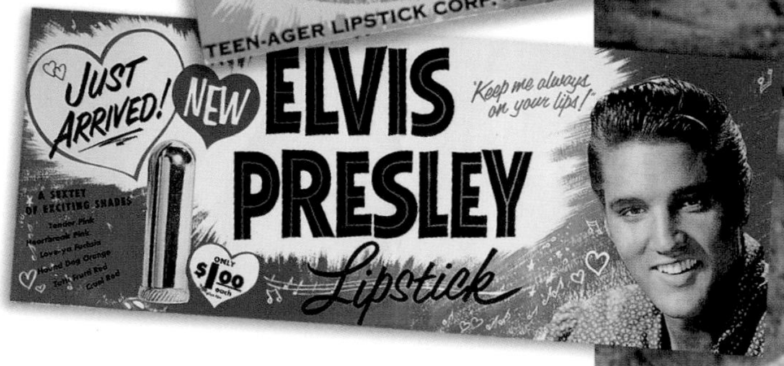

1957 GRACELAND DRIVEWAY The two camera-happy fans, in what looks like a posed picture, greet Elvis as he cruises up the driveway at Graceland. He's driving the 1956 Cadillac Eldorado convertible he bought in July 1957 and had customized with purple paintwork, matching purple and white interior, and monogrammed "EP" floor mats. The car is now one of the major exhibits in the Automobile Museum at Graceland. The purchasing power of his young female fan base was exploited in numerous ways, including the Elvis Presley lipstick.

1957

1957 GRACELAND Elvis stands proud inside his newly acquired home, Graceland (*right*), on Highway 51 in the south Memphis suburb of Whitehaven. He purchased the house for himself and his parents in March 1957 for just over $100,000. The gates (*below*), which he added a month or so later, and which were custom designed with musical notes and a guitar motif, cost another $1,300, and as much again to install. The news story on the front page of the *Memphis Press-Scimitar* illustrates how much local interest there was in the life of the city's most famous resident.

Memphis Press-Scimitar

WEATHER FORECAST: Occasional light rain, high today 50. Partly cloudy, low tonight 33, slightly warmer Wednesday, little change Thursday.

77TH YEAR — MEMPHIS, TENN., TUESDAY, MARCH 26, 1957 — NO. 122

Elvis Looks Over Graceland

Mansion Fit for a (Rock 'n' Roll) King

PENSIVE—Elvis ponders the wonder of a new home.

PERSONAL—Elvis looks over his new bedroom.

PLANS—Elvis checks ideas for his castle.

—Press-Scimitar Staff Photos by William Leaptrott

Presley Is Eager To Redecorate

He Has Plenty of His Own Ideas To Try Out on His New Home

By WILLIAM LEAPTROTT and TOM JOHNSON
Press-Scimitar Staff Writers

Elvis Presley, the boy with the golden voice, and his parents, Mr. and Mrs. Vernon Presley, were to be new owners of one of Memphis' most graciously beautiful homes today.

It marked the long upward climb of a young man who sang his way into the hearts of a nation's young people.

The Presleys were to complete purchase of Graceland at Whitehaven for a price of $100,000.

Elvis already had his own ideas about his own bedroom:

"I want the darkest blue there is for my room—with a mirror that will cover one side of the room.

"I probably will have a black bedroom suite, trimmed in white leather, with a white rug."

Elvis wants the entrance hall of the home decorated with a sky effect—tiny lights for stars, and clouds painted on the ceiling.

"I think it would be great," said Elvis.

The Presleys were at Graceland, making plans.

... in Hollywood, but she and Elvis wouldn't hear of it.

"Elvis said he wanted to stay in Tennessee," Vernon Presley said.

Elvis has ordered purple walls with gold trim for the living room, dining room and sun rooms. There will be white corduroy drapes.

Mrs. Presley said she wasn't too enthusiastic about purple walls — she preferred lighter colors.

But Elvis, "like most young people, likes dark, cozy colors."

The Presleys hope to be in their new home by April 15, when all the re-decorating is done.

BEAUTIFUL HOME of the Presleys, Graceland at Whitehaven, is caught vividly in this picture, with Mr. and Mrs. Vernon Presley, Elvis' parents, and one of the famed Cadillacs in front.

1957

➊ 1957 **QUOTE** Elvis replying to a newspaper reporter: "I ain't no saint, but I've tried never to do anything that would hurt my family or offend God. . . I figure all any kid needs is hope and the feeling he or she belongs. If I could do or say anything that would give some kid that feeling, I would believe I had contributed something to the world".

➋ 1957 **GRACELAND** Elvis outside the Graceland mansion. When he bought Graceland, somehow he seemed to know it was for keeps. Although he would later buy houses on the West Coast, and a ranch in the country, Graceland, the home he bought to please his mother more than anyone else, remained the base for Elvis, his family, and his closest friends.

↑ 1957 JAILHOUSE ROCK A shot from the poolside scene in Elvis' third movie, *Jailhouse Rock.* In real life, one of the first things Elvis did after settling with his family into Graceland was to have installed a kidney-shaped swimming pool. This was very much a status symbol at the time, the kind of thing that Hollywood movie stars indulged in. Contrary to popular myth, Elvis never actually had a guitar-shaped pool, unlike at least one well-known country music star; or indeed like the flamboyant pianist-entertainer Liberace, who had one custom built in the shape of a grand piano! Elvis' main indulgence of this kind seems to have been the musical motifs on the Graceland gates.

1957

1957 AUTOGRAPHS Another fan, another autograph. Rumor had it–again, a popular myth that later grew up around the Beatles as well–that there was an army of scribes in Elvis' publicity and fan club offices, solely employed to sign autographs on his behalf all day. Certainly while he was touring continually [illegible] and 1970s, he must have signed literally hundreds of thousands of autographs–without any assistance from anyone–though it is acknowledged that he did have others authorized to sign for him in some circumstances. Like he'd said earlier about fans scratching his cars, when the autograph hunters stopped pestering him, that was the time to start worrying.

1957

1957

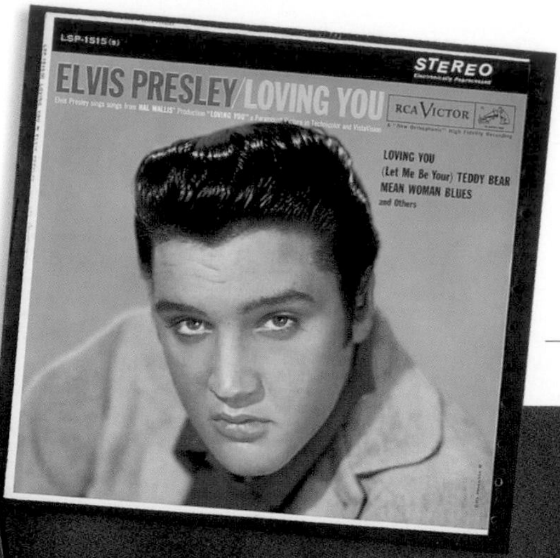

1957 MOVIE MUSIC The records released simultaneously with Elvis' movies contained a number of memorable songs, many of them hit singles—something that couldn't be said of most of his later movies. Below he is shown rehearsing a take during the *Loving You* sessions with the session pianist Dudley Brooks.

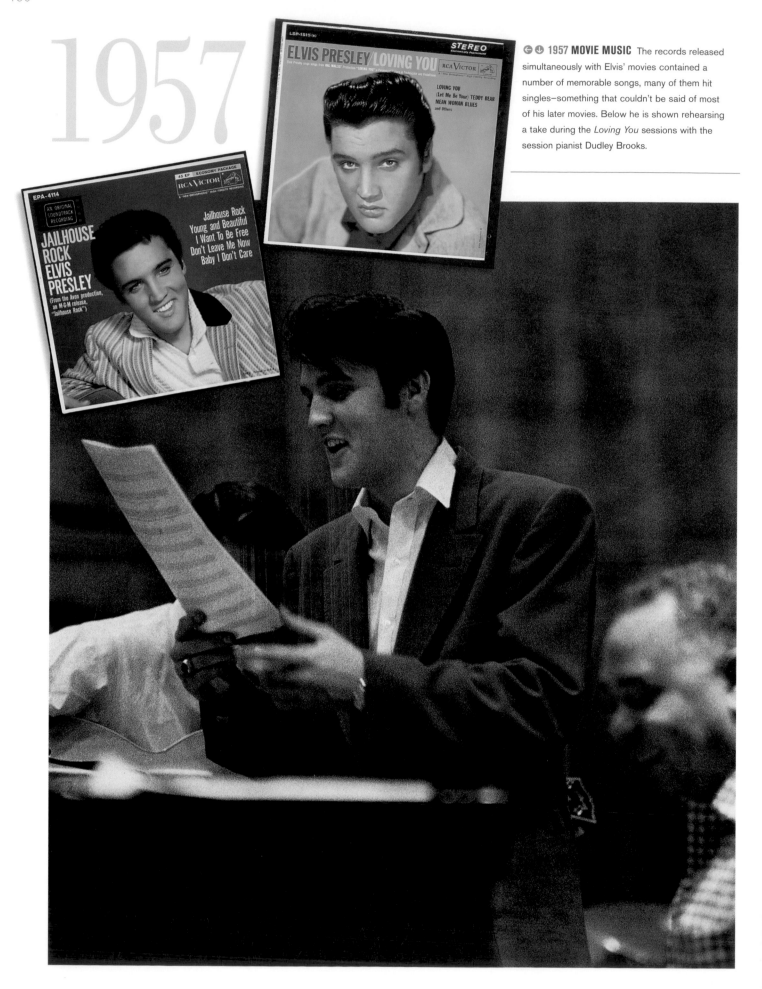

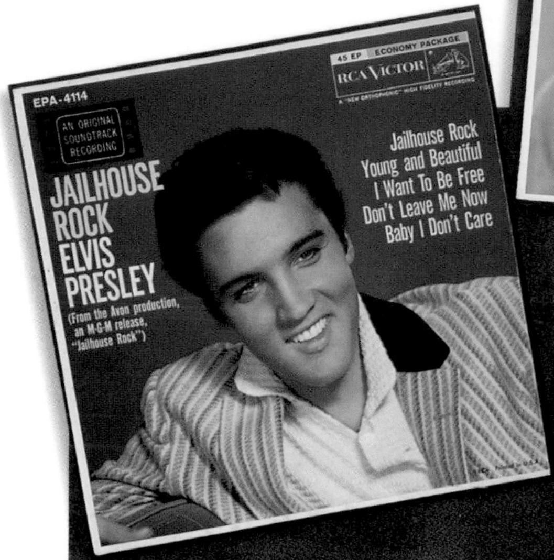

1957 PARAMOUNT Another shot from the *Loving You* music recording sessions. Recordings, which all took place in Hollywood, were split between the Paramount sound stage and the Radio Recorders studios–where this shot of Elvis at the mike was taken, most appropriately on St. Valentine's Day, 1957.

1957

1957

1957 LOVING YOU SESSION Elvis talks to his drummer D. J. Fontana during a break from one of the *Loving You* recording sessions. Also playing on the sessions were (*left*) pianist Dudley Brooks and (*in the background*) guitarist Tiny Timbrell, as well as Elvis' regular musicians (along with Fontana) Scotty Moore and Bill Black.

1958 KING CREOLE SESSION It was back to the Paramount sound stage and Radio Recorders for the *King Creole* sessions, which took place in January and February . An animated Elvis seen here clearly enjoying himself, dubbing his vocals on a largely Dixieland-styled set of songs, employing a brass section for the first time.

0216-2/26

216-2/22

1958

1958 KING CREOLE On the *King Creole* sessions, Elvis was clearly enjoying the luxury of a bigger backing than usual, as can be seen here and on the previous pages, contributing not only as performer but as a genuinely creative part of the record-making process as well.

1958 KING CREOLE Between 1957 and 1960, *Billboard* magazine, the recognized chart source, ran a chart for EP (extended play) records, and Volumes 1 & 2 from *King Creole* hit number one in July and August 1958 respectively. It was also still a time when single sheet music sales were a yardstick of a song's success, as with the three numbers from the movie below.

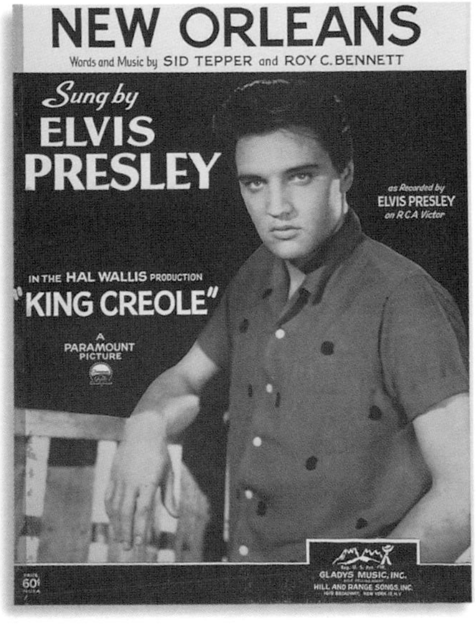

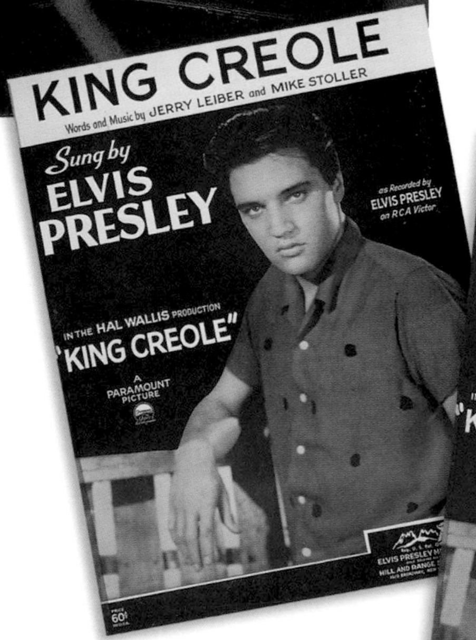

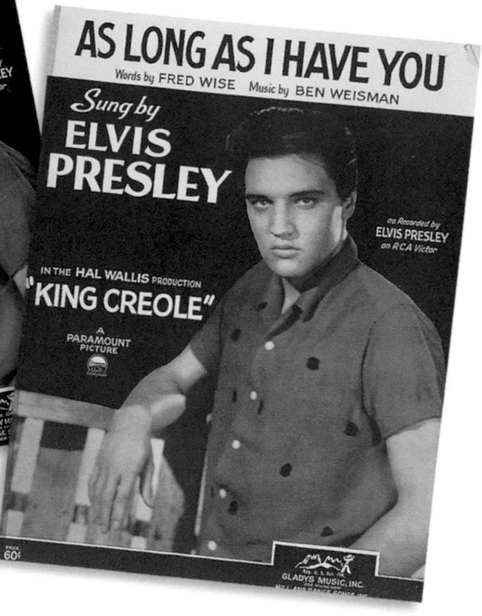

1957

1957 JAILHOUSE ROCK With just six songs performed by Elvis, his third movie could hardly be called a musical, and the dramatic storyline and black-and-white photography underlined this. Indeed, it was billed as "his first big dramatic singing role!" in the movie's publicity. He plays Vince Everett, a singer who gets into trouble with the law, and featured at least three Presley classics in "Treat Me Nice," "(You're So Square) Baby I Don't Care," and the sensational title song which was penned by the now-legendary rock'n'roll tunesmiths Jerry Leiber and Mike Stoller.

1957

1957 JAILHOUSE ROCK Still the hits continued, now via the movies. *Jailhouse Rock* featured a number one single with the title song, in September 1957 plus a number one EP at the end of the year, in time for the Christmas market.

1957 JAILHOUSE ROCK The dramatic role Elvis played in *Jailhouse Rock* required some fight scenes, and to make them as realistic as possible a technical adviser was called in. He was Johnny Indrisano, a former boxer, who had advised similarly in the 1956 movie *Somebody Up There Likes Me*, a biopic of Rocky Graziano starring Paul Newman

1957

1957 JAILHOUSE ROCK The many hundreds of publicity pictures that accompanied Elvis' movies were used to promote not only the movies, but the records that were released at the same time. The pictures then appeared on the inevitable (and often quite extraordinary) merchandise and pinup pictures printed in magazines worldwide.

⬅⬆ **1957 RELAXING** Elvis takes "time out" during the filming of *Jailhouse Rock*, in a series of casual shots taken on the set at MGM's Culver City studios, where the movie was made during the months of May and June. The movie had its premier in Memphis on October 17, and opened nationally across America on November 8.

1957

1957

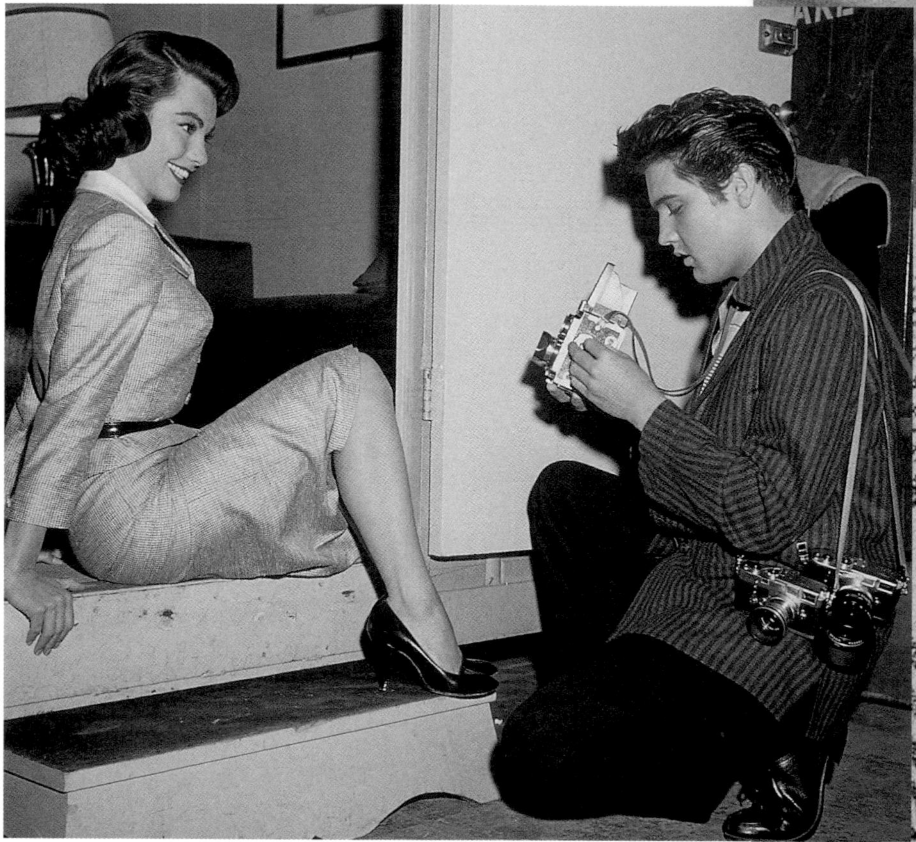

1957 JUDY TYLER Sadly, *Jailhouse Rock* was only Elvis' costar Judy Tyler's second movie when she was tragically killed with her husband of four months, George Lafayette, in a car accident in July 1957, just three weeks after shooting was completed on the picture. Elvis was completely distraught when he heard the news of the 22-year-old actress's death. In the picture on the right she comforts Elvis in a hospital bedside scene from the film, and (*top*) Elvis takes a picture of the glamorous Hollywood newcomer during an on-set break. The film, which presaged the "rock opera" genre by many years, has long been considered by critics–possibly alongside his following motion picture *King Creole*–as Elvis' best-ever performance on the silver screen.

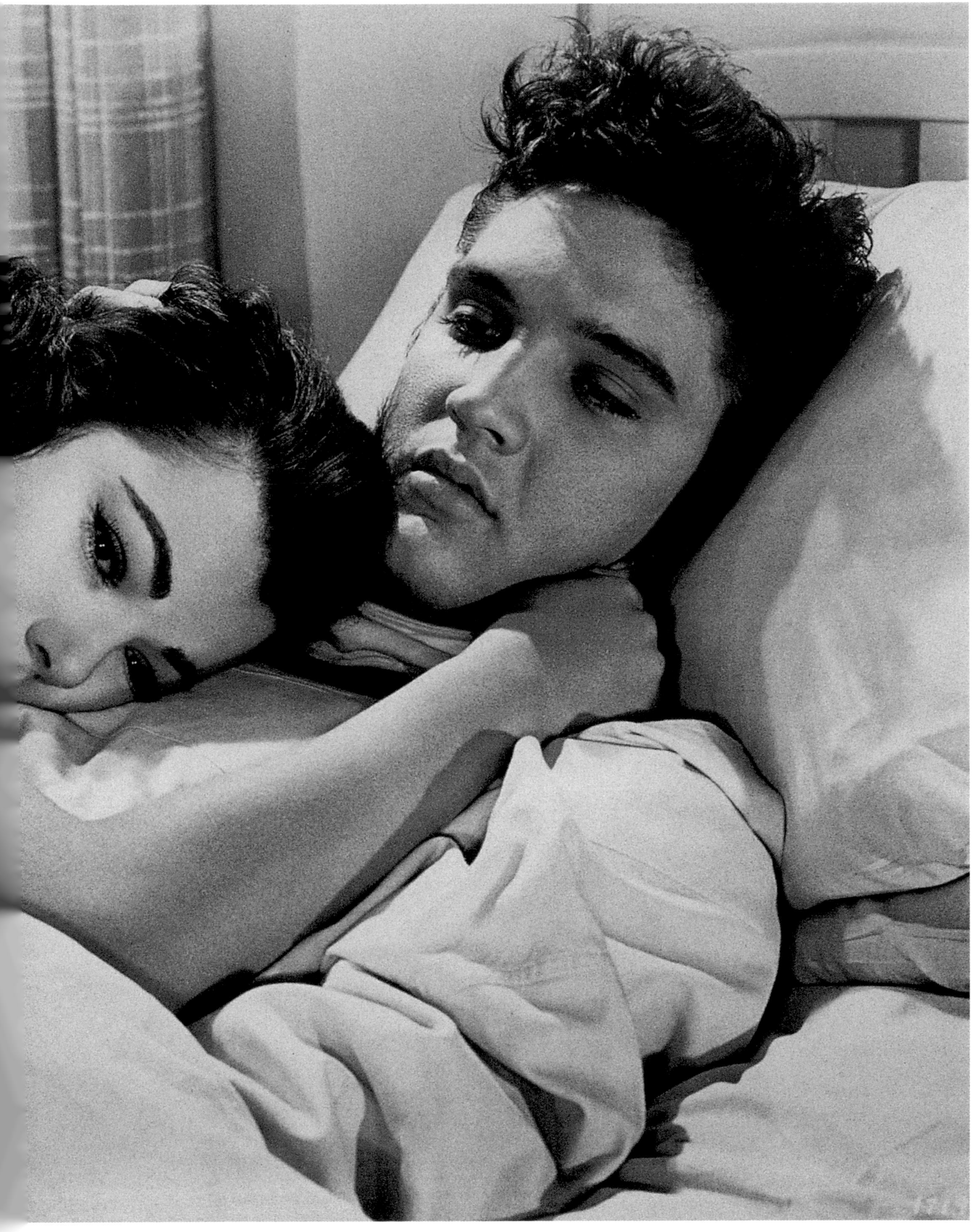

1957

1957 WALLABY Elvis plays with a pet wallaby, a gift presented to him, on the set of *Jailhouse Rock* (it even ended up on a trading card!) It was just one of a number of animals he acquired over the years, at one stage Graceland seemed in danger of becoming a virtual zoo with monkeys, parrots, and other exotic creatures being cared for as pets alongside the more conventional dogs and horses. His pet monkey Scatter became quite a celebrity in the early Sixties, and Elvis later became increasingly involved with horses and riding toward the end of the decade.

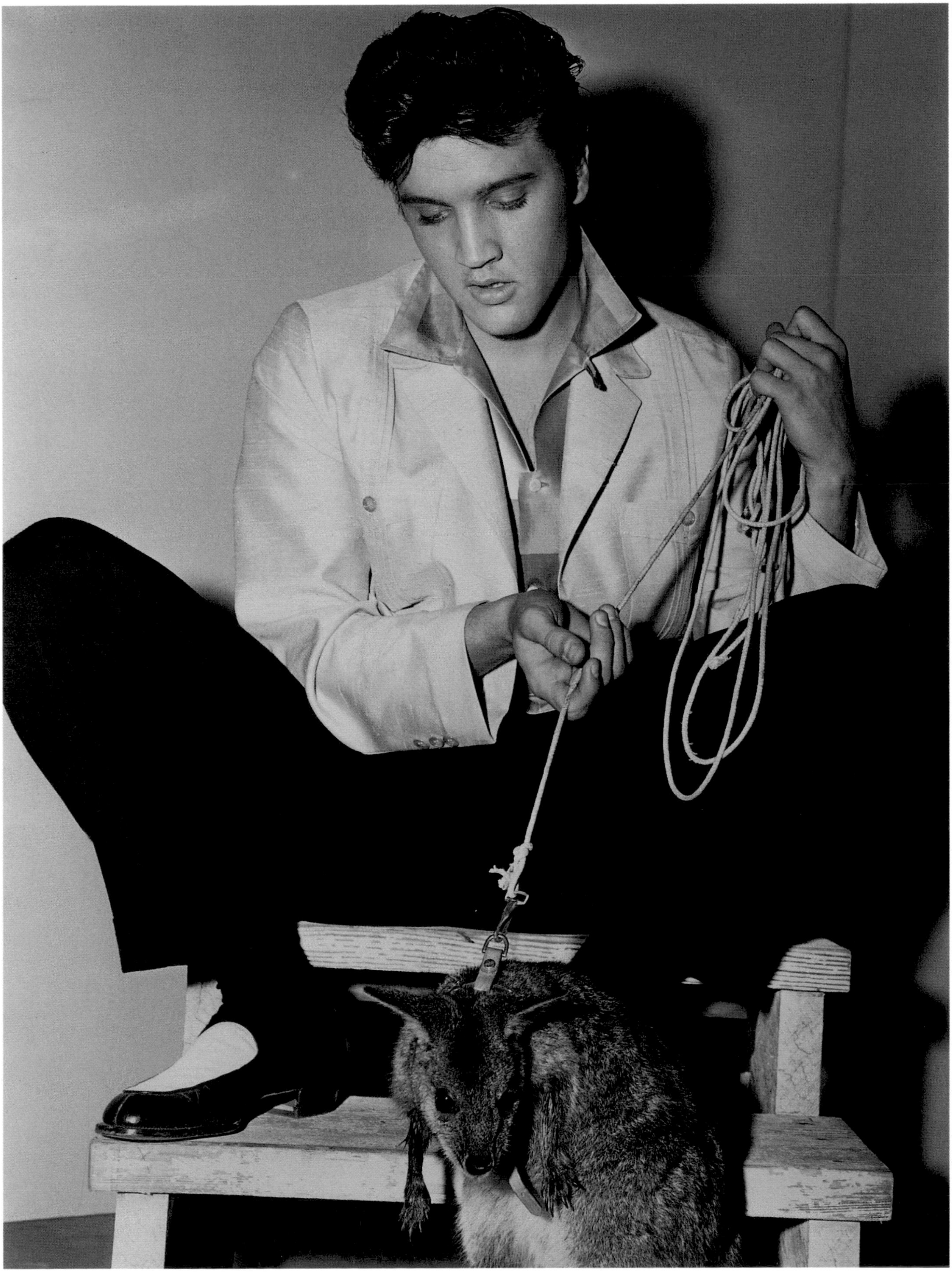

1957

1957 FANS Right through his career, despite the logistical difficulties it sometimes presented, Elvis was very conscious of keeping in personal contact with his fans as far as possible. He knew that without them he would be nothing; they bought the records and the merchandise, and filled the concert venues. They made it all happen.

1957 BOARD GAME The Elvis Presley merchandizing possibilities got more and more imaginative. This Elvis board game was yet another example of his name and image lending itself to marketing a product that had no direct connection with music, films, or other facets of Elvis' success, except of course the image itself.

⬆ **1957 FANS** Elvis loved to goof around with fans, though opportunities got less and less frequent. This "photo booth" style shot was taken around the time he was making *Loving You,* and is simply inscribed "Sadie, Elvis, and Linda."

⬅ **1957 "I LIKE ELVIS"** Typical of the Colonel's many publicity ideas was the "Elvis for President" stunt in which button badges echoed the campaign slogan for the President, Dwight D. Eisenhower, ("I Like Ike") with "I Like Elvis." There was even the "Oy Gevalt Elvis" version for Yiddish speakers!

1957 MEMPHIS CHARITY SHOW In June, TV entertainer Danny Thomas organized a Shower of Stars benefit for a Memphis children's hospital, at which Elvis made a brief stage appearance. Here Elvis poses with two of the shows' celebrity names, screen comedian Lou Costello (of Abbott and Costello fame) and Hollywood actress Jane Russell.

1957 TUPELO CHARITY SHOW Elvis and his entourage backstage at the Tupelo Fairgrounds charity show in September 1957. The blonde girl looking downward in the shot is Anita Wood, a 19-year-old beauty contest winner and would-be actress from Memphis, who was a regular date of Elvis at the time.

1957

1957

1957 JAILHOUSE ROCK Elvis looks at a scrapbook of his own memorabilia and talks to two disabled fans who were with a group on an arranged visit to the set of *Jailhouse Rock*. Always appreciative of his fans, Elvis paid particular attention to those who were in difficult circumstances of one kind or another. This was also reflected in the extensive amount of charity work that Elvis supported. He aided a variety of causes financially and, when his commitments allowed, he gave his time to appearing at many fund-raising events over the years, both in a performing role and just a "personal appearance" capacity.

1957 HAWAII Elvis hugs two young fans during his working visit to Hawaii, just after he has checked in at the Hawaiian Village Hotel. The two shows at Honolulu Stadium were witnessed by no fewer than 14,000 fans, and Hawaii remained a favorite location with Elvis for movies during the 1960s as well as just leisure.

1957 ELVIS DOLL The Elvis doll is an example of merchandise that purported to represent Elvis but did not even look remotely like him. Were it not for the hairstyle, it could have been anyone; but so powerful was Elvis' name that if it was labeled an Elvis Presley doll, then it was an Elvis Presley doll and fans bought them in their thousands.

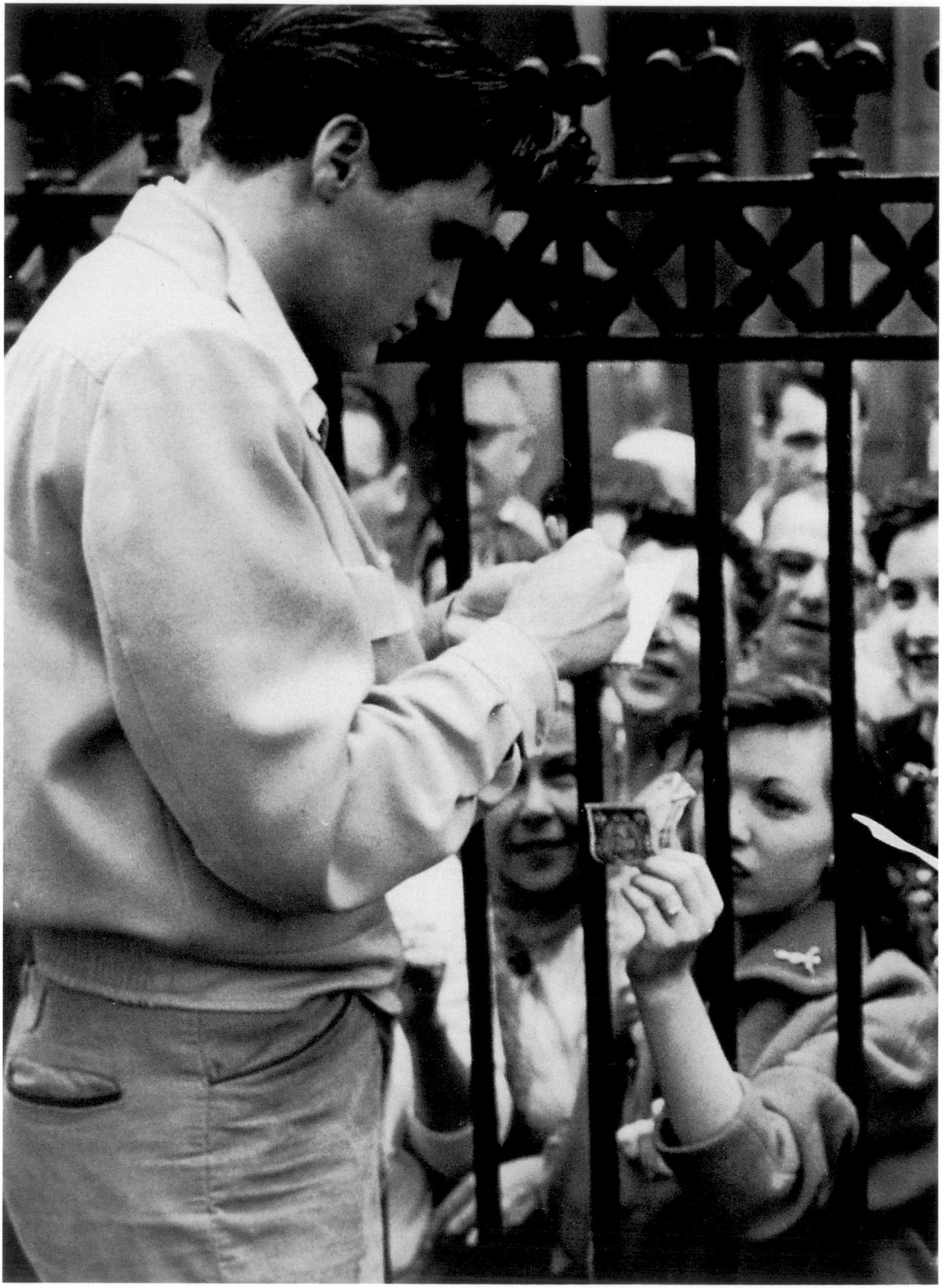

1958 NEW ORLEANS During the location shooting for Elvis' fourth movie, *King Creole,* these fans in New Orleans, Louisiana, were lucky enough to get a glimpse–and autograph–of their idol, albeit through the railings of a cast iron fence. Elvis wasn't always that separated from the crowds, but it probably helped things from getting out of hand.

1958 NEW ORLEANS The Colonel sits and chats with fans who are patiently awaiting the arrival of Elvis, having been allowed onto the *King Creole* location set while shooting took place in New Orleans. As far as many fans were concerned, meeting the Colonel was the second best thing to meeting Elvis himself.

1958

1958

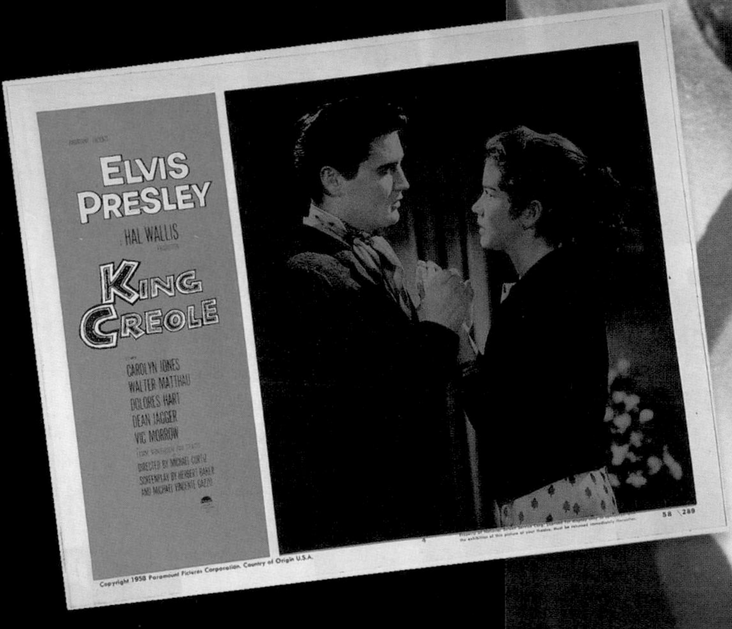

ELVIS PRESLEY
HAL WALLIS
KING CREOLE
CAROLYN JONES
WALTER MATTHAU
DOLORES HART
DEAN JAGGER
VIC MORROW
DIRECTED BY MICHAEL CURTIZ
SCREENPLAY BY HERBERT BAKER AND MICHAEL VINCENTE GAZZO
58/269
Copyright 1958 Paramount Pictures Corporation. Country of Origin U.S.A.

1958 KING CREOLE From time to time during movie shoots, the fans were actually allowed on the set, particularly when it was on location. Studio sets were much more restricted, and visits were by strict invitation only, but on location there was often a period when fans could mingle briefly with the stars. Of course, the only person they really wanted to mingle with was Elvis, seen here greeting fans during the *King Creole* shoots.

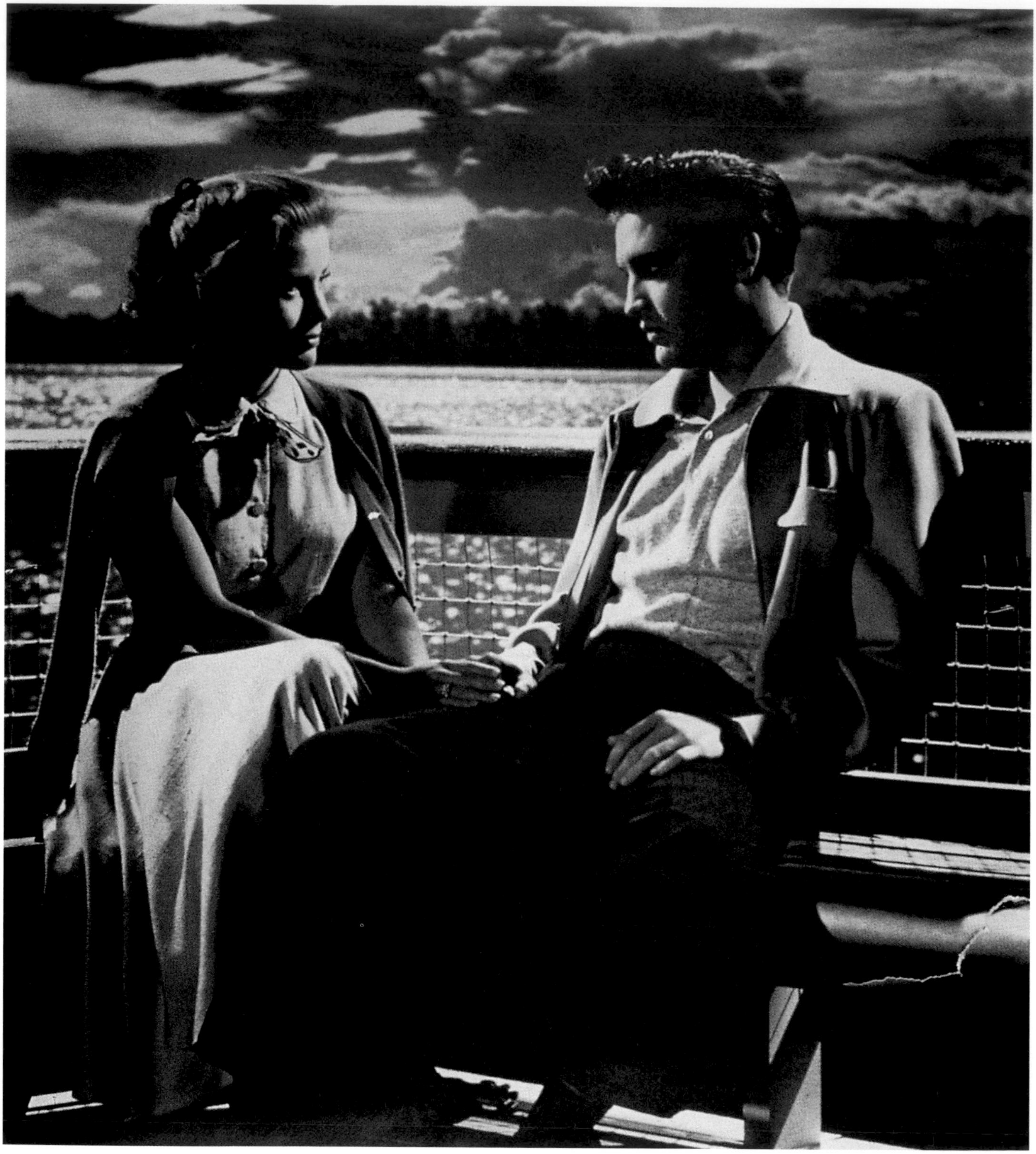

1958 KING CREOLE Based on best-selling writer Harold Robbins' novel, *A Stone For Danny Fisher*, which was also playing in an off-Broadway stage version at the time, *King Creole* certainly had some heavyweight credentials. It was directed by Michael Curtiz–whose long line of successes included *Casablanca,* for which he received an Oscar–and featured established names Carolyn Jones *(right),* Walter Matthau, and Dolores Hart (*above*, who had also appeared in *Loving You).* Like *Jailhouse Rock* it was pitched as a serious drama by the studio, Paramount. Despite this, Elvis managed to get through no fewer than 11 songs during the course of the action!

1958

1958

1958 PORTRAITS All the portraits on these and the following four pages were part of the publicity that accompanied the release of *King Creole* and its associated records. The movie itself was shot between the end of January and early March. To make the picture Elvis had to request a special deferment from the Army draft board. He had received his draft papers just before Christmas 1957, and was granted a 60-day deferment from December 27 in order to be able to make the shoot. The movie opened nationally across the United States on July 2, 1958, and was the first of Elvis' to be made on location—hence the attention paid to local fans visiting the sets.

10216-

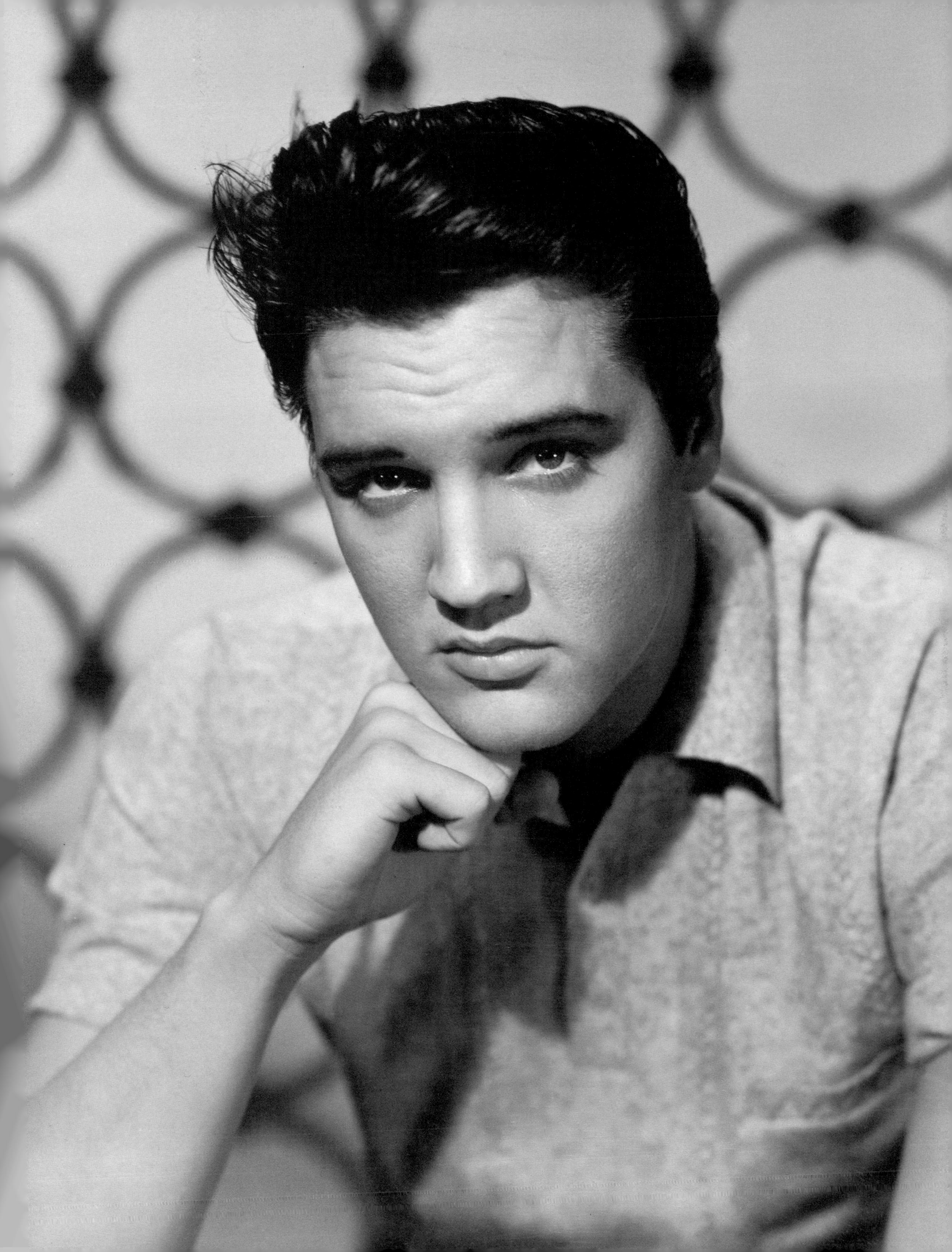

1957

➲ **1957 ARRIVING IN HAWAII** November that year saw Elvis make one of several working trips to Hawaii, when he played at the Honolulu Stadium. The gig was followed by what was to be his last live date before being called up for the Army early the following year, when he appeared before service families at the Scholfield Barracks, Pearl Harbor.

➊ ➔ **1957 HAWAII** Apart from his brief visits to Canada, the only nonmovie working trips that Elvis ever made outside the United States mainland were to the islands of the State of Hawaii. Everytime he arrived there he would be greeted in the traditional manner, with a *lei* hung round his neck (and plenty of lipstick kisses). Elvis took an instant liking to the islands, and played several important dates there during his career, as well as making it the location of several movies and choosing it as the venue for his historic *Aloha* live satellite television link-up in 1973. He also spent leisure time in the islands when he had the chance, and even based the decor of his Jungle Room at Graceland on Pacific Island designs.

1957

1956

1956 END OF THE DREAM? This image from *Love Me Tender* must have become a distant dream for Elvis when, in December 1957, one Christmas present he probably thought he could have done without finally arrived. It was his draft papers for service in the US Army, the documents that were to herald his much-publicized tour of duty as America's most celebrated GI.

Serving Uncle Sam

ARMY DAYS & AFTER

[1958–1961]

1960 DISCHARGE Elvis looks out onto a new future–in many ways an unknown future–in March 1960, as he leaves the United States Army after two years' service and contemplates life in the civilian fast lane once more.

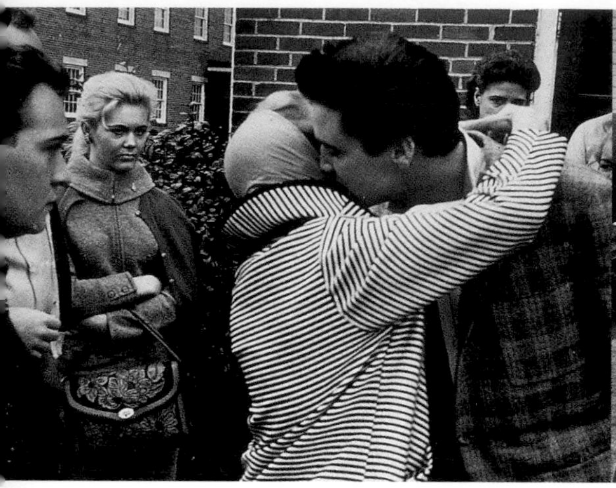

March 1958

March 1958

August 1958

The draft

1958-1961

into the US Army could have been a disaster for Elvis Presley's career. But the combination of a backlog of records and movie material to keep the fans happy, and the positive press he would receive in "doing his duty" like any other GI, ensured that his time in the Army provided him with an even higher public profile than before his recruitment. When he was called up he was the world's number one entertainment personality, and now his hundreds of thousands of fans could watch their hero be a soldier.

Of course, the Colonel and RCA's publicity machine made sure that every aspect of the draft process was exploited for all it was worth—so despite the "ordinary" soldier Elvis was about to become, it was in the full glare of publicity, from formalizing his induction to getting his first Army haircut. And when he was shipped to a base in Germany the reaction was unprecedented—RCA even released an EP of interview material recorded prior to his departure called "Elvis Sails."

All the time he was in Germany, back home it was almost Elvis business as usual. The records were released, hit after hit; he was interviewed via transatlantic telephone (still a novelty in 1959) by Dick Clark on the *American Bandstand* TV show; and before you knew it, Elvis was back, with a new

October 1958

March 1960

March 1961

album aptly titled *Elvis Is Back* and a movie going into production called–again appropriately–*GI Blues.* His homecoming was a media blowout, with a face-to-face interview in front of film and TV cameras, conducted in the office at Graceland, that revealed a confident, relaxed Elvis ready to get back to work. Finally, just to make sure that the message had sunk in that Elvis was indeed back, there was a "Welcome Home, Elvis" edition of Frank Sinatra's TV variety show.

Elvis was now not just a household name, but one with real household appeal. His service in the US Army had helped substantiate a wholesome image as an entertainer suitable for the whole family—one that perfectly fit the Colonel's broader long-term ambitions for his charge, and a million miles from the Hillbilly Cat who seemingly threatened to subvert the nation's youth just five years before.

As if to confirm this status as all-around regular guy, 1961 saw first a Memphis civic lunch in Elvis' honor, followed by two concerts at Ellis Auditorium in aid of over 30 local charities, and finally a benefit performance in Pearl Harbor, Hawaii, to raise money for the building of the USS *Arizona* Memorial. This last event was to be Elvis' final live, non-movie performance until his celebrated "comeback" seven years later.

1958

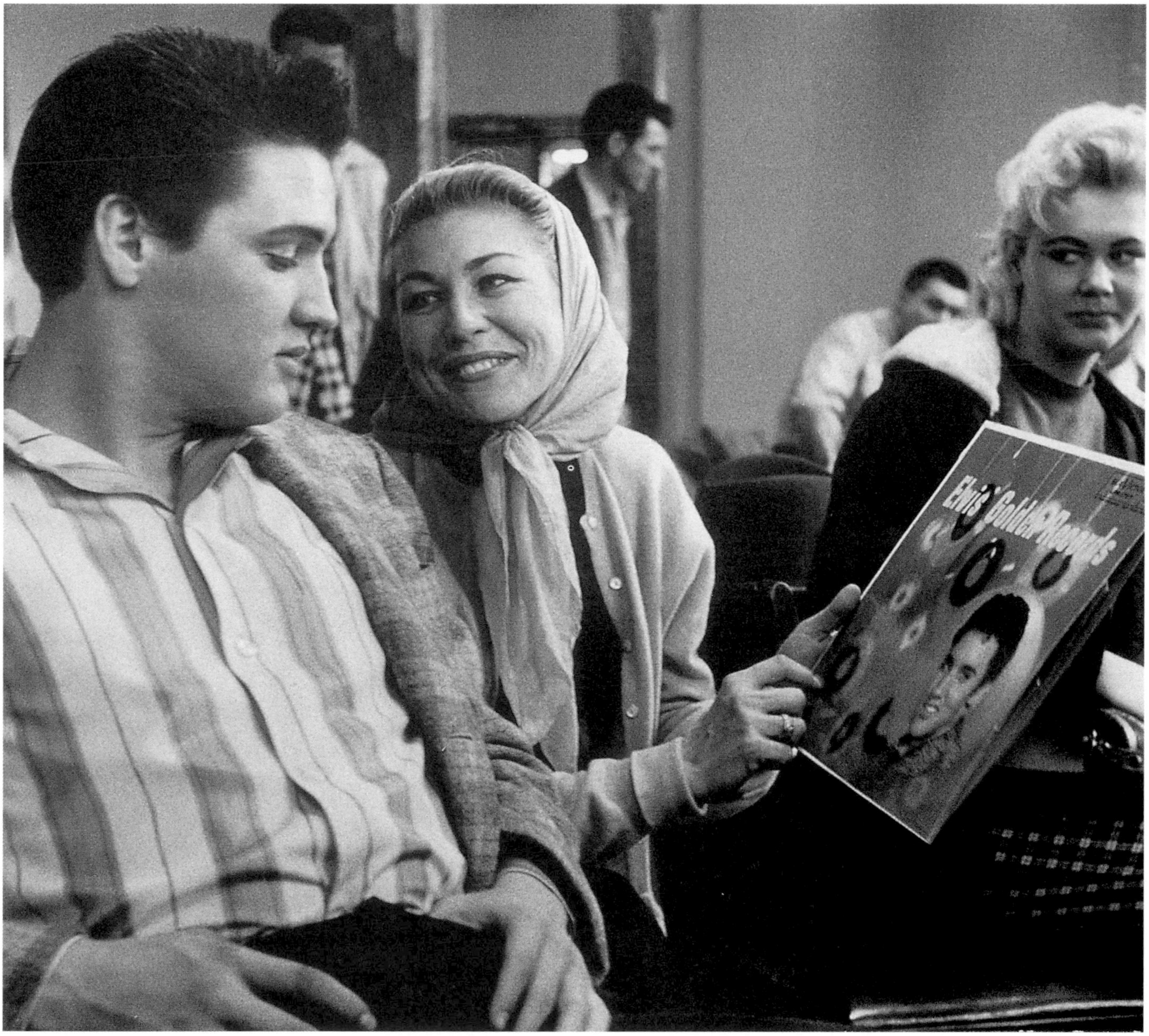

1958 **INDUCTION** The induction process following Elvis' initial reception of his draft papers at the end of 1957 took place on March 24, 1958, at the draft board office on South Main Street in Memphis. Accompanied by his girlfriend Anita Wood and her parents, he reported just after 6.30 AM, along with 12 other new recruits. Also present were his parents, friends, and relatives, dozens of fans (like Judy Spreckles in these pictures) and 20-plus newspaper reporters. The recruits were then bussed to the Kennedy Veterans Memorial Hospital, with the crowd in hot pursuit, where they underwent a physical, after which Elvis was given his Army serial number–53 301 761.

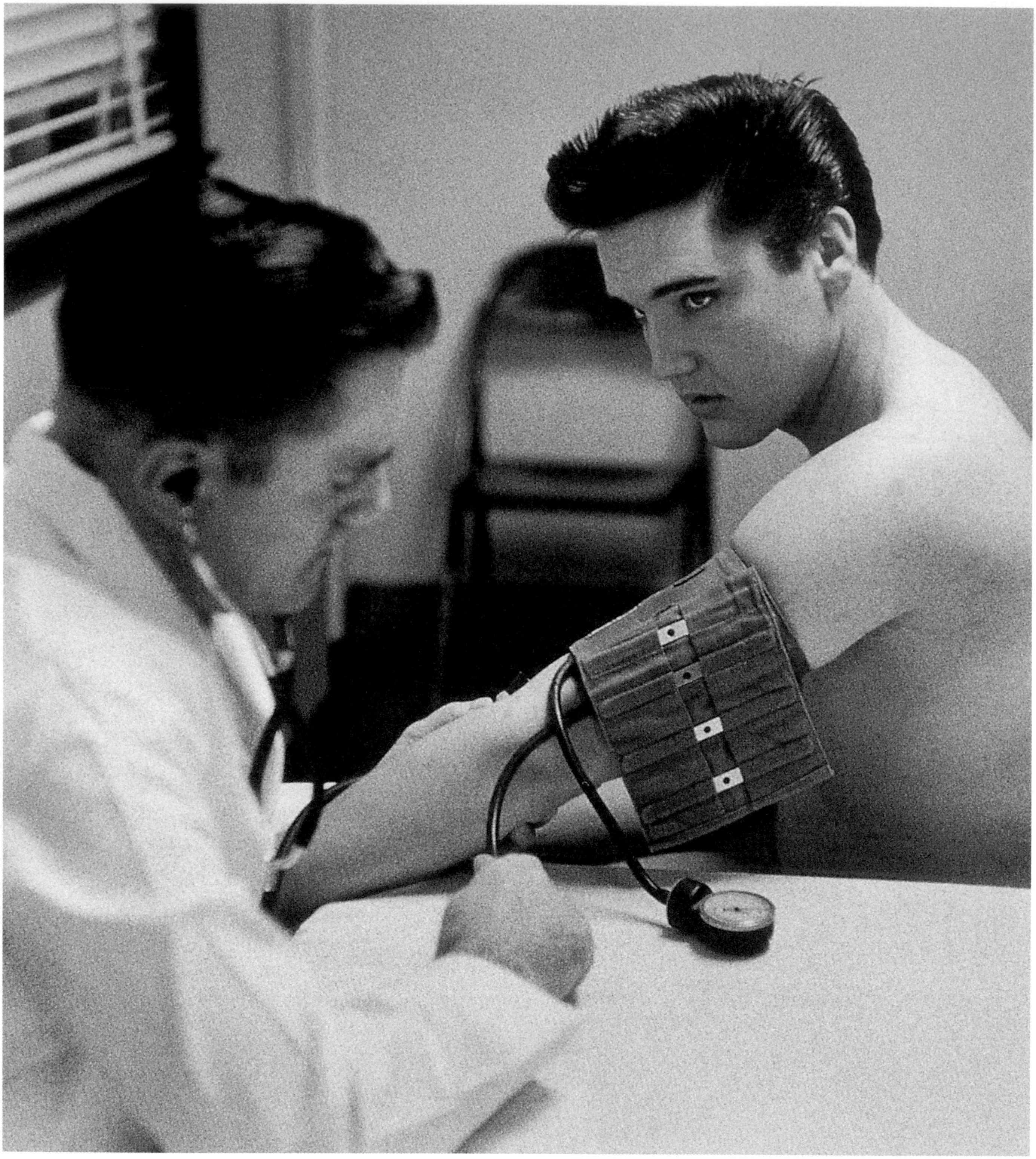

1958

1958 INDUCTION On the previous pages, Elvis sits with his fellow recruits awaiting his medical examination, taking a bite of a roast beef sandwich which the Army had supplied. Typically, while his parents waited outside to say goodbye, the Colonel was handing out balloons promoting *King Creole* to the fans also gathered there. Elvis' actual medical was well documented in the media, including the blood pressure test (*above*). More goodbyes ensued before Elvis and his new partners–some of whom he knew already–were taken to Fort Chaffee, 150 miles away. The following day, again in a blaze of photographers' flashbulbs, Elvis received his first Army haircut.

U.S. ARMY

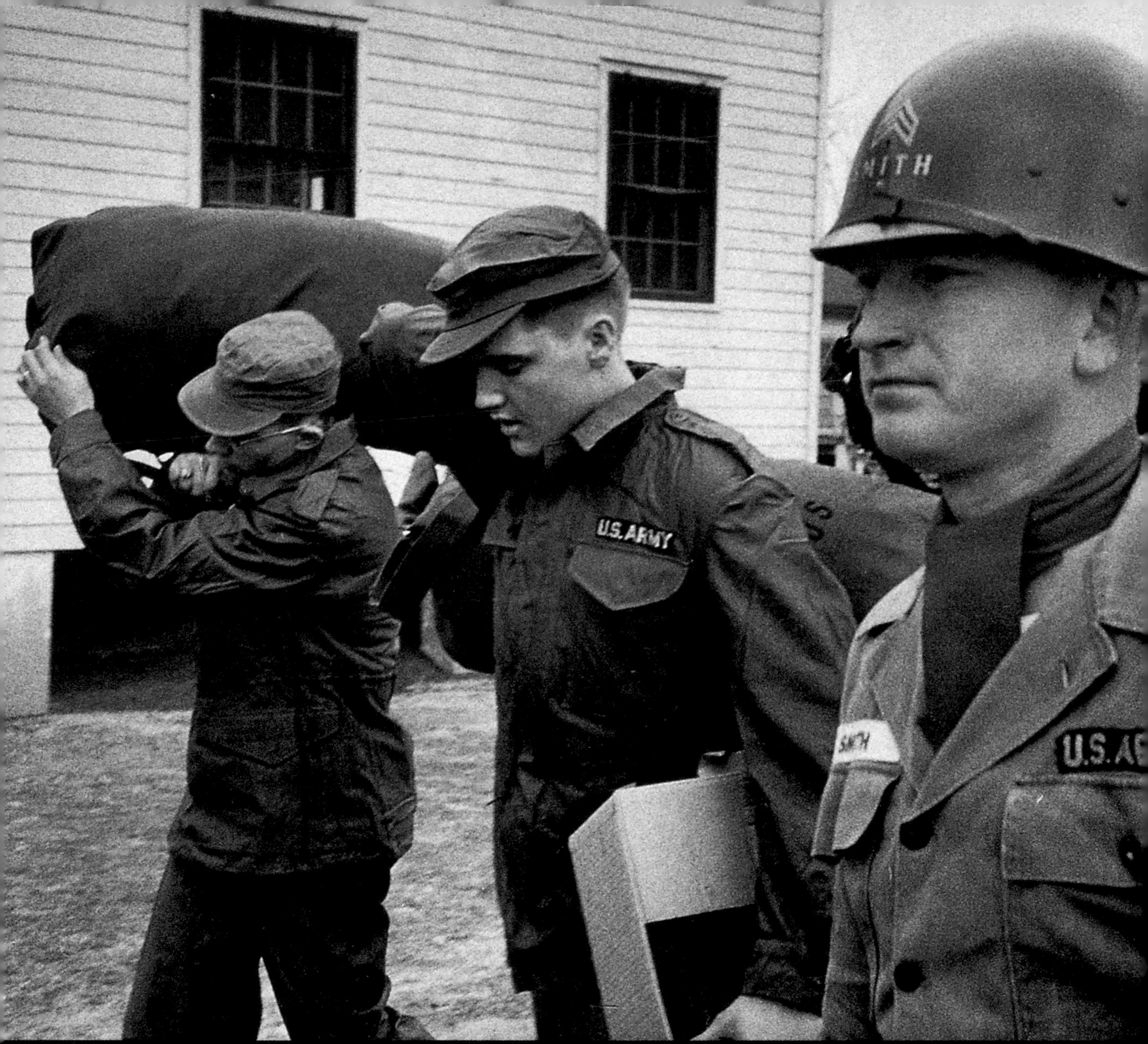

1958 FORT CHAFFEE Army life began at Fort Chaffee in Arkansas, where Elvis and his group–of whom he was put in charge during the induction process– arrived on Tuesday, March 25 (*above*). Very soon the new rigors of military life became a daily routine, not least the chore of shining his boots (*left*)

training, which lasted a full two months through to the end of May, Private Presley had been made acting assistant leader of his squad and also gained a marksman's medal for shooting. After the basic training at Fort Hood, Texas, he was to enjoy two weeks' furlough, which he spent at home in Memphis,

1958

ELVIS' MOM in loving memory

...at he is, she made him. He'll never forget her,
...e'll never be quite the same as he was before.
... were Elvis' hours of tenderness—and torment.

...into the raw earth, where
... to make a place for the
...
...except for a boy and his
...of the grave and crying.
...e," the boy said chok-
...apse, so close that four
...drag him to a car. "Oh,
...thing I have is gone—"
...uld live, and he would
... dark August day, the
...out, and he couldn't
... mother to grow old
...ed to make up to her
...le, years which had
...ful woman.
...e," he'd said a few
...rd way to go. I like
...—"
...ed through Elvis'
... his father got sick
... took a job after
... mother couldn't
...t, sleep, time to
...elf went out and

got a job in a hospital. She emptied bedpans, mopped floors through long grey nights so that Elvis could be educated in peace.

Gladys Presley was a worrier. When Elvis played football, she was afraid he'd get hurt, and when Elvis rode a bike, she was afraid he'd get hurt; her concern never lessened even after her baby had grown up. The day he came home from the Army with a bruised knee and five stitches in his hand, she was ready to go to war with President Eisenhower. "What are they doing with you?" she cried, outraged.

When Elvis made his first record for a disc jockey in Memphis, Gladys sent him off to the movies; she and Vernon sweated out the results by themselves. The record was played, 1600 phone calls came in in less than an hour, and Gladys and Vernon took off for the theatre, went rushing down the aisles calling Elvis' name, the gorgeous news burning their tongues.

Gladys Presley babied her son, and he babied her right back. A relationship so sentimental it might have made other boys flinch was cherished by Elvis. At 23, he was still his mother's "good little boy" and he proved it a thousand different ways. He bought her a house, all air-conditioned, with jukeboxes and swimming pool and great carved gates. He got her a

Nothing can ever compensate Vernon and Elvis for their loss of wife and mother. But, someday, they will realize that Gladys Presley knew a woman's greatest joy in their devotion and the fame her son had won for "my best girl."

Memphis home which Elvis had bought for his parents is an enduring symbol of his love. But such luxury meant less to Mrs. Presley than the good earth where she could plant a garden. "Growing things, son," she said, "is like singing."

A nation which had cheered a son's triumph fell silent in sympathy, as the tragic cortege wound its way to a funeral home. "So young, so young!" mourned Elvis. Only 42—but the short life had been enriched beyond most mothers' dreams.

Dignity and respect marked the final rites. With the best of the past enshrined in their hearts, Vernon and Elvis Presley faced the future—the soldier son's path leading to Army duty overseas, the father hoping to join him there.

By EUNICE FIELD

The house was very still. It seemed to be waiting for the familiar footsteps and voice which would bring it to life again. Relatives and friends whispered sadly in the darkened rooms. Anita Wood, Nick Adams and George Klein, old friends from show business, clustered near a mynah bird that huddled like a bit of charred wood in its cage. Two Negro maids, moist-eyed and weary, brought in armfuls of telegrams and letters and heaped them on the dining-room table, banked with flowers.

On a couch in the living room sat Vernon Presley and his son Elvis, America's singing idol. They sat side by side, limp, brooding, hushed. From time to time, their eyes moved heavily about the room as if unable to believe how unreal, how empty, it all seemed now.

Suddenly the telephone rang, shattering the quiet gloom. The little mynah bird raised its quick black head and shrilled, "Hello, Mama—that's all right, Mama."

A shocked and horrified look passed between Elvis and his father. Their arms went (Continued on page 64)

27

1958 SHARED GRIEF During the summer of 1958, while the family was living in temporary accommodation arranged by Elvis near the Fort Hood base, his mother Gladys became ill. As it became apparent her condition was serious, Elvis sent his parents back to Memphis to consult the family physician. Gladys was rushed from Graceland to the Methodist Hospital on August 9, suffering from an undiagnosed liver complaint. After much pleading (and a threat to go AWOL) Elvis obtained emergency leave on Tuesday, August 12, and rushed straight to the hospital having flown from Fort Worth to Memphis. Gladys died at 3.15 AM on the Thursday morning, and Elvis and his father were inconsolable. At the funeral the next day, Elvis and Vernon were on the point of collapse. It was a grief they could share only with each other.

1958

2
HELL ON WHEELS

← 1958 GRACELAND Elvis at home on leave, marking the end of his basic training at Fort Hood. He arrived at Graceland in full uniform, and took delight in explaining to fans waiting at the gates what the insignia on his uniform represented, including the Armored Division's motto visible on his shoulder, "Hell On Wheels."

↑ 1958 NASHVILLE During his first furlough Elvis took time out to attend the recording session at RCA's Studio B in Nashville. The session was to feature, as well as regular Elvis accompanists D. J. Fontana and the Jordanaires, top session players including star performers such as Chet Atkins on guitar and Floyd Cramer on piano.

195

1958 NASHVILLE The recording session (*previous four pages*), which took place overnight on June 10–11, included, along with the star instrumentalists Chet Atkins and Floyd Cramer, session men Hank Garland on guitar, Bob Moore on bass, and Buddy Harman on percussion. It turned out to be Elvis' last recording session for almost two years.

1958 NASHVILLE The material at the session consisted mainly of up-tempo rockers–"I Need Your Love Tonight," "Big Hunk O' Love," and "I Got Stung" plus the rhythm and blues standard "Ain't That Lovin You Baby," and "(Now And Then There's) A Fool Such As I." Every track was to appear on either the A or B side of a single.

1958

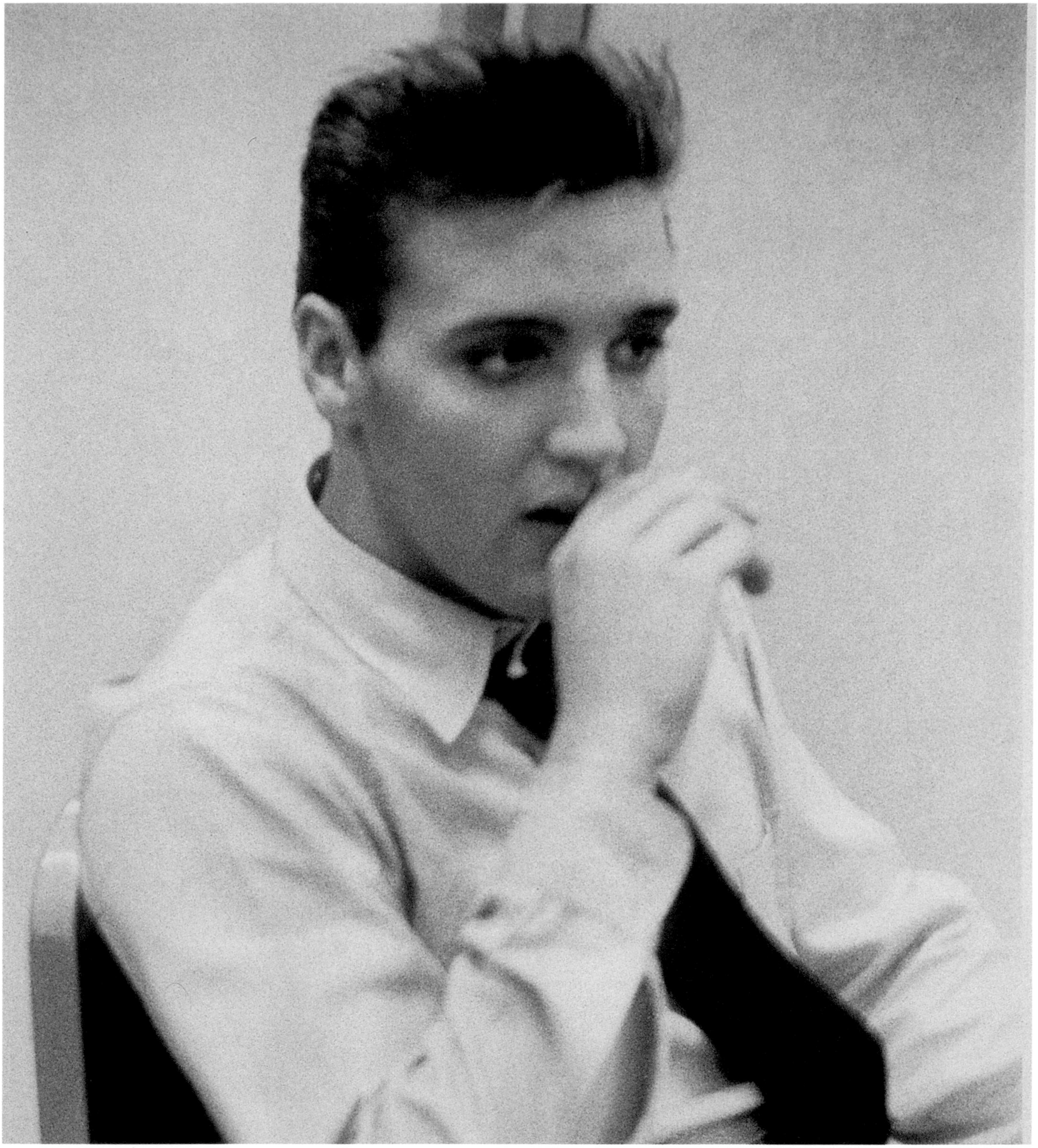

1958 NASHVILLE The fact that Elvis remained in his uniform throughout the entire session at Nashville would seem to indicate just how valuable his recording time was; this (albeit brief) opportunity to lay down some tracks was a rare "window" in a schedule that was dominated by Army commitments, and which would remain so for almost the next two years. Nevertheless, the singles that ultimately came from the session were not all immediately released. "I Got Stung" appeared as a B side later in 1958, while "Ain't That Lovin' You Baby" wasn't released until 1964, with the other three songs hitting the record stores through the following year.

1958

1958 GRACELAND More photographs taken at Graceland during Elvis' first leave in June 1958. The picture in the car was to be used on the cover of the album *A Date With Elvis*. Released as something of a stopgap in the middle of Elvis' Army service, in August 1959, the album featured a collection of vintage tracks including some, such as "Blue Moon of Kentucky," "Milkcow Blues Boogie," and "Baby Let's Play House," that harked back to his earliest recordings on the Sun label. Although recorded in far more "primitive" technical conditions than his later material cut at various RCA studios, the Sam Phillips-produced songs had a raw energy that still sounds fresh today.

1958

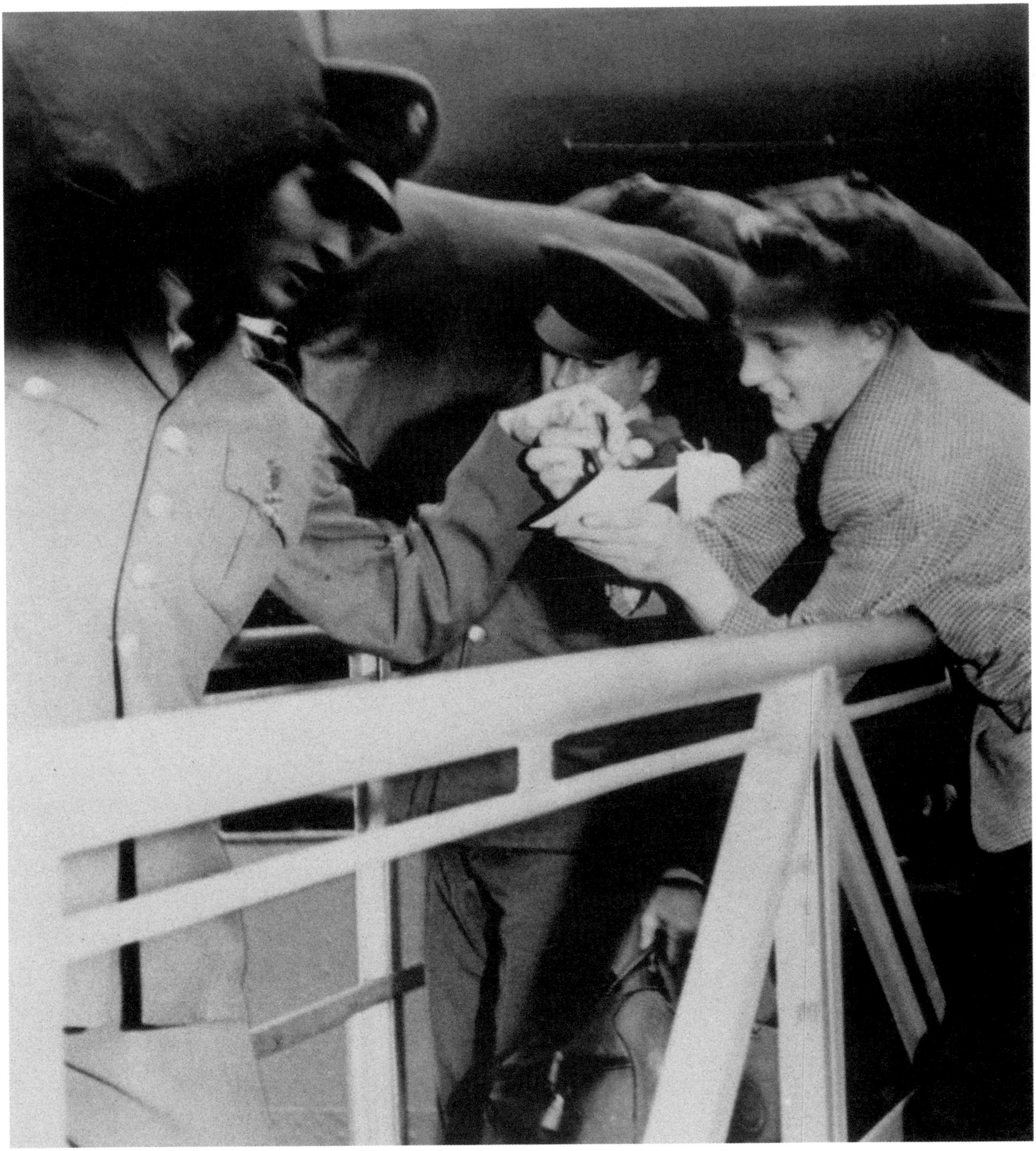

1958

1958 ELVIS SAILS In September 1958, Elvis was assigned to the 3rd Armored Division, based in West Germany. The Colonel was to make sure that, as at Elvis' induction, the publicity surrounding his departure to a foreign country–the first, apart from the concert dates in Canada, in his life–was widespread. He left Fort Hood on September 19, on an overnight troop train to the Brooklyn Army Terminal in New York. From here he was to make his famous departure–after the obligatory press conference–on the USS *Randall*. The shots of screaming fans being held back by military police, and of Elvis signing autographs as he walked up the gangplank, have become part of Elvis' visual history.

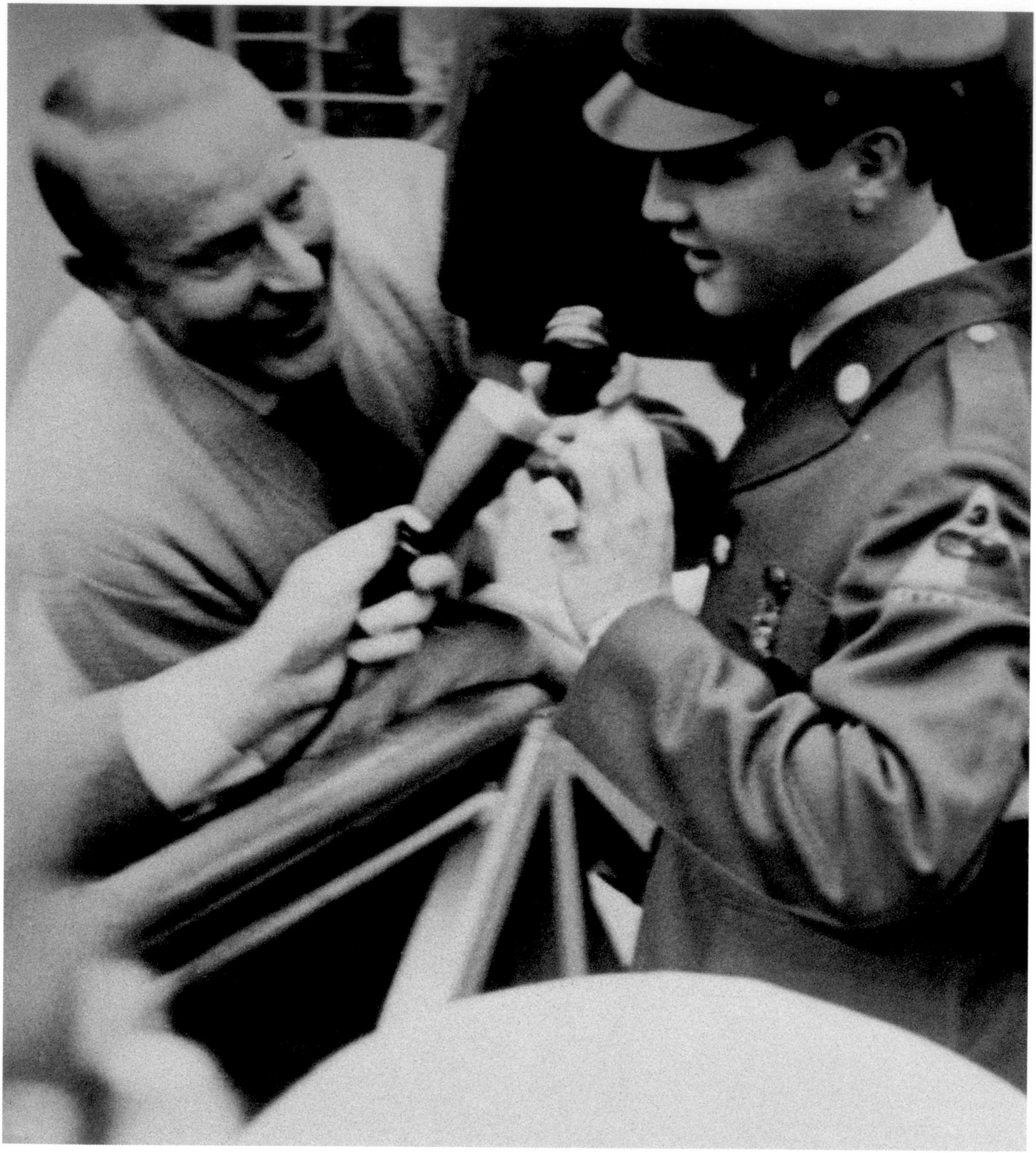

1958 FAREWELL Most of the interviews conducted immedately before and after the nine-day trip to Germany seemed to concentrate on matters concerning the opposite sex. Was he interested in German girls? Did he have a girlfriend he'd left back home? And now he was coming to Europe, would he like to get to know "the sex kitten" Brigitte Bardot? Elvis had already expressed an interest in meeting the French actress, though, the interviewers all asked, was he as eager now that she seemed to be going through so many highly publicized engagements? Little were he or the press to anticipate that it was during his service in Germany that he would meet his future wife.

1958

1958

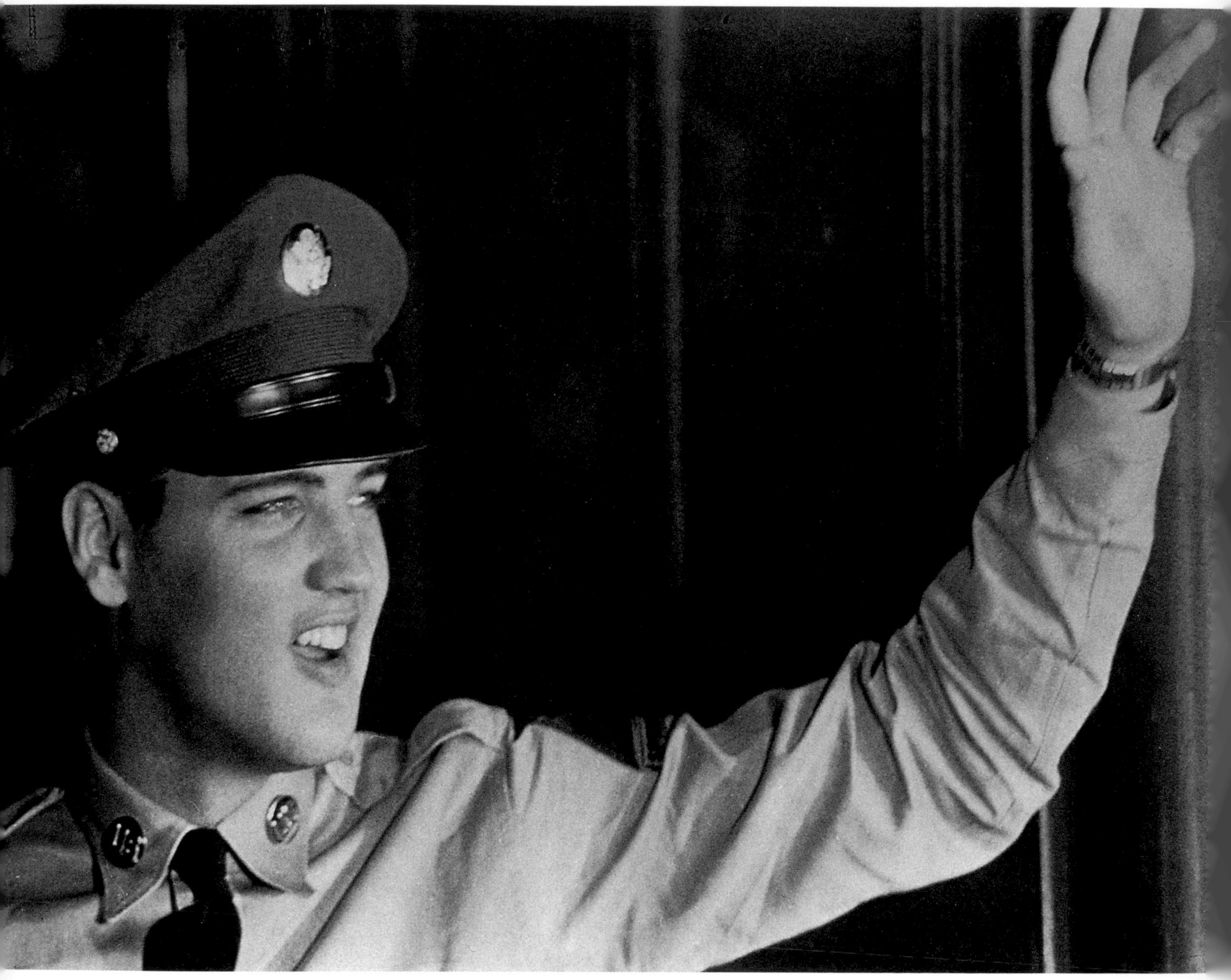

1958 ON BOARD On board Elvis got to know Charlie Hodge, another Southerner with a music background, whom he'd met on the train to New York. During the voyage, the two were put in charge of organizing a talent show for the troops, with Charlie compering and Elvis taking a background role, playing piano in the ad-hoc backing group.

1958 MEMPHIS The train from Fort Hood refueled at Memphis, where Elvis was met by well-wishers (*above*), on its way to New York and the voyage to Germany. The troop ship arrived in Bremerhaven on October 1, 1958 (*overleaf*), after which Elvis—now a member of the 32nd Tank Battalion, 3rd Armored Division—boarded a train bound for Friedberg, not far from Frankfurt. From the start, he tried to blend in with his fellow servicemen as much as possible, but was nevertheless thankful when his father and grandmother arrived, along with buddies Red West and Lamar Fike. He first organized hotel accommodation for them and himself, before providing a more permanent rented house.

1958

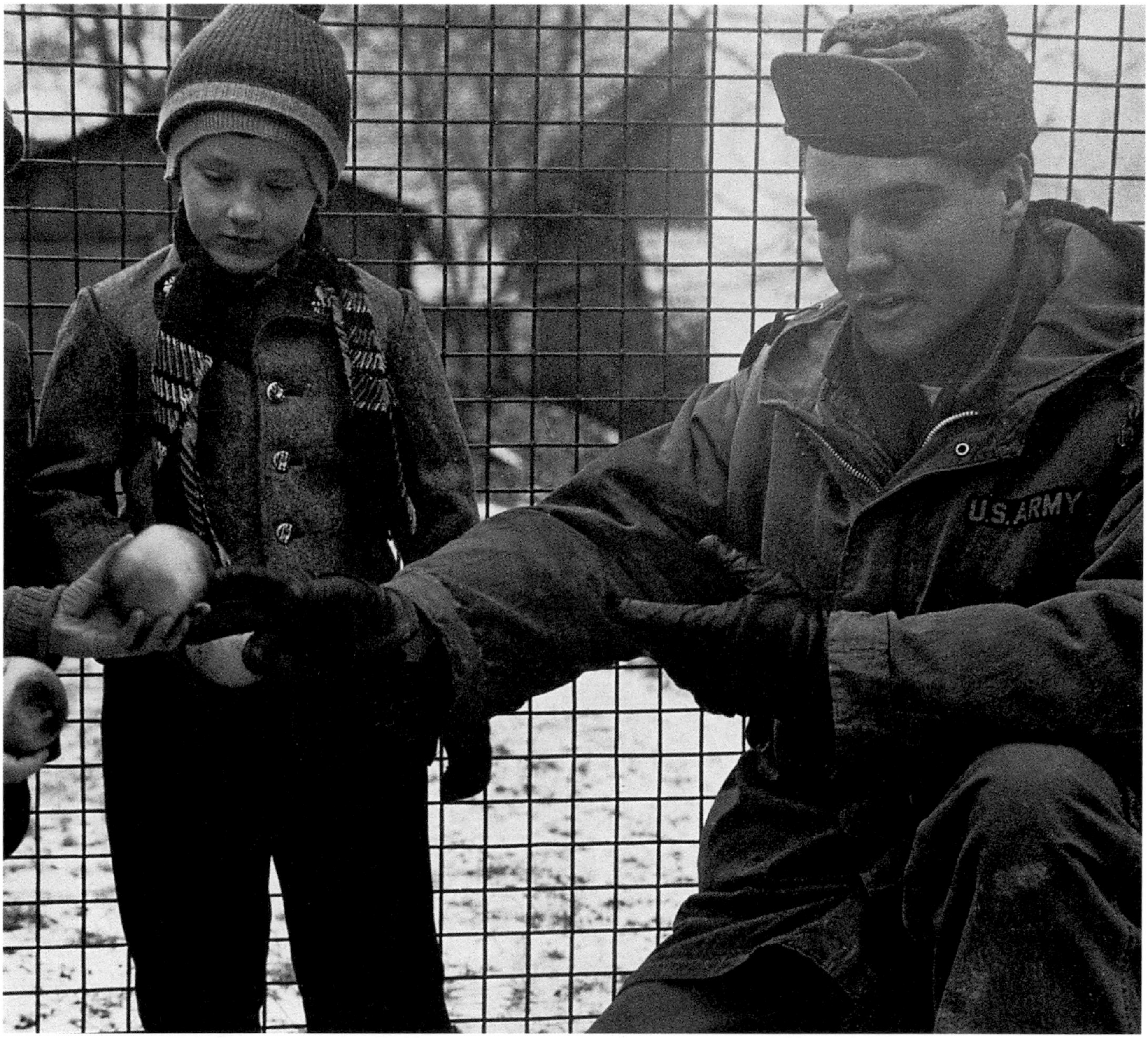

←**1958 NEW RECRUIT** An early picture of Elvis in the Army, not long after his induction, taken during basic training at Fort Hood. Such portraits were much sought after by fans, especially when he was transferred to Germany, since many of his followers in the United States felt as if they might never see their idol again.

↑ **1958 SNOW** The relatively extreme German weather must have come as something of a shock to Elvis. Although snow was not unknown back in Memphis, the hot summers and generally mild winters in the mid-South were a world away from the freezing temperatures and deep snow of central Germany in winter. Nonetheless, as this picture attests, children everywhere love playing snowballs, despite the chill factor; and Elvis, in full cold-weather gear, was happy to join in. Although this was an informal shot, it had the value of being yet another photo opportunity for Elvis, which would do no harm at all to his image with the fans back home, and indeed worldwide, awaiting his return to civilian life.

1958 MANEUVERS After a month or so in the Ray Keserne Barracks at the base in Friedberg, the Army company was transported to Grafenwohr, on the Czech border, for maneuvers. This was the real thing–or as real as it would get. After initially being allowed to cover Elvis on seriously active duty, the press was banned, and he spent the next seven weeks, give or take a weekend leave when he took the bus back to Friedberg, planning mock battles, taking mock prisoners, and shooting real ammo. The press pictures were circulated and syndicated across the world, of course, and the public at large, and Elvis fans in particular, got an intriguing inside glimpse of their idol in action.

1958

PRESLEY
U.S. ARMY

← ↑ **1958 PRIVATE PRESLEY** Elvis during his basic training at Fort Hood, Texas, while still a private before leaving for Germany (*left*), and later on maneuvers near the Czech border when he had gained his corporal's stripe. Shaving in the open air, fixing the engine on a jeep, this was Elvis the soldier as his day-to-day companions in the Army saw him. These latter pictures (*above*) were among those taken by the press corps before they were barred from the whole area due to the military sensitivity surrounding the mock battles and maneuvers. The spectacular color photography sent a wholesome message to the outside world that Elvis was indeed just an ordinary "GI Joe."

1958

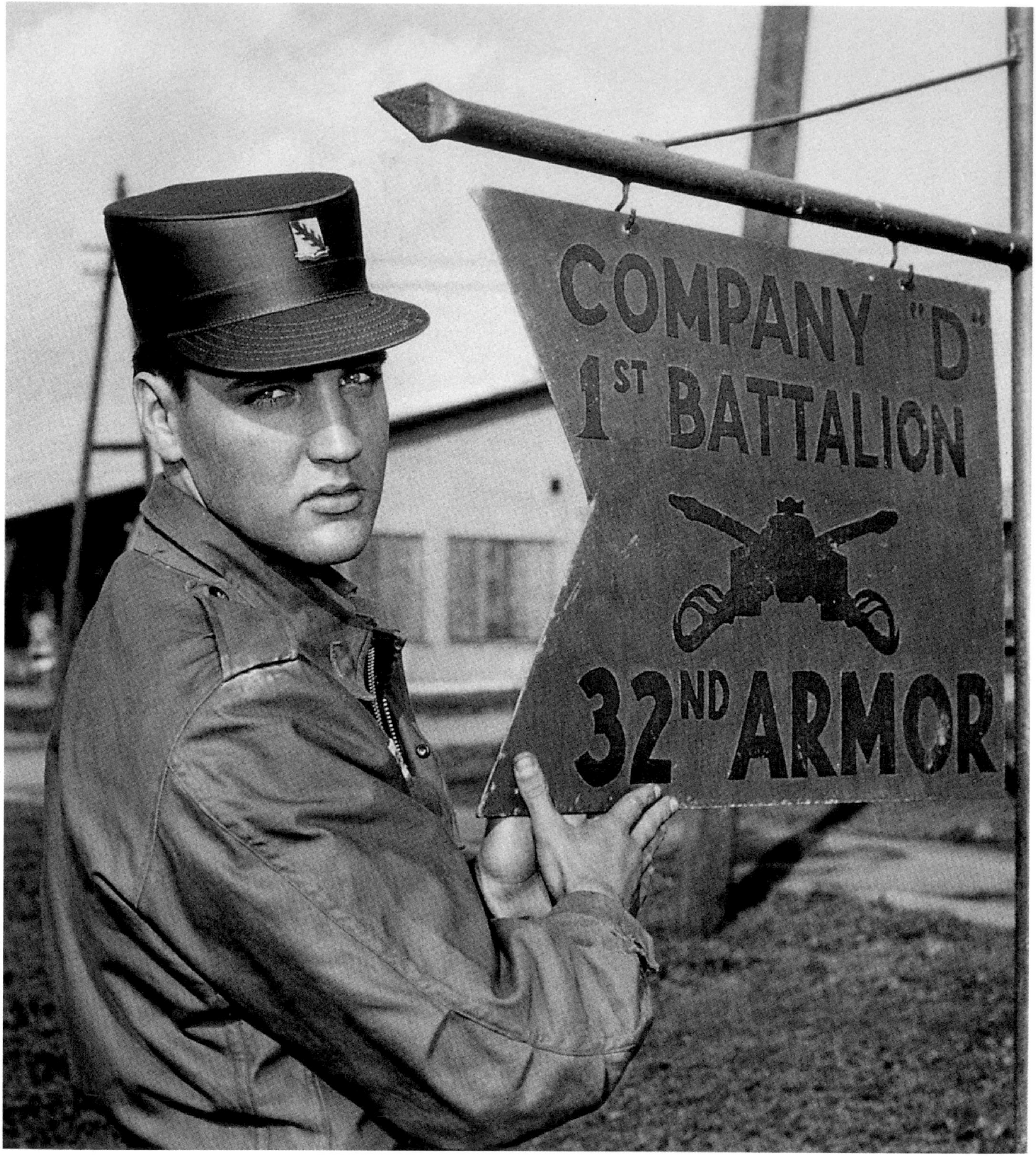

1958

1958 32ND ARMORED Elvis stands by the sign of Company "D" (*above*), 1st Battalion, 32nd Armored Division, while still at Fort Hood. His basic training, during which he undertook Advanced Tank Training, prepared him well for the rigors of the maneuvers (*right*) that were to follow. All in all, Elvis got to enjoy his time in the service, both the social experience of being treated as "normal" as far as possible, and the "masculine" culture of sports and military activity which was to remain a big part of his life from then on. His later interest both in martial arts and the collecting of firearms was evidence of this. In this respect, Elvis was very much "one of the boys" throughout his life.

U.S.ARMY
SPEARHEAD

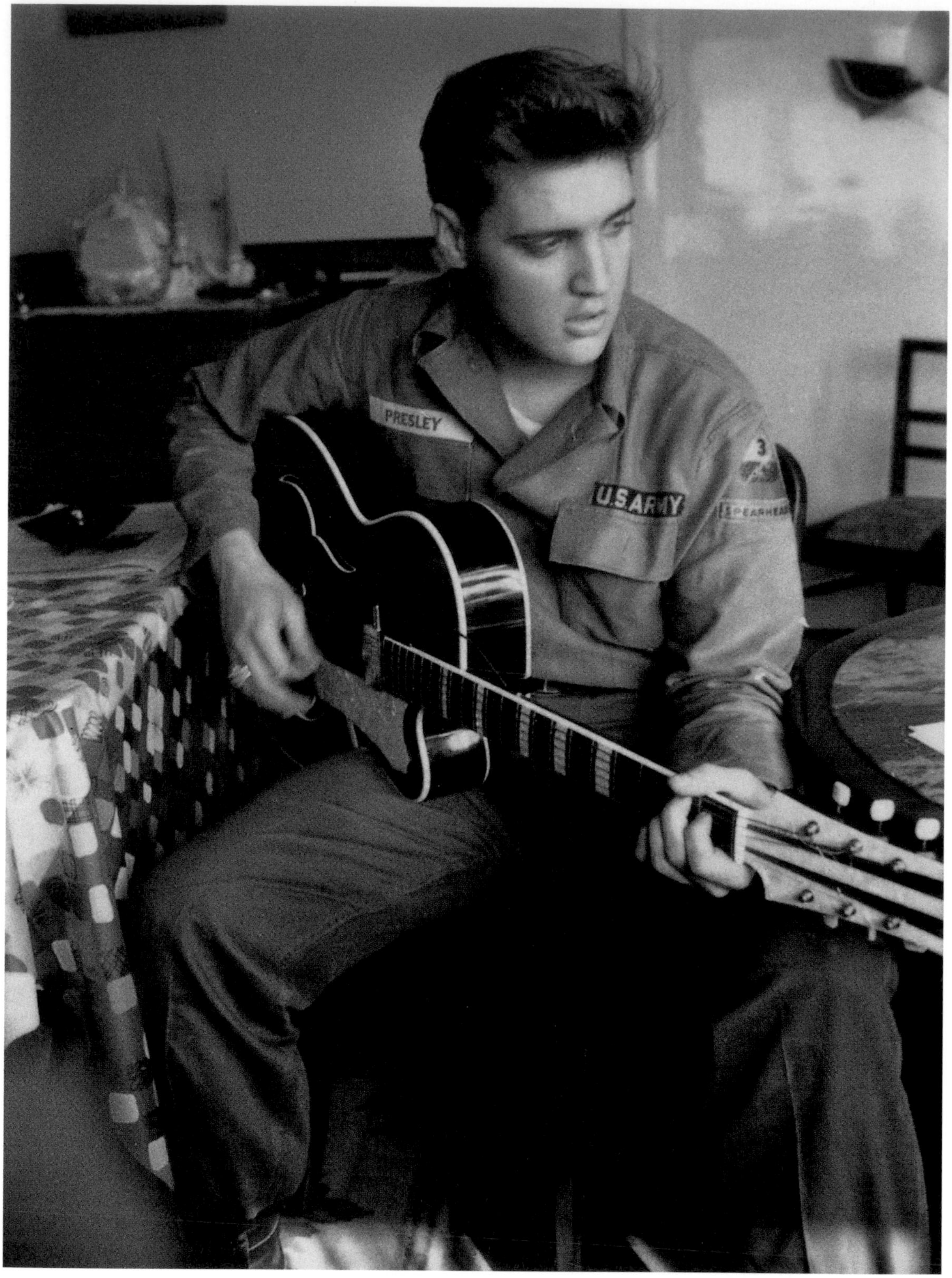

1959 BAD NAUHEIM Elvis got permission to live off base with his dependants, in his case his father and grandmother, so he initially arranged hotel accommodation for them and himself in Bad Nauheim, near the base. He would travel to the base every morning and return to his family in the evening, just like in a civilian job. After a couple of such hotel arrangements, which never proved completely satisfactory, the Presleys moved to a rented three-story house in Goethestrasse, Bad Nauheim, where they lived for the remainder of Elvis' tour of duty in Germany. The pictures here were taken in the house not long after they moved in, during February 1959.

1959

U.S. ARMY
SLEY

1959

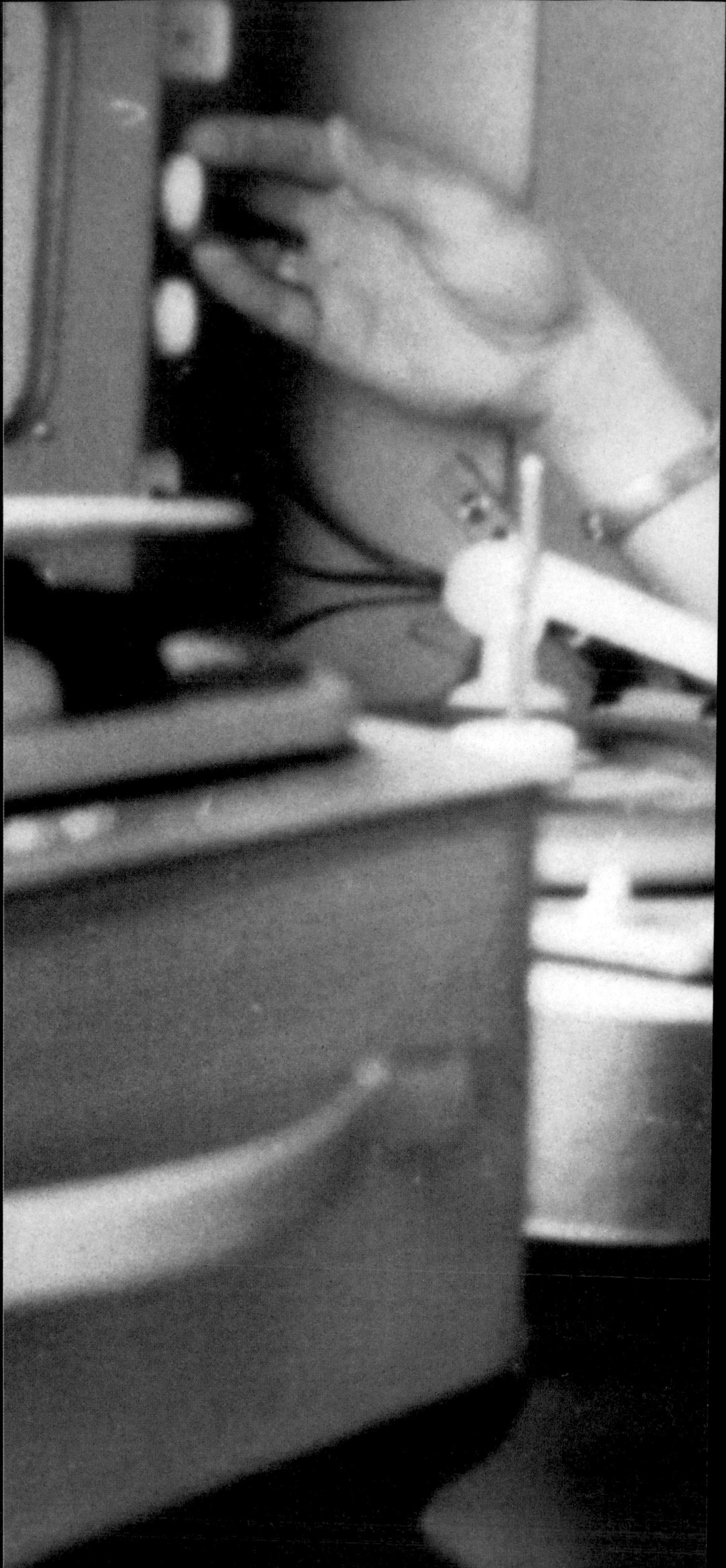

➔ **1959 GOETHESTRASSE** Elvis relaxes listening to records on a small portable record player, in the house at 14 Goethestrasse. He may have had the bonus of his own accommodation to alleviate Army life to a degree, but the modest record machine (and the tape recorder just visible in the foreground) show how life was a lot less luxurious than that to which he had become accustomed at Graceland.

1959

1959 PARIS On June 15, 1959, Elvis, along with Army buddies Charlie Hodge and Rex Mansfield, plus Lamar Fike, spent most of a two-week leave period in Paris. They traveled to the French capital by train, and were booked into the Prince de Galles (Prince of Wales) Hotel, just off the then-fashionable Champs-Elysées, by an executive of Elvis' music publishers, Hill & Range. After a brief press conference, Elvis–with Army-short haircut and white T-shirt–hit the streets, hoping to enjoy a welcome degree of anonymity. Within minutes, a couple of hundred people were mobbing the party, which retreated to the hotel. Thereafter sightseeing was done by limousine, though Elvis was reported to be more interested in the fabled Paris nightlife, visting world-famous venues including the Moulin Rouge and the Folies Bergère. These pictures were taken as Elvis met the press outside his hotel, just minutes before the abortive attempt at trying to be an "ordinary" party of tourists, during which they were mobbed sitting outside a nearby café.

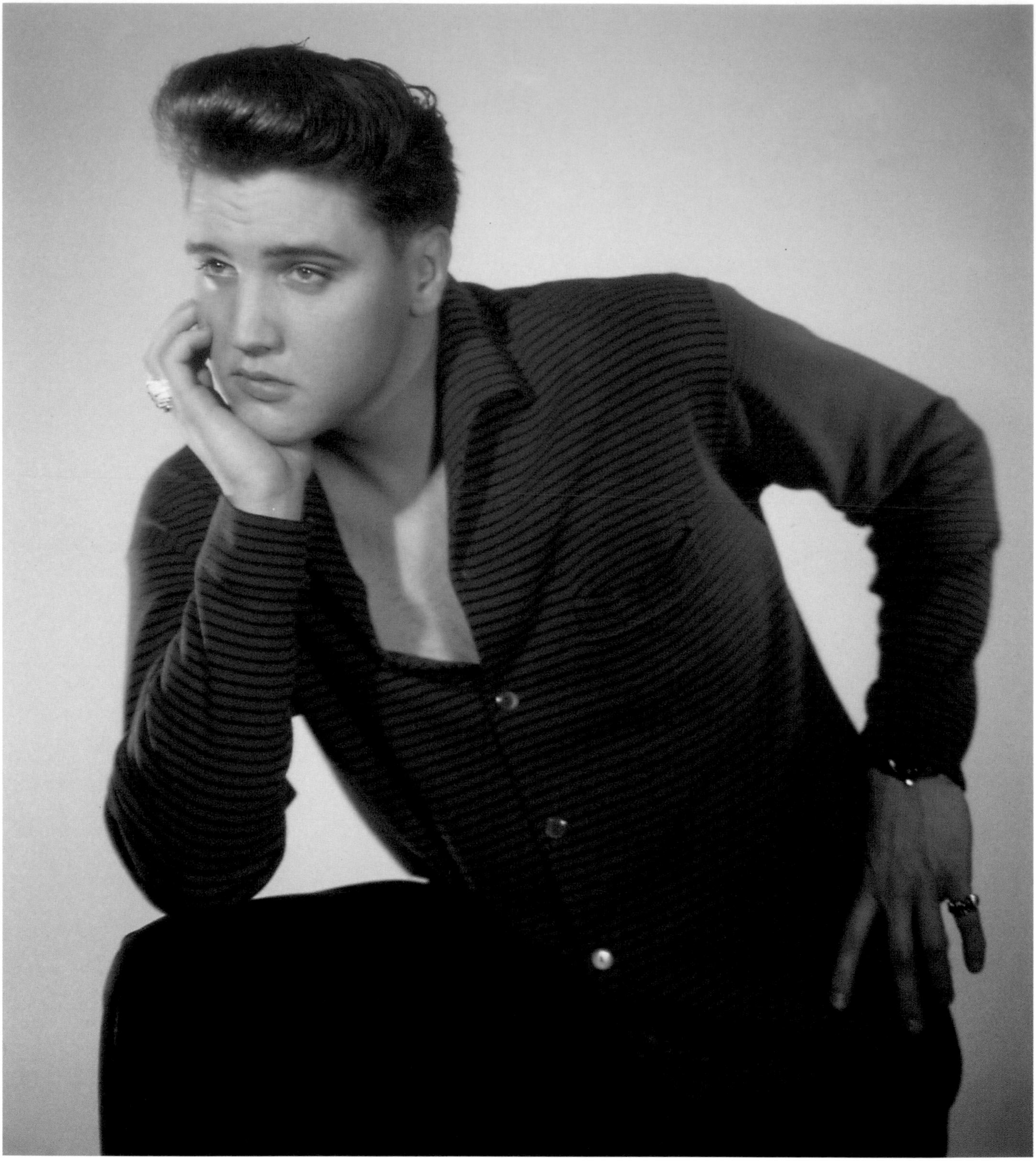

1959 PUBLICITY On this page and the two overleaf, another studio photo session staged during the time Elvis spent in the Army. The Colonel continually lobbied the military to allow his client to finish his tour of duty in the United States rather than in Europe, arguing that the photographs they had allowed to be shot in Germany would make great publicity for the Army, as would Elvis spending the rest of his service time at home, concentrating on recruitment. The portrait on the right was taken some time later, during a publicity session for Elvis' collection of gospel songs *His Hand In Mine*, which was recorded in October 1960, seven months after his Army discharge, and released that November.

1959

U.S. ARMY

1960 MERCHANDISE The Army years provided more raw material for Elvis merchandising and promotion. As well as the trading cards featuring Elvis in various military poses (*left*), there was even an “Elvis Dog Tag” (*below*) similar to the nametag worn by all US service personnel (*bottom*), engraved with Elvis' picture and actual Army number.

1960 PUBLICITY To keep the fires of fanaticism fanned brightly, a surprisingly large number of fan-oriented pictures continued to stream out of Elvis' and RCA Records' publicity departments. Among them was this particularly topical example–a rather kitsch setting for Elvis posing in full Army fatigues atop a mountain peak. With the news pictures, in-uniform recording shots, studio portraits like this, and the post-Army movie *GI Blues*, it was often hard to tell “Elvis in the Army” fact and fiction apart.

I'M FOR ELVIS
NAME
STREET
CITY
© COPYRIGHT 1956 ELVIS PRESLEY ENTERPRISES
ALL RIGHTS RESERVED
VARI-VUE® PAT. APPL'D FOR • by PICTORIAL PRODUCTIONS, INC.
TUCKAHOE 7, NEW YORK, N. Y.

↑ **1960 PUBLICITY** In fact during his whole time in the Army, the Colonel and Elvis made sure that the publicity machine didn't grind to a halt. As well as squeezing as many photo opportunities out of his actual military activity as the Army authorities would allow, there were also a number of studio photography sessions, as this posed and autographed portrait demonstrates. The momentum generated by high-profile public relations was such that although Elvis was, in theory, "out of the picture" for two years, he remained constantly in the public eye. With a major movie and record releases also during that time, it was like he'd never been away.

→ **1958 MIDGET FANS** The Colonel pulled out all the stops to keep everyone aware of Elvis during his Army service. At the Chicago convention of the Music Operators of America he even put together an Elvis Presley Midget Fan Club and provided a photo opportunity for the press, ever eager to seize on any new angle on the phenomenon that was Elvis.

WELCOME!
MUSIC OPERATORS OF AMERICA
ELVIS PRESLEY'S MIDGET FAN CLUB
ELVIS & THE COLONEL
Let's Don't Forget
ELVIS

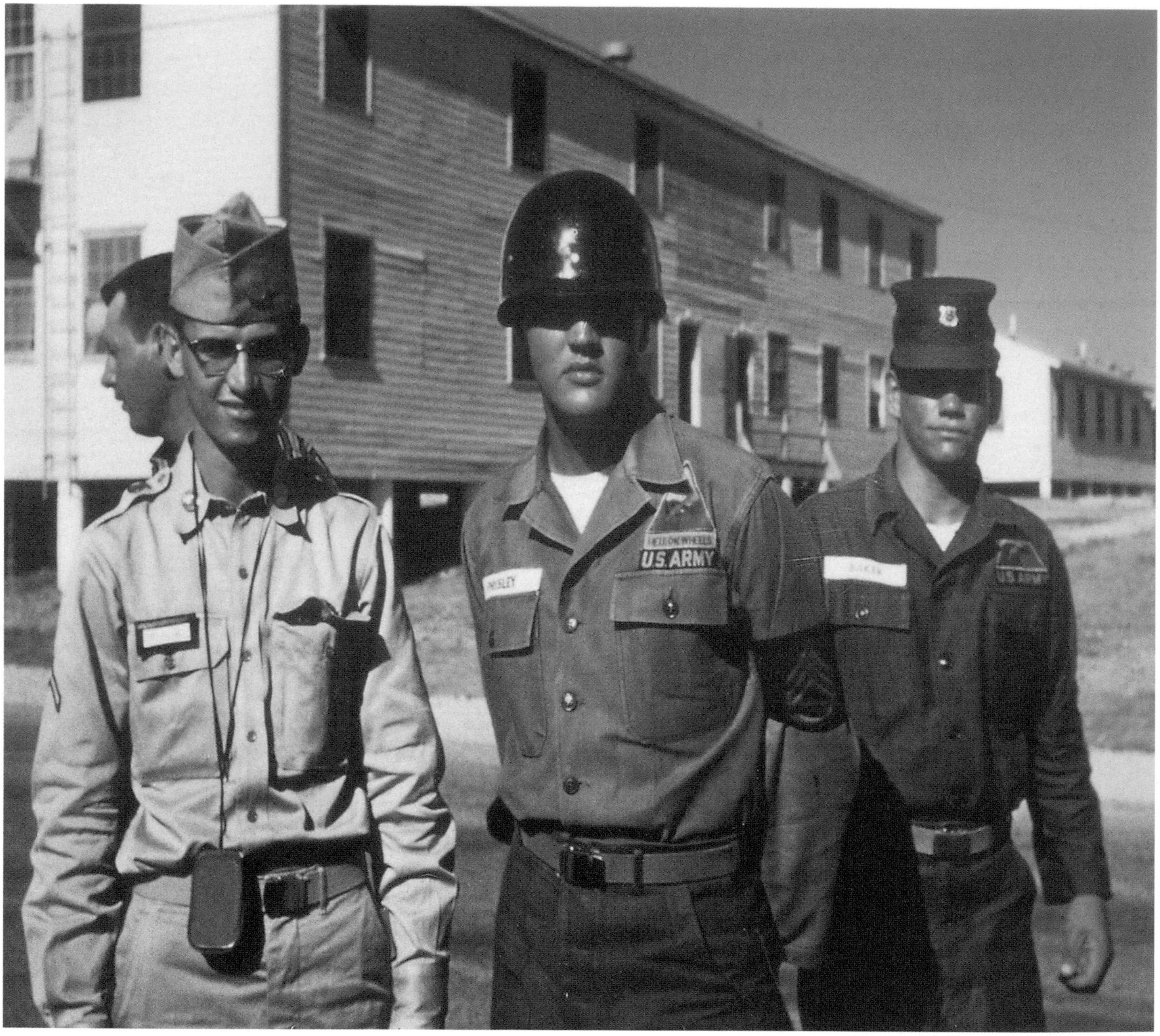

1959

1959 **BAD NAUHEIM** Looking more militaristic than usual in his shiny helmet, Elvis poses in a rare color photo taken at the base in Bad Nauheim. One thing the experience of his Army service did for the star was to allow him to rub shoulders, albeit in a limited way, with "ordinary" guys who were not chosen friends, relatives, or business associates–nor, for that matter, were they necessarily fans. He was discovering for the first time in his adult years the kind of relationships with work and leisure acquaintances that don't all bond into close friendships, but are nevertheless a part of normal, everyday life. That was probably the greatest legacy of his Army years.

1960 GI JOES Elvis and some of his Army buddies in winter maneuvers in Grafenwohr, January 1960. The picture is inscribed on the back "Ed – Elvis – Al Ha Ha Velsect 1960, to Elvis, Eddie," while the front gives liitle more clue to the identity of the two soldiers on each side of Elvis, just reading "Me –The Twist – Ha Ha." One can assume that Al's nickname was Ha Ha, and Elvis was dubbed "The Twist," by these guys at least. Certainly he seems to be doing a joke mime of the Twist dance craze, which was just becoming popular via hits by Hank Ballard, Joey Dee, and later Chubby Checker. Not one to jump on bandwagons, Elvis never made a Twist record to cash in on the fad.

1960

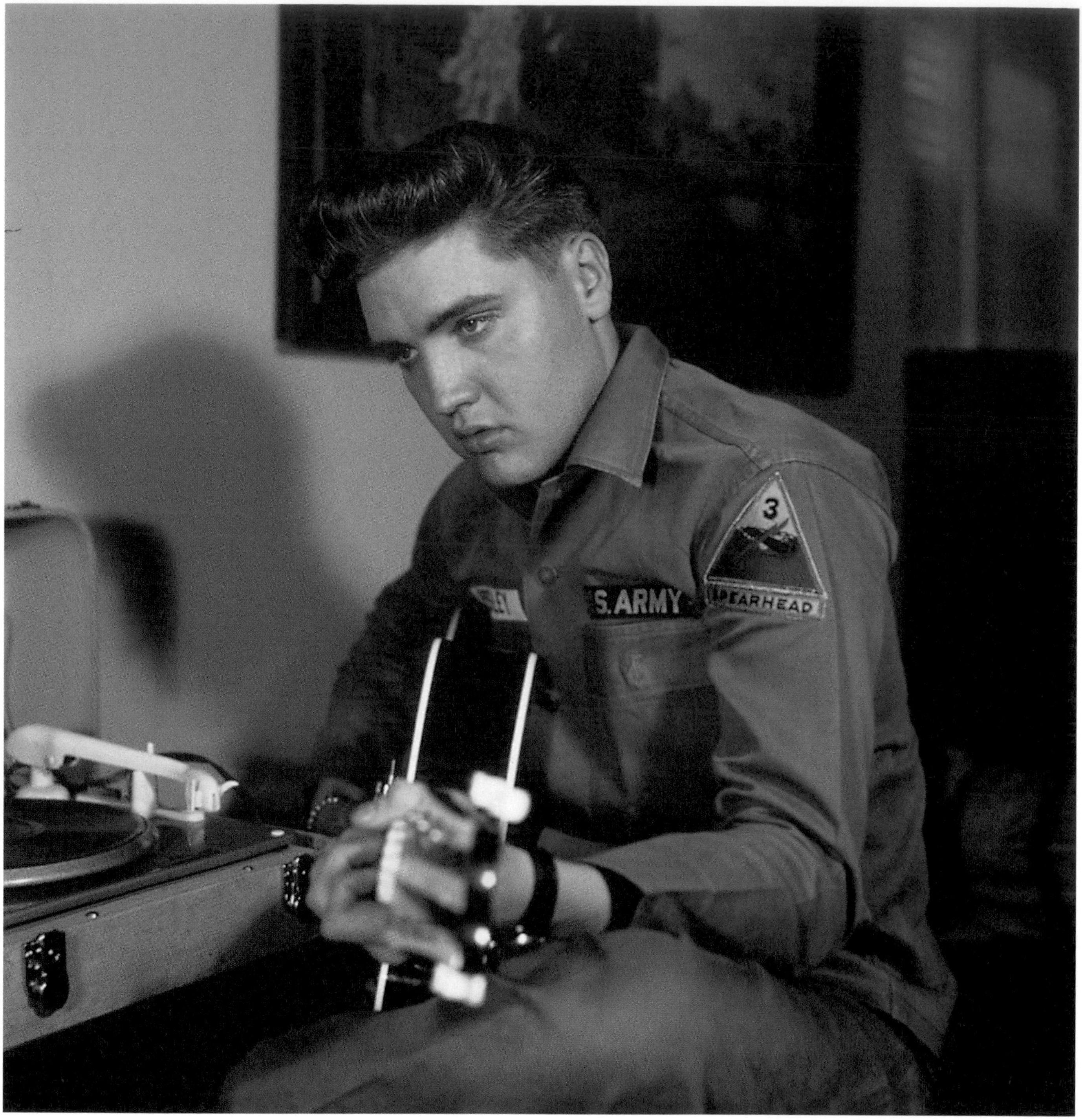

1960 GOETHESTRASSE Relaxing at home in Germany. Regardless of the fact that it was within Army regulations for a soldier to live off base with dependent relatives, it's fair to say that Elvis was in a privileged postion as far as his living arrangements were concerned. Very few draftees, indeed probably none other, were in a position to bring over to Germany two members of their family plus friends, and to rent an entire house for them to live in. As in Texas, it enabled (maneuvers apart) Elvis to travel to "work" every morning, almost as if it was another day at the office. But even that daily routine would of course have been a radical change of lifestyle for the superstar.

1960 BREAKFAST Grandmother Minnie Presley stops for the camera as she serves breakfast for Vernon and Elvis in their modest kitchen at 14 Goethestrasse, Bad Nauheim. The picture, perhaps surprisingly, has ended up on postcards, alongside rather more iconic images of the King of Rock'n'Roll.

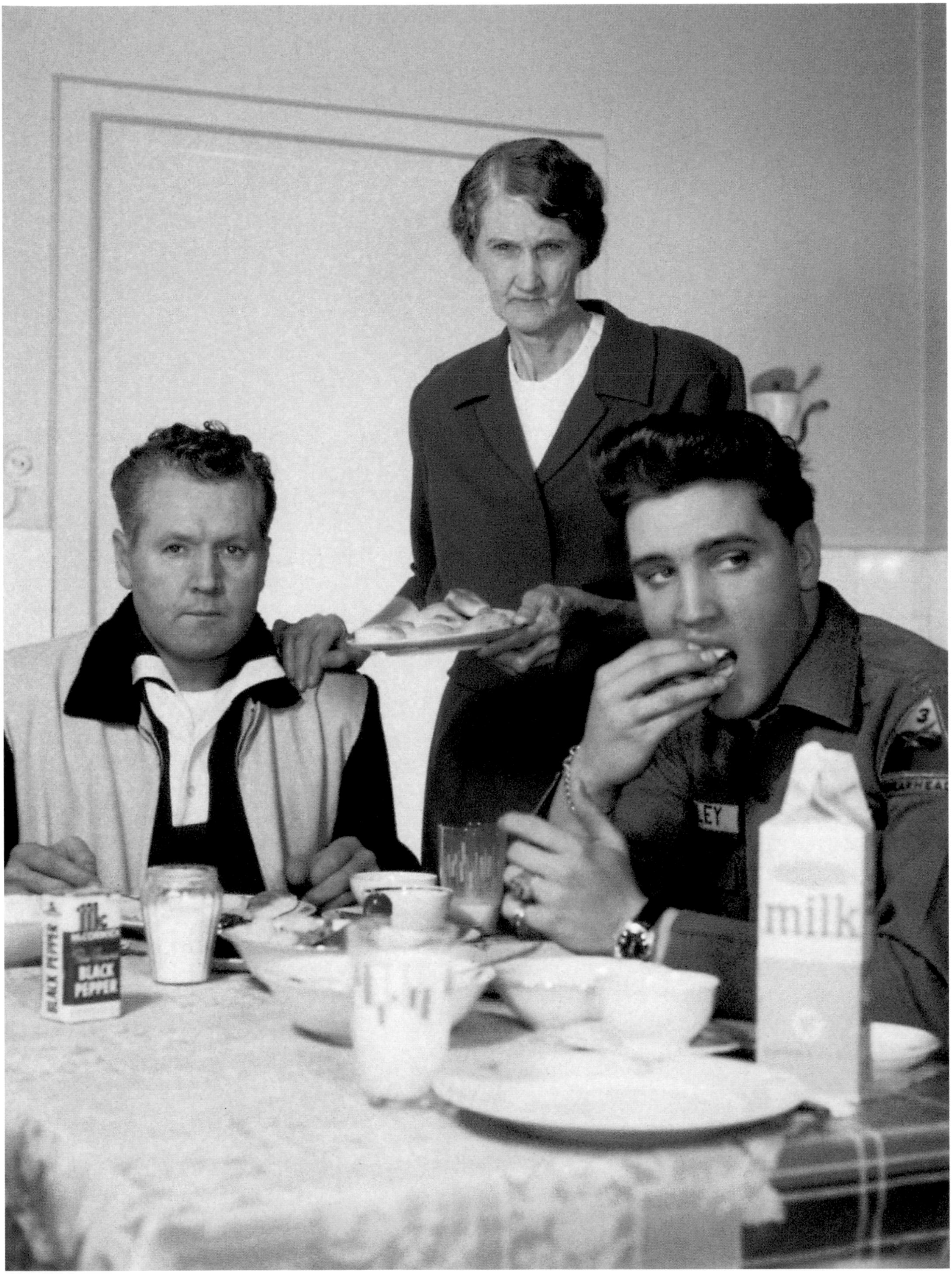
BLACK PEPPER
milk

1960

➔ **1960 PRISCILLA** Priscilla Beaulieu was only 14 when she met Elvis in the house in Bad Nauheim on September 13, 1959. The daughter of a full-time Air Force captain, she had arrived in Wiesbaden, another small town near Frankfurt, a month earlier. A mutual acquaintance had brought her around to the Presley family home in Goethestrasse, and she and Elvis immediately struck up a rapport. After just four dates he met her parents, and from then on in they saw each other constantly. The picture at right was taken as Priscilla bade farewell when Elvis left Germany from the Rhein-Main airbase on March 2, 1960.

1960

1960 HOME Seventeen months later and Elvis has left Germany. On March 3, 1960, he landed at McGuire Air Force Base near Fort Dix, New Jersey, having flown from the Rhine-Main airbase, with his official separation papers clutched under one arm. He flew into a heavy snowstorm, something he'd started to get used to in Germany.

1960 HOMECOMING The major publicity event to mark Elvis' homecoming from the Army was the press conference that the Colonel staged on his return to Graceland. It was held in Vernon's office, which was located in the outbuildings of the house, and the filmed session can still be viewed by visitors to the mansion, where it plays on a video monitor placed near the actual desk. During the very relaxed interview Elvis articulated his feelings about his time in the Army and his return to civilian life. At least one questioner raised the issue of whether he'd had a regular girlfriend in Germany, to which Elvis coyly replied that there *was* someone he'd been seeing, but would give away no more.

1960

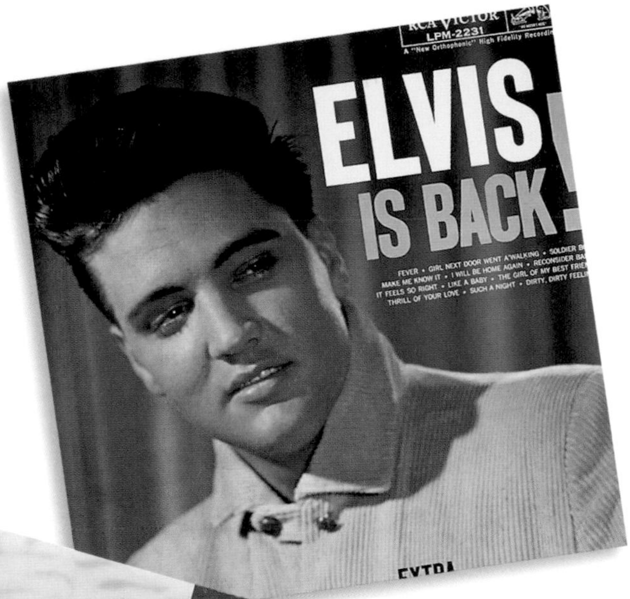

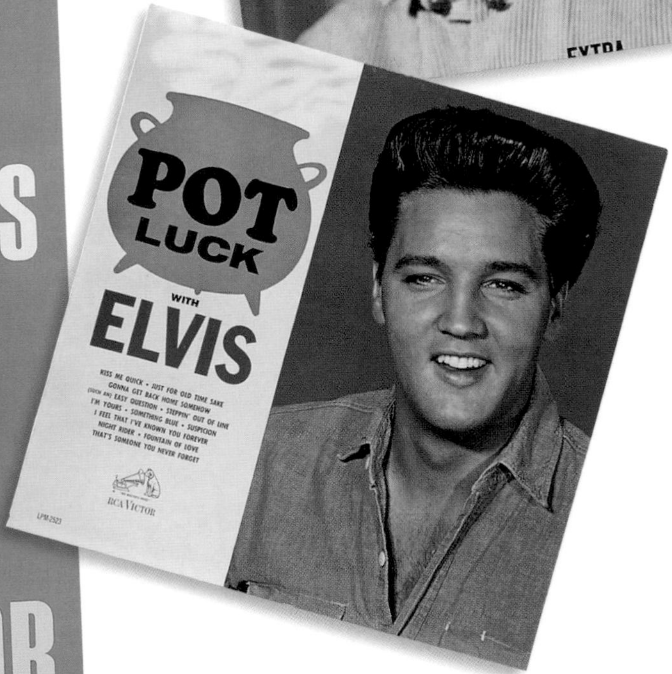

1960 50 MILLION RECORDS When Elvis got home, one of the first accolades he was to receive was from his record company, RCA, which had delivered to the front door in Graceland a huge state-of-the-art TV and record player console to commemorate the sale of more than 50 million records worldwide (*left,* Elvis greets its arrival).

1960 RECORDS April 1960 saw the release of the first major album marking Elvis' return to civilian life, the aptly titled *Elvis Is Back!* As if making up for lost time, RCA Records was to release another five LPs over the next two years, the fifth being *Pot Luck*, which appeared in June 1962. One of the most important releases was the collection of gospel songs, *His Hand In Mine,* which appeared in November 1960, well timed for the Christmas market. Two singles taken from the album were to appear six years later in February 1966, "Joshua Fit The Battle"/"Know Only To Him" and "Milky White Way"/"Swing Low Sweet Chariot", this time being pitched as "Elvis For Easter."

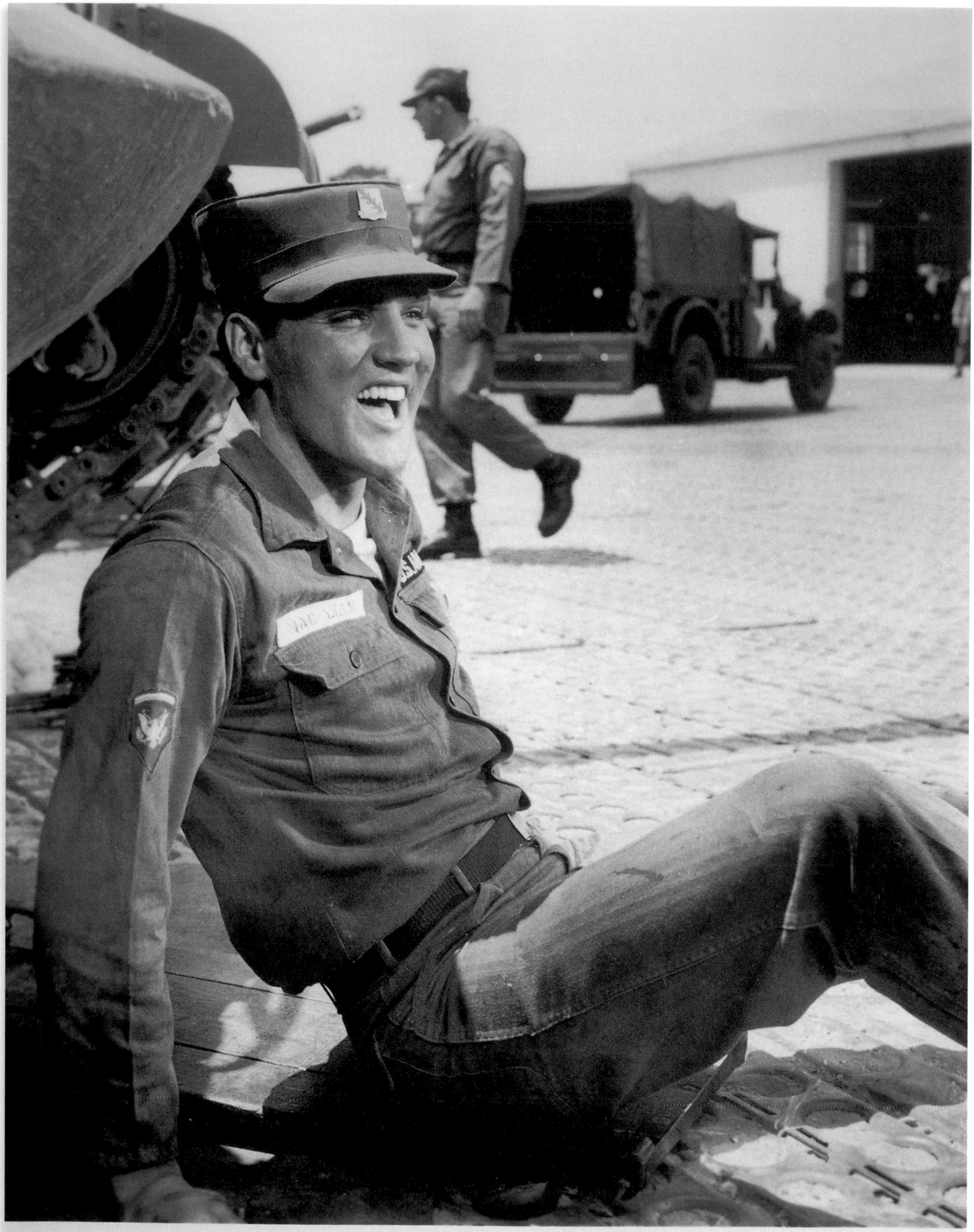

Copyright © 1960 by Hal B. Wallis and Joseph H. Hazen. Permission granted for newspaper and magazine reproduction. (Made in U.S.A.)

"G. I. BLUES"

A Hal Wallis Production   A Paramount Picture   Technicolor®

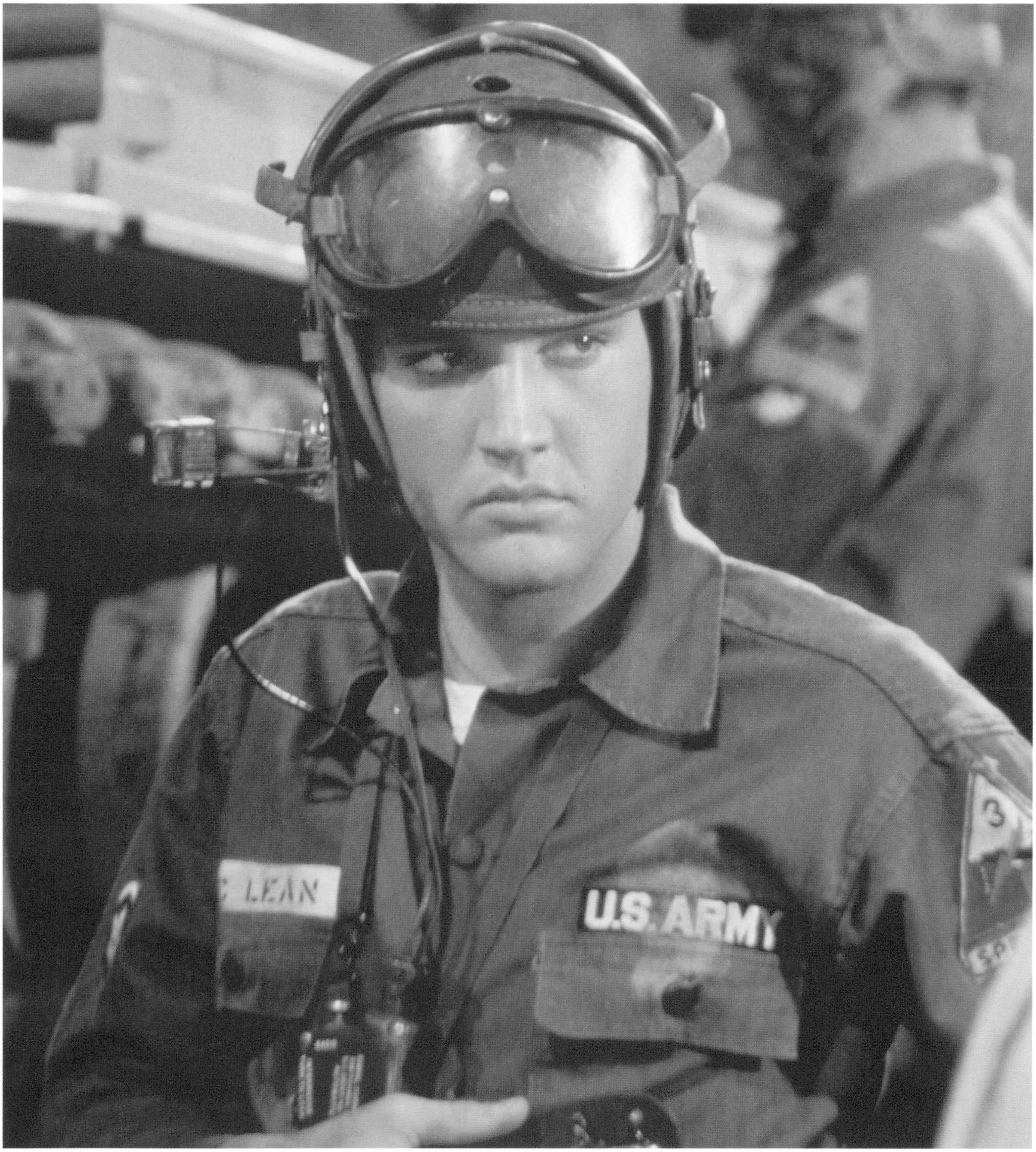

1960 GI BLUES A prudently timed cash-in on Elvis' return to civilian life after his Army service, the movie *GI Blues* was set in a US Army unit stationed in West Germany. The songs proved fairly lightweight in terms of memorable hits, and a scene in a club where Elvis sings "Doin' The Best I Can" is eclipsed musically by someone playing "Blue Suede Shoes" on the jukebox! The biggest hit from the picture was the somewhat sentimental "Wooden Heart," which Elvis delivered, accompanied by an accordian (and including some lines in German), to a group of children watching a puppet show. Nonetheless, the film did well at the box office, and was among the 15 top-grossing movies of 1960.

1960

HAPPY

1960 GI BLUES Elvis dons an Army uniform once more, here on the set of *GI Blues.* Filming ran through May and June, not long after Elvis' return to America and civilian life, so location shots in Germany were probably out of the question for him. He did all his scenes in the Paramount studios, while the cameras went to Germany for some authentic atmosphere photography. It was certainly one of Elvis' most successful movies in commercial terms, reaching number two in the weekly list of top-grossing films published in *Variety* magazine, and taking more than $4 million in the last six weeks of 1960. His costar was Juliet Prowse, who, after her second movie *Can-Can* earlier in 1960, was being acclaimed as a bright new singing-and-dancing Hollywood talent. The allusions to Elvis' own recent tour of duty in the Army were reinforced by the inclusion of a song called "Frankfort Special," during which Elvis and the Jordanaires are seen singing on a train heading for "Frankfort," presumably a veiled reference to his own Army location near Frankfurt.

1960 SINATRA TV SPECIAL The biggest "welcome back" event the Colonel negotiated to mark Elvis' return to civilian life was the Frank Sinatra TV special, sponsored by Timex watches, and billed as "Frank Sinatra's Welcome Home Party for Elvis Presley." The show, for which Elvis received $125,000, a record then for a TV guest spot, was recorded on March 26, 1960, and also featured three of Sinatra's "rat pack" buddies Sammy Davis Jnr., Peter Lawford, and Joey Bishop, plus Nancy Sinatra, who was to costar with Elvis in the movie *Speedway* a few years later. For Frank Sinatra it was an about-face as far as his attitude to rock'n'roll was concerned. The crooner had famously criticized the music in 1957 as being "sung, played, and written for the most part by cretionous goons," yet now he was accommodating in no uncertain terms its biggest figurehead. When the show was broadcast on May 12, it captured nearly 70% of the audience share. Elvis was certainly back, and everyone knew it.

1960 HIS HAND IN MINE Two publicity pictures, one used on the cover of the album of gospel songs *His Hand In Mine*. Recorded in RCA's studios in Nashville on October 30, 1960, it featured such traditional religious items as "Joshua Fit The Battle" and "Swing Low Sweet Chariot," and included among the musicians Scotty Moore, D. J. Fontana, the "Yaketty Sax" man Boots Randolph on tenor saxophone, and, as well as Elvis and the Jordanaires, Millie Kirkham on vocals. The release of "Crying In The Chapel" and "I Believe In The Man In The Sky" as a single from the album came in April 1965. Interestingly, Elvis' only Grammy awards were for gospel recordings.

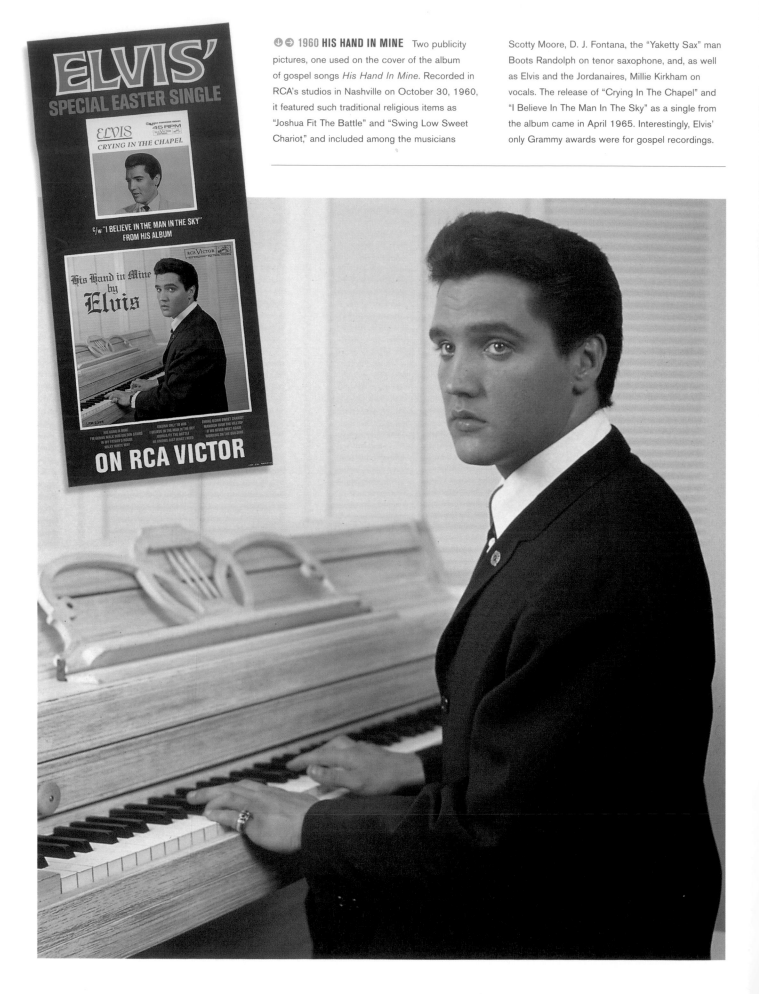

1961

1961 HONOLULU On March 15, 1961, Elvis played a benefit to raise money for a memorial to the 1,102 men entombed in the World War II battleship USS *Arizona*, which was sunk at Pearl Harbor 20 years before. The spectacular was promoted by the Pacific War Memorial Commission and held at the Bloch Arena in Honolulu, Hawaii. For such an important and sensitive cause Elvis was prepared to waive his $150,000 performance fee. As well as raising actual funds for the project, Elvis' participation was invaluable as a means of generating publicity and raising public awareness of the proposed memorial, which, although having had problems up to that point, was then completed within a year.

1961 HONOLULU Accompanied by full-page welcomes in every local newspaper, Elvis arrived at Honolulu airport to mayhem. More than 3,000 fans and 75 police were there to greet him; second-on-the-bill star, the country singer Minnie Pearl, later described her reaction to the scene: "We got off the plane, girls were screaming. He walked over to sign autographs, I'd never seen anything like it before, I was just horrified . . . I thought they were going to kill him . . ."

PARADE THE SUNDAY NEWSPAPER MAGAZINE

CONGRATULATIONS TO ELVIS ON HIS U.S.S. ARIZONA MEMORIAL FUND SHOW

BLOCH ARENA – PEARL HARBOR

SATURDAY ONLY, MAR. 25–8:30 P.M., DOORS OPEN 7:15

ELVIS REMEMBERS PEARL HARBOR

Hawaii Next Charity Stop

By DON WALKER

BLOCH ARENA, PEARL HARBOR

Saturday MARCH 25TH

Symbol of Freedom

USS ARIZONA MEMORIAL U.S. NAVY PROJECT

BUREAU OF YARDS & DOCKS

A Proper Tribute

Film To Follow

Parker Answers Plea

All For Arizona

"See Elvis in Blue Hawaii" A Hal Wallis Production—Paramount Release. Soon to be filmed in Hawaii.

THE PACIFIC WAR MEMORIAL COMMISSION Proudly Presents

IN PERSON

ELVIS AND HIS SHOW

SPECIAL GUEST

MINNIE PEARL

WITH AN ALL STAR CAST

★ THE JORDANAIRES

★ D. J. FONTANA

★ SCOTTY MOORE

BLOCH ARENA, PEARL HARBOR

Saturday MARCH 25TH

TICKETS NOW AT SEARS

HONOLULU, HAWAII

NOTICE THIS IS A GUARANTEED 100% BENEFIT PERFORMANCE NOTICE

Absolutely all receipts from ticket sales must go to The USS Arizona Memorial Fund.

RCA VICTOR

EXCLUSIVE MANAGEMENT COL. TOM PARKER

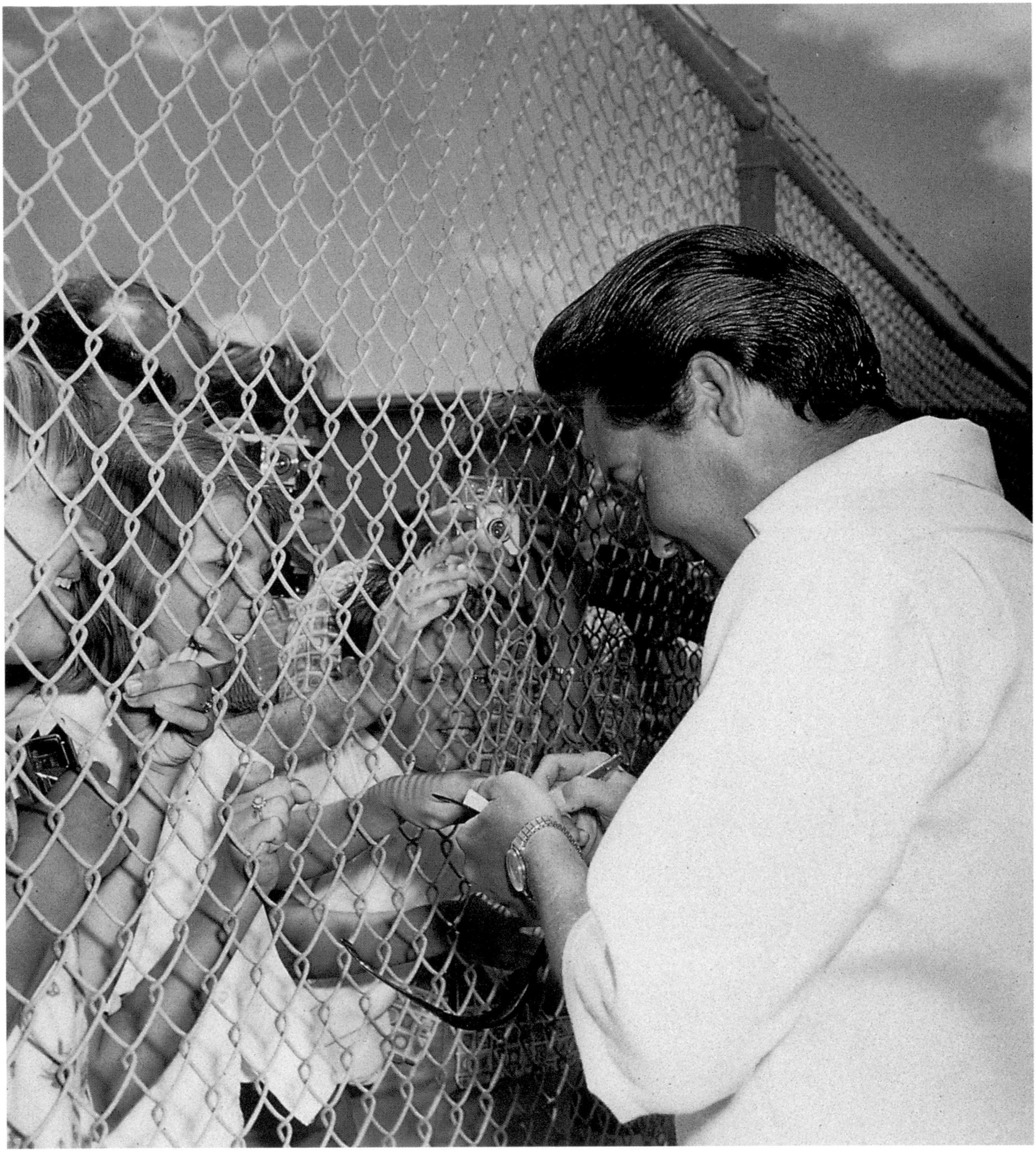

⊖ **1961 HONOLULU** The USS *Arizona* benefit concert raised more than $62,000, and the Hawaii House of Representatives formally thanked Elvis and the Colonel for their efforts. Many accolades were received from the US Navy, including one from the admiral who actually introduced Elvis at the concert.

⊕ **1965 HONOLULU** Elvis visits the USS *Arizona* Memorial. Never one to let an opportunity pass, after the gratitude expressed by the authorities in Hawaii, the Colonel wrote to Vice President Lyndon Johnson in 1961, offering his and Elvis' services to their country "in any capacity, whether it is to use our talents or help load the trucks."

1961

196

1961 HONOLULU Elvis contemplates Honolulu harbor from the balcony of his room in the Hawaiian Village Hotel. The Colonel and Elvis stayed on in Hawaii to commence shooting on the movie *Blue Hawaii*, which was to mark the beginning of his movie-only career through the next seven years. The *Arizona* date was his last live performance until his TV "comeback" show at the end of 1968.

ELVIS PRESLEY

Elvis™

Hollywood Calls

IN THE MOVIES

[1960–1969]

← **1965 PARADISE, HAWAIIAN STYLE**
Elvis relaxes on the exotic location set in Hanauma Bay, Hawaii, during the filming of his 21st movie, which was released worldwide in July 1966.

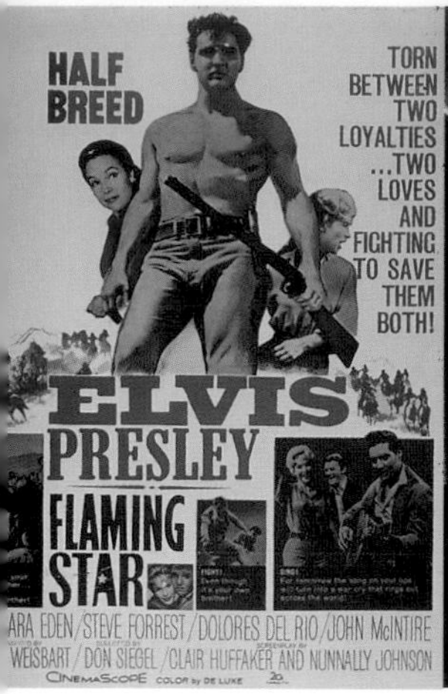

December 1960

August 1968

April 1961

April 1967

1960-69

From early on in his career, Elvis' name was suggested for roles in a number of "serious" movies, including *The Defiant Ones, Cat On A Hot Tin Roof*, and the late-Seventies remake of *A Star Is Born*. But despite encouraging early performances in *Love Me Tender*, *Jailhouse Rock,* and *King Creole*, his potential as a dramatic actor was never to be realized.

Most of Elvis' activity through the 1960s was centered on a plethora of (mainly lightweight) movies that by and large presented an increasingly anodyne image of the singer. There were some exceptions, of course. In *Flaming Star* and *Charro!* (interestingly, both Westerns) he played parts that stretched him as an actor, giving him situations and plots that didn't require him to burst into song at the drop of a clapper board. But mostly the audiences saw a happy-go-lucky Elvis, with immaculate hair and clothes to match, in a variety of contrived situations, and always with glamorous female costars.

There were "travelog" movies, with romantic locations providing backdrops to song-and-dance routines with interchangeable Sixties starlets. Likewise, there were Elvis-on-wheels plots, ranging from motorcycles to race cars to water skis, in roles that again were an excuse for him to pursue, be pursued by, and serenade a seemingly never-ending line of Hollywood lovelies.

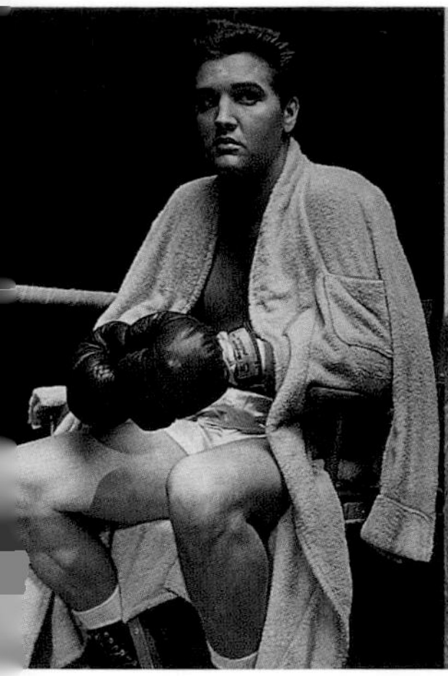

December 1961

August 1963

April 1961

Nevertheless, within the confines of this quickly-established formula, some memorable moments were captured on celluloid, like the double part he played in *Kissin' Cousins,* the raunchy dance sequences with Ann-Margret in *Viva Las Vegas!,* and the boxing scenes (in which Elvis didn't use a stand-in) in *Kid Galahad*.

Interestingly, Elvis came to work with a surprising number of Hollywood greats, alongside the newer names who dominated the cast lists of most of the movies. *Blue Hawaii* featured Angela Lansbury, who was first nominated for an Oscar for *Gaslight* in 1944. Gig Young, who appeared in *Kid Galahad*, was nominated three times. Hollywood veteran Barbara Stanwyck shared the honors for *Roustabout*, while 1967's *Easy Come, Easy Go* featured Elsa Lanchester, who was twice nominated for an Oscar.

What the Hollywood years did establish, once and for all, was Elvis' prime position in the very upper echelons of the showbusiness establishment elite, evidenced by the many celebrities who visited him on- and off-set during his long sojourns in California. Whether it was legendary names like Jimmy Durante and Mahalia Jackson, or new pop-chart stars (everyone from Tom Jones to the Beatles), they all came to pay homage to the King of Rock'n'Roll.

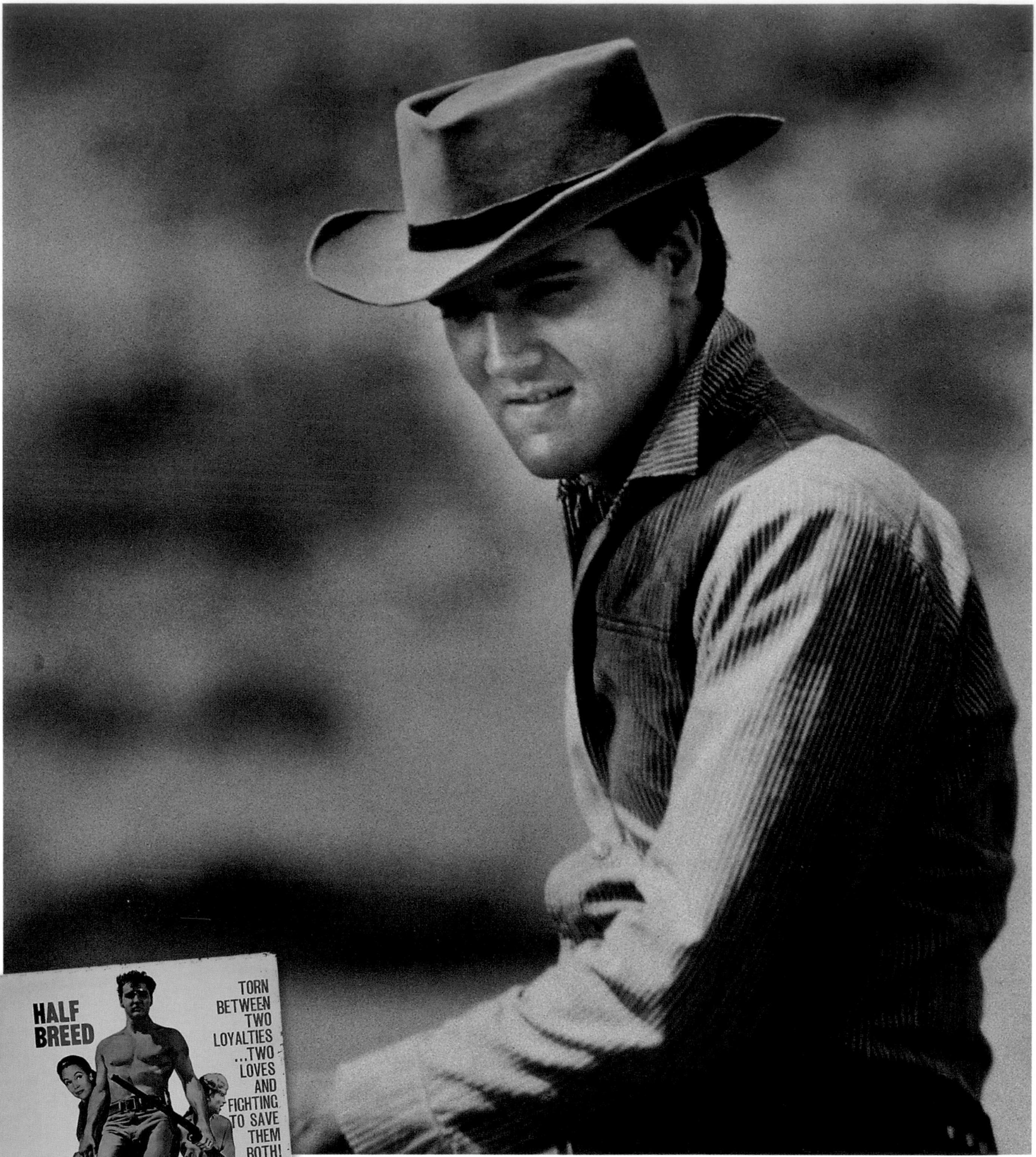

1960 FLAMING STAR Elvis' sixth film–in which he played a Native American–was, with the exception of *Charro!* later in the decade, the nearest he got to a nonsinging role. It features only the title song (over the credits) and "A Cane and a High Stitched Collar" in the opening minutes of the movie. In fact, director Don Siegel didn't want any songs in the film, but producer David Weisbart won the day. *Flaming Star* was based a book called *The Brothers of Broken Lance* by Claire Huiffaker, and was originally going to be filmed in 1958 as *The Brothers of Flaming Arrow* with Marlon Brando and Frank Sinatra as the two brothers. These roles were eventually taken by Elvis and Steve Forrest.

A Scene from the 20th Century-Fox Production
"FLAMING STAR"
In CinemaScope
Printed in the U.S.A.

1960 FLAMING STAR Elvis' role in *Flaming Star*, as the mixed-ethnicity Native American Pacer Burton–described in the language of the time, including on the front-of-house posters, as "half breed"–was a serious if not exactly controversial one, dealing with a clash of cultures, and therefore a clash of loyalties facing the hero.

1960 FLAMING STAR This portrait of Elvis from *Flaming Star*, actually a posed studio photograph produced for publicity purposes, was one of the many images of him that were to become pure iconography, especially when it was later the subject of a 1964 painting, *Single Elvis*, by the pop artist Andy Warhol.

1960

1960 FLAMING STAR Elvis relaxes on one of the outside location sets during the filming of *Flaming Star*. Much of the movie was shot on three ranches in the San Fernando Valley near Los Angeles, and the rest was shot in the studio. It was directed by Don Siegel, famous for many cult classics including the 1956 film *Invasion Of The Bodysnatchers*.

1961 BLUE HAWAII On location shooting the early scenes of *Blue Hawaii*, in which he played a serviceman leaving the army, Elvis shares a joke with the film's producer Hal Wallis. Wallis was a Hollywood veteran whose productions ranged from *Casablanca* and *Gunfight At The OK Corral* to John Wayne's *True Grit*. He died in 1986, aged 88.

1961

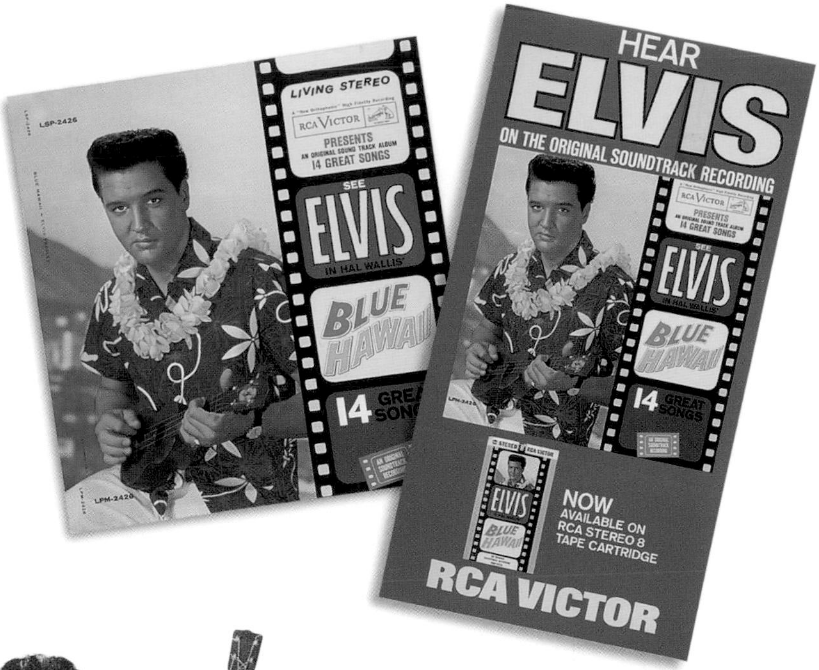

1961 BLUE HAWAII An all-singing, all-dancing Technicolor blockbuster, the first in Elvis' trilogy of "South Seas" movies and the first of the lighthearted genre of films that became the stereotype for much of his subsequent Hollywood output (*here and overleaf*). The trite plot served as a backcloth for no fewer than 14 songs, and the film grossed over $4 million at the box office, not to mention the tie-in soundtrack album, which went gold immediately on release. Costarring Joan Blackman, who appeared again with Elvis in *Kid Galahad*, the movie also featured Angela Lansbury as the mother of Elvis' character Chad Gates, although in real life she was only 35 years old.

"BLUE HAWAII"

A Hal Wallis Production A Paramount Picture Panavision® Technicolor®

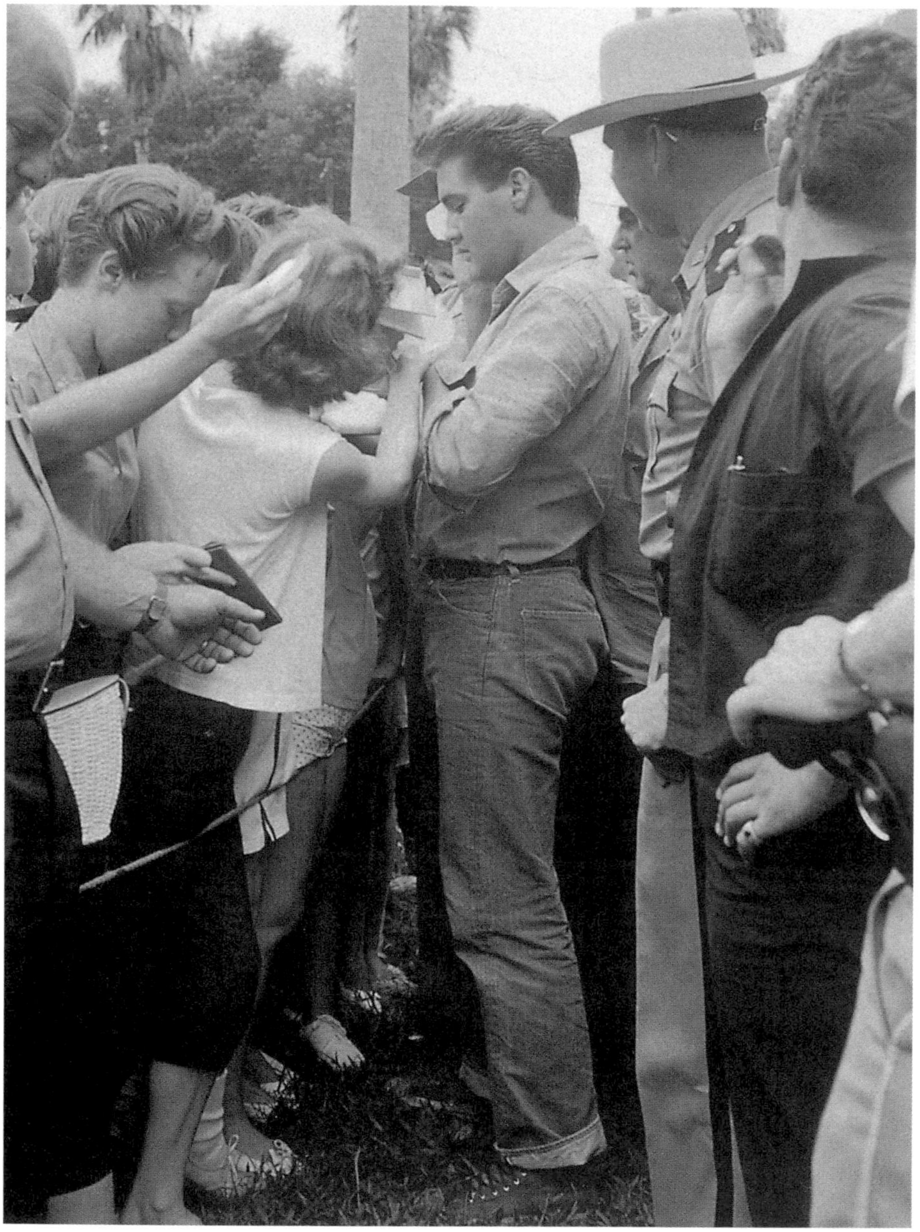

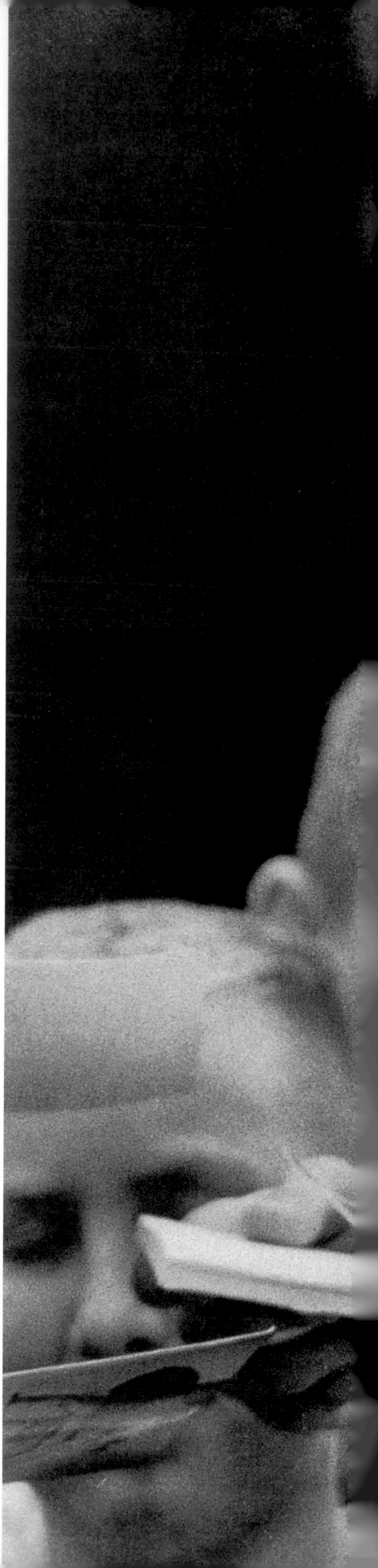

1961

1961 FOLLOW THAT DREAM Location shooting for Elvis' films often provided lucky fans with a rare chance to get close to their idol. Florida was the chosen site for *Follow That Dream*, and–as usual, under close supervision by the local cops–eager kids got their autographs from Elvis, who was always happy to oblige.

1962 FOLLOW THAT DREAM Released in 1962, the film was distinguished by a well-received stab at comedy on Elvis' part. Based on a novel entitled *Pioneer Go Home!* by Richard Powell, the plot followed the adventures of an itinerant family down on their luck, setting up a new home and fishing business in Florida. Elvis played Toby, the son, and romantic interest was provided by Anne Helm as his adopted sister Holly. The film's premiere was staged in Ocala, Florida, on April 11, 1962, and the film was released nationally–and worldwide–at the end of May. With only five complete songs, the disc spin-off was restricted to a 45 that got to number 15 in the US singles chart.

1961 FOLLOW THAT DREAM Principal photography on *Follow That Dream* took place in July 1961, a few days after Elvis had checked into the Port Paradise Hotel in Crystal River, Florida. Here Elvis plays with one of his costars on the set, the child actress Pam Ogles, who played the youngest member of the family, Ariadne.

1961 FOLLOW THAT DREAM By all accounts it seems that Elvis had a particularly good time while on location shooting *Follow That Dream*. Arriving at the Florida set in a privately-rented bus, he brought along with him–for recreation purposes only–a 20-foot speedboat, a motorcycle, and two of his cars.

1961

ORTH
SY. 6-7173

1961 KID GALAHAD The outdoor locations for the 1962 boxing movie *Kid Galahad* were shot primarily in the popular California resort of Idylwild. The film, costarring a trio of Hollywood stalwarts–Lola Albright, Gig Young, and Charles Bronson–was shot in the winter of 1961 and released during August of the following year.

1961 FOLLOW THAT DREAM Filming away from the studio on location, whether it was in the South Seas or the more localized regions of the mainland US (in this case Florida), always provided an excuse for Elvis to indulge in his passion for various forms of outdoor activity, particularly his love of high-powered motorcycles.

1961

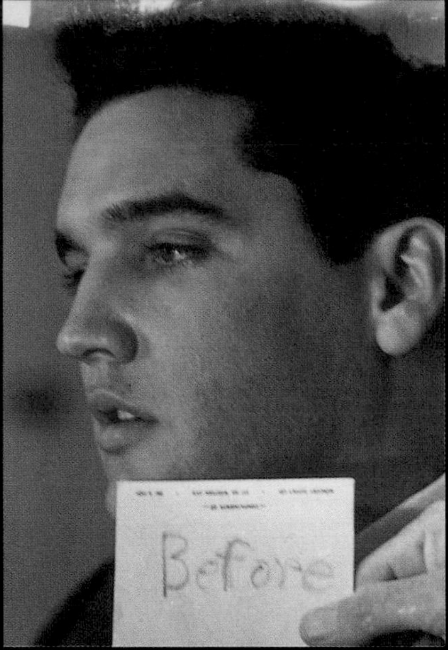

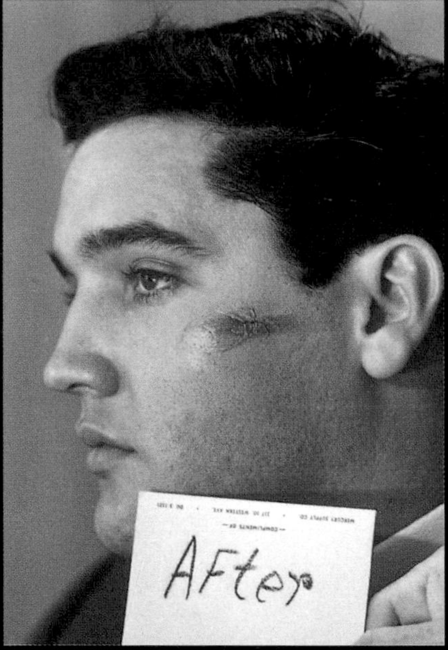

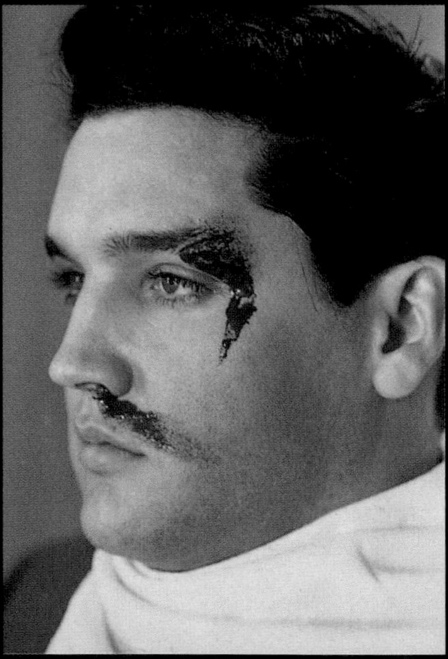

962

↑ → **1962 KID GALAHAD** A boxing movie based on a 1930s story, which had previously been adapted for the screen in 1937 by Michael Curtiz—who directed *King Creole* in 1958—starring Edward G. Robinson and Bette Davis. Some of the most sensational images in the film are those of Elvis with fight wounds on his face. These were also captured in a series of before-and-after snaps taken in the makeup unit while preparing for shooting. Elvis declined to have a stand-in for the actual fight sequences; instead, he was coached by the former world junior welterweight champion Mushy Callahan and Al Silvani, extrainer to such boxing luminaries as Floyd Patterson and Rocky Graziano.

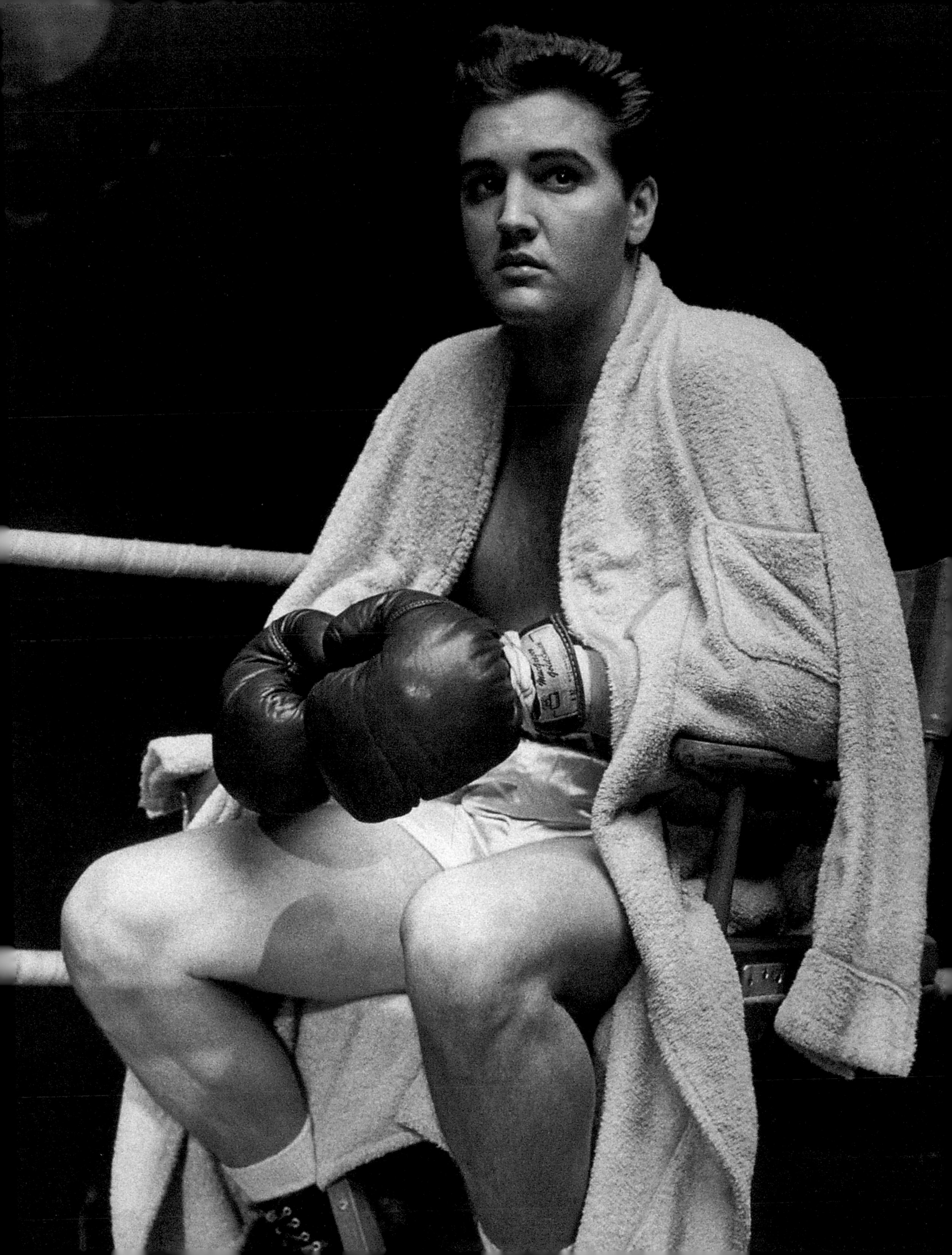

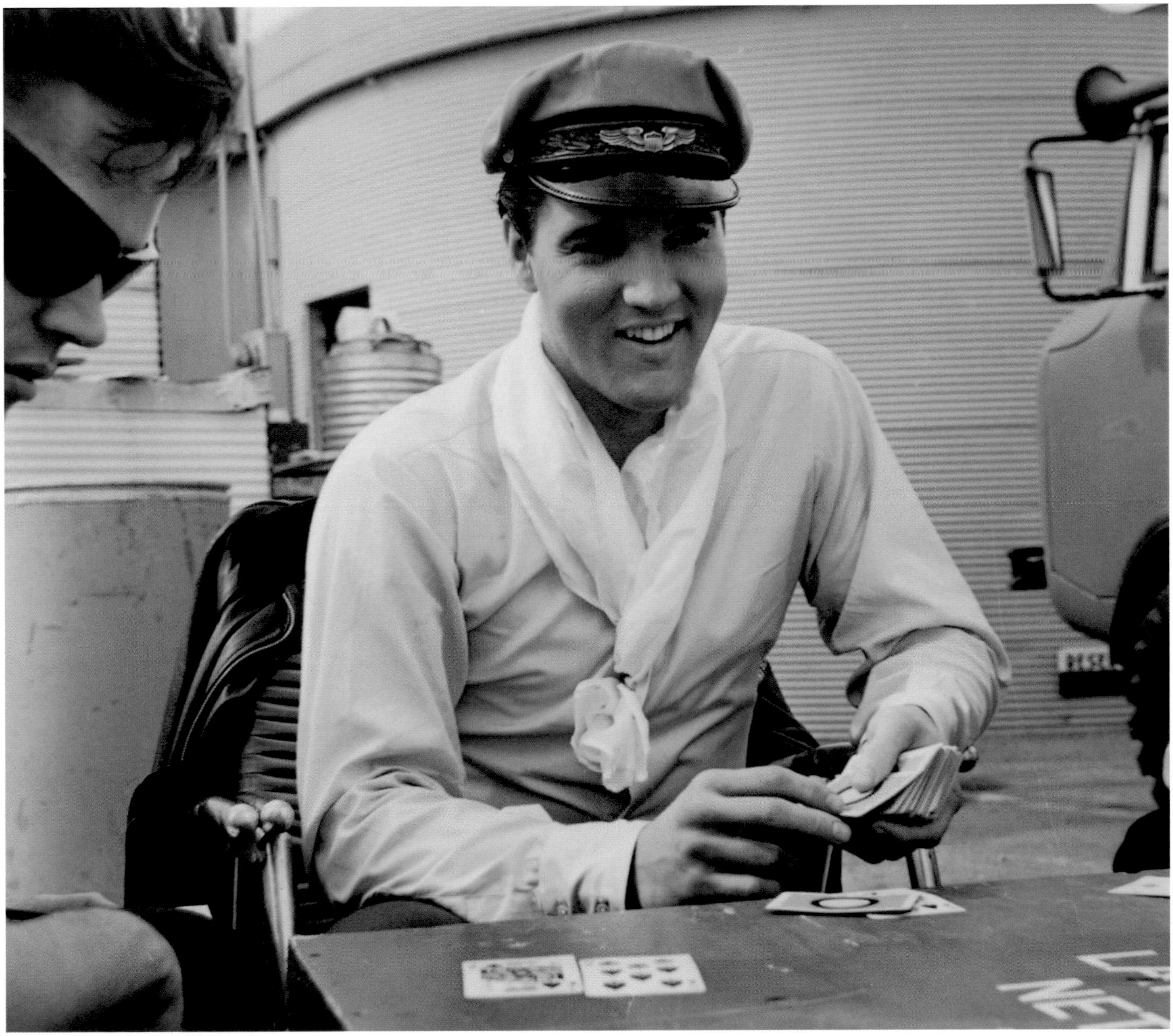

1962 GIRLS! GIRLS! GIRLS! Archetypal of Elvis' "all-singin', all-lovin'" vehicles, and one of many films in which he was surrounded by plenty of girls in musical routines held together by a lightweight storyline. He plays a charter fisherman who sings in a nightclub to raise money for a boat, torn between the affections of Stella Stevens and Laurel Goodwin.

1962 IT HAPPENED AT THE WORLD'S FAIR Elvis relaxing on set during filming at the Seattle World's Fair for his 12th film. Shooting began in September 1962, and the movie was released the following April. Interior scenes were shot at the MGM Culver City studios. Though not one of his biggest films, it grossed over $2 million at the box office in 1963.

1962

← **1963 CALENDAR** During the years in which his main occupation was making movies at the rate of two or three per annum, Elvis still made records. He had at his disposal the combined publicity machines of film studios, RCA Records, and Colonel Tom Parker, so his image was prominent on fan magazines, postcards, and other merchandise.

↑ **1964 RCA PUBLICITY** RCA Records couldn't go wrong with Elvis. As well as albums that were produced to accompany the movies, there were also studio albums made in their own right, and, most lucratively in the long run, there was his huge back catalog–a treasure trove in terms of sheer quality as well as quantity.

1963

➊ 1963 IT HAPPENED AT THE WORLD'S FAIR
Along with cars, motorcycles, and speedboats, it was inevitable that Elvis would get involved with aircraft in at least one of his movies. He portrays a crop-dusting pilot, who, along with his partner (played by Gary Lockwood), gets involved at the Fair with Joan O'Brian and Vicky Tiu.

➋ 1963 IT HAPPENED AT THE WORLD'S FAIR
As well as the the local Seattle police and the World's Fair security organizations, MGM hired 100 special policemen to shield Elvis from the crowds while filming took place. Additionally, six Pinkerton plainclothes detectives were at his side when he wasn't actually in front of the cameras.

MIKE EDWARDS

1962

↑ → 1962 IT HAPPENED AT THE WORLD'S FAIR

The movie appeared to be nothing more than an excuse for a conducted tour of the Seattle World's Fair of 1962, and, of course, for Elvis to run through a collection of songs. Shooting at the location proved difficult, as the actors and crew were hampered by genuine visitors to the Fair who suddenly realized that Elvis was there too. Unlike other Elvis shoots, at which fans could be strictly monitored and kept away from the set if necessary, the crowds were there anyway–the Fair was the set, and the crowds were part of the scenery. Local police and Fair security staff were probably relieved when shooting ended.

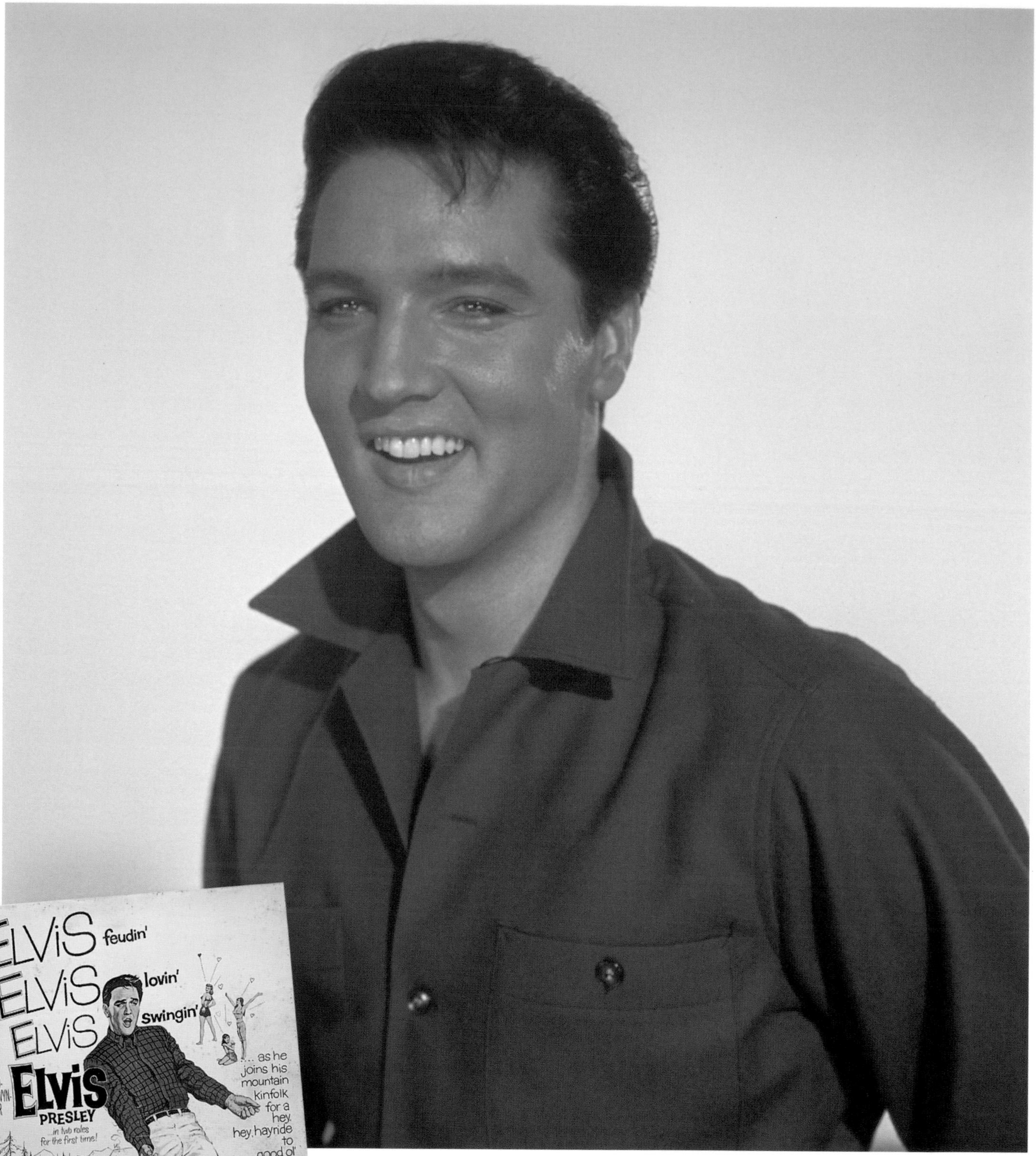

1963 MOVIE PUBLICITY Every Elvis movie—and in most cases the simultaneously released soundtrack album—was accompanied by a new series of publicity shots, coordinated by the film studio and RCA Records. Previous pages: a portrait *(left)* from *Fun In Acapulco*, another "travelog" movie (its title was originally to be *Vacation In Acapulco*), this time set in Mexico; and *(right)* *Kissin' Cousins*. The shot above is also from this film, in which Elvis fans got twice the value for the price of a ticket, as the movie featured him in two roles—one with dark hair, one blonde—as long-lost cousins. The picture opposite, with Elvis in race-driver gear, was posed for *Viva Las Vegas*.

JACKSO

1812-

1964

1963 **VIVA LAS VEGAS** Despite the routine plot of this 1964 release, involving a race-car driver's adventures in the casino capital, the stand-out features of *Viva Las Vegas* are Elvis' song-and-dance routines with his vivacious co-star, the Swedish–American actress Ann-Margret. The film's success was helped in no small way by the director George Sidney, whose achievements included the classic MGM musicals *Annie Get Your Gun*, *Show Boat*, *Kiss Me Kate*, and *Pal Joey*. Ann-Margret, who was romantically linked to Elvis during shooting, had already briefly made her mark on the music scene in 1961, when she made the US Top Twenty chart with her single "I Just Don't Understand."

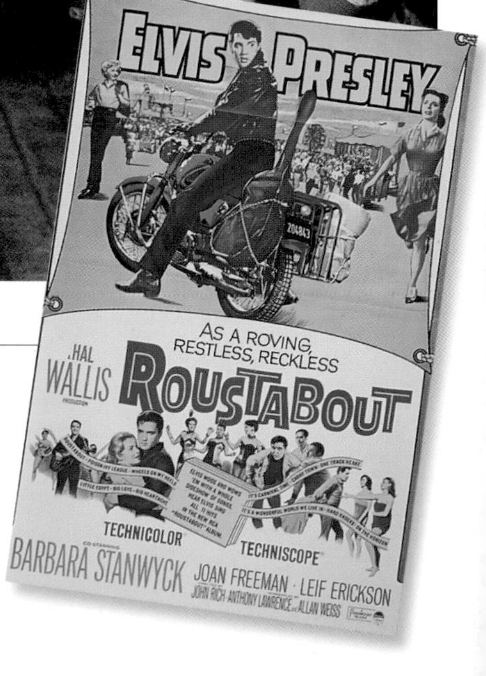

1964 ROUSTABOUT From race cars in *Viva Las Vegas* to motorcycles in *Roustabout*: Elvis played a wandering singer whose musical contribution rescues a traveling carnival from bankruptcy. The carnival proprietor was played by Barbara Stanwyck *(above)*, a Hollywood veteran with four Oscar nominations behind her, including one for the 1944 thriller *Double Indemnity*. The best musical number was undoubtedly "Little Egypt," already a Leiber and Stoller classic as recorded in the 1950s by the Coasters. The film also featured Sue Ane Langdon—best known for a number of popular American TV series, and pictured (*right*) with Elvis on set—as the carnival's fortune-teller.

1965 GIRL HAPPY Elvis' costar in *Girl Happy* was Shelley Fabares, an early Sixties pop star in her own right, who had had a number one record in the US singles chart with "Johnny Angel" in 1962. She went on to star with Elvis in two more movies, *Spinout* and *Clambake*, while other "juvenile" movie roles included parts in *Summer Love* (1958) and *Ride The Wild Surf* from 1964. His other romantic interest in the film was played by a former Miss America, Mary Ann Mobley; they are seen here together in an on-screen clinch. She also appeared opposite Elvis in *Harum Scarum*, and later starred in the Eighties television series *Diff'rent Strokes*. The portraits overleaf were publicity material for the film

1965

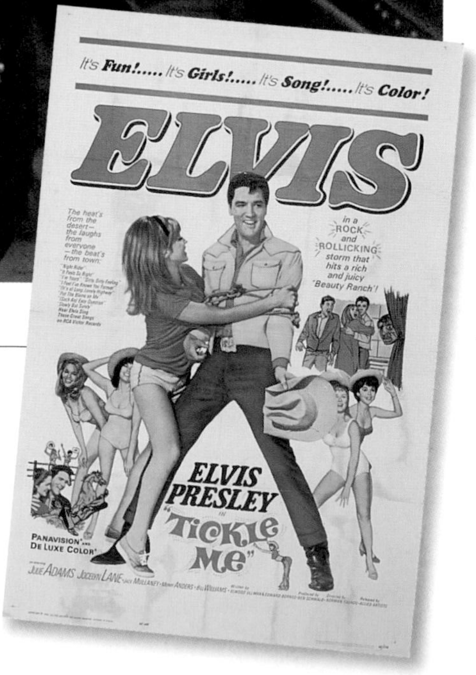

1965 TICKLE ME Another lightweight affair in which a bevy of man-crazy beauties–led by Julie Adams–vied for Elvis' attention. At least Elvis probably enjoyed the making of the film, his 18th, in which he played a rodeo rider–he got to ride a lot, and also engage in fistfight scenes, including one involving one of his "Memphis Mafia" buddies, Red West. West, who had been a close friend of Elvis since their days together at Hume High School, also appeared in *Wild In The Country* and a number of other Elvis films. The film is said to have saved its studio, Allied Artists, from financial ruin–it was the company's third-highest earner, after *55 Days at Peking* and *El Cid*.

1965

↑ → → 1965 HARUM SCARUM Without doubt the most ludicrous setting for a Presley film, the Kismet-style fantasy-land of Lunakahn is visited by an American actor, Johnny Tyronne (played by Elvis), who is on a goodwill tour of the Middle East promoting his movie, *Sands Of The Desert*. Predictable crazy adventures ensue, involving every "Arabian Nights" character stereotype known to Hollywood, and culminating in a spectacular finale back in Las Vegas, complete with a host of exotically garbed Harem beauties. The shots here (*right*, signing publicity photographs) were taken in Elvis' studio dressing room, while the stills overleaf show Elvis in full "Rudolph Valentino" sheik mode

ELVIS PRESLEY

1966

1966 PARADISE, HAWAIIAN STYLE Filmed largely on location, *Paradise, Hawaiian Style* was another movie that allowed Elvis to enjoy working in an exotic environment. Given the fact that he was not performing live in the mid-1960s, these outings afforded the only opportunity, in his working life at least, for Elvis to get in touch with the "real" world. While on location in Hawaii in August 1965, Elvis was interviewed for a local radio station during an end-of-shoot party at the Polynesian Cultural Center by Peter Noone, the lead singer with the then hugely successful UK beat group, Herman's Hermits. The interview has since appeared on various "bootleg" releases over the years.

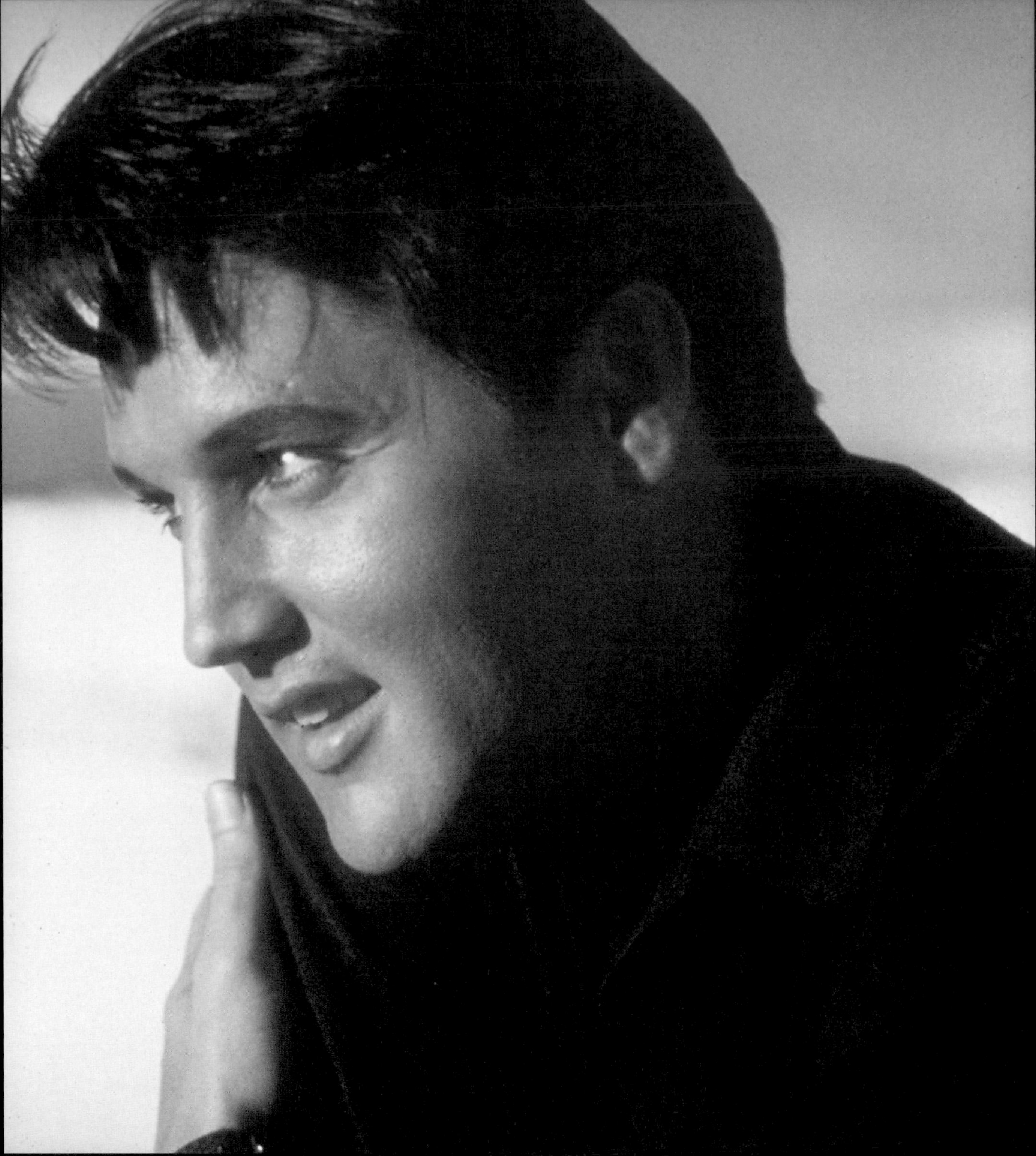

↑ → 1966 **EASY COME, EASY GO** The only Elvis movie to contain references to hippies–who were about to become a major factor in US youth culture in the mid-Sixties–was this 1967 release. In the picture, a genuine Hollywood legend–Elsa Lanchester, who was the original *Bride of Frankenstein* in 1935–runs a yoga class. The candid pictures shown here were taken during the shoot, which took place in October 1966 in Hollywood and at Long Beach Naval Station. Elvis played a naval frogman, Ted Jackson, who becomes involved in a hunt for sunken treasure in the wreck of an old ship–a quest that, bizarrely, leads him into the yoga class.

1966

1966 SPINOUT Another movie in which Elvis plays a race-car driver (who also happens to be a singer with a rock'n'roll band). MGM studios mounted a huge publicity campaign for *Spinout* to mark Elvis' tenth year in the movie business. The literature included press kits, theater competitions, and advertisements that read "With His Foot on the Gas and No Brakes on the Fun!" The on-set picture *(right)* sees him with one of his costars, Deborah Whalley. The female lead was played by Shelley Fabares, in the second of her three films with Elvis, and two members of the race-track pit crew were played by Elvis' buddies, members of his "Memphis Mafia" entourage, Red West and Joe Esposito.

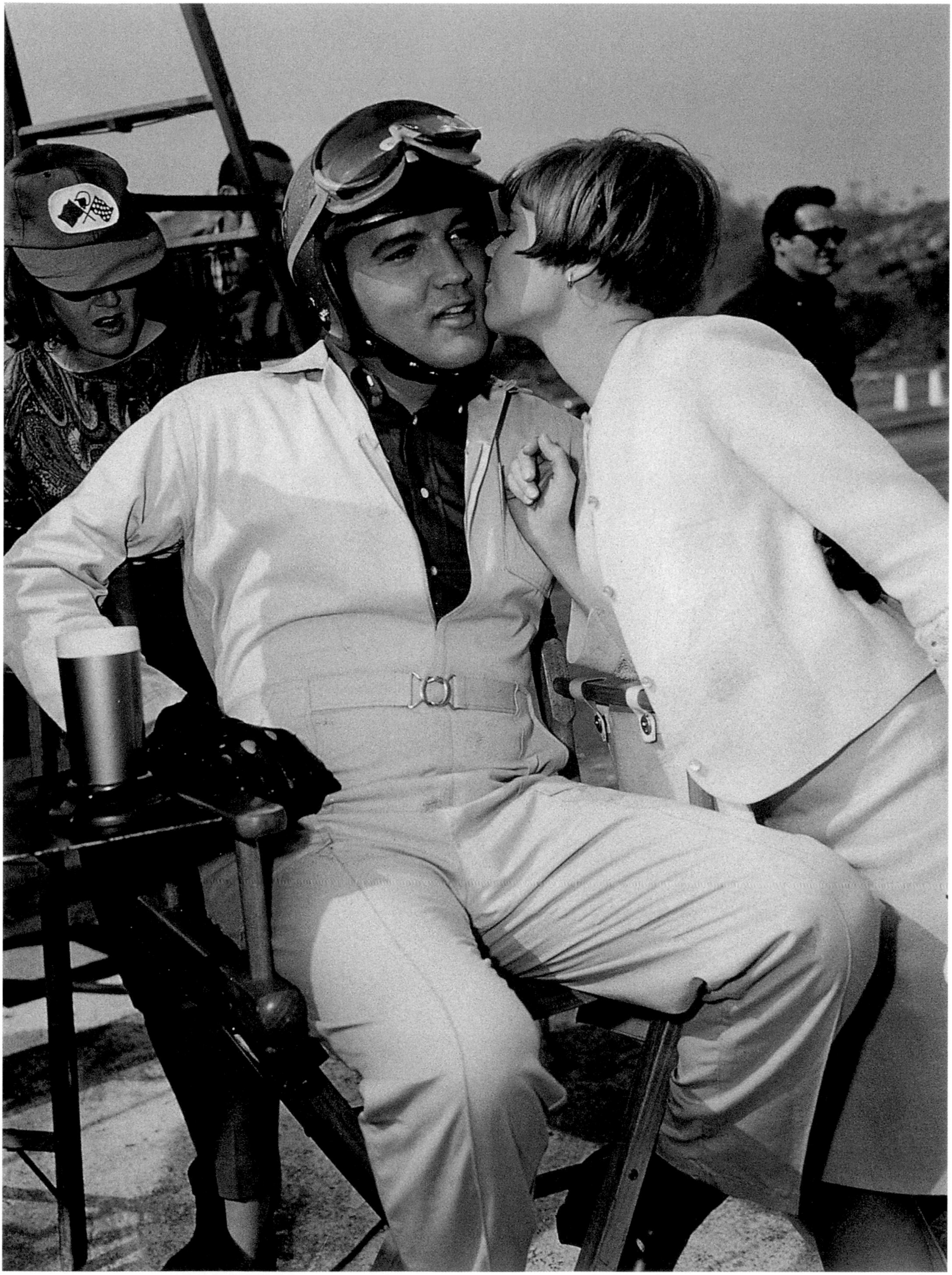

222-1
222-5
222-2
222-6
222-3
222-7

1967 STAY AWAY JOE During the location shooting for his 26th film, *Stay Away Joe*, which took place in Sedona, Arizona, Elvis was interviewed by *Cosmopolitan* magazine. In the piece he put a modest spin on his acting ability, insisting that he had learned most of what he knew from other, more seasoned professionals playing alongside him. In the case of *Stay Away Joe*, these included the great Burgess Meredith, whose track record involved dozens of films and, at that time, the *Batman* television series. Also in the film was Katy Jurado, the spirited Mexican actress whose long line of great films included *High Noon, One Eyed Jacks,* and (in the 1970s) *Pat Garrett and Billy the Kid.*

1967

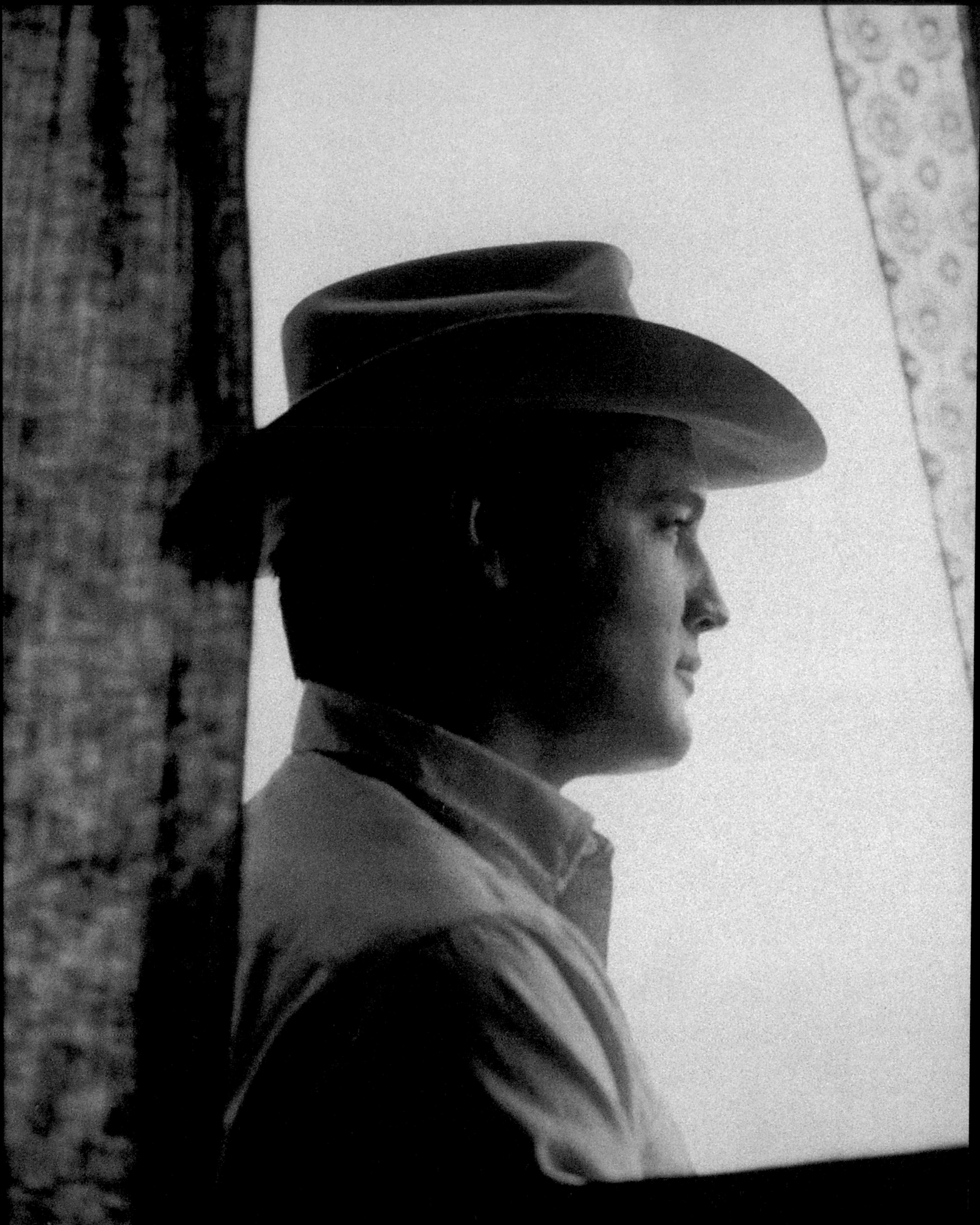

1968

1967 STAY AWAY JOE As the hell-raising, hard-drinking, Native American Joe Lightcloud, Elvis was back in almost dramatic territory with *Stay Away Joe*, a 1968 release, which featured only three songs after the credits had rolled. As the location was Arizona, with plenty of horse riding (plus a motorcycle thrown in), Elvis was able to mix work with play.

1969

1968 CHARRO! Like *Flaming Star*, *Charro!*, a 1969 release, was a dramatic, nonmusical Western. The only song in the film was featured over the credits. It was certainly a one-of-a-kind as far as Elvis' image was concerned. Appropriately for a "serious" Western, all the soundtrack music, apart from Elvis' credit-sequence song "Charro," was composed by Hugo Montenegro, famous for the theme music for Clint Eastwood's 1968 "spaghetti Western" *The Good, the Bad and the Ugly.* Equally well-suited was the film's director and script writer, Charles Marquis Warren, who made the classic television Westerns *Gunsmoke, Rawhide,* and *The Virginian.*

11

1969 THE TROUBLE WITH GIRLS Set in the late 1920s, Elvis' penultimate fiction movie had him playing the manager of a traveling tent show. Elvis had in fact first been lined up for it in 1961; it was originally called *Chautauqua*–the name for traveling "shows" that combined education with entertainment that were popular across the US before the days of talking pictures and television. Undoubtedly to Elvis' delight, there was a football sequence in the movie, in which he was able to indulge in his favorite sport, albeit wearing an antiquated helmet and shirt. The full title of the film was *The Trouble With Girls (And How to Get Into It)*, and it was directed by the man who made *Stay Away Joe,* Peter Tewksbury.

1969

1969

1969 THE TROUBLE WITH GIRLS Released in 1969, Elvis completed shooting *The Trouble With Girls* in December 1968, by which time he had already completed the TV special for NBC. Aired on December 3, it was to represent his much-awaited "comeback" to live performance, and the end of the Hollywood period of his career.

1969 CHANGE OF HABIT The plot of Elvis' final fictional picture (poster, *bottom right*) was unusual to say the least; he played a doctor in an inner-city clinic who accepts the help of Mary Tyler Moore and her two friends, not knowing they are novice nuns in "civilian" clothes. After enjoying huge success in *The Dick Van Dyke Show* in the 1960s, Mary Tyler Moore had her own successful series in the early Seventies. Other movies in Elvis' final total of 31 included *Clambake* in 1967, and *Speedway* and *Live A Little, Love A Little*, both 1968. As seen in the posters–in true Sixties graphic style–they were full of the same predictable mix of songs and girls, making a "change of habit" inevitable.

Intermission

RELAXING

[1967–1973]

1968 HAWAII Priscilla and Elvis relaxing in Hawaii, the island paradise where he had performed and filmed throughout his career. The couple spent a two-week vacation there in May 1968 with their daughter Lisa Marie and five friends.

May 1967

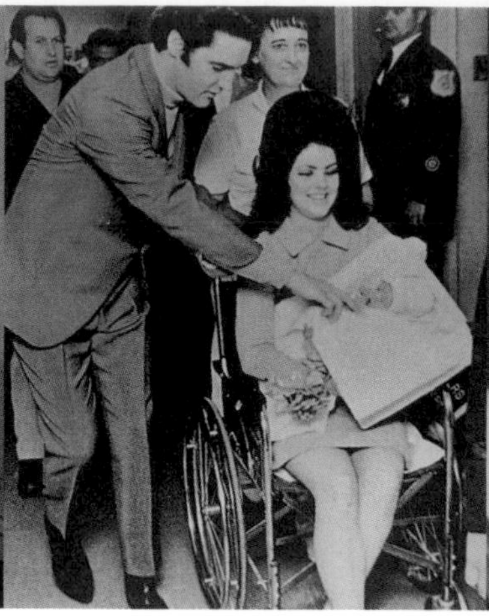

February 1968

February 1970

1967-1973

Movie making, by its very nature, involves a lot of spare time between shoots for those involved. Consequently, although he was taking part in feature films at a rate of two or three a year in the mid-1960s, Elvis had a lot more leisure time on his hands than when his life was preoccupied with touring concert venues across America for live performances. Pictures from home, fan shots, newspaper "paparazzi" photographs—a variety of "candid" pictures allow us a peek into the Presley private life during a period when he was sharing his domestic time between homes in California and Memphis, Tennessee.

The most significant change in his family arrangements, of course, was his marriage in May 1967 to Priscilla Beaulieu, whom he had first met during his draft duty in 1959, when he was stationed in Germany. Significantly, the wedding ceremony was held in the showbiz capital of Las Vegas, not Memphis.

There were few guests invited to the ceremony, but among them, acting as best men, were Joe Esposito and Marty Lacker, two of a small group of the so-called "Memphis Mafia" in attendance. The Colonel, however, arranged a post-ceremony press conference to make the event headline news around the world.

February 1970

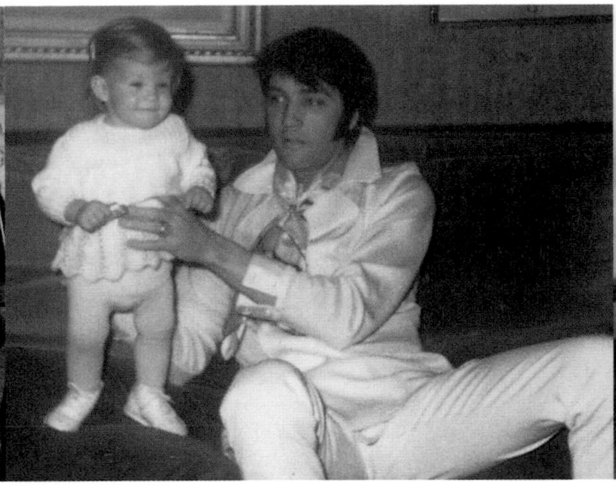

February 1969

February 1967

At the same time that he was dividing his residence between Palm Springs and Graceland, Elvis purchased a 163-acre cattle ranch near Walls, Mississippi, cutely called Twinkletown Farm, to indulge his passion for horses. He renamed the property the Circle G (for Graceland) and adopted an almost "cowboy" lifestyle for himself and his entourage whenever he was there. Elvis added "Flying" to the name when he discovered a ranch called the Circle G already existed.

Another leisure activity which was occupying Elvis more and more, and was captured photographically at various times, was karate. He had developed basic skills during his time in the Army, and at his "welcome home" press conference after his service ended, he offered to demonstrate for reporters if someone could find a piece of wood! By the end of the decade, karate had become so much a part of Elvis' private lifestyle that he began to incorporate the poses and moves into his stage act when he resumed live performances.

Then, in February 1968, Priscilla gave birth to a baby girl, Lisa Marie, and for the rest of the 1960s, the "family album" photographs invariably featured the three of them—Elvis at ease and relaxed, a "normal" home life that was in stark contrast to the hectic professional pressures that persisted in the world outside.

1967

1967 MARRIAGE May 1,1967, at 11.45 AM Elvis and Priscilla are married by Nevada Supreme Court Chief Justice David Zenoff at the Aladdin Hotel in Las Vegas, after obtaining a $15 license at the Clark County Courthouse. The ceremony was held in a room that would only accommodate a handful of people. Though called at short notice, the wedding announcement came as no surprise, for the couple had been engaged since the previous Christmas. Elvis had presented Priscilla with a ring purchased from Memphis jeweler Harry Levitch. Harry was one of a select group of non-family guests at the ceremony in Las Vegas, along with Marty Lacker and Joe Esposito.

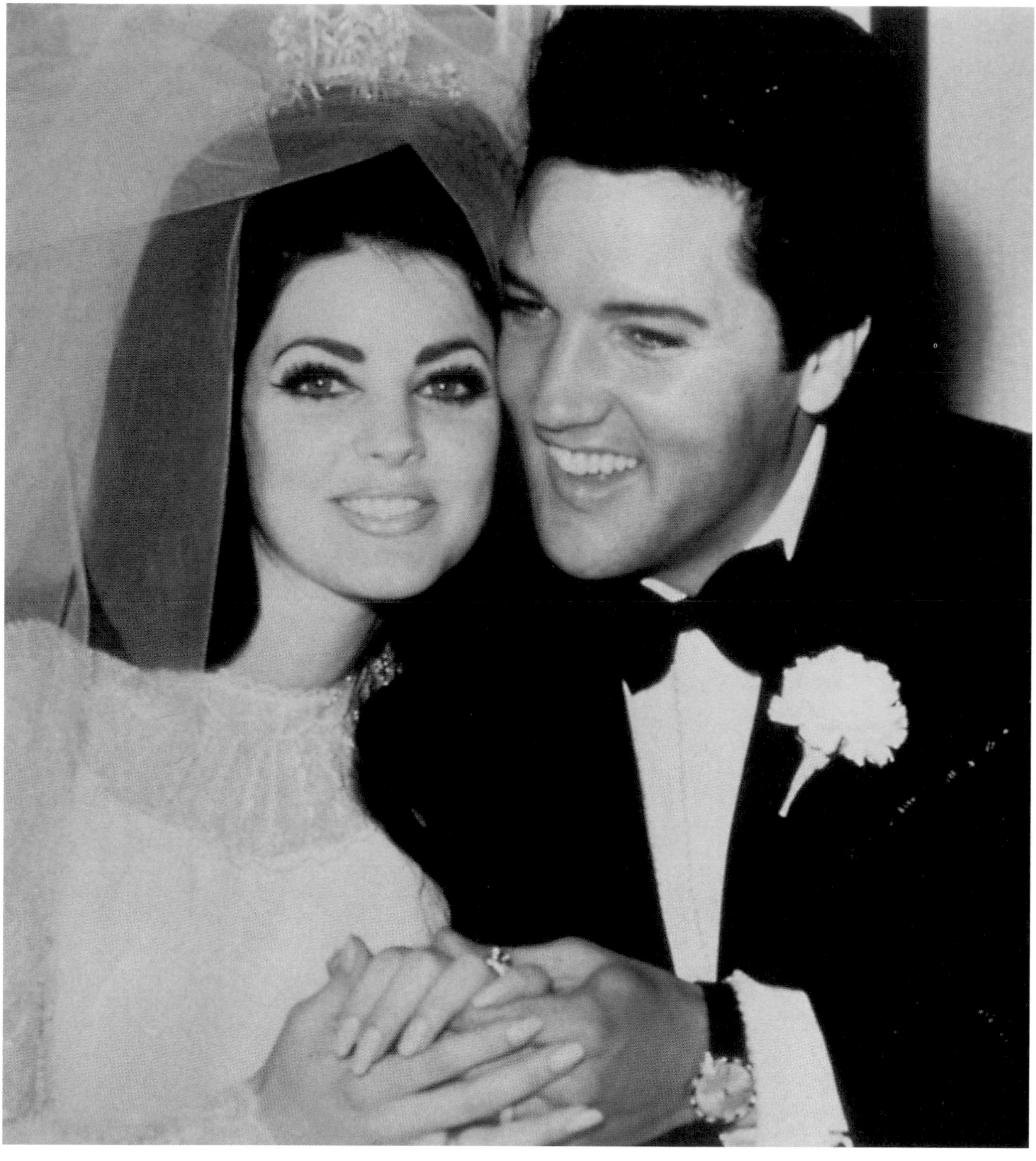

1967 RECEPTION The wedding rites were followed by a brief press conference that the Colonel had arranged, in which Vernon and Priscilla's father, Colonel Beaulieu, took part as well as the bride and groom. Following the press conference came a lavish reception in the hotel, attended by about 100 people. They included family, many of the Memphis entourage, their wives and at least one celebrity, comedian Redd Foxx. The buffet banquet at the reception was said to have cost over $10,000. The guests enjoyed salmon, oysters, and champagne, as well as more traditional Southern fare such as fried chicken, and ham and eggs.

1967

1967

1967 **WEDDING CAKE** The bride and groom sample the wedding cake at the reception. They then spent two days in Palm Springs, California, at the house that Elvis had leased at 1350 Ladera Circle. A quick visit to Memphis was followed by a more extended vacation at their Circle G ranch in Mississippi, though it could hardly be called a honeymoon as all the Memphis guys also went along.

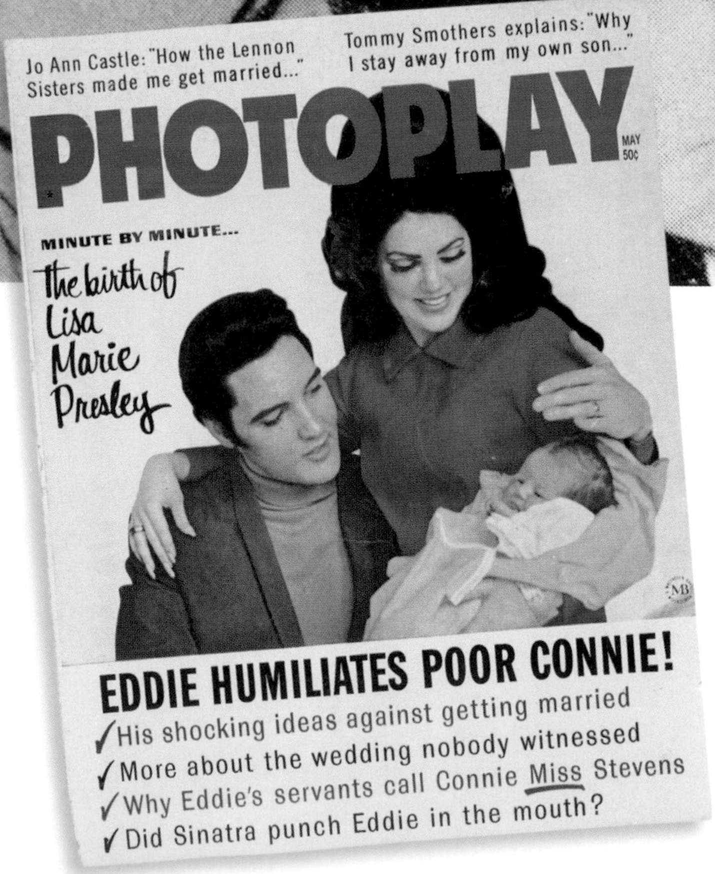

Jo Ann Castle: "How the Lennon Sisters made me get married..."
Tommy Smothers explains: "Why I stay away from my own son..."
PHOTOPLAY
MAY 50¢
MINUTE BY MINUTE...
the birth of Lisa Marie Presley
EDDIE HUMILIATES POOR CONNIE!
✓His shocking ideas against getting married
✓More about the wedding nobody witnessed
✓Why Eddie's servants call Connie Miss Stevens
✓Did Sinatra punch Eddie in the mouth?

1968 LISA MARIE On February 1, 1968, just after 5.00 AM, Priscilla Presley gave birth to a baby girl, Lisa Marie, at the Baptist Hospital in Memphis. Elvis hired a special squad of police to watch over her room there until she left the hospital (*above*) four days later. Their departure was, as to be expected, an unprecedented event for the hospital. While fans and student nurses crowded outside, the staff and patients waved from the windows as the Presleys, now a threesome, and their entourage were whisked away by car. Over the next few months an avid press worldwide–whether in the newspapers, the gossip magazines, or Elvis' fan publications–followed the progress of the infant Presley and her proud parents. Elvis, once a symbol of rebellious youth, was now truly the family man.

1968 HAWAII Elvis and Priscilla indulging in some horseplay on the beach (*above*), and wading into the water (*right*), while relaxing in Hawaii in May 1968. Ever since his first working visits on movie shoots, Elvis enjoyed the sea and sunshine of both the Hawaiian islands and California. In fact by the end of the 1960s he had rented or purchased a string of properties on the West Coast. These included a house designed by Frank Lloyd Wright (the former home of the actress Rita Hayworth) in Bel Air, which he left in 1965, two more homes in Bel Air, and two locations in the Los Angeles suburbs where he and Priscilla frequently stayed. The couple also spent a lot of time at two properties inland at Palm Springs.

1968

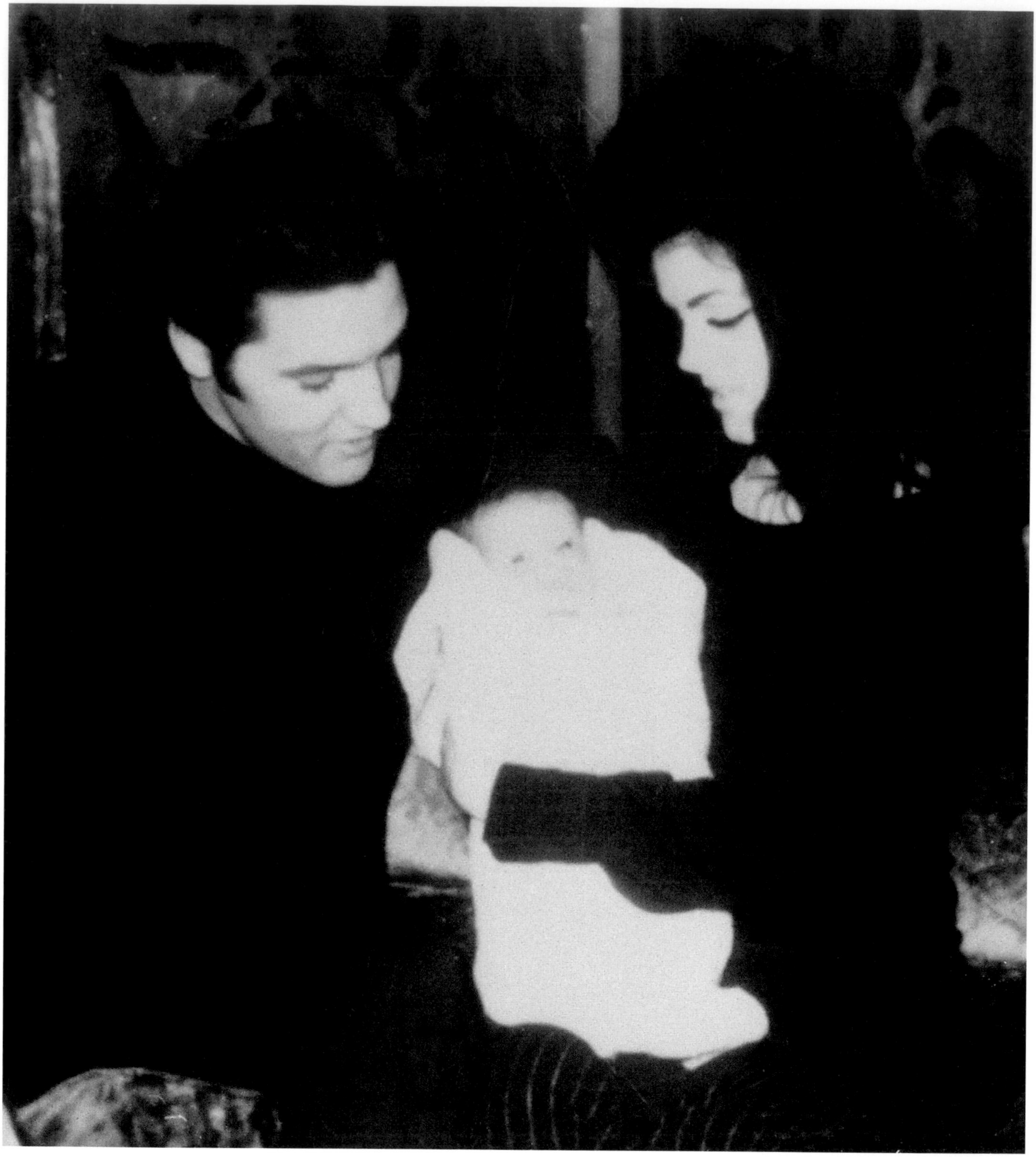

1968 MEMPHIS Father and mother with the newborn Lisa Marie. It was still a convention in the 1960s, and has remained so since to a lesser degree, for pop stars with a large following of the opposite sex to avoid marriage or even steady relationships–in public at least. But by the time Elvis finally got married, it was in the context of the "family entertainer" image that the Colonel had fostered over the years, substantiated by the innocuous movies. So when he became a father, it fit perfectly with his "mature" persona as a regular family man. And, of course, for the media it was another stage in the Presley saga, and one that could just run and run.

1968

1969

1969 GRACELAND Playing the proud parents, Elvis and Priscilla play with one-year-old Lisa Marie. The photo was taken in the den at Graceland. It was the time of the "comeback" in Elvis' career as live performer, and also a period, despite their delight with Lisa Marie, when the strain was starting to show in the short-lived marriage.

⊖⊕ **1970 FAMILY PICTURES** Lisa Marie not long before her third birthday, in more family pictures, taken at one of their homes in California. When photographs like these (*above and following pages*) were released, the Presleys' obvious delight in their daughter was shared by Elvis' legions of fans worldwide. A couple of years before Lisa Marie's birth, Elvis had declared in a newspaper interview that he would name any daughter he might have after his mother Gladys, but this was not to be. During the 1970s Elvis would name his private jet (which now stands across the highway from Graceland) the *Lisa Marie* after his daughter, who was to be his only child and heir to his estate.

1970

1970

← **1970 ROYALTY** To the outside world, not yet aware of the difficulties besetting their marriage, Elvis and Priscilla were the royal couple of show business. She was a natural beauty, later to succeed as both a model and actress. Elvis was reemerging from what many considered his Hollywood exile to establish himself once again as the undisputed King of Rock'n'Roll.

1970

⬆ **1970 CLOSE-UP** A close-up shot of Mr. and Mrs. Presley. The couple spent as much time as possible together, given the responsibilities of parenthood and Elvis' career. In 1969 they even planned a trip to Europe, as a continuation of a brief vacation in Hawaii. However, the influence of the Colonel was to be apparent when he dissuaded them on the grounds that it would be bad for Elvis' image with his fans in Europe, should he be seen visiting the Continent just as a tourist rather than in a long-awaited professional capacity. The vacation plans then switched to the Bahamas. In the event, Elvis Presley never did get to perform live in front of his millions of loyal European fans.

1970

1971 THE "JAYCEE" AWARD Priscilla and Elvis taking their seats at a special prayer breakfast that preceded the prestigious "Jaycee" Award for the nation's Ten Outstanding Men of the Year for 1970, an honor selected annually by the Junior Chamber of Commerce, and on this occasion presented in Memphis in January, 1971.

1967

1967 PRIVACY Elvis in a car, somewhere, 1967. The privacy that most of us take for granted was not to be enjoyed by Elvis very often. Even in the chauffeured security of the back seat of a limousine, passersby would rubberneck, the cameras would intrude, and the curious gawp. That was the price of ultimate fame, and he paid dearly. There is a picture that could be constructed which describes his fame, his absolute celebrity, purely from the myriad candid camera shots of him getting in and out of cars, traveling in cars, sometimes in the back, sometimes driving up front.

1964

1964 ESCAPE By 1964, the touring was over for a while. Work meant a closed film set rather than the open obstacle course of hotel-to-limo-to-dressing-room-to-stage. It should have been easier to escape for a while, hit the streets as he'd tried to in late 1950s' Paris. But it would never happen. There were the furtive excursions to favored hamburger joints in the middle of the Memphis night, rented movie theaters, empty of people, for private showings of the latest releases. Entire amusement parks were reserved for his pleasure, stores opened specially so he could browse uninterrupted, just like anyone else. But he was Elvis, he simply wasn't like anyone else.

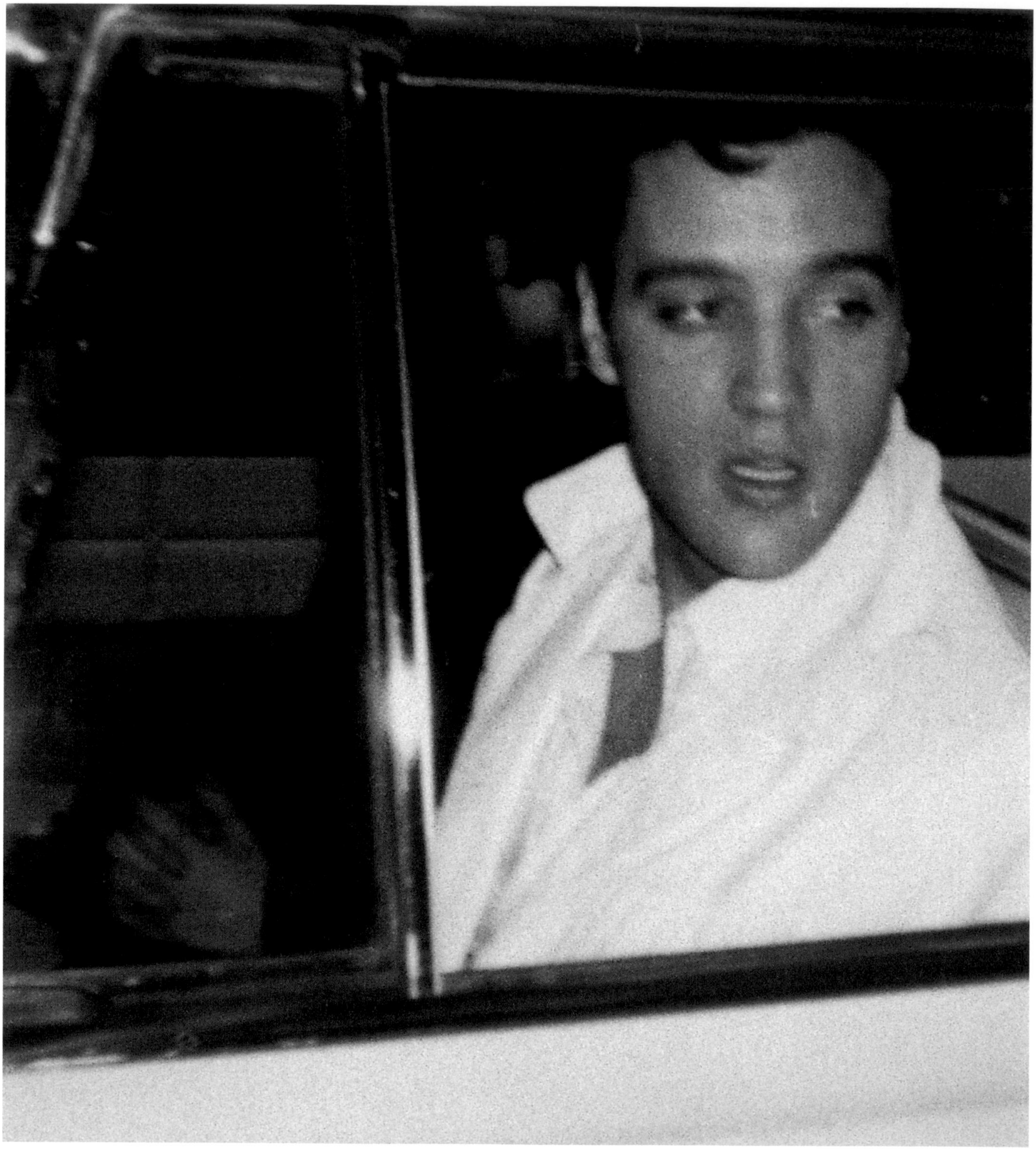

1968 GRACELAND The mansion on the hill overlooking Highway 51 (the immediate stretch of which was renamed Elvis Presley Boulevard in 1971) was his sanctuary, the one place where he could rely on being alone, or not alone, as he wished. But he only had to venture out of the gates (*below*) and the world outside was waiting for his every appearance. As his car halted at the bottom of the driveway, there would be the inevitable tap on the window, the smiling face, that he couldn't–and certainly wouldn't–ignore. He was the star, and these were his public. They made him what he was. Sometimes the sanctuary must have seemed more like a prison.

1968

↑ c1969 **COMEBACK** When Elvis made his celebrated comeback to live performance, via the TV special at the end of 1968, it was also a return to an even more pressured lifestyle than he had been used to for some years. From here on in, the schedules would be more hectic, the bodyguards more necessary, and privacy more precious.

1969 MEMPHIS Things were beginning to speed up again. Before he embarked on live recordings from his new performance base of Las Vegas, Elvis was working on his first significant studio recordings in years. For the first time he used a studio in Memphis, called American, and session players that included the Memphis Horns—famous for their work on the Stax soul label in the 1960s. Elvis created a fresh sound for himself in February 1969 that ended up as the album *From Elvis In Memphis*. It was recognized to be as much of a comeback as his TV show just a couple of months before. Above, Elvis leaves American Studios in the small hours of the morning.

1969

1967

⬆ 1967 HORSES The early months of 1967 saw Elvis indulging in another of his favorite pastimes, horseback riding. In fact, for a time it became something of an obsession with him. He acquired a taste for equestrian activity in some of his movie roles, and when it took off as a part of his personal life there was no stopping his enthusiasm. Between Christmas 1966 and the end of February 1967, he purchased no fewer than 25 horses, knocking down a whole group of outbuildings at Graceland to make more room for riding next to the extensive stables there. In the early months of that year he took on a totally "western" persona, even turning up to a recording session in cowboy attire, complete with chaps! In the picture above, Elvis is seen riding at Graceland on his favorite horse, a golden palomino called Rising Sun, which he had bought in January 1967. The stable had written on its front door "The House of Rising Sun" (like the song) and when the horse died he was buried in the pasture outside, facing the rising sun.

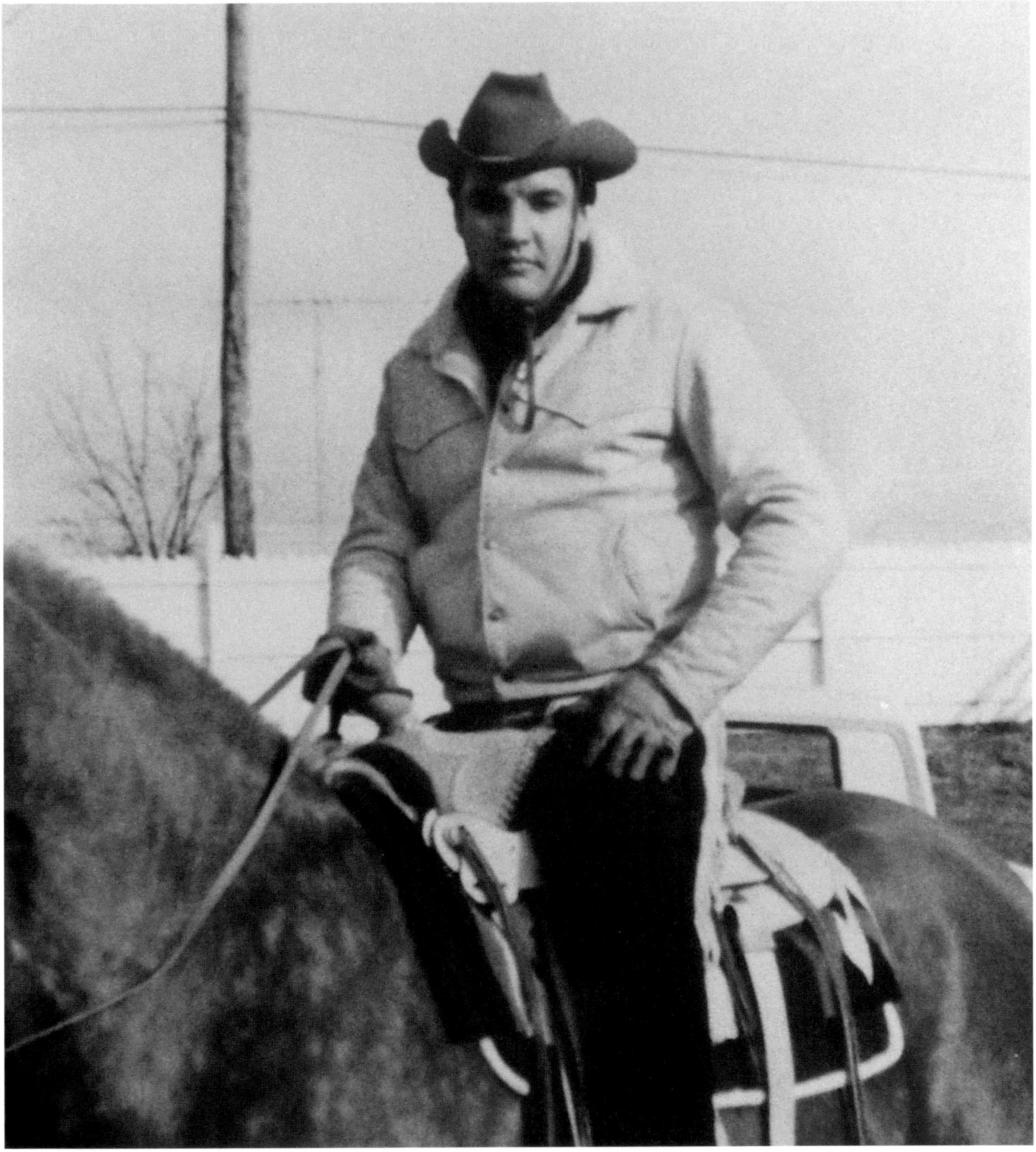

1967 CIRCLE G RANCH During this period Elvis bought what was later to become known as the Flying Circle G ranch, primarily in order to accommodate his growing herd of four-legged friends. Elvis paid $437,000 for the 163-acre Twinkletown Farm, just 10 miles south of Graceland in De Soto County near Walls, Mississippi, and immediately renamed it the Circle G, the G of course standing for Graceland. The ranch rapidly became a new playground for him and his (two-legged) friends, and for a time it threatened to become a serious distraction from his professional work. He eventually, and reluctantly, sold the ranch two years later in May 1969.

1967

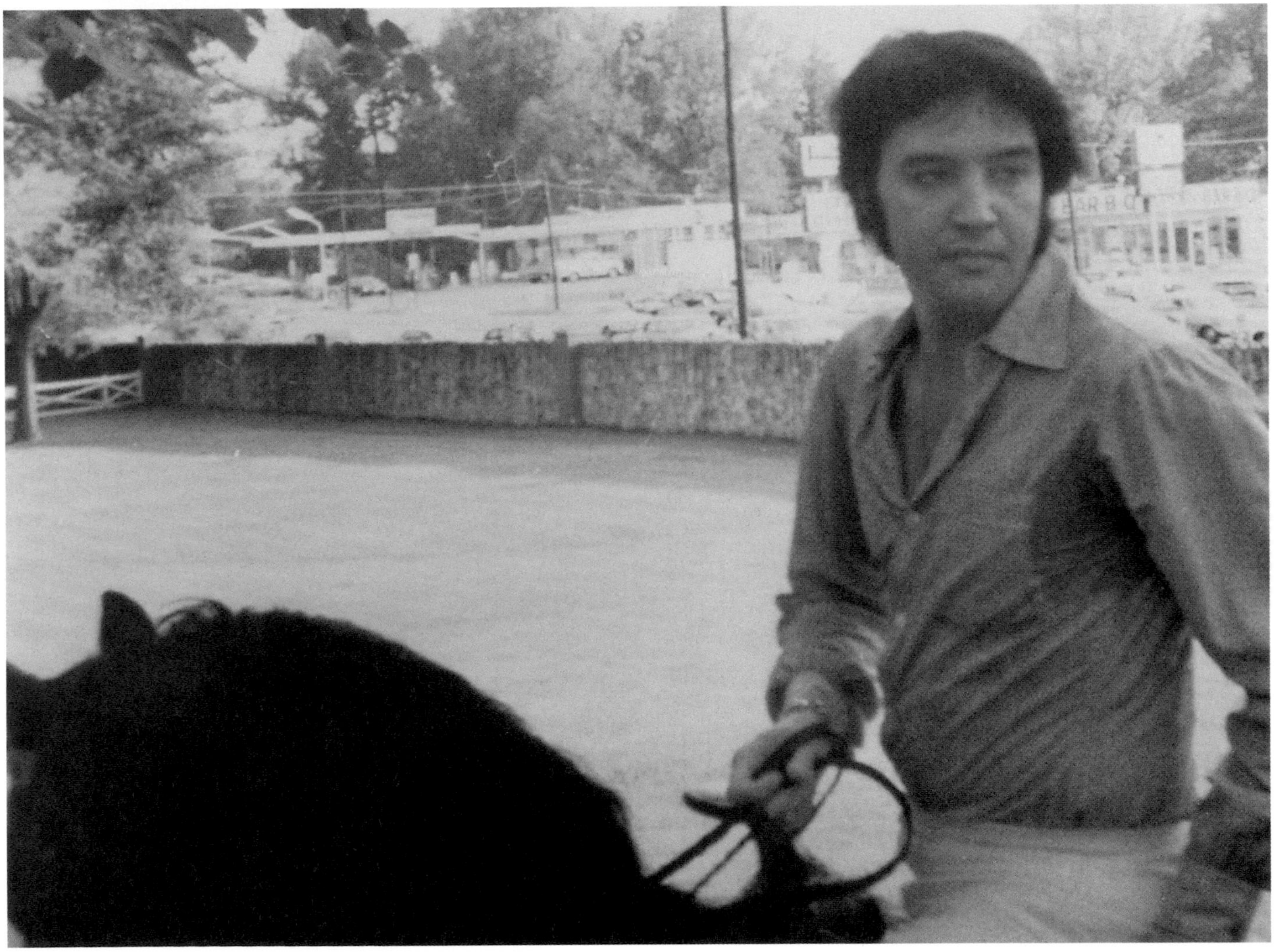

1969–70 GRACELAND HORSES Elvis riding in the grounds at Graceland. Elvis got seriously involved in horses and horseback riding after he had bought Priscilla a quarterhorse for Christmas 1966. They named it Domino on account of the white spot on one leg of an otherwise completely black animal. In the picture at left Elvis is riding Rising Sun, and above another favorite, Bear, a black Tennessee walker. In the stables at Graceland, Elvis personally supervised where everybody's tack and gear would be hanging in the barn. It is his writing that is still to be seen in red marker in the back "tack room," the scribbled names indicating whose riding equipment was to be hung exactly where.

1970 CHRISTMAS CARD A hand-made Christmas card to Elvis; fans often used photographs they had taken of Elvis on the cards they sent to him, this one was taken outside Elvis' Hillcrest home in California. Christmas was a favorite time of year for Elvis, and Graceland was, and indeed still is, decorated in spectacular fashion.

1969

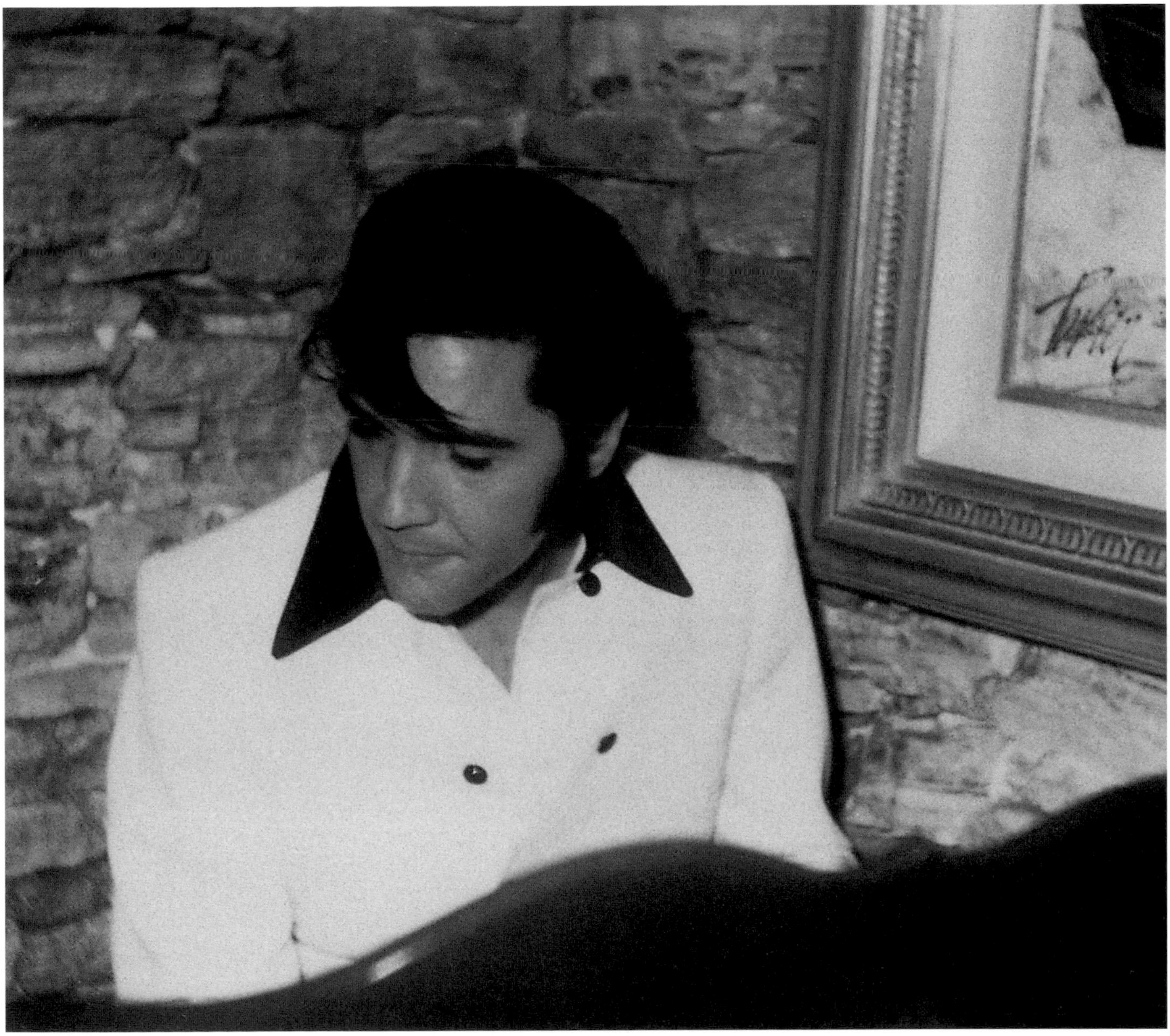

1969 HILLCREST Elvis outside his Hillcrest house in California, wearing the suit in which he performed "If I Can Dream" during the 1968 TV special. The month-long run at the Showroom of the International Hotel grossed a record figure in excess of $1,500,000, during which Elvis performed in front of more than 100,000 people.

1969 RELAXING Elvis is not thought of as a pianist, and certainly among the most memorable images are those of him with a guitar slung around his neck. Yet one of Elvis' favorite forms of relaxation was to sit at the piano and run through songs, old and new, in company or just on his own. Many of the stories and anecdotes of Elvis backstage involve him "jamming" at the piano with other artists. Similarly, people remember private parties when he would find the nearest keyboard and just play along. And of course there was the "Million Dollar Quartet" session in 1956, in which he accompanied Jerry Lee Lewis, Carl Perkins, and Johnny Cash in an impromptu musical get-together.

1974

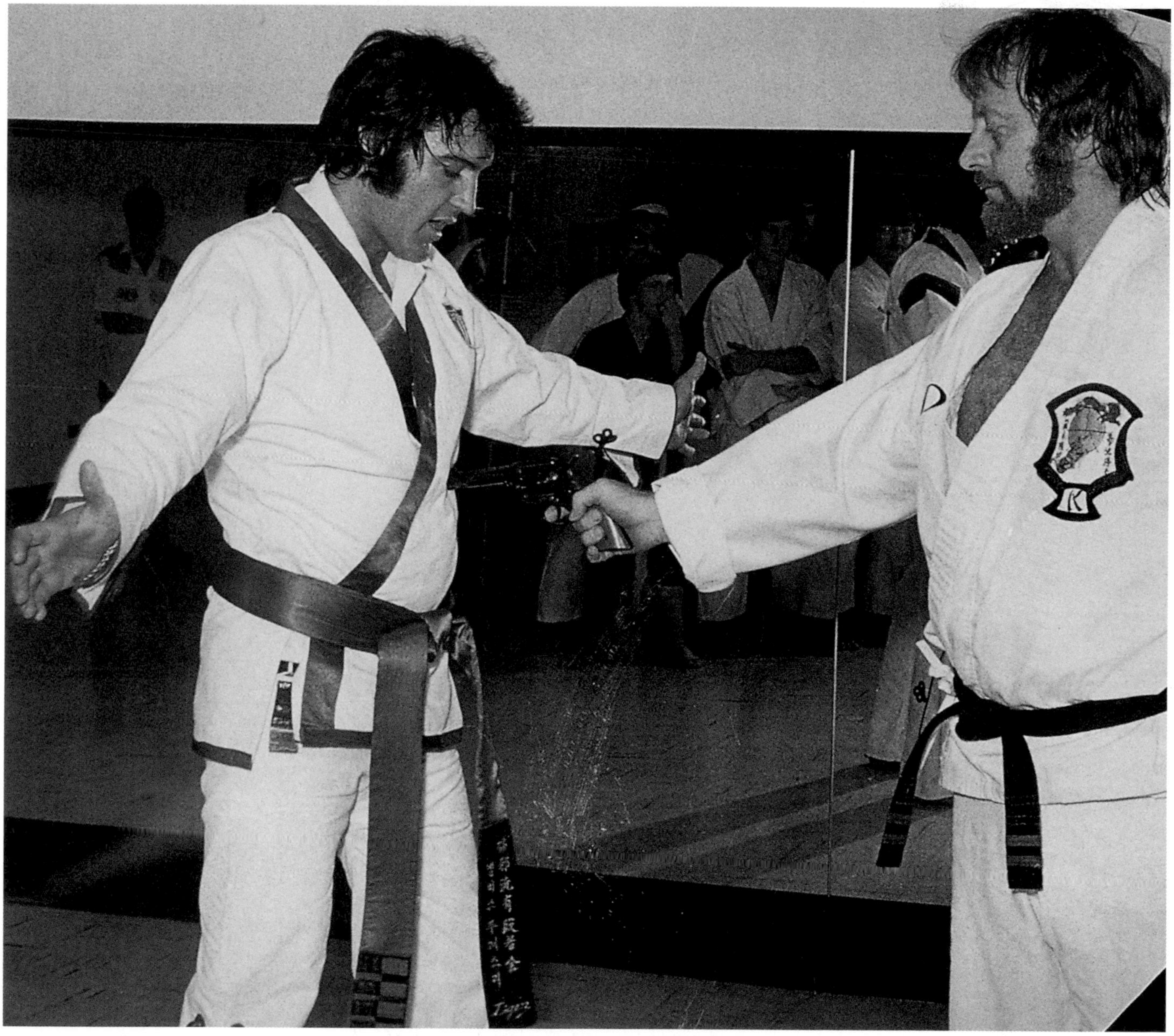

1974 FAVORITE HOBBY By the 1970s, Elvis was even more involved with his favorite hobby of karate, incorporating a lot of the moves and poses into his flamboyant stage act at the time. Here (*left*) he is striking a characteristic pose, while (*above*) Red West points a pistol at him during a mock fight they are demonstrating before the rest of the class. Elvis, whose karate title was Tiger, received his black belt in 1960 and went on to get an eighth degree–making him a "master of the art." He also put the skill to good use in some of his movies, perfoming convincingly in fight sequences in *GI Blues*, *Blue Hawaii*, *Kid Galahad,* and several other films.

1974

1976

1974 LINDA THOMPSON Previously crowned Miss Memphis State and then Miss Tennessee in 1972, Linda Thompson was 22 when she started dating Elvis in July of that year. This was not long after his final separation from Priscilla was formalized. Everyone around Elvis liked Linda, with her unpretentious natural charm and down-to-earth sense of humor. By the time this romantic vignette was taken, the couple were involved in a regular relationship. Linda accompanied Elvis on most of his concert dates, changed her lifestyle to match his, and moved into Graceland. She became what the guys in the entourage called themselves–a "lifer."

1976 ELVIS AND LINDA Linda and Elvis boarding his private jet, the *Lisa Marie*. By 1976 his health was becoming more of a problem, and Linda's presence was often a calming factor in traumatic times. She was seen by all as providing great support and security during what was becoming a period of real crisis in Elvis' life and career.

1970

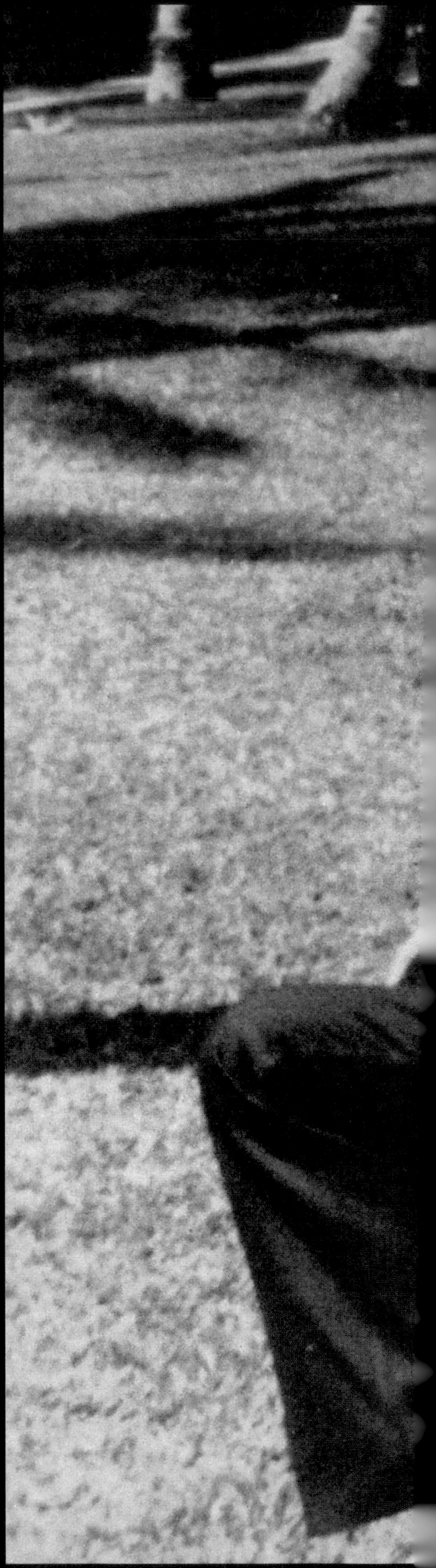

➔ 1970 **CALIFORNIA** Elvis takes in the sun in the grounds of one of of his California homes. Much of the visual record of Elvis, his family and close friends at leisure, has survived either from personal snapshots, home movies, or "paparazzi"-style photos. The latter in most cases were not taken by an intrusive media trying to grab an exclusive picture of Elvis' private life, but more often by well-meaning fans who were lucky enough to grab a "personal" picture of their idol. Elvis appreciated this, and over the years treasured hundreds of such shots which fans sent to him at Graceland.

TV & Vegas

THE COMEBACK

[1968–1969]

1968 NBC SPECIAL Elvis in a big production number on the "comeback" TV special; the historic program was taped before a live audience on June 27 and 29, 1968, at NBC Studio 4 in Burbank, California, and broadcast across America on December 3.

June 1968

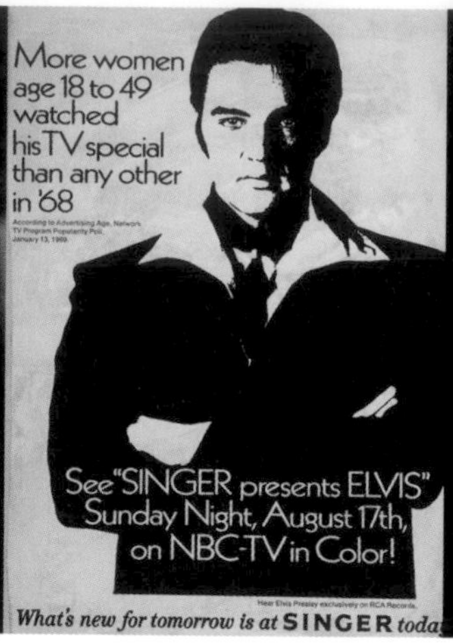

August 1969

June 1968

1968-69

Just when the world thought Elvis was forever consigned to only appearing in front of the movie cameras, he made a sensational comeback to live performance in December of 1968. It took the form of an NBC TV spectacular that would be seen worldwide, in which he reestablished himself in the mold of classic rock'n'roll singer, a stereotype that he himself had created a decade and a half earlier.

The original plan—at least as far as the Colonel was concerned—was to make it a Christmas special, typical of the ones seen on television during that period. But the show's director, a young TV whizz-kid called Steve Binder, who at the relatively tender age of 23 had already produced the top rock TV show *Hullabaloo*, had other ideas. Binder wanted a one-man show that would reveal to the audience the various sides to Elvis' music in a loosely biographical way; he envisaged the show to include a rock'n'roll section, a gospel section, a big production number, and so on.

Months of preparation included, in June, the taping of various segments of music, starting with the big "Guitar Man" production number and the show-closer "If I Can Dream" that featured a backing outfit of the very best studio session musicians. But it was the rock'n'roll

June 1968

August 1969

August 1969

August 1969

era of the Fifties that was acknowledged most potently. Dressed in black leather, Elvis went through his great rock hits of the period with his old buddies (including Scotty Moore on guitar and D. J. Fontana on drums, the two surviving members of the original touring quartet), in an "informal" session surrounded by a live audience, Elvis and the boys performing "in the round."

The show, when it was broadcast across America on December 3, confirmed him once more as a live (albeit in a recorded program) performer without equal.

He even made it to the front cover of *Rolling Stone*, which in the late Sixties was considered the mouthpiece of the new "alternative" youth culture. This wasn't as surprising as it might have seemed; the movement the magazine represented identified strongly with rock, and after the TV special Elvis was once again recognized as being a prime force and figurehead in that musical constituency.

And never one to let the grass grow under his charge's feet, the Colonel followed the public (and critical) acclaim for the TV Special—which was simply entitled *Elvis*—with a series of live dates in Las Vegas that created a template for much of Elvis' live performances for the remainder of his career.

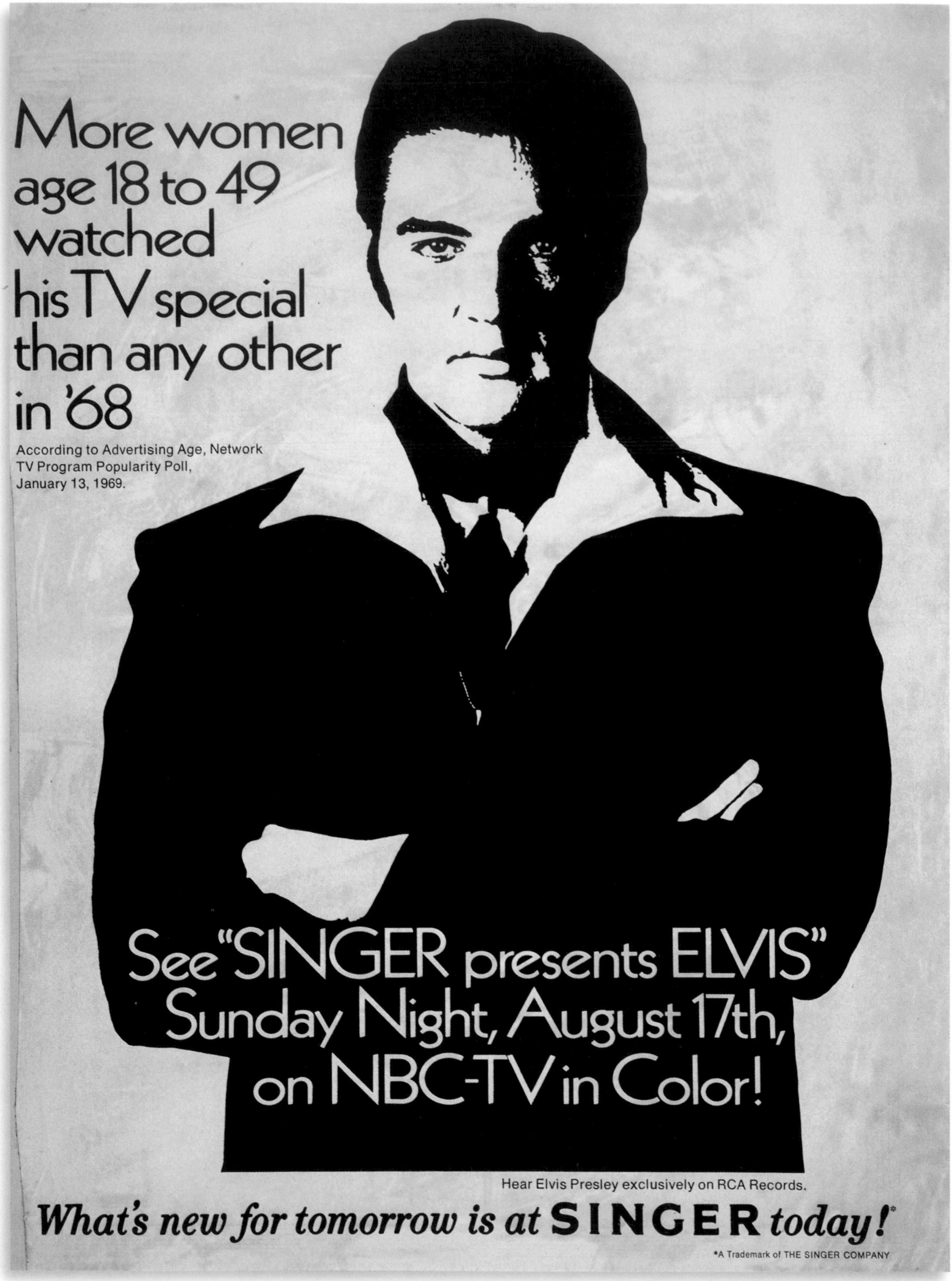
More women age 18 to 49 watched his TV special than any other in '68
According to Advertising Age, Network TV Program Popularity Poll, January 13, 1969.
See "SINGER presents ELVIS" Sunday Night, August 17th, on NBC-TV in Color!
Hear Elvis Presley exclusively on RCA Records.
What's new for tomorrow is at SINGER today!*
*A Trademark of THE SINGER COMPANY

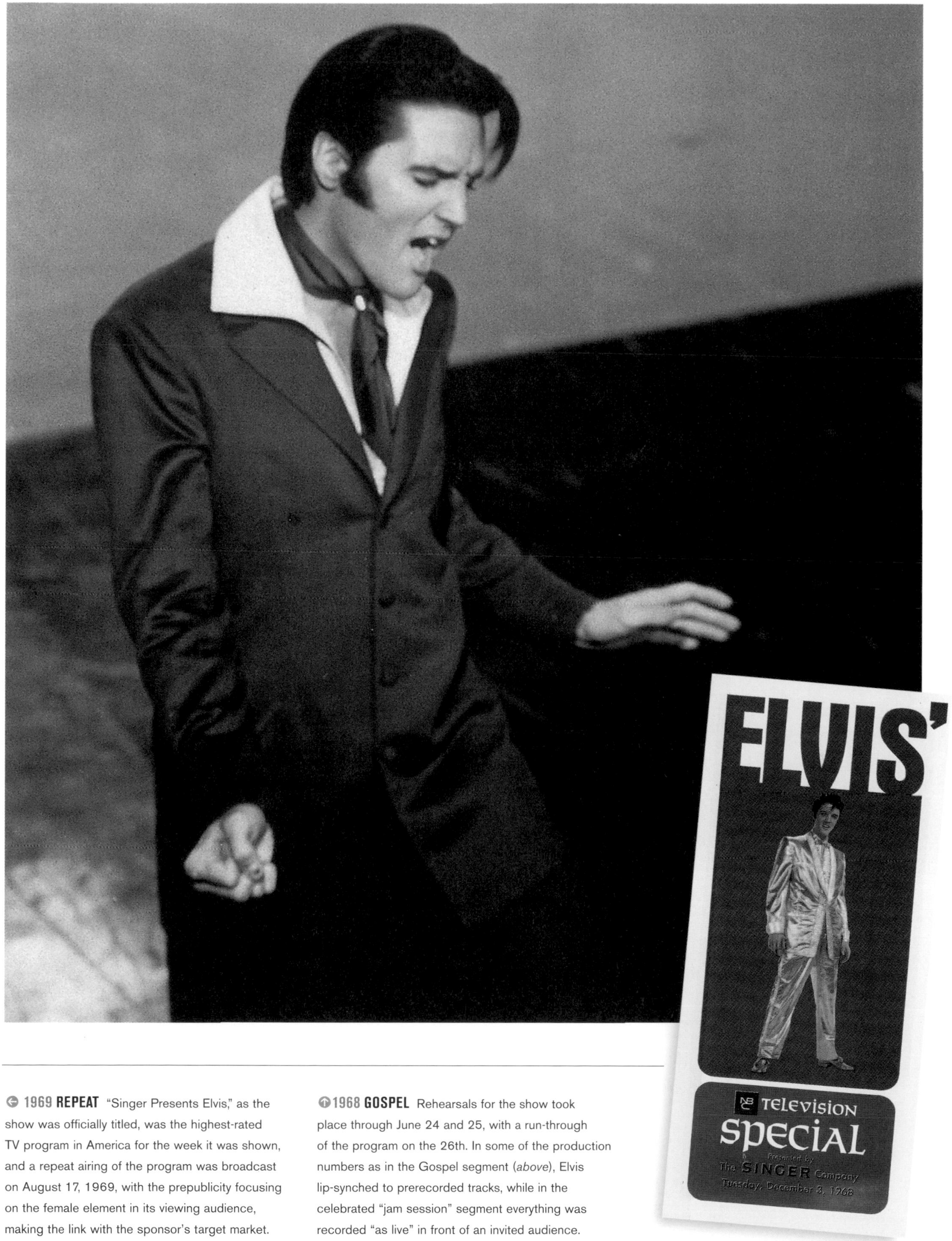

1969 REPEAT "Singer Presents Elvis," as the show was officially titled, was the highest-rated TV program in America for the week it was shown, and a repeat airing of the program was broadcast on August 17, 1969, with the prepublicity focusing on the female element in its viewing audience, making the link with the sponsor's target market.

1968 GOSPEL Rehearsals for the show took place through June 24 and 25, with a run-through of the program on the 26th. In some of the production numbers as in the Gospel segment (*above*), Elvis lip-synched to prerecorded tracks, while in the celebrated "jam session" segment everything was recorded "as live" in front of an invited audience.

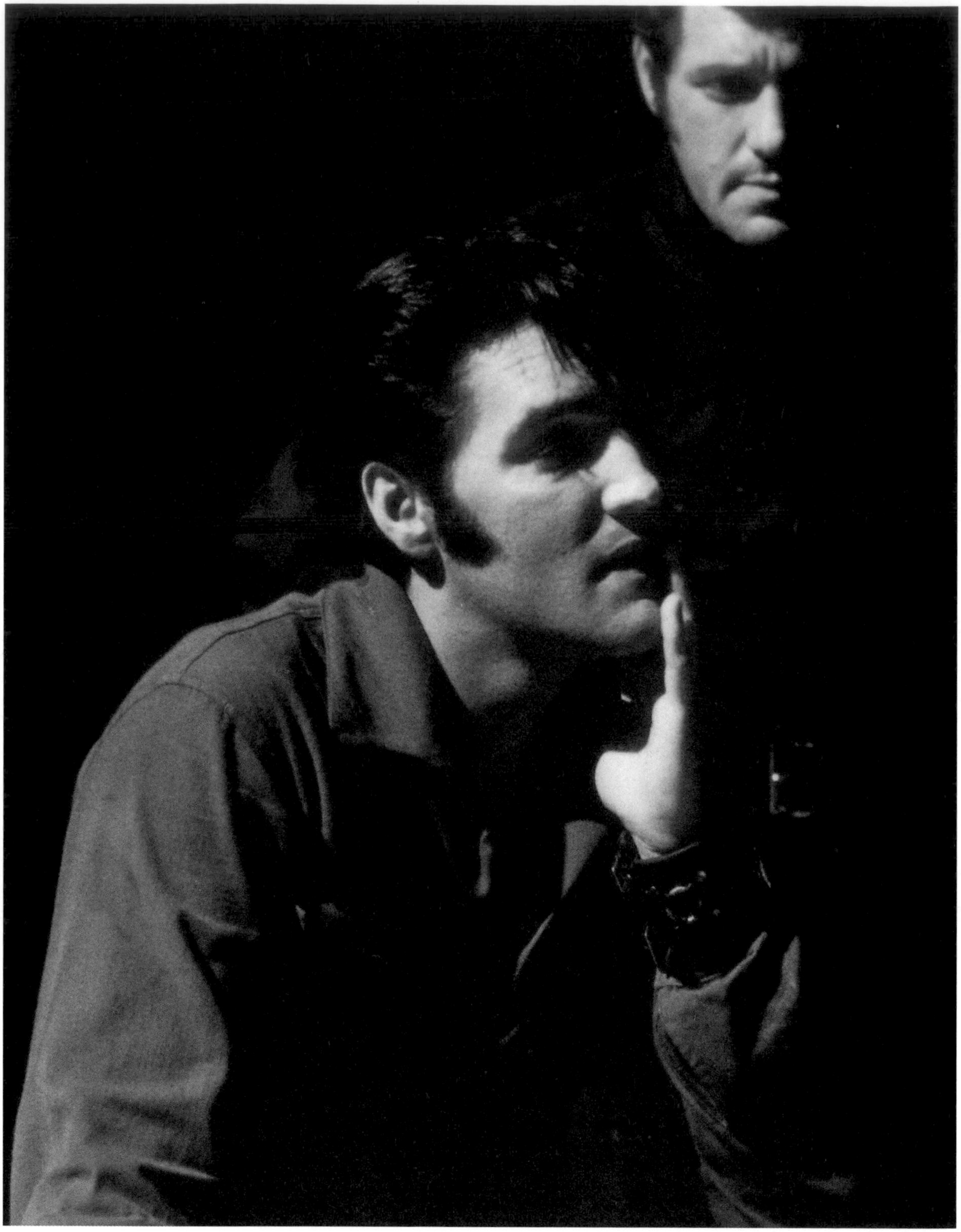

1968

1968 PRODUCTION Elvis discusses the "informal" segment of the show with ex-Army buddy and subsequent member of Elvis' close circle Charlie Hodge (*above*). Charlie played guitar on the set, along with Elvis' original musical colleagues Scotty Moore and D. J. Fontana. Also involved in the "jam" were "Memphis Mafia" road manager and entourage member Alan Fortas, tapping the back of a guitar case, and Lance LeGault, who had doubled for Elvis in many of his movies, playing tambourine. It was this set that delighted fans and critics more than any other part of the show, where Elvis truly demonstrated that he was back, singing rock'n'roll like nobody else ever could.

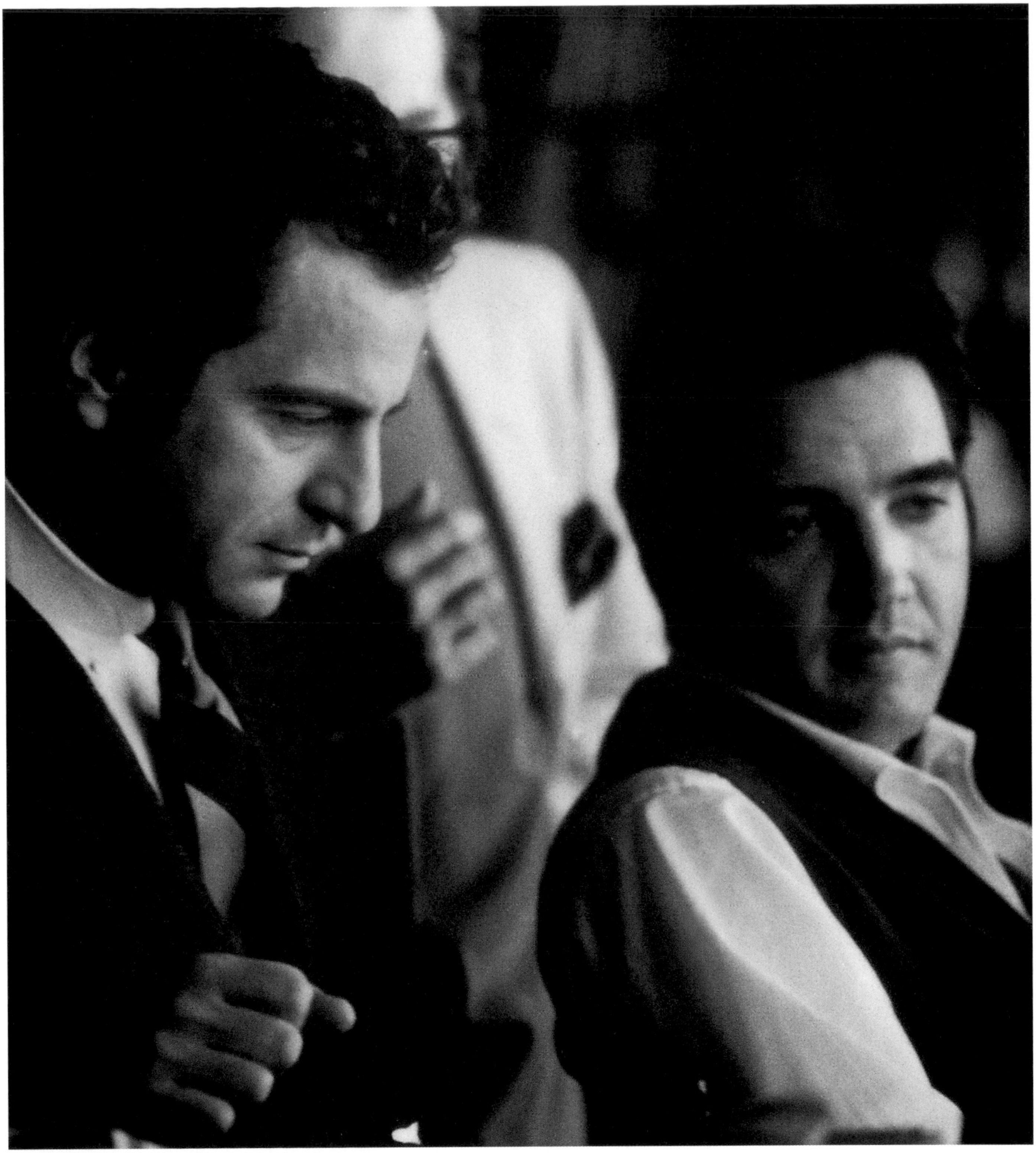

1968 BOB FINKEL Run-throughs and rehearsals were supervised by director Steve Binder and NBC executive producer Bob Finkel (seen *above* with Elvis). It was Finkel who commissioned Binder, who in turn persuaded Elvis that it would be a good idea to make a program that featured all aspects of Elvis' music.

1968

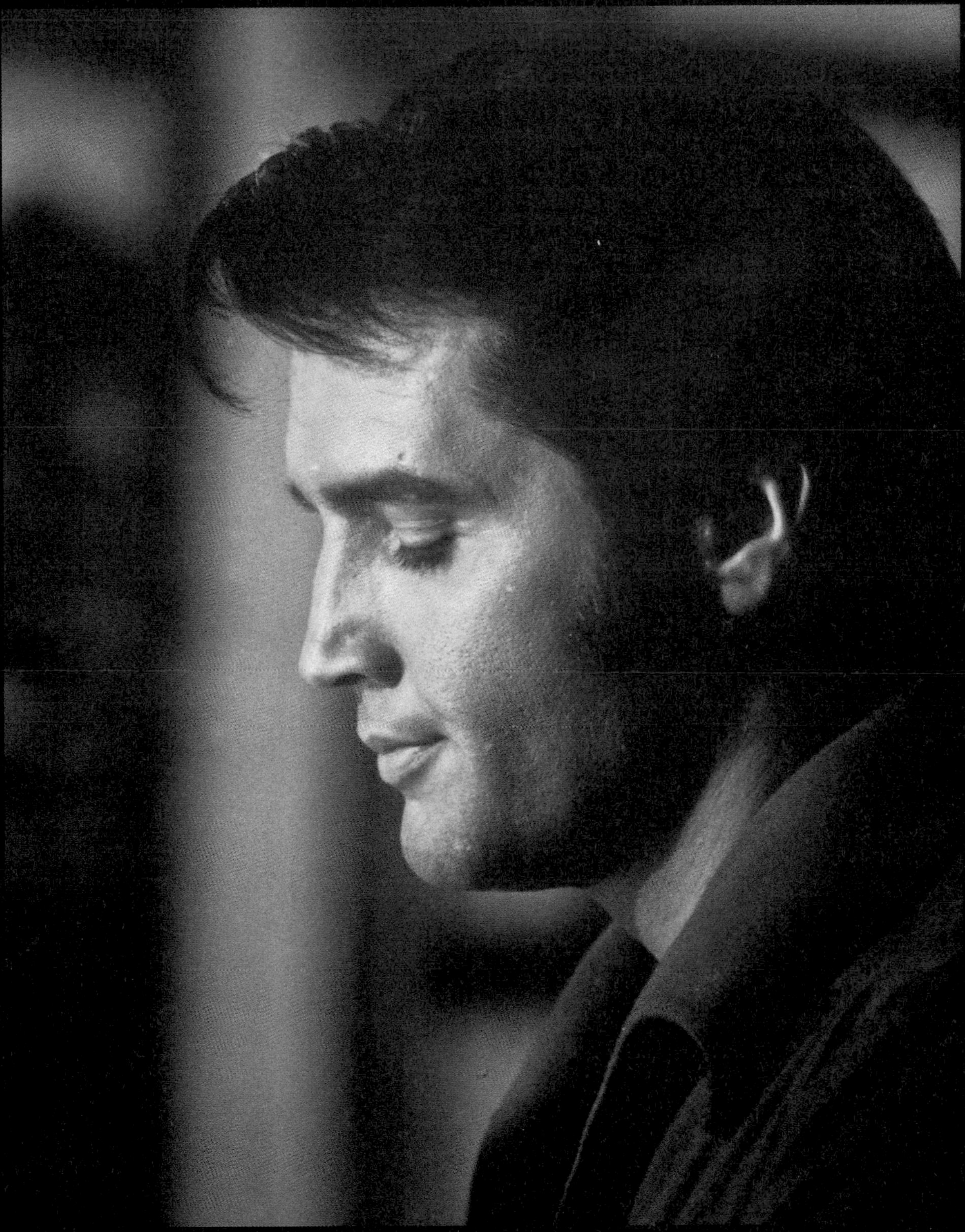

1968 TV STUDIOS As well as rehearsals, script conferences, production meetings, and run-throughs, the days leading up to the actual recording of the TV special included a press conference in which Elvis and the Colonel came over as a skilled double act. When Elvis suggested, "I thought I'd better do it before I got too old," the Colonel added, "We also got a very good deal." Elvis informed the press he would be "singing the songs I'm known for" to which the Colonel commented, "If he sang the songs he's known for, that would take a couple of hours." Asked whether his audience had changed much, Elvis observed, "Well, they don't move as fast as they used to."

1968

1968

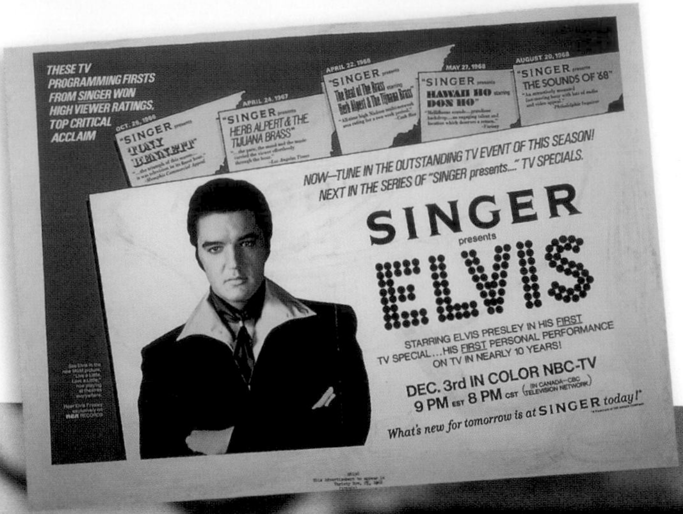

1968 PRODUCTION Taping the big gospel production number for the TV special, in which Elvis is backed musically by a band of the top session players including Tommy Tedesco and Al Casey on guitars, Larry Knechtal on keyboards, and Hal Blaine on drums. He also had a backup vocal group, the Blossoms, and a full orchestra conducted by Billy Goldenberg. In addition, he was accompanied by male and female dancers. The show's director, Steve Binder, was quoted as saying: "This show is a matter of video history significance . . . Presley is one in a lifetime. We had Joe Louis in the boxing ring and we had Manolete in the bullring. In his arena, Presley is the champ."

1968

➲ **1968 "STAND UP"** Throughout the show, with various changes of set and costume, Elvis had the studio audience–and millions at home–in the palm of his hand. But the highlight was undoubtedly the second section, when, clad in black leather, he ran through his old rock'n'roll classics with long-time colleagues Scotty Moore, Charlie Hodge, and D. J. Fontana. This has come to be referred to as the "sit down" show, and was recorded on June 27, followed by a "stand up" segment (*right*) on June 29, in which he also ran though his hits in a live environment, in the same "boxing ring" arena with the audience all around, but this time backed by the full studio band, orchestra, and vocal group.

1968 "STAND-UP" In the "stand-up" show, Elvis went though a selection of his greatest hits including "Heartbreak Hotel," "Hound Dog," "All Shook Up," "Jailhouse Rock," and "Blue Suede Shoes." It was taped in two sessions, one at 6.00 PM, one at 8.00 PM, and the televised version was made up of bits from both. Significantly, a still from the "stand-up" show was used on a 1969 cover of the "Bible" of the so-called counterculture, *Rolling Stone*. Although youth culture at the time had moved a long way from the mainstream that Elvis seemed to represent in most of his movies, rock music was at its center, and this was a telling acknowledgment that he was back as a potent force.

1968

1968

1968 "SIT DOWN" In the "sit-down" session Elvis, Scotty, D. J. Fontana, and the rest of the boys delved even further back into his early repertoire, with other songs he had first recorded in his earliest days with RCA Records. Among them were "Lawdy Miss Clawdy," "Trying To Get To You," and "When My Blue Moon Turns to Gold Again." To the delight of fans of his earliest work, he began the first of the two evening sessions with the very first title he had released on the Sun label back in July 1954, 14 years before (though so much had happened, it seemed like it could have been a hundred years), the old rhythm and blues classic by Arthur "Big Boy" Crudup, "That's All Right."

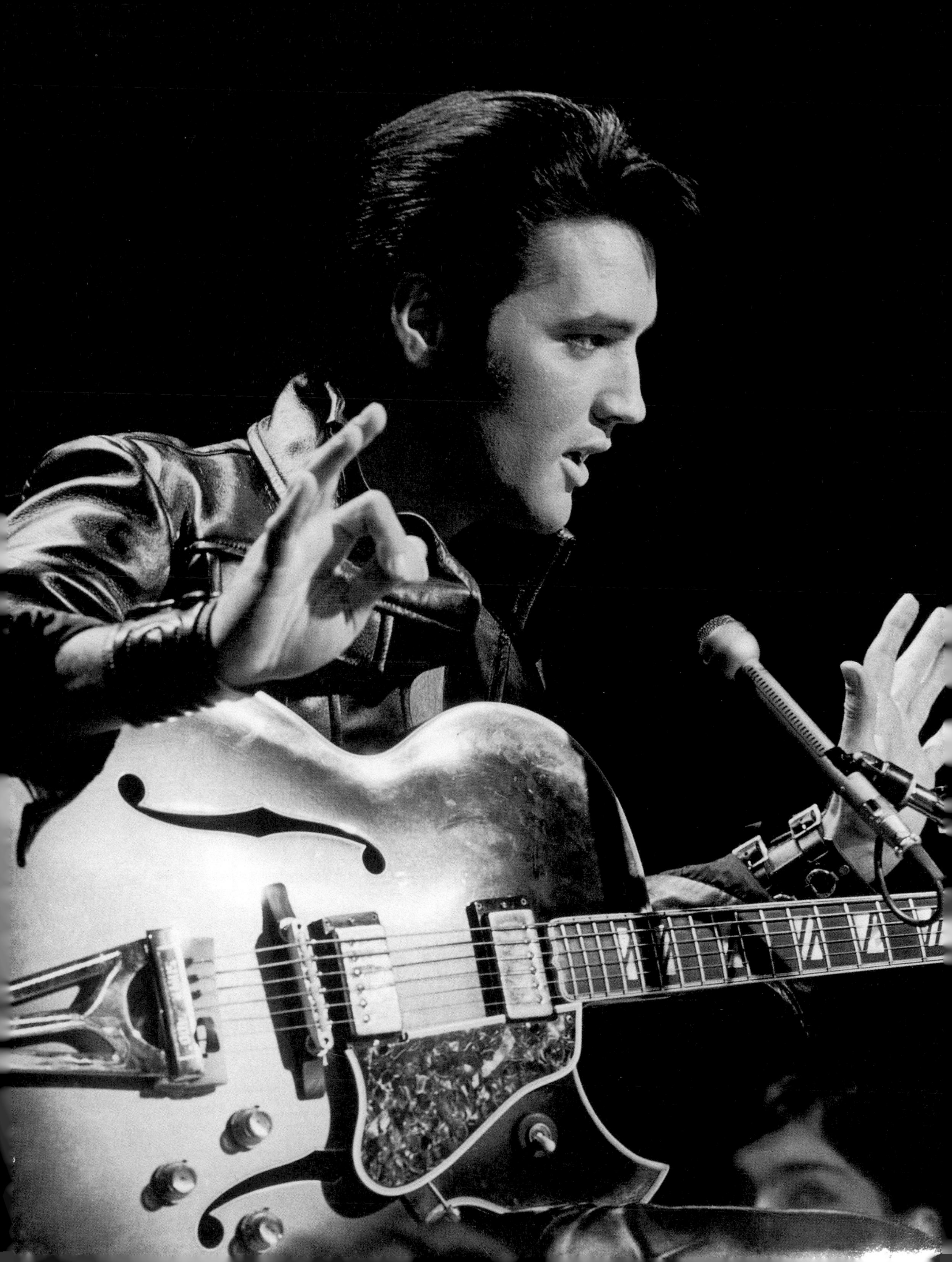

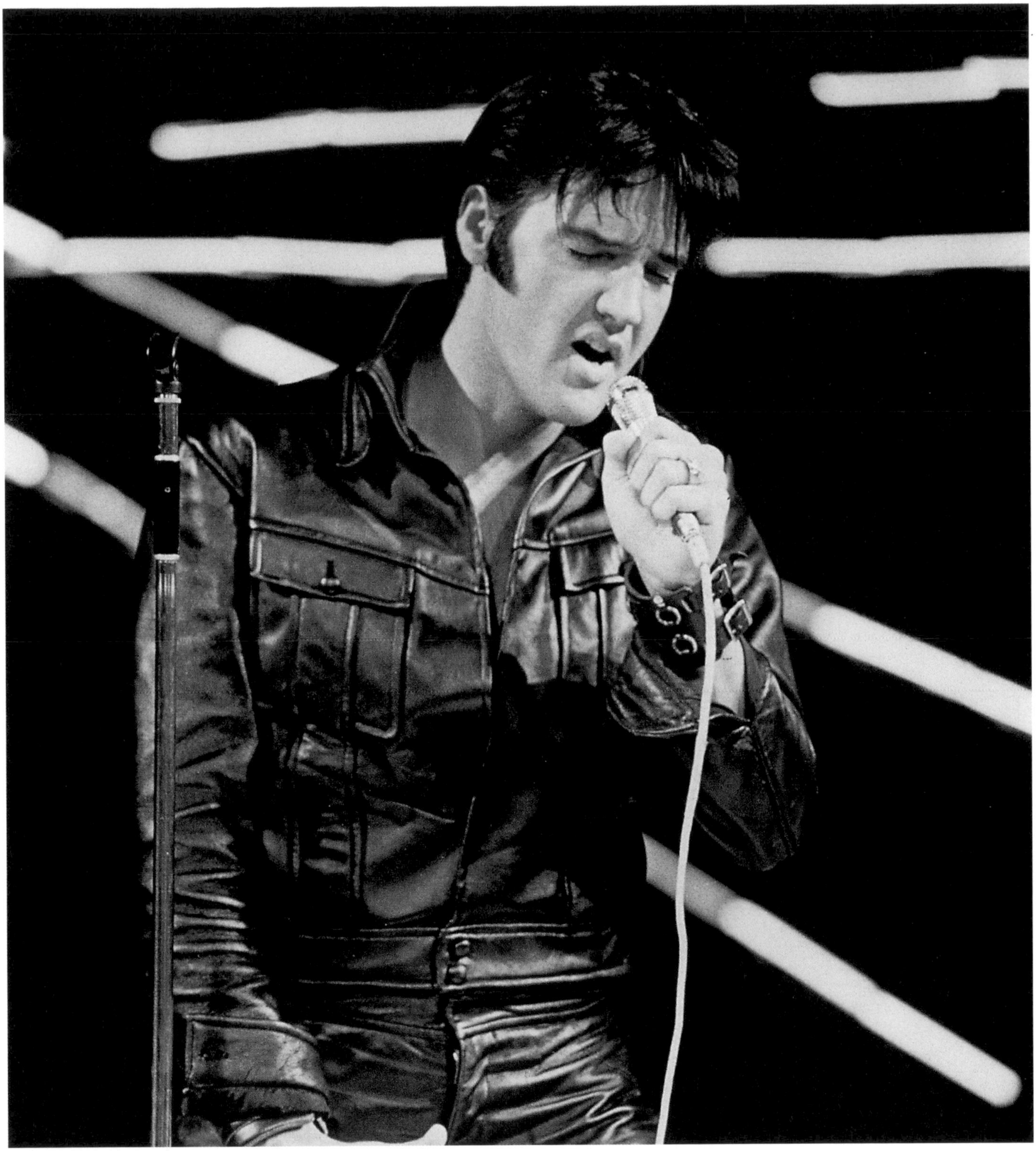

1968 BLACK LEATHER All Elvis' outfits (*see also overleaf*) on the program were made for him by the show's costume designer Bill Belew, who went on to design his famous jumpsuits in the Seventies. That included the black leather suit for the "informal" sessions. Elvis was sweating so much after the first "sit-down" set that Belew had to get the leathers cleaned and pressed before he went on again an hour later. Wearing black leather for these most intimate segments of the show was a shrewd move; it was a look that personified youth, and rebellious youth at that, from Marlon Brando in *The Wild One* through Elvis' "biker" shots in the Fifties, and even the earliest images of the Beatles.

1968

1968

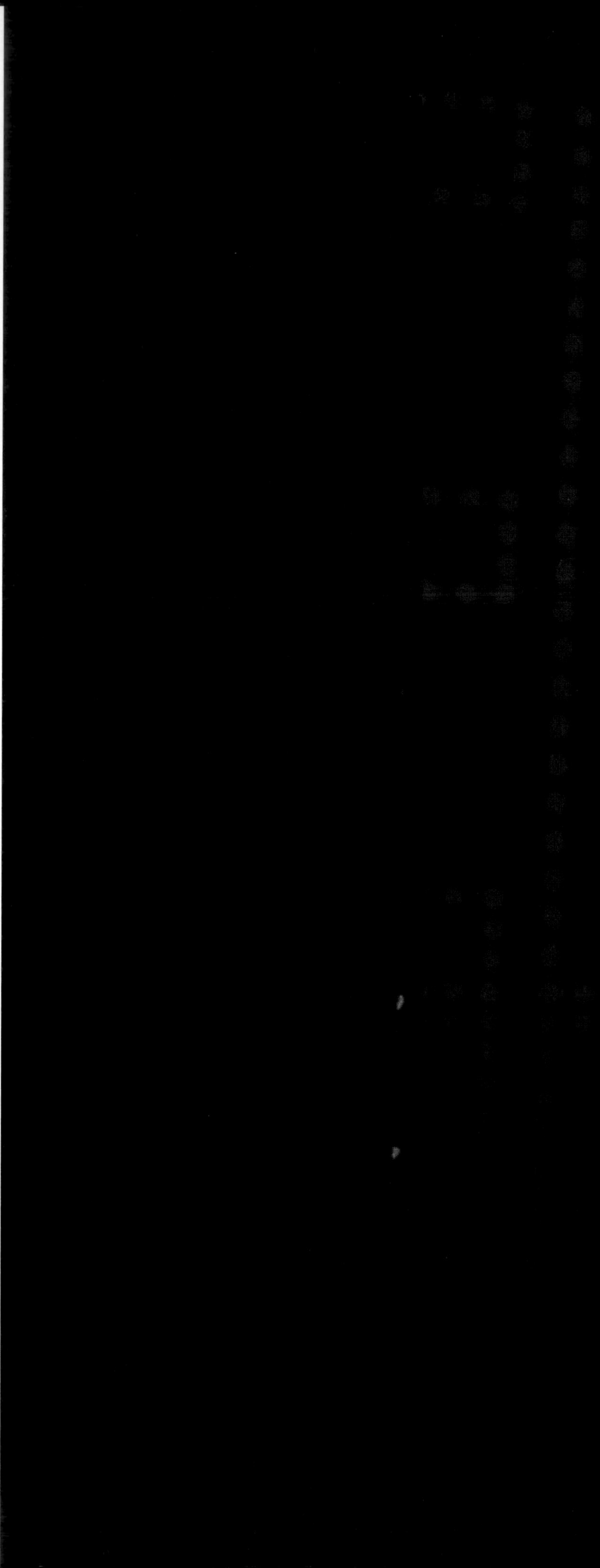

1968 FINALE The show concluded with one of the most spectacular and enduring images of Elvis, with a white suit and red scarf standing in front of the vast ELVIS in red lights, which has become part of Presley iconography. The final song in the special was "If I Can Dream," after which he raised his arms in triumph, and bade his audience, through the lens of the TV camera, a simple "Thank you, good night."

1968 IF I CAN DREAM Despite Colonel Parker's insistence that there should be at least one Christmas number in the show, the proposed notion to end on a seasonal note was rejected by Steve Binder. He favored something that reflected the feeling of optimism that he wanted to run through the whole program. Exactly what that something was to be, he wasn't at first sure. He then asked the show's vocal arranger, Earl Brown, if he could come up with something suitable, and overnight "If I Can Dream" was born (*see also overleaf*). Binder loved it, more importantly Elvis loved it, and the song–which rounded off the whole spectacular perfectly–was in as the closer.

1968

1968

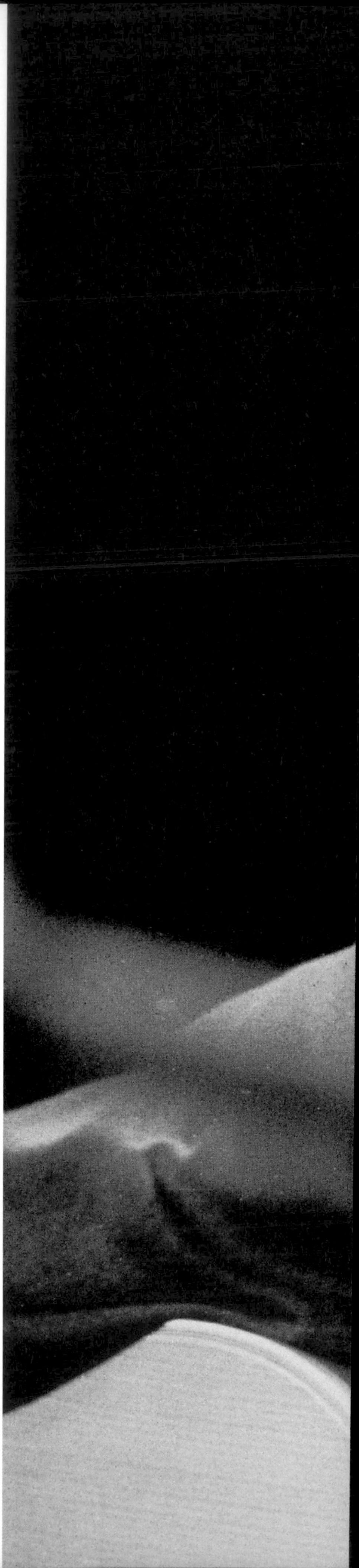

1968 BREAKTHROUGH The biggest influence of the show, and hence it being forever after dubbed the "comeback" TV show, was on the public perception of Elvis as a performer of hit popular music. After "Return To Sender" in 1962, the subsequent movie-dominated years had only yielded a few really big chart singles, with "Devil In Disguise" (1963), "Bossa Nova Baby" (1963), and "Crying In The Chapel" in 1965 making the Top Ten. The TV show, despite all its showbiz trappings of long-legged dancing girls, fight sequences, and dramatic set pieces, represented a tangible breakthrough for Elvis' credibility. He was seen by the world to be able to "cut it" on stage as dynamically as ever.

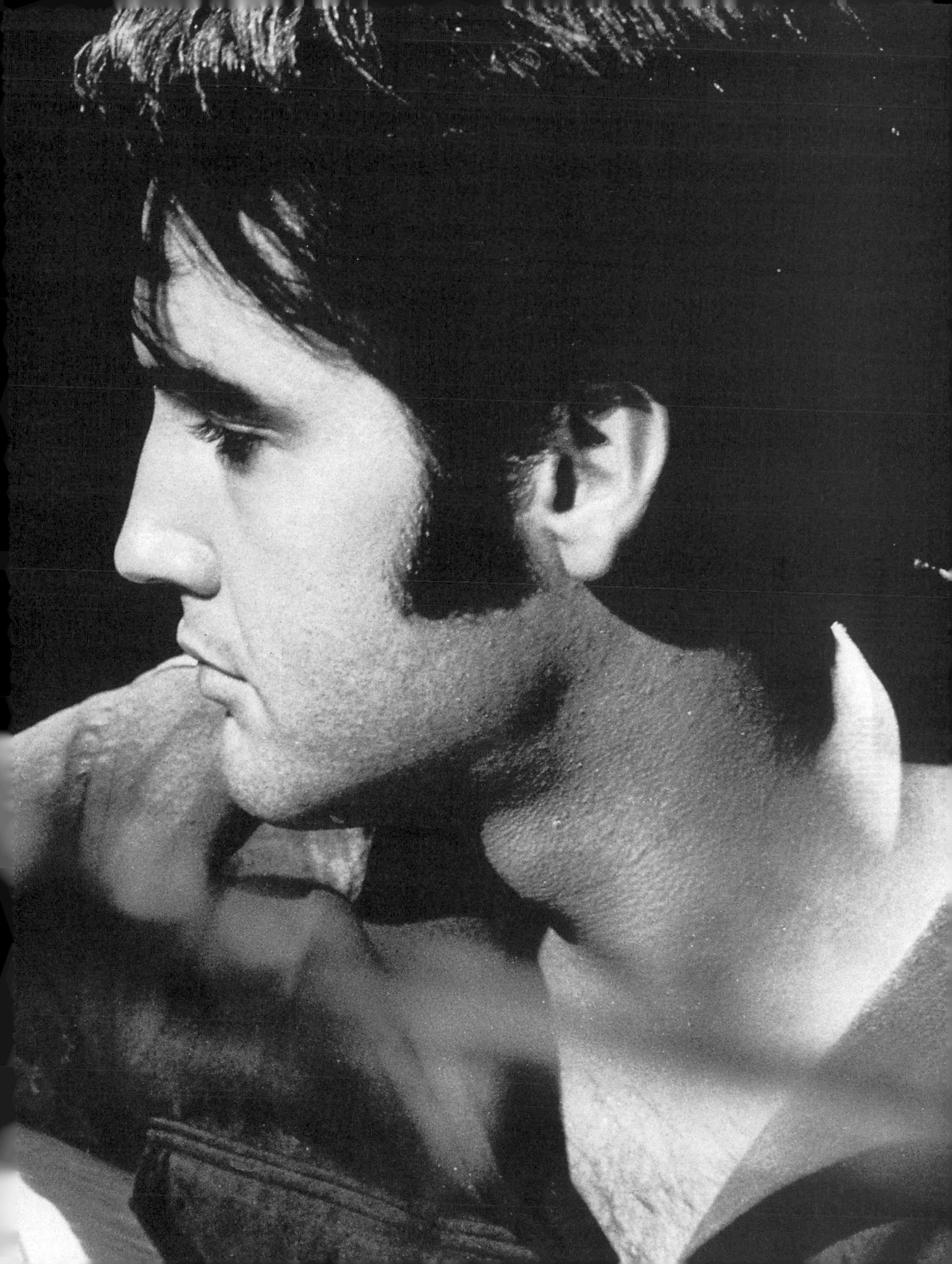

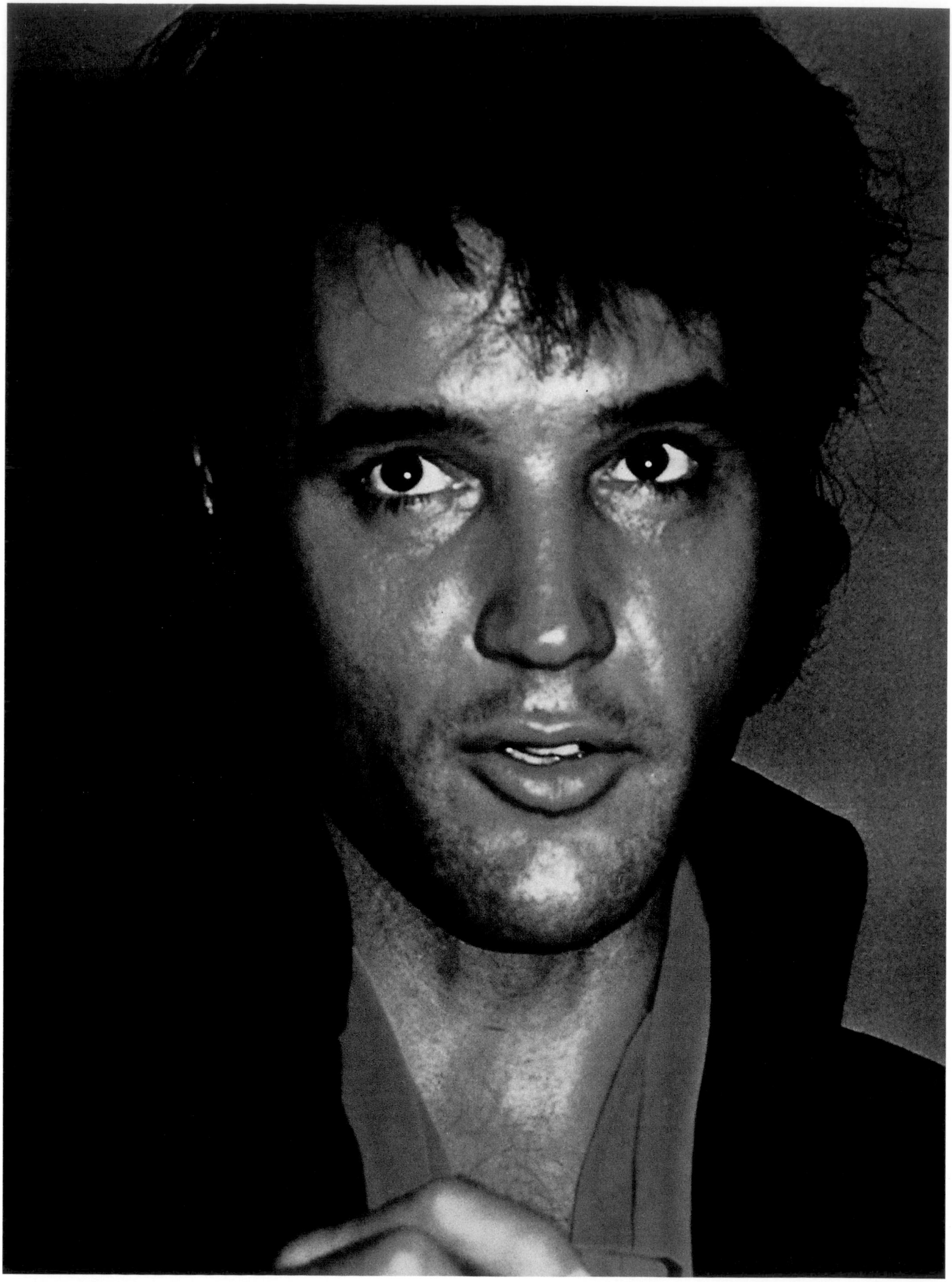

1969 CHANGES Elvis during the time of his Las Vegas "comeback" at the end of July 1969. Months before this live debut, in fact between the recording and the broadcast of the TV special, he had told a journalist for UPI that he was contemplating a return to live concerts: "I'm planning a lot of changes. You can't go on doing the same thing year after year. It's been a long time since I've done anything professionally except make movies and cut albums. Before long I'm going to make some personal appearance tours. I'll probably start out here in this country and after that play some concerts abroad starting in Europe. I miss the personal contact with audiences . . . "

1969

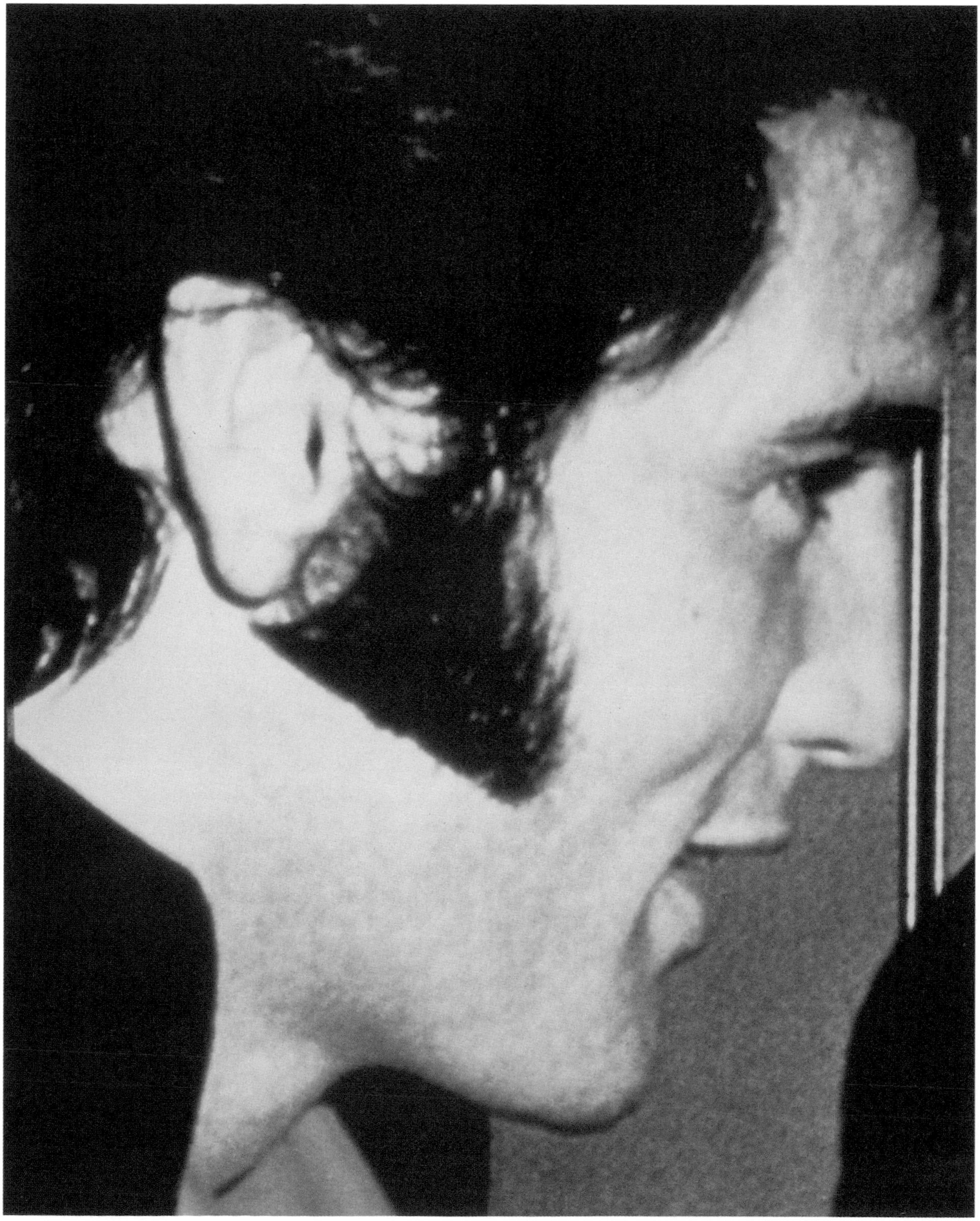

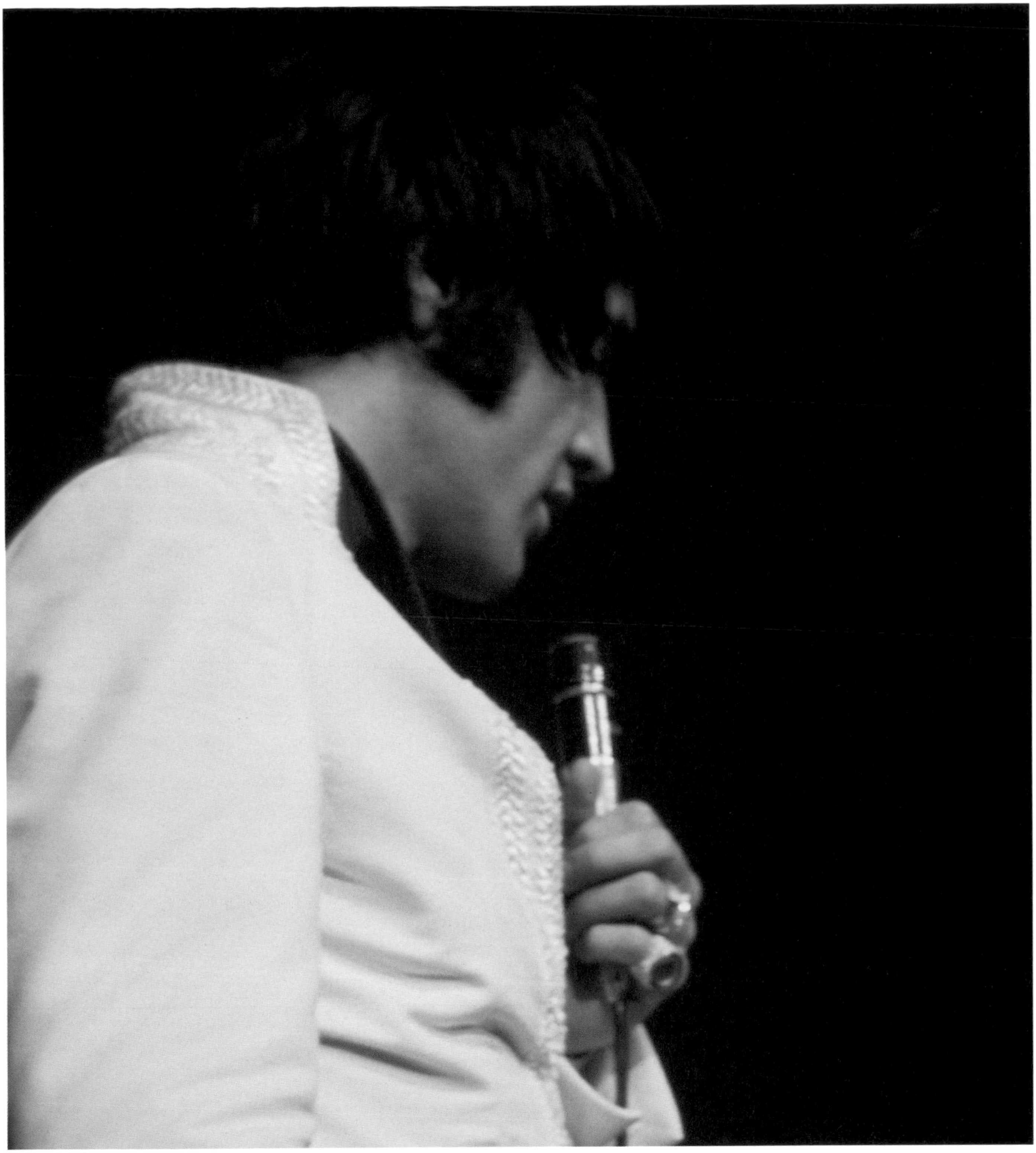

1969 LAS VEGAS The immediate impact of the TV special was clear by the offers of work that started flooding into the Colonel's office. One much-quoted instance was when a proposal came for Elvis to play the prestigious London Palladium, offering $28,000 for the week. The Colonel replied, "That's fine for me, now how much can you get for Elvis?" The offer that did bear fruit was when the new International Hotel in Las Vegas announced in May 1969 that Elvis would open there for four weeks commencing July 31. He was to play two shows a night, for a reported $100,000 a week, and this was to represent the second phase of his comeback, this time in live concerts. The invite-only opening night saw Elvis perform in front of a star-studded crowd, plus a huge press contingent, which the Colonel had flown in on the hotel owner's private jet. Reflecting attitudes that were the norm at the time, the invites read: "Elvis and the Las Vegas International Hotel take pleasure in inviting you and your lady to our opening show . . . "

1969

1969 FANS, GRACELAND During the period leading up to his "comeback" appearances in Las Vegas, Elvis was increasingly in the habit of walking down to the gates at Graceland to sign autographs, talk, and even on occasion sing to the fans waiting there–in preparation, perhaps, for his return to live performance.

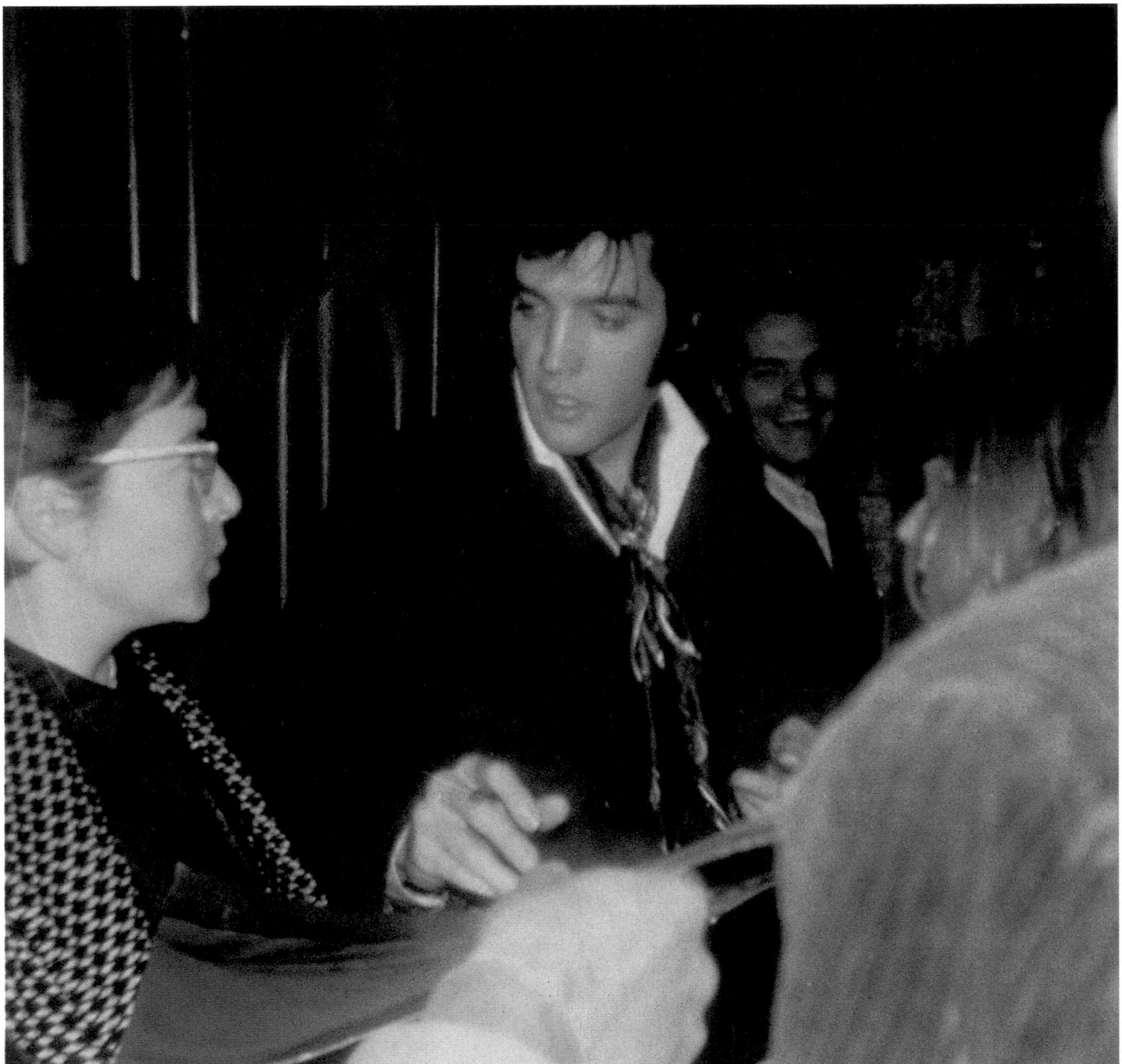

1969 FANS, LOS ANGELES Elvis meets with some fans who are gathered outside his West Coast home located at 1174 Hillcrest Road, in the exclusive Trousdale section of Beverly Hills, Los Angeles. Elvis and Priscilla bought the three-bedroom, multi-level house in November 1967—their first purchase of a home in the Los Angeles area—for around $400,000, and were able to entertain friends not just in the house but also in the guest cottage that was attached. The elegant home, which was just one of no less than seven properties that Elvis rented or purchased in California over the years, was built in 1961 in the French Regency style, and included an Olympic-size swimming pool.

1969

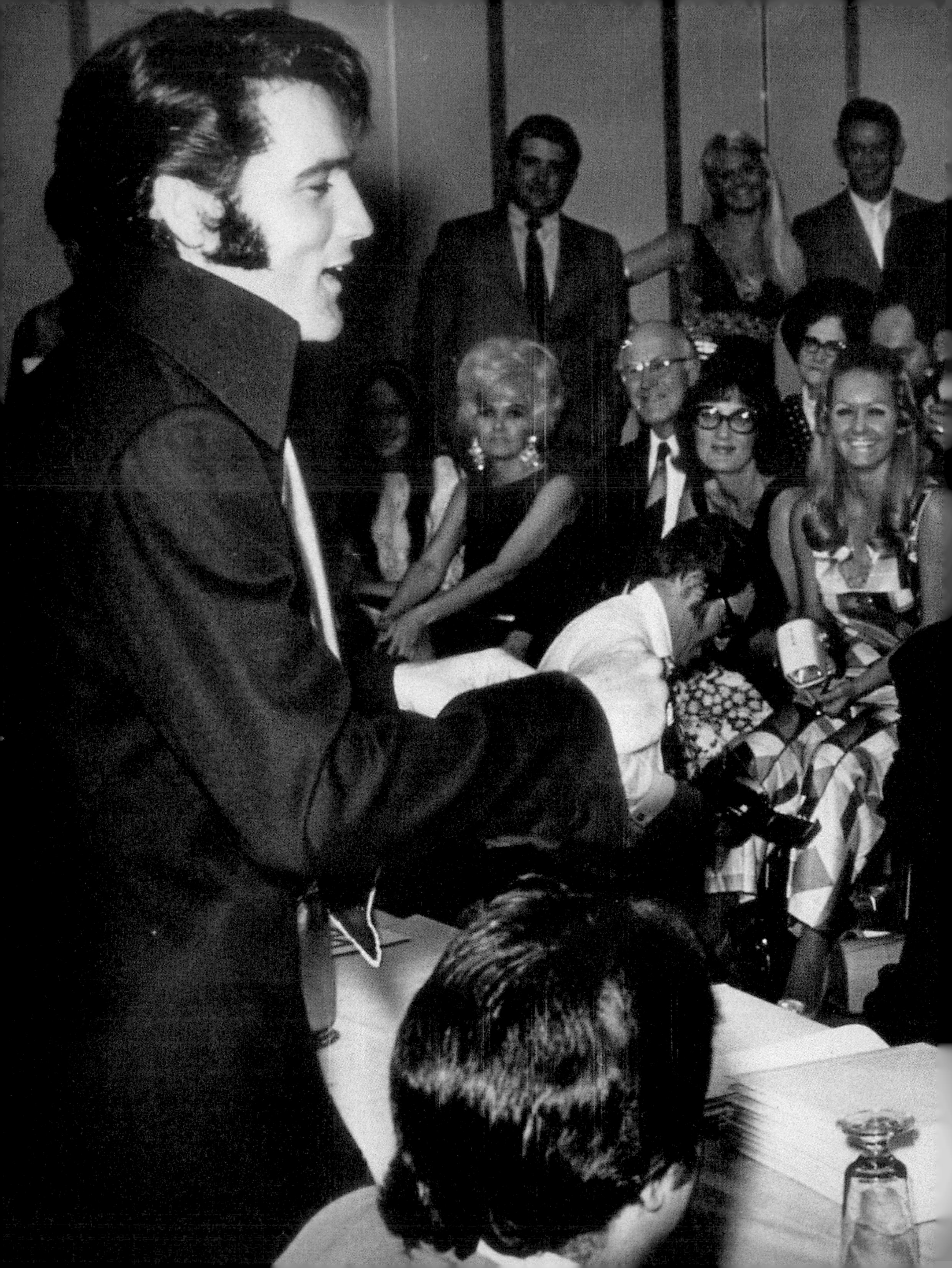

1969

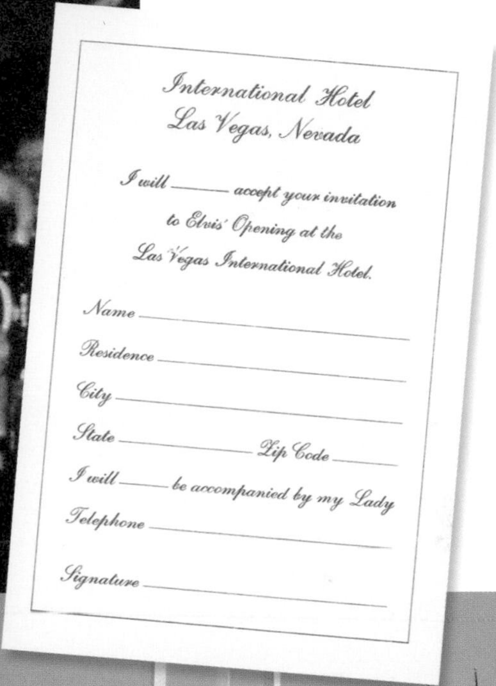

International Hotel
Las Vegas, Nevada

I will ______ accept your invitation
to Elvis' Opening at the
Las Vegas International Hotel.

Name ______________________
Residence ______________________
City ______________________
State __________ Zip Code __________
I will ______ be accompanied by my Lady
Telephone ______________________

Signature ______________________

1969 PRESS CONFERENCE The very morning after his opening night Elvis staged a press conference (*left*), at which he admitted that he had suffered some first night nerves. Nonetheless, the press reaction to his comeback was as favorable as that of his fans. It augered well for future seasons of live appearances in the Nevada desert city (*above*).

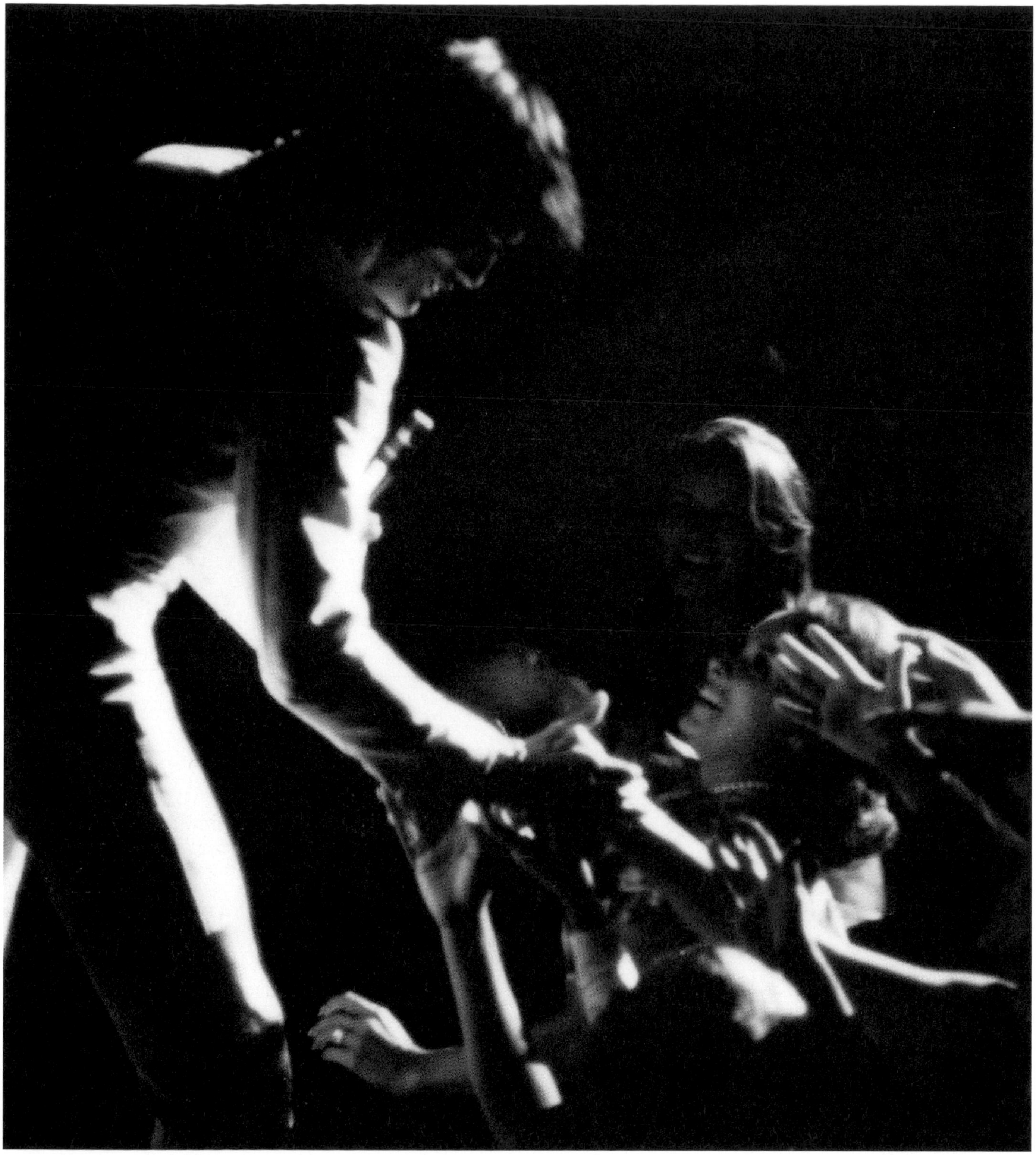

1969 THE FANS The reaction of the female members of the Las Vegas audience got wilder as the season progressed. They started throwing underwear at the stage, no doubt encouraged by Elvis who, leaning over to the front row, would kiss a fan here, touch a hand there, and after a few shows–noted by the ever-present press of course his pants split for the first time. It was all good-natured fun, though sometimes the level of enthusiasm approached the point of hysteria. Unlike the restrained "supper club" type of audiences at his Las Vegas debut at the New Frontier Hotel back in 1956, the crowds at the 1969 comeback season were redolent of the demonstrative fans he encountered during his touring concerts in the Fifties, screaming at his every gesture (*see also overleaf*), physically moved by his music. When he reached out to them, they reacted as his fans always had, they stretched forward to touch him, hung on every word he uttered, every lyric he sang. They moved with him, as one.

1969 GUITAR MAN For the International season Elvis was backed by a handpicked band, featuring the great James Burton on guitar, Jerry Scheff on bass guitar, Larry Muhoberac on piano, John Wilkinson on rhythm guitar, and Ronnie Tutt on drums. Plus, of course, on many numbers, Elvis also accompanied himself on guitar.

1969

1969 THE MUSIC The core of the set for the opening Las Vegas shows (*see also previous pages*) consisted of the following numbers: "Blue Suede Shoes," "I Got A Woman," "Love Me Tender," "Jailhouse Rock," "Don't Be Cruel," "Heartbreak Hotel," "All Shook Up," "Hound Dog," "Memories," "In Tne Ghetto," "Yesterday," "Hey Jude," "One Night," "Johnny B. Goode," and "Suspicious Minds." It was a selection that relied on his own vast back catalog of hits, but also included songs made famous by rock greats Chuck Berry and the Beatles. As well as Elvis, his band and orchestra under Bobby Morris, the show featured comedian Sammy Shore and two vocal groups, the Imperials and Sweet Inspirations.

1969

➔ 1969 RENAISSANCE The "comeback" period of the late Sixties (*see also previous pages*) represented a true renaissance for Elvis, not just some nostalgia-driven retrospective but a true revival of his art in fresh terms. This was no live version of a "greatest hits" package, carbon-copied classics rolled out for the faithful fans–and that would have been easy, for there were certainly millions of them. This was an Elvis for a new decade, freed from what was had become the artistic straitjacket of his movies. His ambitions to act were frustrated by plots usually constrained by the commercial demands of making "musical" films, while his musical horizons in the films were limited to these same often sterile scenarios. Hollywood had served its purpose, but it was time to move on. And with the TV special of 1968 and the Las Vegas season in 1969, Elvis had signaled in no uncertain terms that he had made that move.

Showtime

ELVIS ON TOUR

[1970–1977]

1972 **ON STAGE** Following the "comeback" TV show and live dates at the close of the Sixties, the rest of Elvis' career was characterized by his spectacular stage act.

July 1970

September 1970

Spring 1972

1970-1977

Once he had made his comeback, there was no going back for Elvis. The Seventies opened with him in the center of the action again as far as live appearances were concerned, with a new image rather than the slightly retro-Elvis that was a feature of the TV special. Honed to what quickly became a new Elvis look, just as his image in the Fifties had become the look for a thousand would-be-rock'n'roll singers, the Elvis of the Seventies—parodied by Elvis impersonators forever after—was indeed regarded by some as a parody of himself by the middle of the decade. But as the jumpsuits became more rhinestone-encrusted and the capes more flamboyant, it was his own self-created image that he was building on. It was not modified or copied from elsewhere: this was Elvis, and noone else.

And, like his voice, no matter how the look was parodied, satirized, or simply imitated, it could never be duplicated. All the white-suited impersonators in the world can't come near to reproducing the way he moved, the way he used the clothes, the way he occupied the stage—and the way he was at one with the audience.

Elvis had become an icon once again, not in some "Fifties revivalist" mode, harking back to a past era he had indeed helped to define, but a true icon for the times.

Summer 1971

Summer 1975

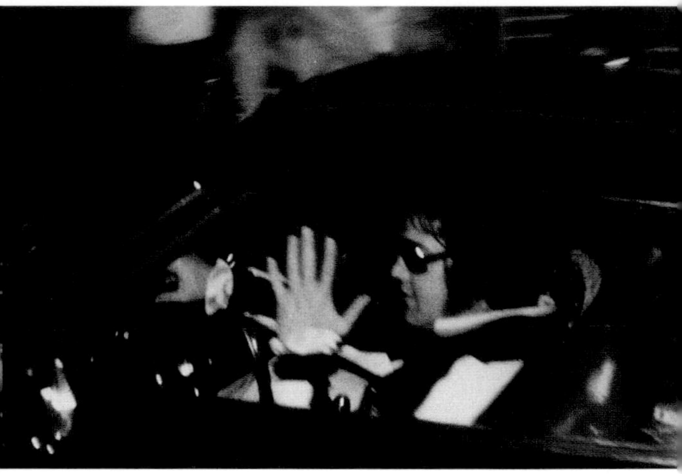

August 1977

As with his stage shows, every aspect of Elvis' working life in the Seventies was spectacular to say the least. While the touring became more grueling, and undoubtedly took its toll, media-driven events, including the "Aloha" satellite link-up and two major movie documentaries, took the Elvis stage show to fans around the world.

And as he became, once more, a pillar of the showbusiness establishment, so he received more and more accolades from the social establishment. An award as one of the Ten Outstanding Young Men of 1970 was followed at the end of that year by his unprecedented meeting at the White House with President Richard Nixon; in the light of subsequent history, it's not hard to guess which of them is more fondly remembered.

But by the middle of the decade, it had become apparent that things were not as they should have been. Elvis often looked physically tired on stage, his performances were frequently sloppy, and they increasingly lacked the surefire dynamic that had been their trademark.

When his death on August 16, 1977 was announced by a stunned media, the world was shocked, but many who had observed his career over the previous few months were not truly surprised. The King was dead. Long live the King.

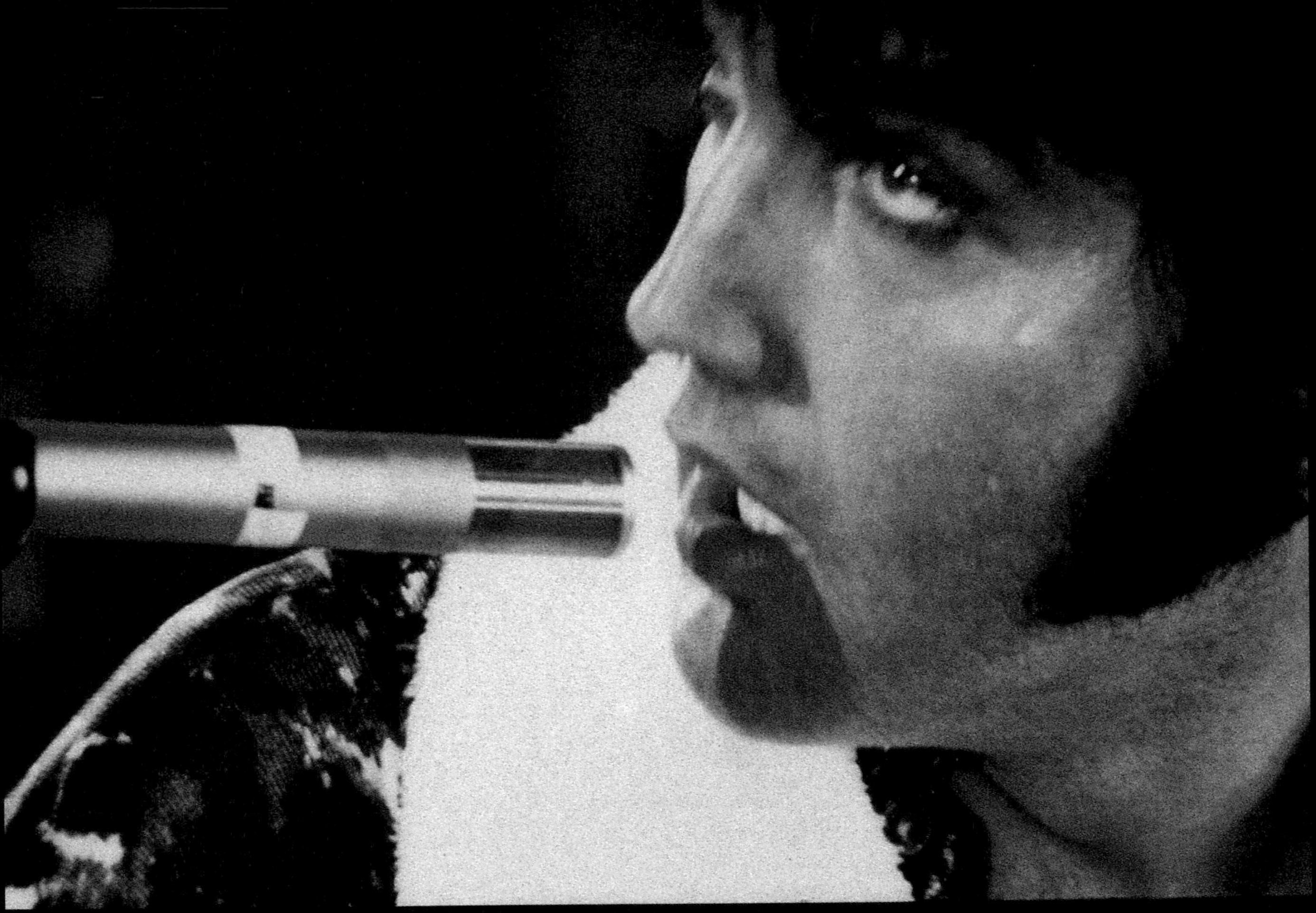

1970

1970 MGM STUDIOS In July 1970, MGM started filming what would become a major movie documentary of Elvis as a live performer. This included rehearsals, life backstage and on the road, and the concert performances that were part of Elvis on tour, as well as his showcase–which was to become something of a home from home–at the International Hotel in Las Vegas. The director was Denis Sanders, who had won two Academy Awards, including one for *A Time Out Of War*, a 1954 short set in the American Civil War that is now considered a classic antiwar film. His other credits included three well-remembered television series: *The Defenders*, *Route 66*, and *The Naked City*.

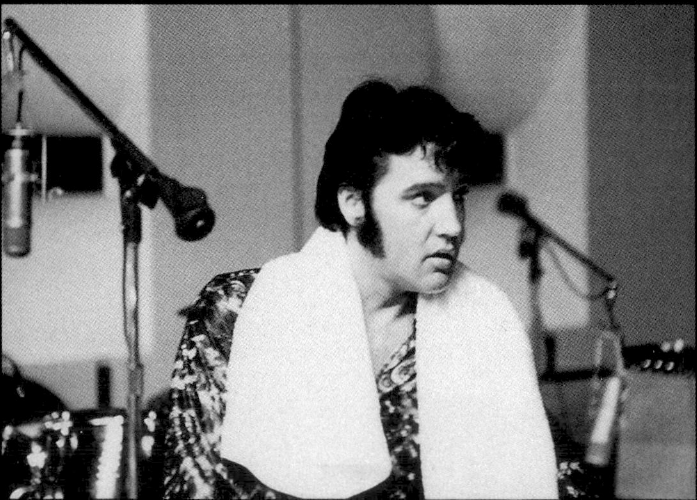

⊖⊕ 1970 **MGM STUDIOS** The rehearsal session musicians were the core of Elvis' onstage band. They included Ronnie Tutt on drums, Charlie Hodge on guitar, Glen D. Hardin (from Buddy Holly's Crickets) on piano, Jerry Scheff on bass (*opposite*, behind Elvis), John Wilkinson on rhythm guitar, and James Burton on lead guitar. Burton (*top*, behind Elvis) cut his teeth on Ricky Nelson's seminal records in the Fifties, and went on after his work with Elvis to feature on tracks by such artists as Emmylou Harris, John Denver, and Elvis Costello.

1970 MGM STUDIOS Although doubtless under the close scrutiny of both Elvis' record company, RCA, and of course the Colonel, who was as publicity conscious as any manager could be, the film's director Denis Sanders managed to produce a candid portrait of Elvis doing what he undoubtedly did best–making live music. This was never more the case than during the rehearsal sequences. The 97-minute movie, the first of two produced in the Seventies that followed Elvis' working life "on the road," was released in November 1970 with the slightly cumbersome title *Elvis:That's The Way It Is.* It was originally to be simply called *Elvis*, which was the working title throughout the film's production.

1970

1970

1970 MGM STUDIOS The rehearsal sequences for the documentary were filmed on the MGM sound stage at Culver City studios on July 15 and 29. The vast range of songs covered included early favorites from Elvis' days at Sun Records, among them "Baby Let's Play House" and "That's All Right," rock'n'roll standards such as "Johnny B. Goode," country classics like "I Can't Stop Loving You," the Beatles' hits "Yesterday" and "Hey Jude," and Elvis' own classic hits, ranging from "Love Me Tender" to "Suspicious Minds"–over 50 songs in all. Subsequent rehearsals took place at the RCA Studios in Hollywood, and then in the convention room and on stage at the International Hotel.

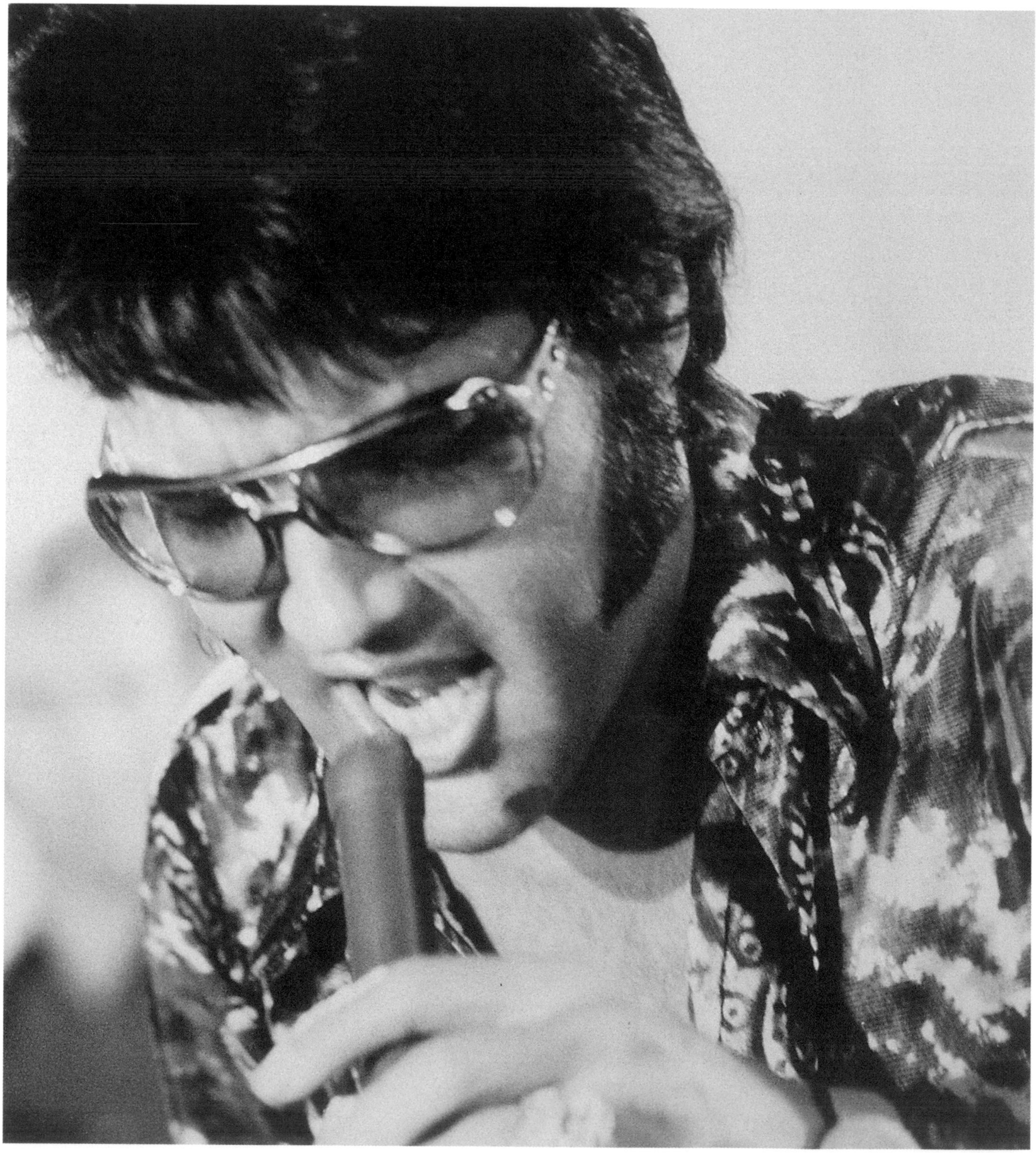

BY REQUEST
ELVIS
BY REQUEST
3 A.M.-SUN.-SEPT. 6
SPECIAL
PERFORMANCE
SPECIAL
SHOWROOM INTERNATIONALE
ELVIS RECORDS AND TAPES AVAILABLE AT RECORD DEALERS EVERYWHERE
Special ELVIS Special
POLK SALAD
With
Corn Muffins & Honey
$1.95
INTERNATIONAL
HOTEL PRESENTS
ELVIS
SWEET INSPIRATIONS
JOE GUERCIO CONDUCTING
WELCOME
TICKETS NOW AVAILABLE
HAIR
AMERICA'S #1 MUSICAL
IN OUR LEGITIMATE THEATRE
9:15PM-5:30AM

1970 LAS VEGAS At the end of February 1970, Elvis began a four-week season at the International Hotel, Las Vegas, opening with an invitation-only date that garnered enthusiastic press reviews, many drawing attention to his new stage act and its use of Elvis' almost choreographed dance movements.

1970 POLK SALAD A table card from the International Hotel Las Vegas, offering a "polk salad" with corn muffins and honey for $1.95. It was named after a song in Elvis' repertoire at the time, "Polk Salad Annie," which had been a 1969 hit for its composer, the Nashville-based "swamp rock" country singer Tony Joe White.

1970

1970 EARLY JUMPSUITS This white suit with tasseled rope neckties featured in the Las Vegas shows, and was among the first of the jumpsuits that were to become Elvis' trademark in the Seventies. The suits, designed by Bill Belew and made by I C (Ice Capades) Costumes of Los Angeles, were later to become even more flamboyant.

1970

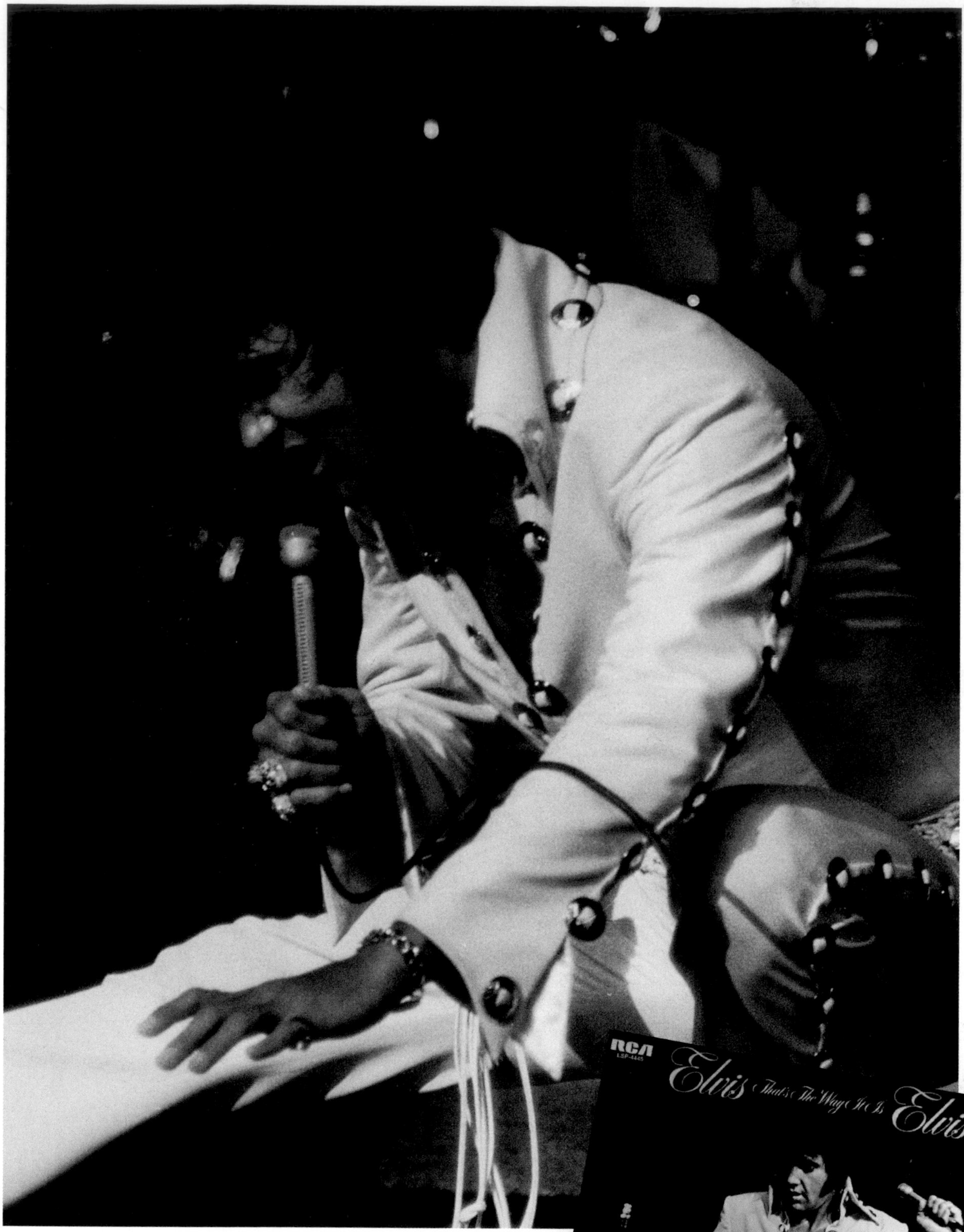

1970 SUMMER SHOW Shot as part of *Elvis: That's The Way It Is*, the image (*above*) shows Elvis reestablished after his "comeback." The soundtrack album appeared at the same time as the film's release in November. The image on the facing page and those on the following four pages were taken during Elvis' February 1970 engagement in Las Vegas.

1970

1970 TOURING Virtually all of Elvis' jumpsuits (*here and overleaf*) were made out of 100% wool gabardine from Milan, Italy. Bill Belew chose this fabric for its flexibility (the same reason that ice skaters used it for their outfits). The flared legs were typical Seventies, while the turned-up collar was inspired by military styles from the Napoleonic period.

1970 WINTER The choice of Las Vegas as the central location for Elvis' return to live performances was initially seen as curious, to say the least. The gambling capital was regarded as a haven for cabaret-style supper club audiences rather than for Elvis' fan base, which would have been more familiar with the country's concert stadia.

1970 SUMMER The summer dates at the International Hotel were presented by Colonel Parker as the "Elvis Presley Summer Festival" with thousands of specially printed menus, postcards, catalogs, and photo albums—not to mention 3,600 specially-made imitation straw boaters for the hotel staff to wear during his season there.

1970

1970 **WINTER** Even the Colonel doubted whether the success in Las Vegas could be reflected nationwide. However, after the Houston shows he was confident enough to set up a six-day tour in September that took in Phoenix, St. Louis, Detroit, Miami, Tampa, and Mobile. During this tour, Elvis appeared before a total audience of over one million. The photos on this page and the following four pages are all from 1970 Las Vegas shows.

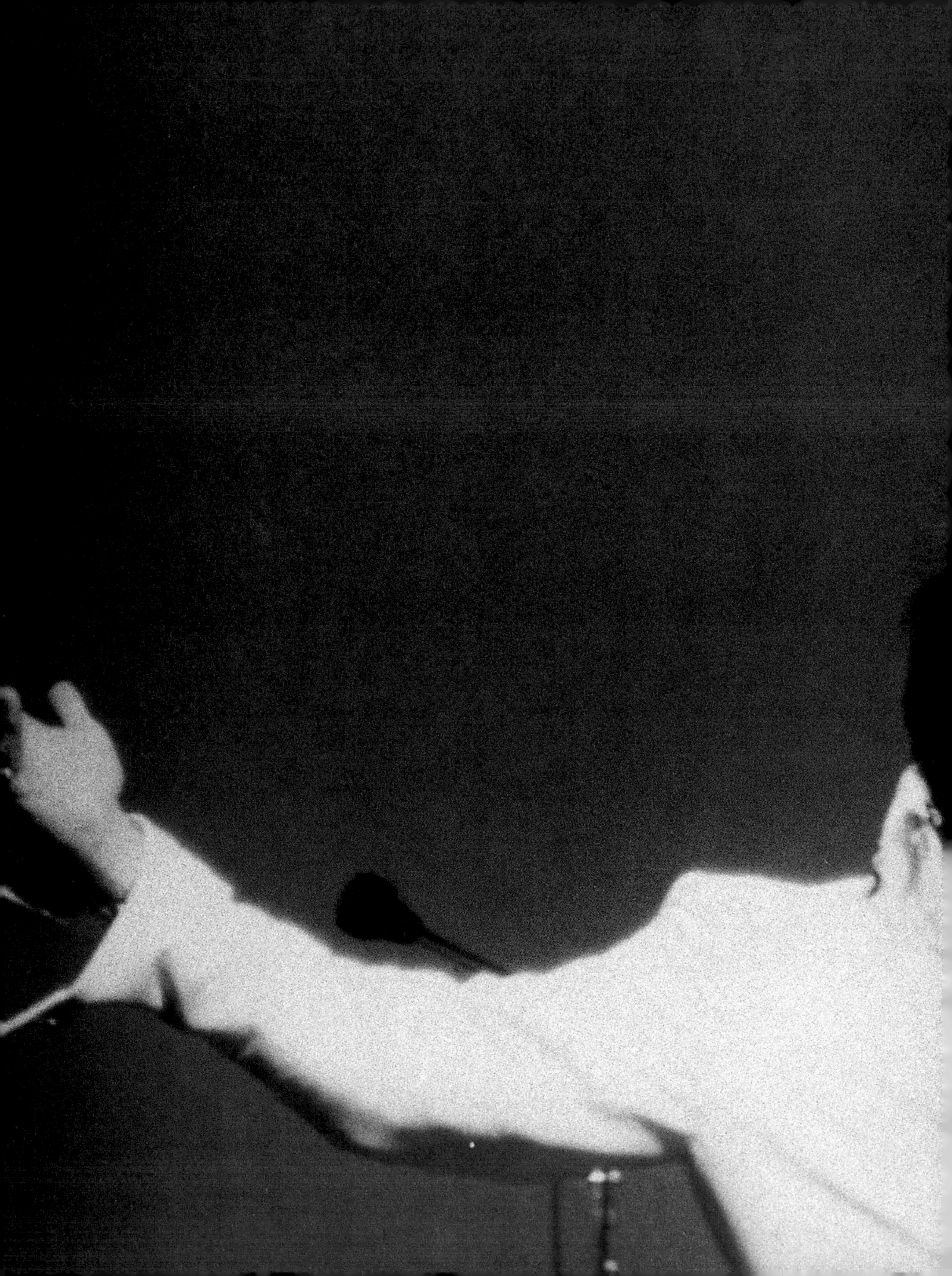

1972

➲ 1972 **COLLARS** Inspired by the European military styles of the late 18th and early 19th centuries, the collars on Bill Belew's creations got bigger and bigger, as did the capes and the flares on the pants. These are parts of the Elvis Presley "stereotype" that has persisted–particularly with Elvis impersonators the world over–ever since.

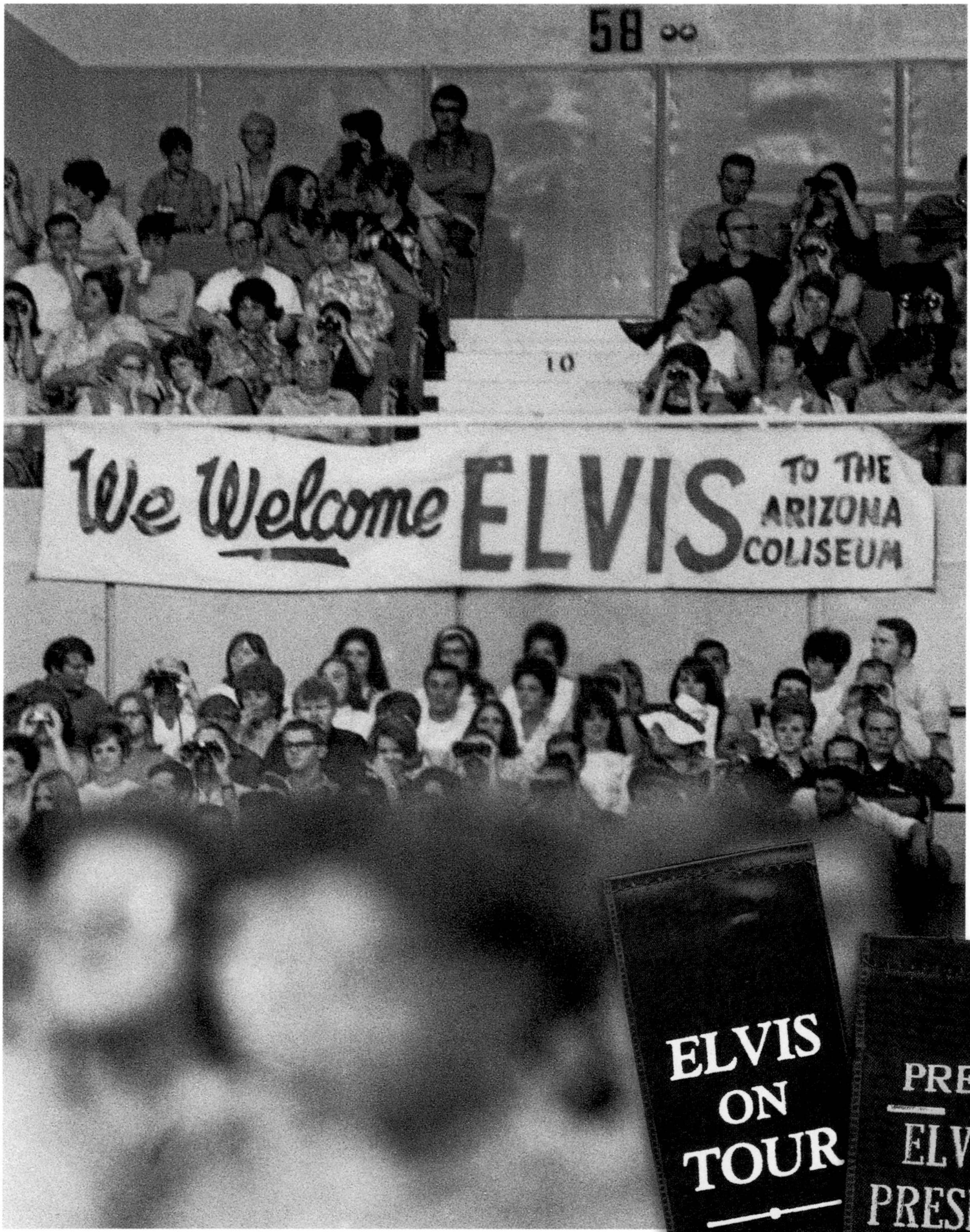

1970 PHOENIX, ARIZONA Just two of many sensational audience shots from *Elvis:That's The Way It Is*. One shows a huge banner saying "We Welcome Elvis to the Arizona Coliseum;" the other is the view from the back of the stage. For the first time in a decade, Elvis fans across the length and breadth of the US were being afforded the opportunity to see their idol in the flesh. With a supporting band, vocal groups, and full orchestra–plus a newly honed stage act–it could be said that Elvis certainly gave them what they wanted. Some of the sensational performances in the early years of the Seventies have rightly become the stuff of legend. Were you there?

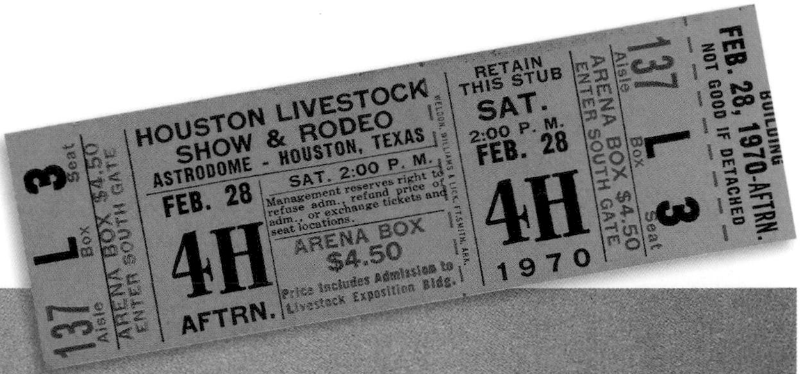

1970 HOUSTON PRESS CONFERENCE Elvis held a press conference after his final show at the mammoth Houston Astrodome on March 1, 1970. Here he was presented with a Stetson, a gold watch, and a gold deputy's badge from the local sheriffs' department, adding to what was becoming a huge collection of honorary law-enforcement decorations. As Elvis admires his gifts (*left*)–wearing a military-style jacket probably influenced by the Beatles' "Sergeant Pepper" look of the late Sixties–the Colonel looks on, sporting what can only be described as a jaunty tweed cap, plus of course the ever-present cigar. Whatever, the Texans look mighty proud.

1970

FORD

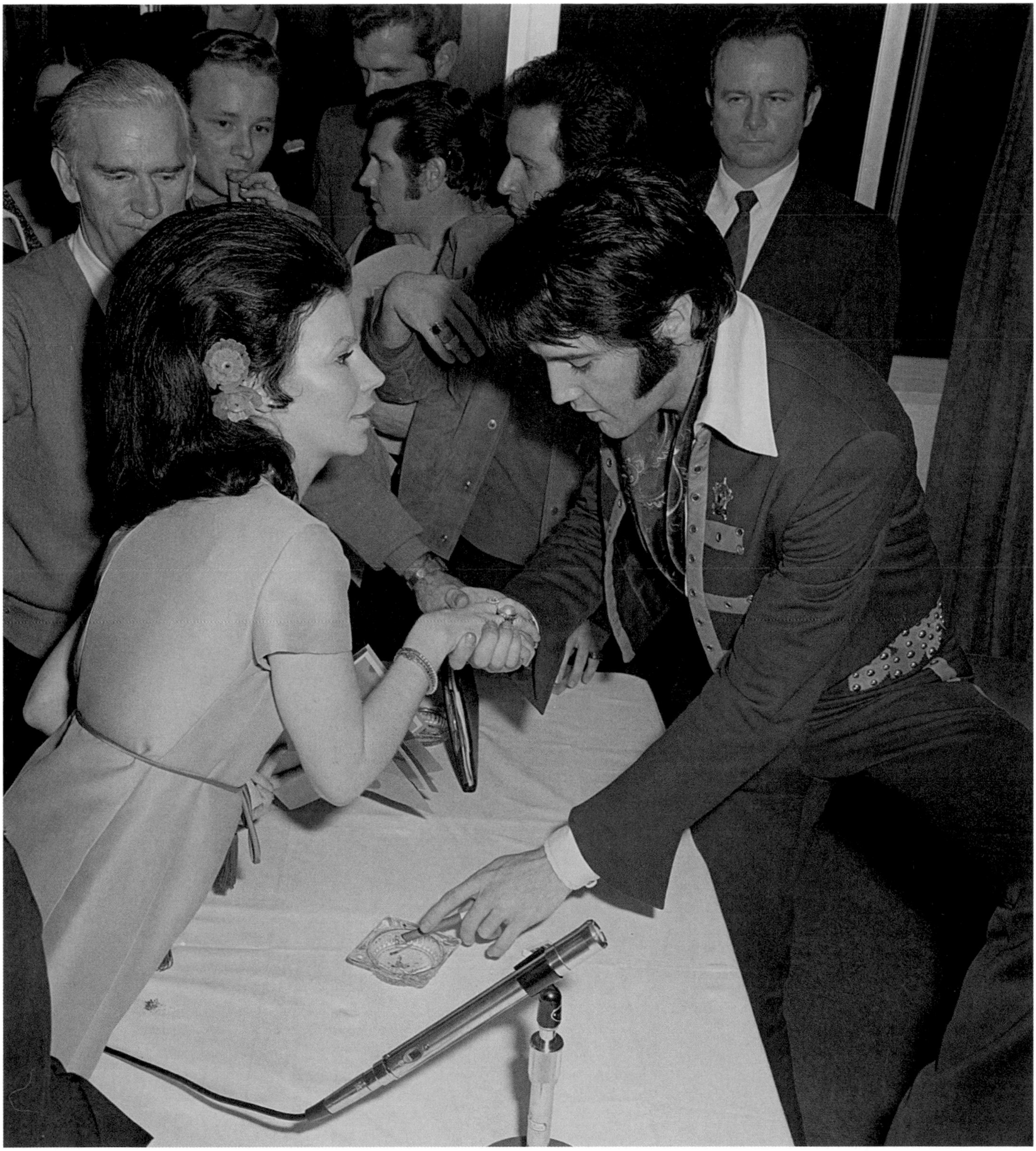

1974 HOUSTON ASTRODROME In 1974, Elvis returned to the Houston Astrodome on March 1 for two shows, starting at 2 PM and 7 PM respectively. Together the shows set a world audience record for any indoor arena. As always he preceded the shows with a "lap of honor" around the auditorium in a jeep.

1970 HOUSTON ASTRODROME Elvis prepares for the Houston press conference, at which, as well as the gifts from the sheriffs, he also received gold records for five of his 1969 releases–"Don't Cry Daddy," "In The Ghetto," "Suspicious Minds," and two albums, *From Elvis In Memphis* and *From Memphis to Vegas/From Vegas to Memphis.*

1970

ELVIS
BIG
50
Records
ELVIS
SUMMER
FESTIVAL
ELVIS
50
ELVIS
PERSON
NOW!
NOW!

1970s

1970 SUMMER FESTIVAL Captured on film in *Elvis: That's The Way It Is*, the Las Vegas Hilton Hotel lobby, pictured during what Colonel Tom Parker dubbed the "Elvis Summer Festival." The Colonel spared no effort in his promotion of the dates and in the marketing of spin-off product, and the hotel lobby was filled with Elvis souvenirs–T-shirts, straw boaters, mugs, photographs, concert programs, and stuffed animals. In the shot opposite, the Colonel is seen reviewing some of the 3,500 straw boaters he had provided for the hotel staff to wear. This was the logical extension of licensing merchandise, in which the Colonel organized the manufacture and sale of a variety of items.

1972 SUMMER FESTIVAL A virtual army of stuffed hound dogs line the way, like some guard of honor, to the inevitable souvenir stand in the Hilton lobby. In many ways the stuffed pooches were pure Colonel–one of Elvis' toughest rock'n'roll records became the inspiration for kiddies' playthings, akin to prizes at a fairground.

1973

↑ **1973 THAT'S THE WAY IT IS** A shot from the film; the Colonel, as always, is watching over Elvis. His relationship with his charge was complex; he was business organizer, public relations man, father-figure, financial adviser, and–despite many suggestions to the contrary–a long-term friend.

→ **1973 ON THE ROAD** Hotel room, limousine, dressing room, stage, and then back again: the story of Elvis' frenetic life on the road. Here Elvis leaves a hotel on his way to a concert date, as always becoming the center of attention with the passing crowds.

⬆ **1970 SAMMY DAVIS BACKSTAGE** Elvis met with Sammy Davis Jr.–whom he had known since his earliest years in Hollywood when Elvis was shooting *Love Me Tender*–backstage at the opening night of his summer season at the International Hotel. The event was recorded on film in *Elvis: That's The Way It Is*. Other celebrities who attended the opening–and can be seen in the film–included Juliet Prowse (who had starred with Elvis in *GI Blues*), Cuban bandleader Xavier Cugat, and the actor Cary Grant. Backstage encounters with celebrities, ranging from movie stars and pop singers to ex-Presidents of the US, were a constant feature of his appearances in Las Vegas.

1970

1973 ELVIS AND ALI When Elvis was appearing at the Las Vegas Hilton in February 1973, he met up with Muhammad Ali–formerly Cassius Clay–simply the greatest boxer of his generation. Of course the meeting with Ali couldn't pass without a photo of the two kings sparring. Here, the King of the ring is wearing a stud-encrusted robe presented to him by the King of rock'n'roll. In this posed picture (*left,*) Elvis is wearing the pendant he was presented with in appreciation of his work through the Aloha project for the Kui Lee cancer fund.

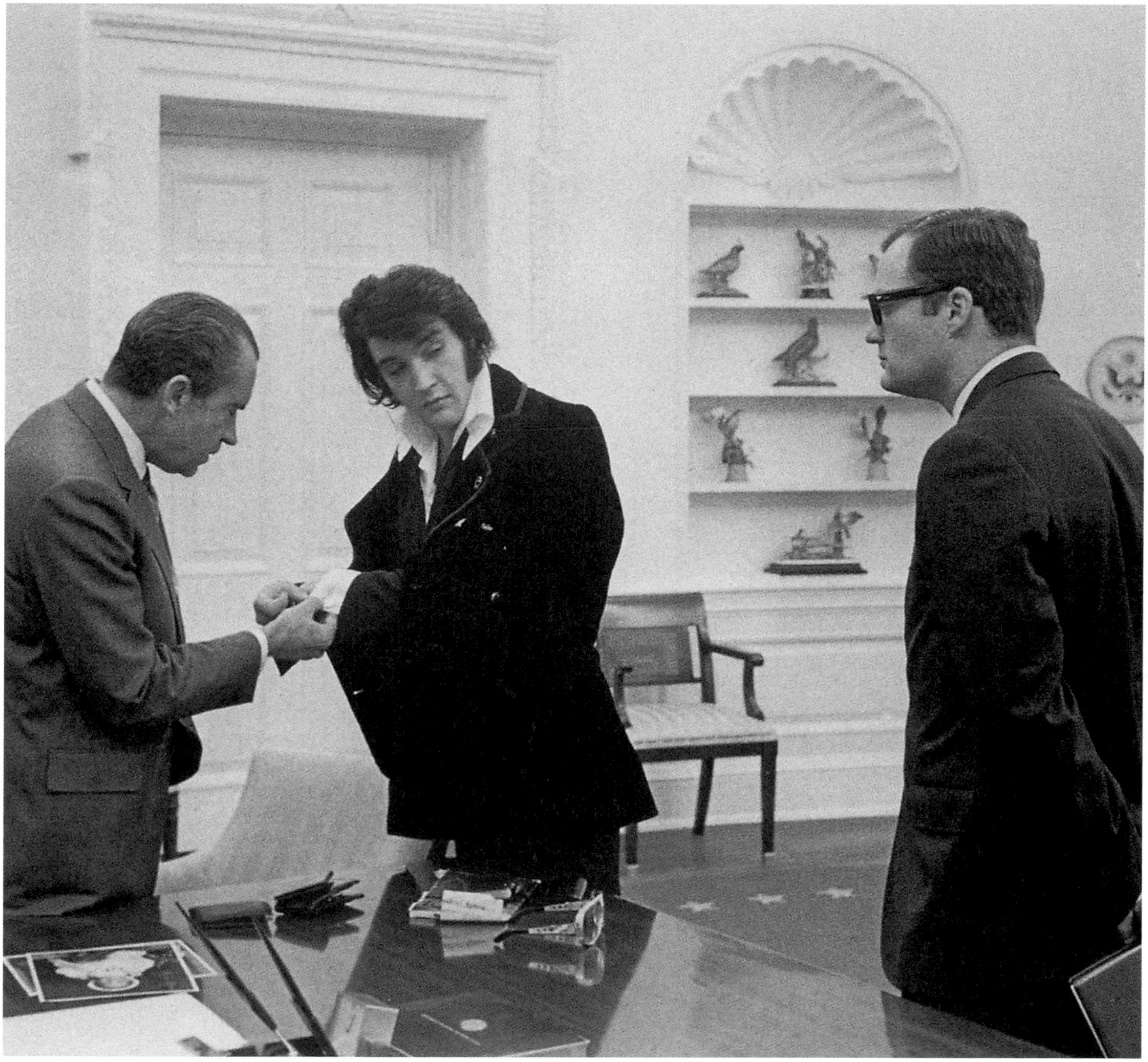

1970 THE WHITE HOUSE On December 21, 1970, after much personal lobbying of the President, Elvis had his famous meeting with Richard Nixon in Oval Office of the White House. After presenting the President with a World War II Colt .45 in a wooden case, he received the much sought-after badge as an honorary member of the Federal Narcotics Bureau, having written to the President voicing his concern about "the drug culture," and offering to use his status as a top entertainer in the war against illicit narcotics. Also in the picture below, as the President looks with interest at Elvis' cufflinks, is the President's deputy counsel, Egil Krogh.

1970

1971 DENVER, COLORADO An informal shot of Elvis taken in a motel room in Denver, Colorado. Life on the road, regardless of a star's status, is not all glamor. As well as the best hotels in town there were more modest motels, though smart restaurants were the rule rather than roadside diners, and a private plane hop rather than an overnight drive.

1974 THE TELEVISION ROOM Elvis in the television room at Graceland. The room had housed television, hi fi, and movie equipment since the Fifties, and was redecorated in 1974 by the designer Bill Eubanks. With its mirrored ceiling, it was pure Seventies; the row of three sets meant that Elvis could watch three sport events at once!

1971

↑ 1971 **THE "JAYCEE" AWARD** In January, Elvis was selected by the Junior Chamber of Commerce as one of the nation's Ten Outstanding Men of the Year for 1970. Other recipients of the award, which was inaugurated in 1939, include conductor Leonard Bernstein, actor and film director Orson Welles, and

→ 1970 **BEST MAN** Elvis was best man, and Priscilla matron of honor, at the Memphis wedding of Sonny West—who had been a friend since the late 50s and long-time member of Elvis' entourage—on December 28, 1970. After an initial church reception, Elvis hosted a second

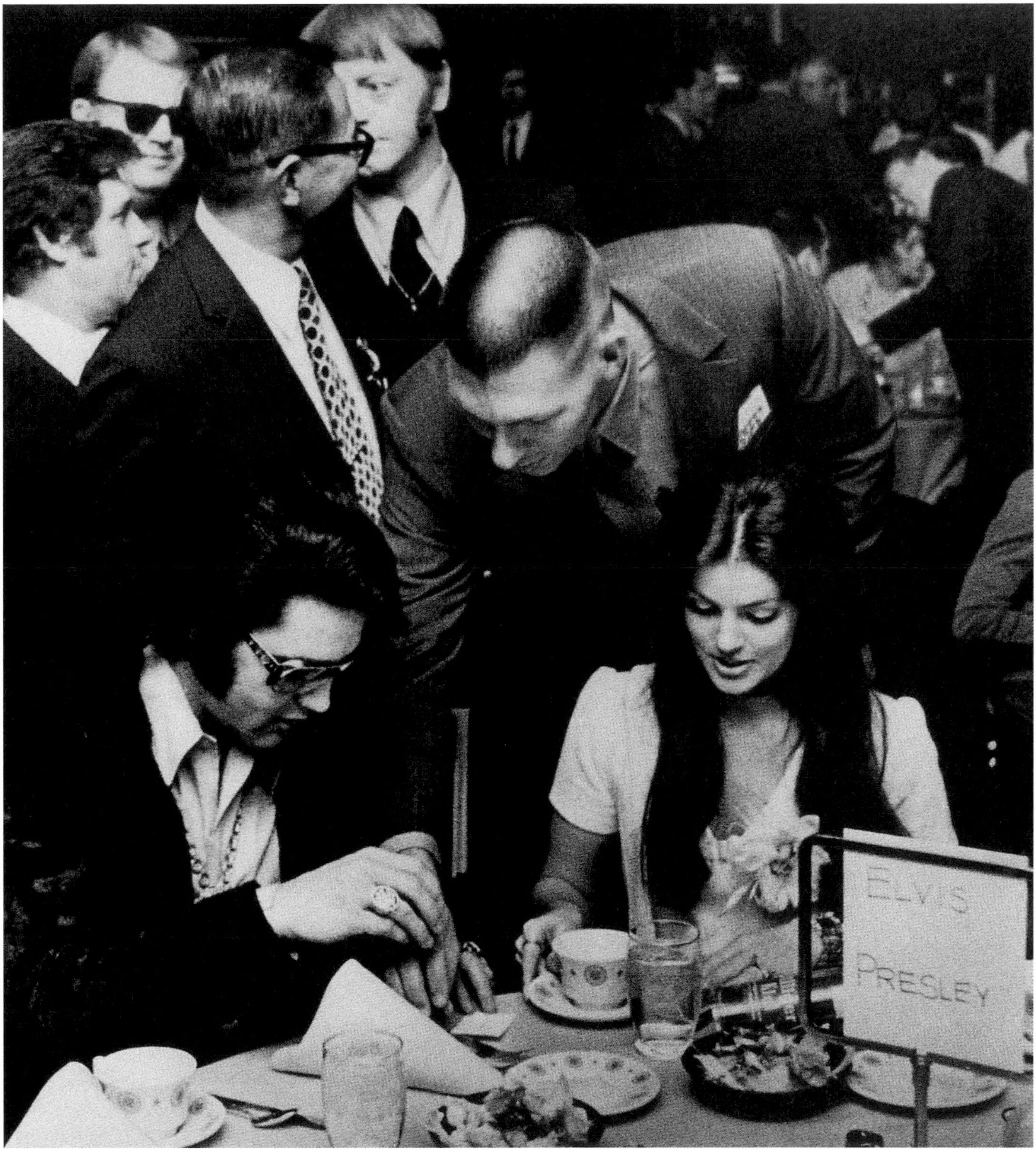

1971

1971 ELLIS AUDITORIUM Elvis and Priscilla attended the closed-circuit broadcast of the first Ali-Frazier fight at Memphis' Ellis Auditorium on March 8, 1971. Elvis wore his Jaycee Award medallion and a "championship" belt that had been presented to him in September 1970 for record attendances at the International Hotel, Las Vegas.

1971 THE "JAYCEE" AWARD Elvis and Priscilla at the "Jaycee" prayer breakfast, January 16, where Elvis spotted Sam Phillips' former office manager Marion Keisker. It was she who had encouraged Elvis to make his first recording tests at the Sun studios. He rushed over to her and introduced her to Priscilla, declaring that "without her I wouldn't be here."

1971

➊ ➋ **1971 THE "JAYCEE" AWARD** Elvis' award speech ran: "When I was a child, ladies and gentlemen, I was a dreamer. I read comic books, and I was the hero of the comic book. I saw movies, and I was the hero of the movie. So every dream that I ever dreamed has come true a hundred times. These gentlemen over here, these are the type who care, are dedicated. You realize that if it's not possible they might be building the kingdom, it's not far-fetched from reality. I'd like to say that I learned very early in life that 'Without a song the day would never end / Without a song a man ain't got a friend / Without a song the road would never bend / Without a song' So I keep singing a song. Good night. Thank you."

1970

1970 ALL THE KING'S MEN During 1970 Elvis became more and more interested in police work, receiving many deputy badges from sheriffs' offices. After getting one such badge from Shelby County Sheriff Roy Nixon, Elvis acquired them for his entire entourage. Here, displaying their badges after Sonny West's wedding in December, is one of the most complete pictures of the so-called "Memphis Mafia"– plus local law officers. *(Standing, left to right:)* Billy Smith, former Sheriff Bill Morris, Lamar Fike, Jerry Schilling, Sheriff Roy Nixon, Vernon Presley, Charlie Hodge, Sonny West, George Klein, and Marty Lacker. *(Front, left to right)* Dr. George Nichopolous, Elvis, and Red West.

c1974 ON THE ROAD Another city, another hotel. Leaving with Elvis, on the way to another concert, are Jerry Schilling (to Elvis' right), Joe Esposito (behind Schilling), Red West (behind Elvis), and Dick Grob (to Elvis' left). All were regular members of the entourage that traveled with him everywhere.

1974

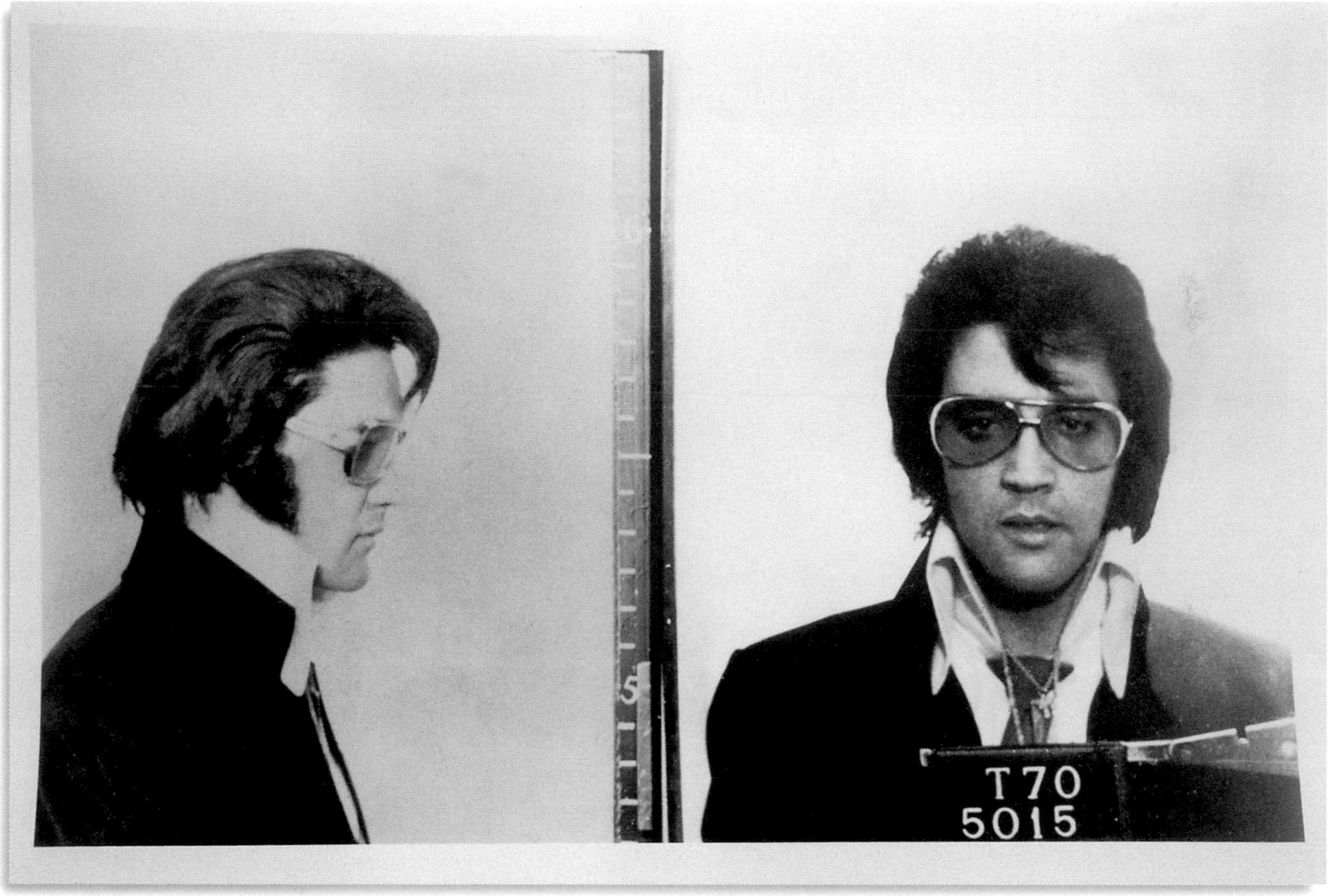

1975 CALIFORNIA Elvis astride one of his beloved Harleys outside the gates of his West Coast California home in Hillcrest Street, Bel Air. During and after his movie-making period, Elvis spent a lot more time on the West Coast than he had done previously, but Memphis and Graceland remained his permanent base and home.

1970 "MUG SHOTS" After making friends with the off-duty policemen assigned by the local law enforcement to protect him, Elvis poses straight-faced in these "mug shots" taken for an honorary police badge with which he was presented in Denver, Colorado, before playing the Coliseum there on November 17.

1970

PHOENIX

1970s

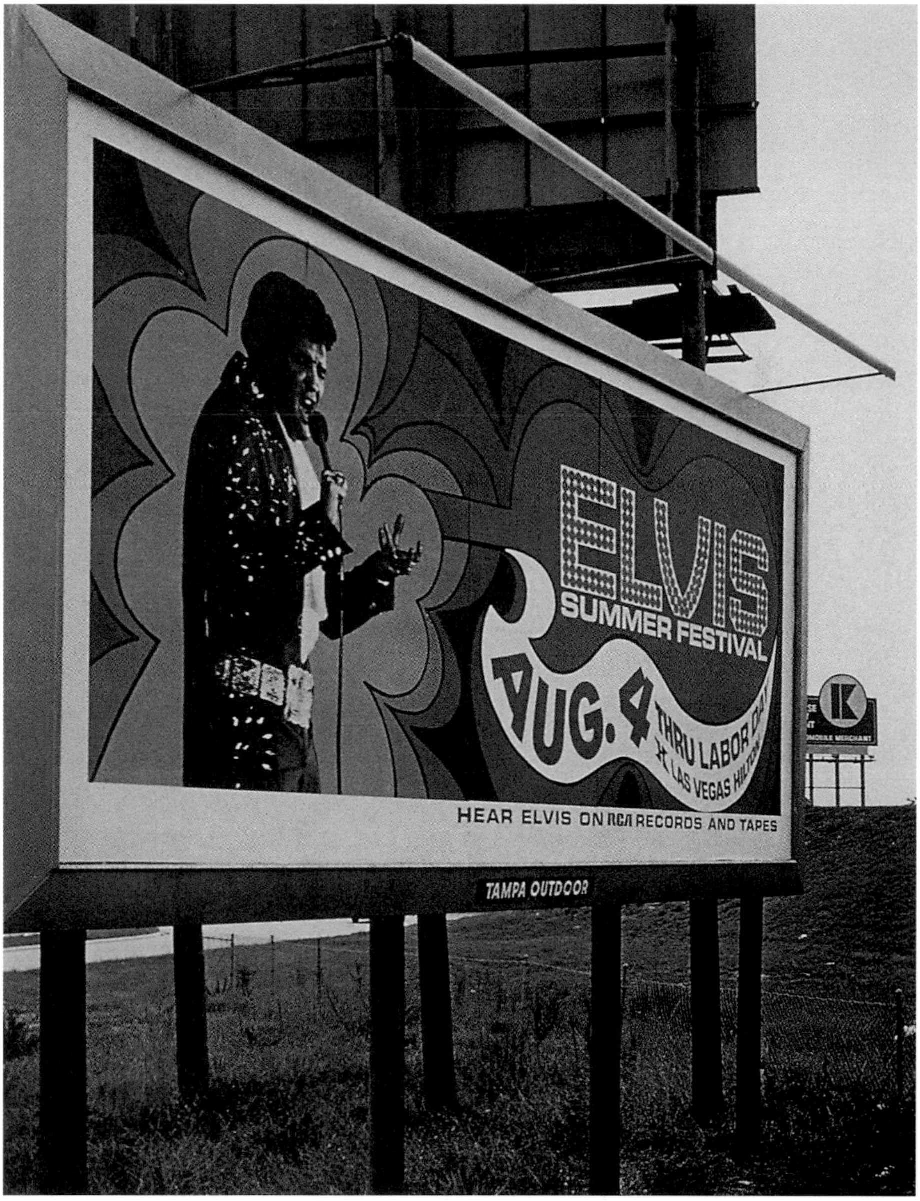

1970 PHOENIX, ARIZONA September 9: Elvis and the Colonel disembark from an aircraft at Phoenix, Arizona, at the beginning of a six-day "pilot" tour arranged by the Colonel during his season at Las Vegas. Parts of the concert at the Phoenix Coliseum were filmed by MGM for the documentary *Elvis: That's The Way It Is.*

1972 BILLBOARDS, LAS VEGAS One of the most spectacular sights when driving into Las Vegas from the Nevada desert is the huge array of billboards that announce current attractions as you approach the entertainment capital. The Elvis concerts held there during the 1972 "Summer Festival" were always prominently advertised in this way.

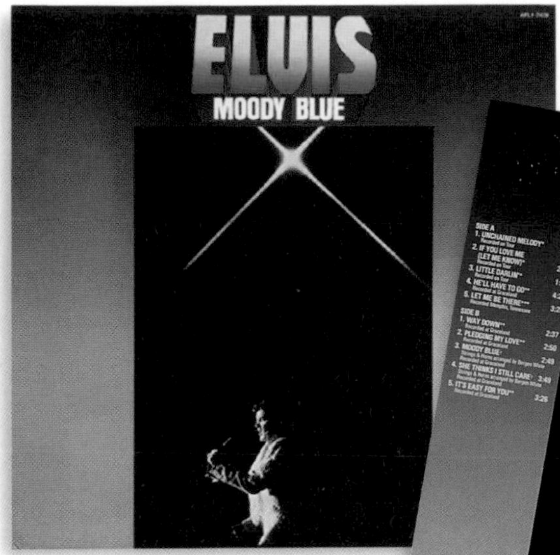

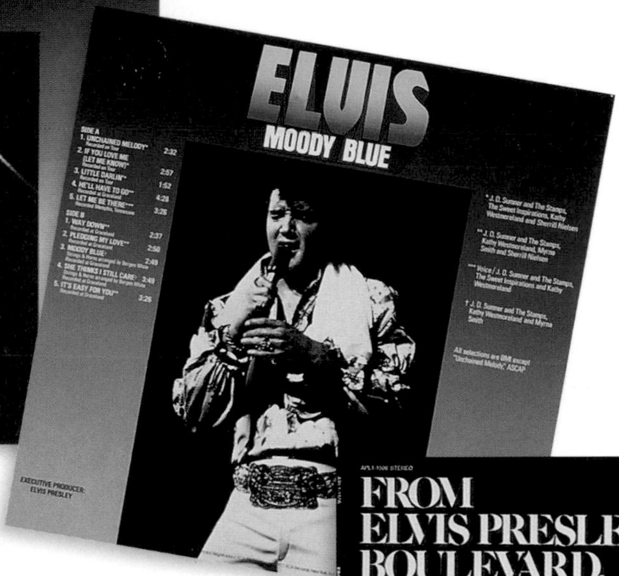

1970s THE RECORDS Through the Seventies, Elvis kept up his output of albums and singles, recorded both in the studio and live on the road. Memorable among them was the single "Steamroller Blues," taken from his *Aloha From Hawaii* LP (1973), *Back In Memphis* (1970, half of the 1969 double album), *Elvis as Recorded at Madison Square Garden* (1972), *From Elvis Presley Boulevard, Memphis Tennessee* (recorded in 1976 in the Jungle Room at Graceland), and the penultimate Elvis album released during his lifetime, *Moody Blue* (1977).

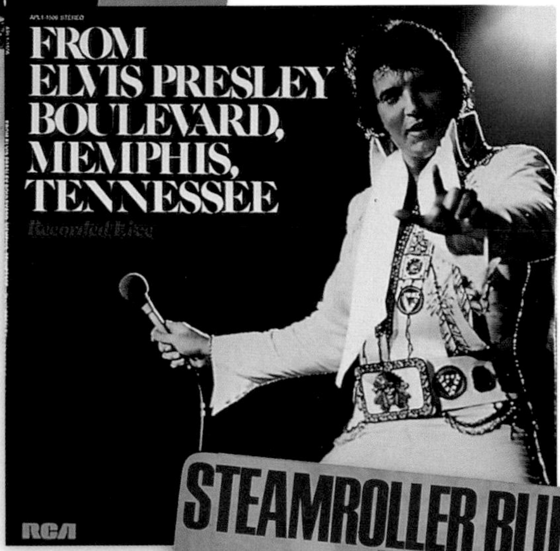

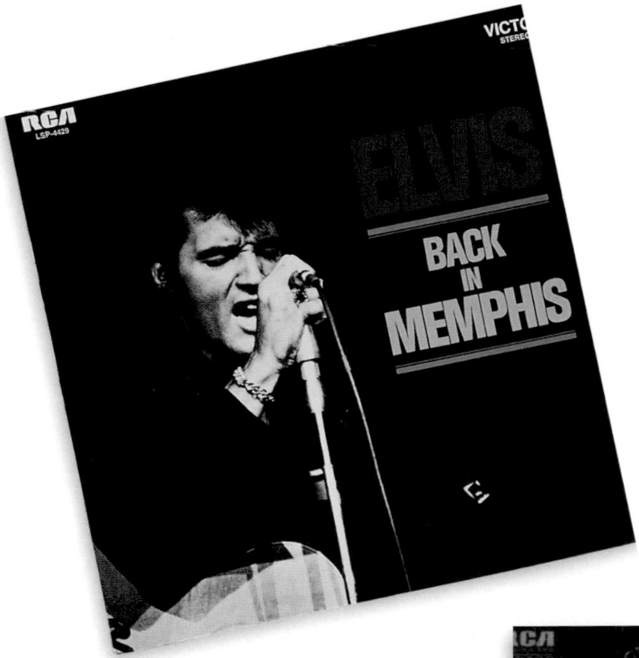

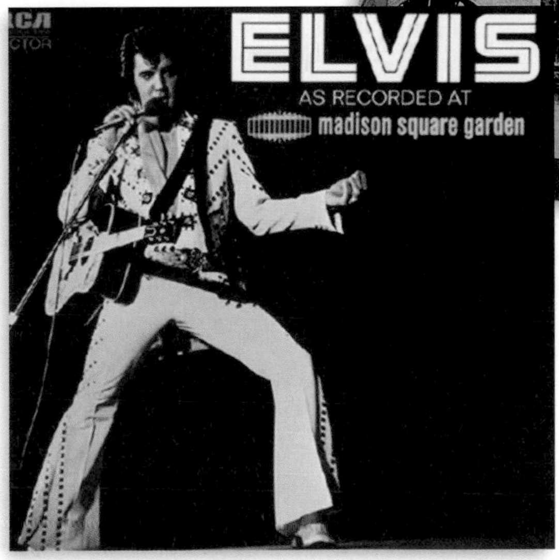

1976 ON STAGE For many of his touring dates between March and September that year, Elvis wore what became known as his "bicentennial" jumpsuit, designed by Bill Belew to mark the US bicentennial year. The patriotic tone of the red-white-and-blue outfit was emphasized by the number that was the highlight of many of the shows, a rendition of "America The Beautiful." During this period, the physical toll of the touring was beginning to show in many live performances.

1972 CAPES The famous capes (*also see over*) first appeared in the early Seventies. They got heavier and more unwieldy as they were encrusted with more metal and rhinestone studs, and were phased out by 1975 when it became apparent that more and more fans were grabbing at them, threatening in some instances to pull Elvis off stage.

The capes shown opposite were captured on film during the spring of 1972 in the *Elvis On Tour* movie; the image above is from Honolulu in November. *Elvis On Tour*, which opened November 1, was the second MGM documentary to follow Elvis on the road, emphasizing the dynamics of touring with candid shots and effective split-screen sequences.

1972

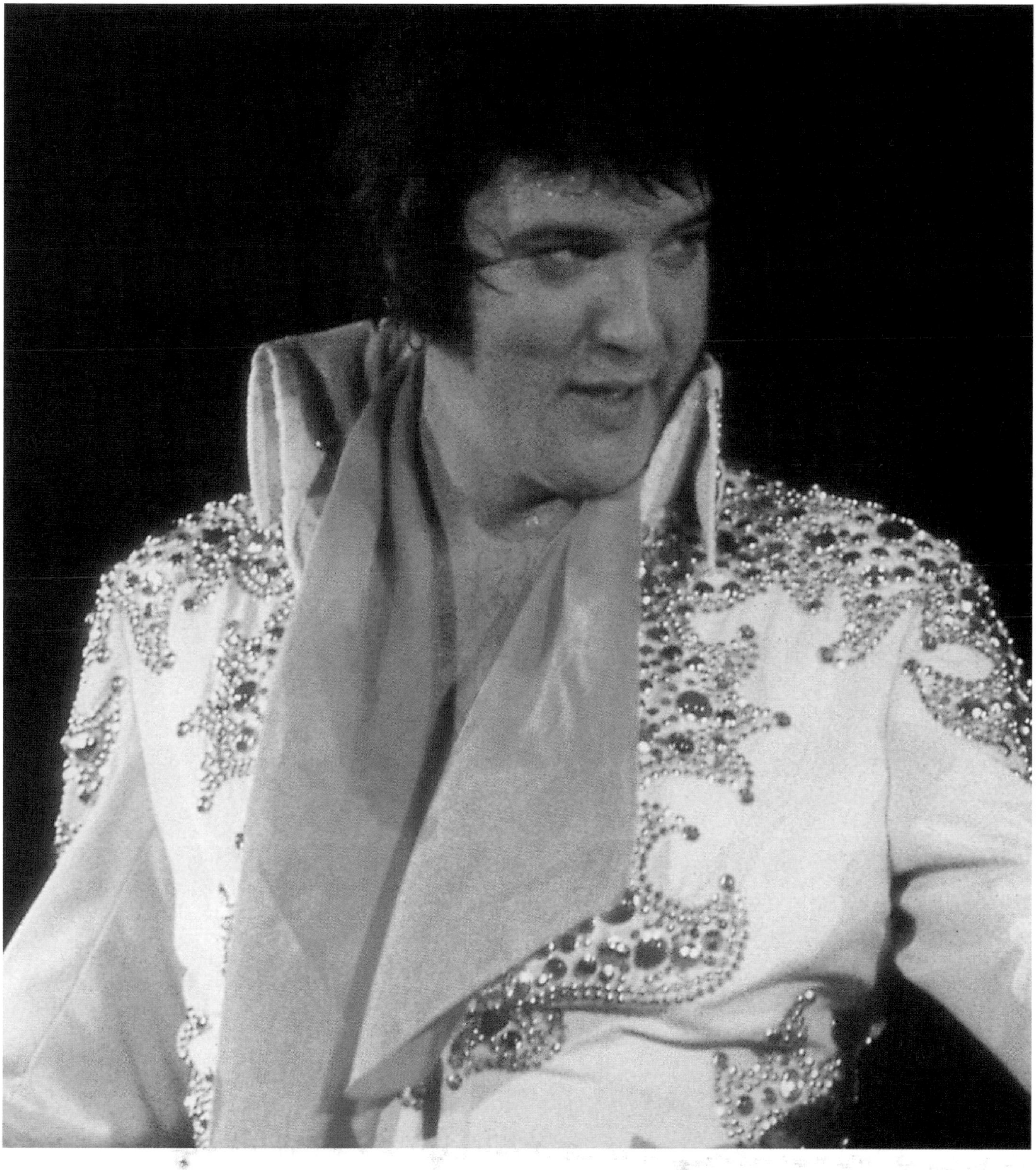

c1974 **SCARVES** A feature of Elvis' stage dress–which can be seen in the documentary movie *Elvis On Tour*–scarves had become another fashion accessory during the live shows. In February 1973 the movie itself was honored with a prestigious Golden Globe Award, co-winner with the film *Wheels of Fire* as the best feature documentary of 1972.

1972

1973

1973 ALOHA Elvis made television history with the "Elvis: Aloha From Hawaii Via Satellite" special. He appeared at the International Center Arena in Honolulu on January 14. The show was broadcast live at 12.30 AM Hawaiian time, and via the innovative Globecam satellite link-up it was seen live in Australia, Japan, Thailand, South Korea, South Vietnam, the Philippines, and other territories. It was also seen on a time-delay basis in another 30 countries across Europe. It was not seen in the US until April 4, when, with 57% of the nation's television audience tuned in, it was seen in more US households than the live transmissions of man's first walk on the Moon.

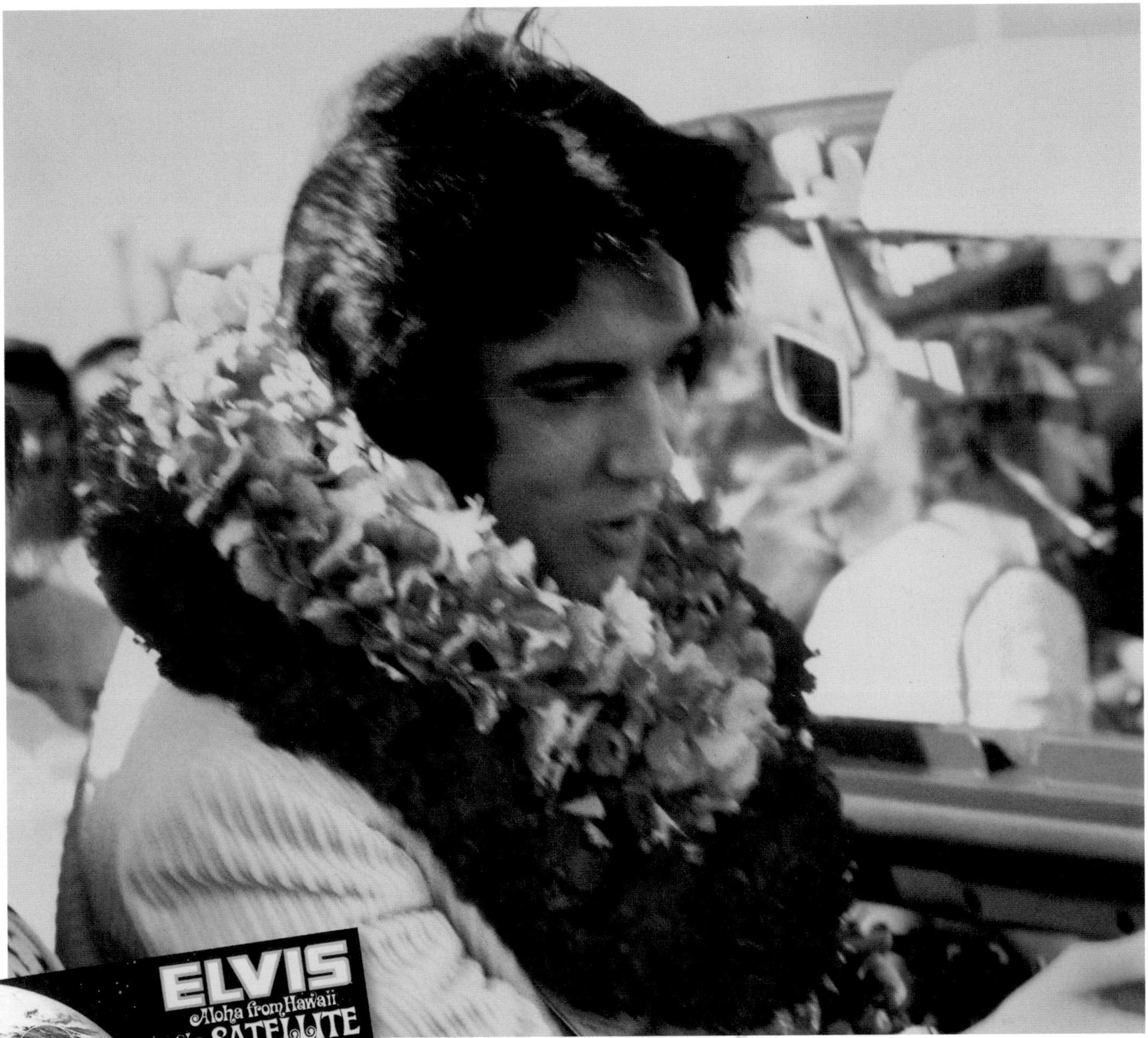

1973 ALOHA ALBUM The double LP from the "Aloha" broadcast made record industry history when it became the first-ever album to be released simultaneously worldwide. As a failsafe mechanism, in case anything had gone wrong with the broadcast, almost the entire set of 21 numbers (plus the "2001" theme) was recorded in two separate shows.

AR ELVIS
A RECORDS
DENMARK
MEXICO
SWEDE
NORWAY
FRANCE
ARGENTINA
PHILLIPPINES
KOREA

1972 LAS VEGAS Between Elvis' dinner and midnight shows at the Las Vegas Hilton on September 4, the Colonel organized a press conference at which Elvis and RCA Records president Rocco Laginestra (*above*) announced the *Aloha From Hawaii* broadcast planned for January 14. The familiar Hilton straw boaters were displayed, this time emblazoned with the names of the countries that the satellite link-up was going to reach. It would be seen by an estimated 1.4 billion viewers in total. Elvis sounded astounded by the scale of the broadcast and simultaneous worldwide album release, but concluded "It's my favorite part of the business, a live concert."

1972

1973

1973 ALOHA JUMPSUIT The regular jumpsuit designer Bill Belew was called by Elvis with a request for something special for the planned worldwide "Aloha From Hawaii" broadcast. He said he wanted something that would represent the US. The designer decided that, apart from the Stars and Stripes, all he could think of was the American eagle–so the spectacular eagle, outlined in studs on the front and back of the Aloha jumpsuit, was born. At the end of the broadcast show, Elvis flung both his belt and the jewel-laden "eagle" cape into the audience, providing one of the highlights of a sensational performance. The image above was shot straight from a TV screen.

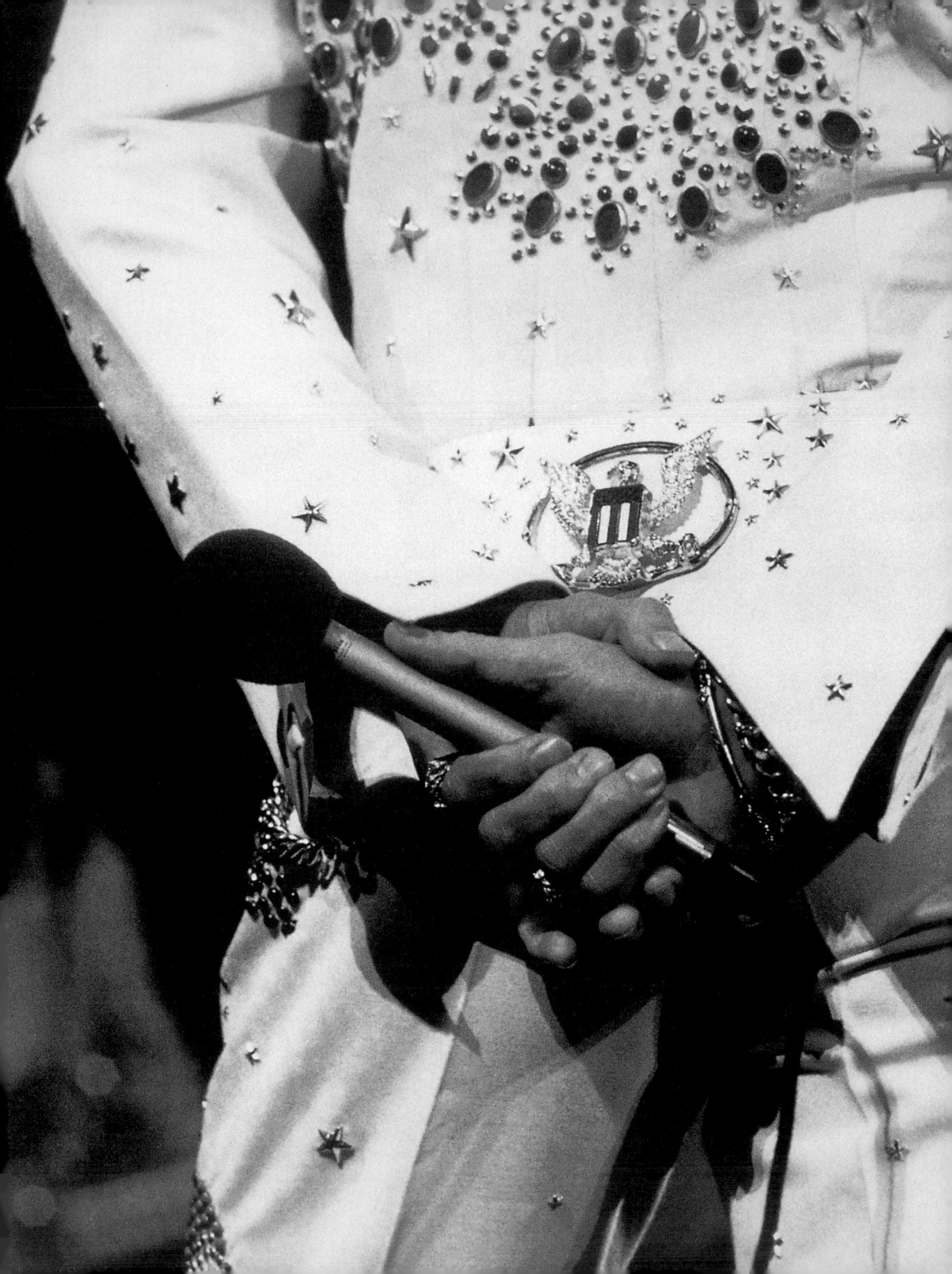

1973 ALOHA A back detail of the Aloha "eagle" suit. The show was a fund-raising event for the Kui Lee Cancer Fund (Kui Lee was a Hawiian composer who had died of cancer while still in his thirties). During the broadcast, Elvis was delighted to announce that they had raised $75,000 from audience donations at the show.

1975 HUNTSVILLE, ALABAMA A June 1 concert during his April–July tour this year, Elvis–clearly starting to gain weight–is wearing what was referred to as the "blue phoenix" jumpsuit. All the Bill Belew outfits acquired specific names, dreamed up originally by the fans, though many outfits were given more than one name in this way.

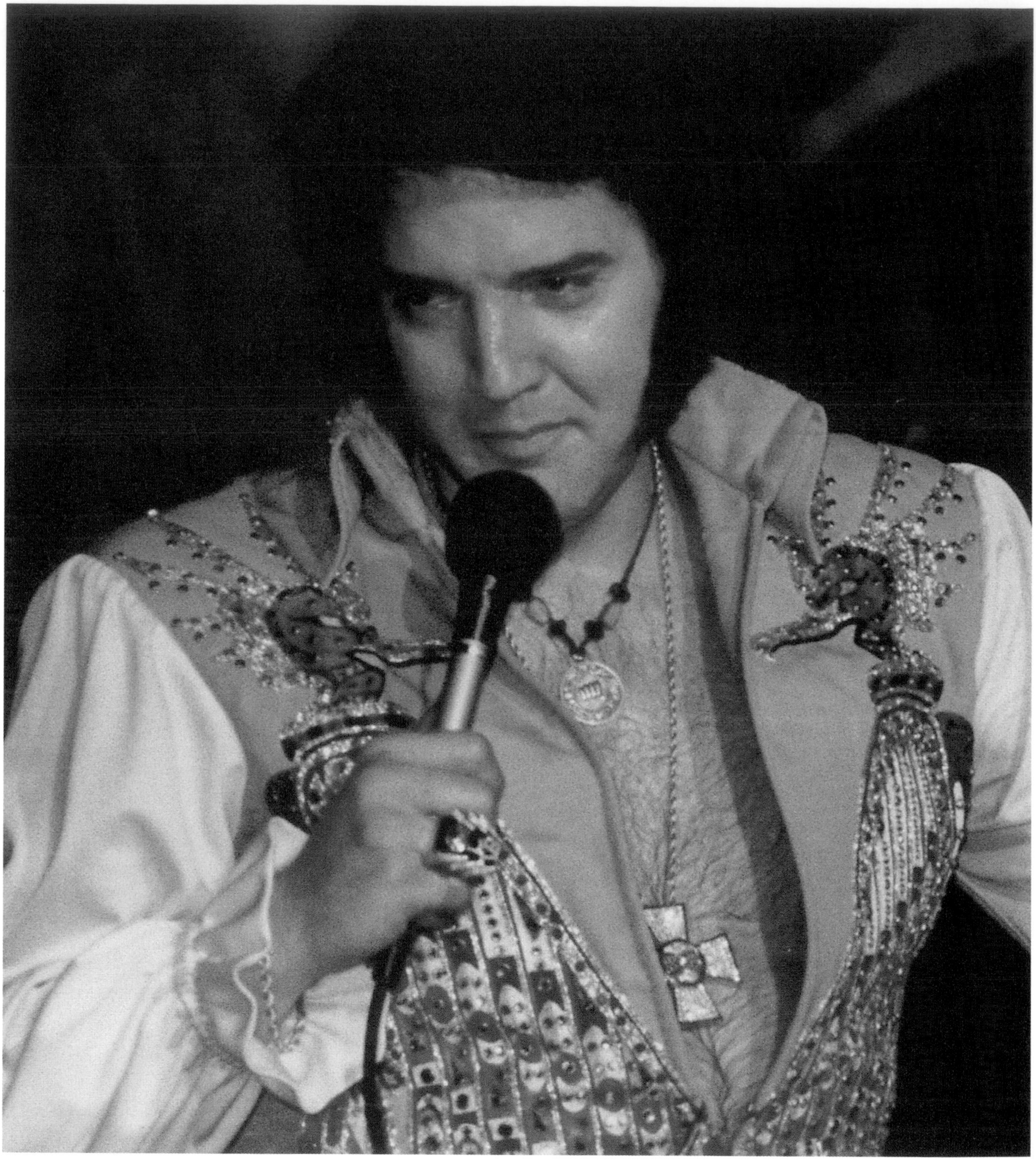

1970s

⬆ **1976 ON STAGE** During the bicentennial year tour, Elvis is photographed wearing the bicentennial "twin birds" jumpsuit. Given the very physically demanding nature of his stage routines, it's not surprising that the heavy rhinestone-studded suits had given way to the lighter embroidered oufits by the mid-Seventies.

➡ **1977 "AZTEC" JUMPSUIT** The very last jumpsuit that Elvis was to wear on stage was the Mexican-inspired "sundial" suit, with its gold Aztec-style calendar design on the front and back, which he wore for the entire 13 days of his May–June tour. Some of this tour was filmed for a CBS television special.

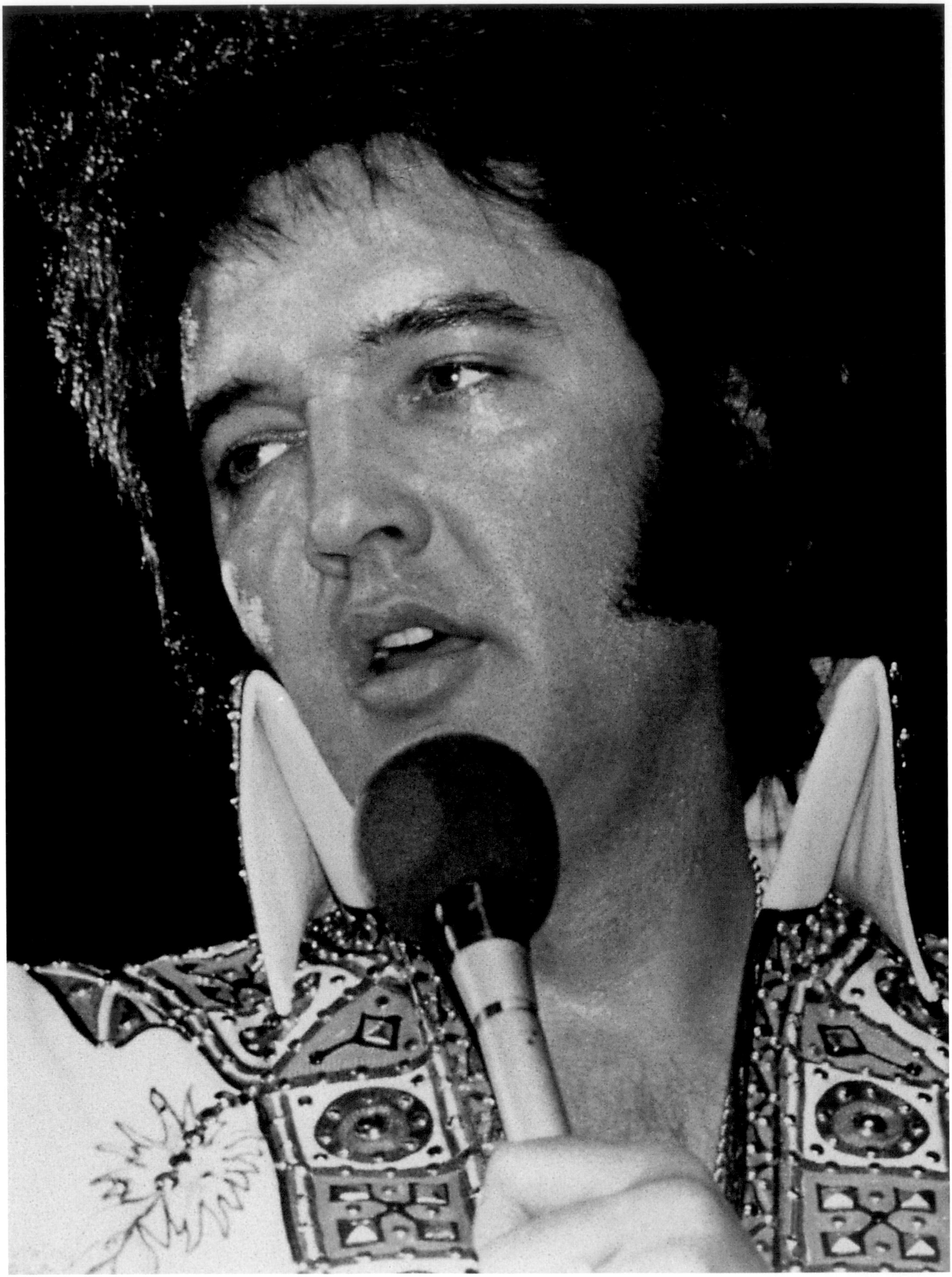

1975 "AMERICAN INDIAN" JUMPSUIT Through the Seventies, Elvis' jumpsuits just got more and more flamboyant. The elaborate embroidery on this particular outfit incorporated elements of Native American design and culture, hence the name of the outfit most often used by Elvis afficianados to describe it.

1970 WEBBED JUMPSUIT This photograph shows the webbed jumpsuit that Elvis had made, worn during the Fall concert dates of 1970. This early example of the jumpsuit fashion predates his outfits that featured a cape, instead having a web of fabric from sleeve to torso with a long fringe hanging from the web.

1975

1975 "BLACK PHOENIX" JUMPSUIT Identical to the "blue phoenix" outfit, except for a different color combination, Elvis appeared in the "black phoenix" jumpsuit on the same midyear tour in 1975. It was a period when his health was beginning to cause some concern among those close to him, and a short period of hospitalization was soon to follow.

1975 "GYPSY" JUMPSUIT For many of his performances during the tour dates in mid-1975–a period when he also seemed to be wearing more and more jewelry on stage–Elvis wore the so-called "gypsy" outfit. This shot is thought to have come from a concert appearance in Asheville, North Carolina, on July 23.

1974

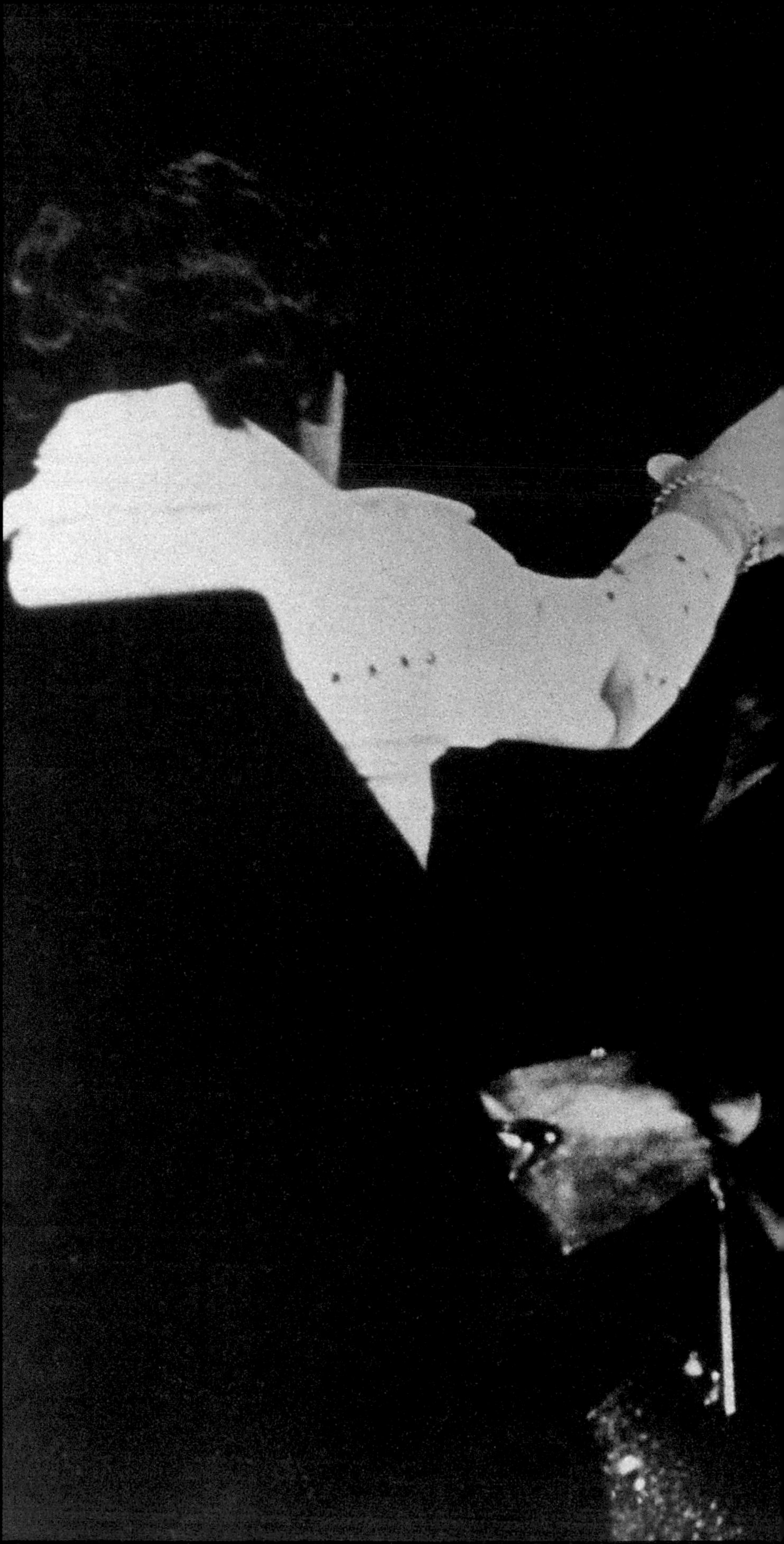

➔ **1974 ON TOUR** Elvis in the Seventies, during the last few years of his life, is typified by this shot of him reaching out with the guitar on stage. His life was music, and in this period, despite the lows that often followed the highs, he expressed that in the most direct way possible, and the way he knew best—performing in front of live audiences. When he decided to go back on the road at the beginning of the decade, it was a way of reaching out once more for that contact with his fans that he had enjoyed 10 years before. This communication with his public could never be achieved via a movie camera or studio microphone. During the last years of his life that contact was made once again, and, perhaps fittingly, that is how he is best remembered.

1977

1977 THE FINAL WAVE Thought to be the last ever picture of Elvis Presley alive, this candid shot was taken as he entered Graceland in a car on August 15, on his way from an evening dental appointment, and just hours before he was found dead the next day.

Epilogue

ELVIS LIVES: THE LEGEND CONTINUES

1957 **PHOTO PORTRAIT** This portrait is what used to be called a tinted photograph, a photo made to look like a painted portrait. For years it was thumbtacked to a wall in Vernon's office at Graceland, being framed and moved into the house itself when the tours began in 1982.

August 1977

August 1977

October 1977

Once on a scratchy acetate disc recording, "My Happiness" backed with "That's When Your Heartaches Begin"—made by Elvis at the Memphis Recording Service—now appear on the modern marvel of the digital compact disc, packaged with jewel-box care and elegantly designed with a postmodern knowingness of early-Fifties style. And true to the archivist fan's insistence on authenticity, this is no "cleaned up" job—the detail is there, hisses and all. But what astounds across the years is the detail of the 18-year-old voice, the purity of sound that someone once described as the "voice of an angel."

Strutting on stage at the Fort Homer Hesterly Armory in Tampa, Florida, in 1955, Elvis can be seen hitting that brand new Martin guitar, proclaiming his youth, reaching for the sky. That image burned in the imagination of millions, from the first 12-inch album cover through nearly 50 years of posters, postcards, theater programs, T-shirts, snow-globes, children's coloring books, lampshades, ballpoint pens, and pillowcases.

Down on Memphis' Beale Street, a young kid is casually leaning on a pink-and-white Cadillac outside of Lansky's clothing store, shirt collar turned up, with a draped jacket, cuffed pants and two-tone shoes in open imitation of the zoot-suit rhythm and blues singers who crackle across

August 1992

July 1992

August 1998

the airwaves from the car radio. Now 21st-century Beale has a whole nightspot dedicated to the kid, right where Lansky's used to be. Who'd have imagined it?

The lights dim, and as a hugely amplified rhythm section riffs an intro, a sudden spotlight reveals a virtual, almost holographic, image looming huge over the stage. Diamanté and rhinestone glint off the white jumpsuit with the flowing cape and high collar, jet black hair and sideburns as familiar as family. It's the Mid-South Coliseum in Memphis on August 16, 1997, and, 20 years after his death, Elvis is "back."

Through video images, and accompanied live on stage by over 30 of his former band-mates and the Memphis Symphony Orchestra, the concert became the prototype for the touring production *Elvis—The Concert*. By being the first performer ever to headline a live concert tour while no longer living, Elvis made history again. The 1998 tour included three shows at Radio City Music Hall in New York and Elvis' "return" to the Las Vegas Hilton. The 1999 European tour opened with a sellout at London's Wembley Arena and, in effect, marked Elvis' first-ever concerts outside of North America.

It looked like Elvis was back but like all true icons, he never really went away.

FORD
55

FINAL THE COMMERCIAL APPEAL FINAL

138th Year No. 229 Memphis, Tenn., Wednesday Morning, August 17, 1977

Death Captures Crown Of Rock And Roll
—Elvis Dies Apparently After Heart Attack

Memphis Press-Scimitar

SPECIAL EDITION

97TH YEAR MEMPHIS, TENN., WEDNESDAY, AUGUST 17, 1977

Memphis Leads the World in Mourning the Monarch of Rock 'n Roll

A Lonely Life Ends on Elvis Presley Boulevard

A Tribute to Elvis

Mourners In Waiting For Last Homecoming Of Revered Singer

1977 FUNERAL By the afternoon of Wednesday, August 17, as the news of Elvis' death had reverberated around the world, more than 50,000 fans had gathered outside the gates of Graceland as his body was returned from the Memphis Funeral Home, Vernon having arranged for it to be viewed by mourners in the hallway of the mansion. The funeral was held the next day, when the body was carried in a white hearse followed by a cortège of white limousines, to the Forest Hill Cemetery where after a short ceremony Elvis was interred in a crypt a few hundred yards from his mother's grave.

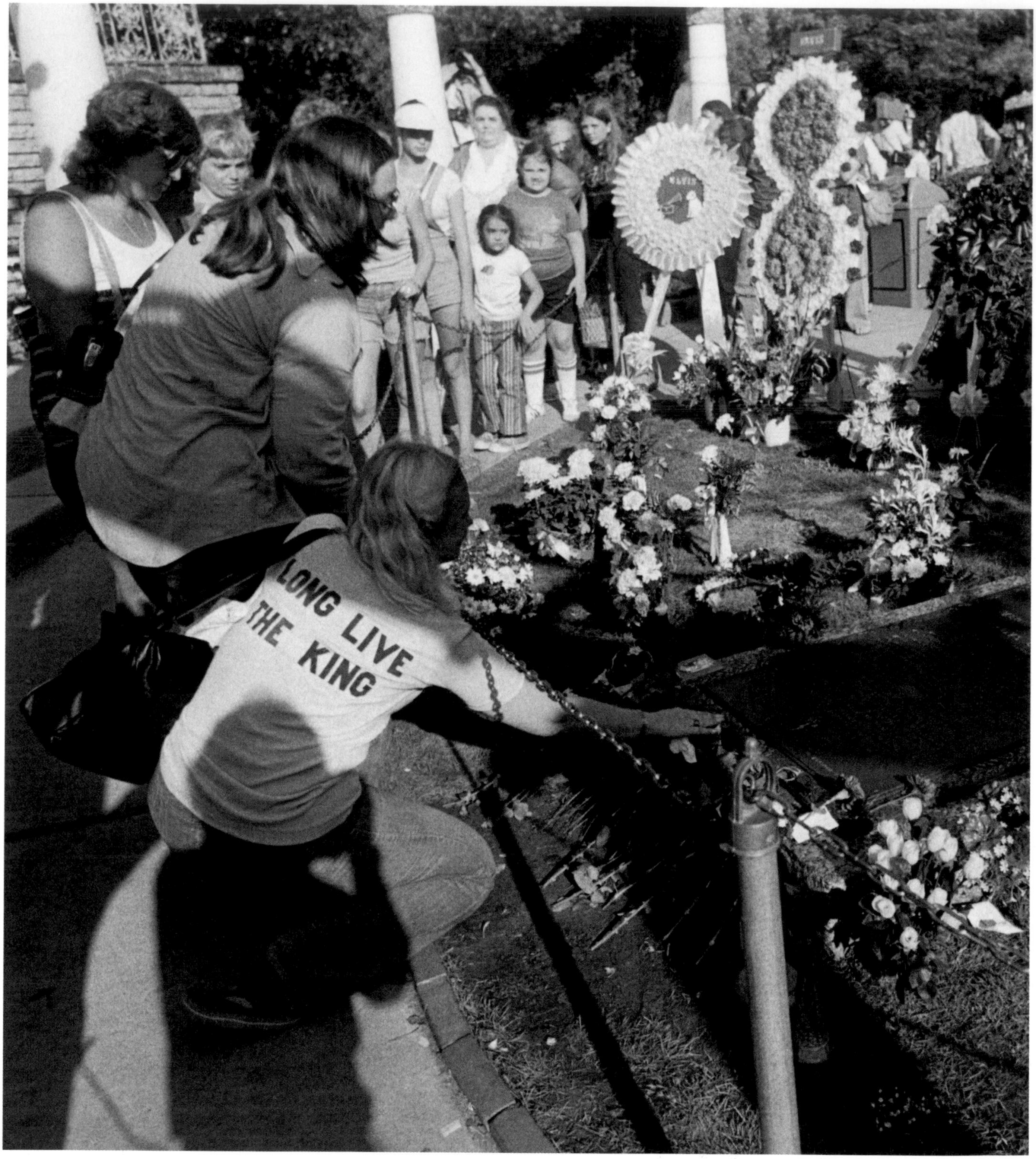

1977

⬆➡ 1977 **RESTING PLACE** On October 2, the bodies of both Elvis and his mother were moved–after Vernon had obtained special permission from the city authority–to the Meditation Garden on the south end of the Graceland mansion grounds, their final resting place. Fans then immediately treated it as a place of pilgrimage, which of course they still do today. Since then, grandmother Minnie and Vernon subsequently have died and they too were buried in the garden. In addition, there is a plaque to the memory of Elvis' twin brother Jesse Garon, who was stillborn and is actually buried in Tupelo, Mississippi.

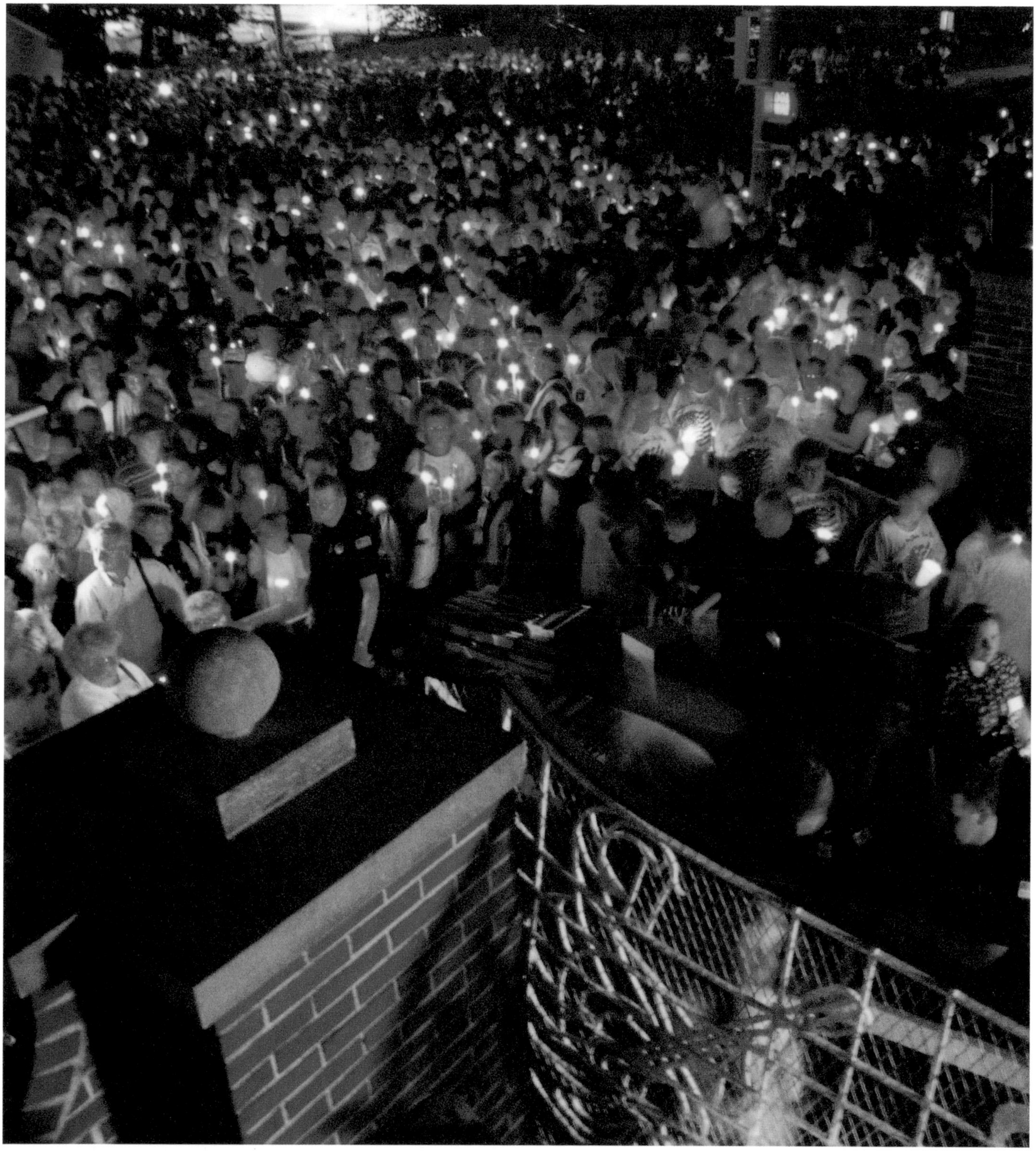

CANDLELIGHT VIGIL Every year, during Elvis Week in the middle of August, which commemorates the anniversary of Elvis' death, thousands of fans take part in the candlelight vigil that centers on the Meditation Garden at Graceland. After Gladys' and Elvis' bodies were moved to the garden, the original Presley family monument was relocated from the family's plot at the Forest Hill Cemetery to the Meditation Garden. With the stained glass windows at the back of the garden already having a reverential feel about them, the monument brought to the garden a sacred element that made it even more a focus of pilgrimage for fans over the years.

⊖ **1992 GRACELAND** Elvis Presley's home and refuge for 20 years, Graceland is one of the most visited homes in America today, attracting over 600,000 visitors annually. It is also the most famous home in America after the White House. In 1991, Graceland mansion was placed on the National Register of Historic Places.

⊕ **1992 MEDITATION** The Meditation Garden was originally inspired by Elvis' interest in various Eastern philosophies during the Sixties, and was built under his personal supervision. The garden was never intended as a place of burial; it was simply a quiet retreat where he enjoyed periods of solitude or engaged in private conversation.

SOME GO TO
WE GO TO
GRACEL
FOR OUR
PILGRIMAG

1992

1992 **GRAFFITI** Ever since Elvis had it built in 1957, people have been writing graffiti on the Alabama flintstone wall that runs along the front of the Graceland property on Elvis Presley Boulevard (Highway 51), and the writing has become more dense in the years since Elvis' death. Originally the messages were of the "I Love You" and "My Phone No is"... variety. Since his death they have been more along the lines of tributes. A pressured water system is used by the Graceland staff to thin out the writing from time to time. Writing on the wall, like posing for a photograph outside the famous gates, has become part of the ritual of visiting the mansion for many fans.

Heartbreak Hotel
RESTAURANT

1990s MERCHANDISE Still the merchandise appears. As with these dolls, the representation of Elvis spans all the iconic phases of his life, from the early rock'n'roll period of the Fifties to the jumpsuit "Las Vegas" image of the Seventies.

1992 HEARTBREAK HOTEL Right across the highway from the Graceland mansion, in the visitors reception area, which also includes the automobile museum, Elvis' private aircraft, and various souvenir shops, stands the 128-room Elvis Presley's Heartbreak Hotel and Restaurant. The neon sign (*at left*) now occupies a spot in the Graceland Visitor Center. Another development and popular visitor attraction, and right in the heart of downtown Memphis, is Elvis Presley's Memphis restaurant and nightspot, a huge entertainment complex right on the corner of Second Street and Beale, on the site that was once Lansky's clothing store where Elvis used to shop.

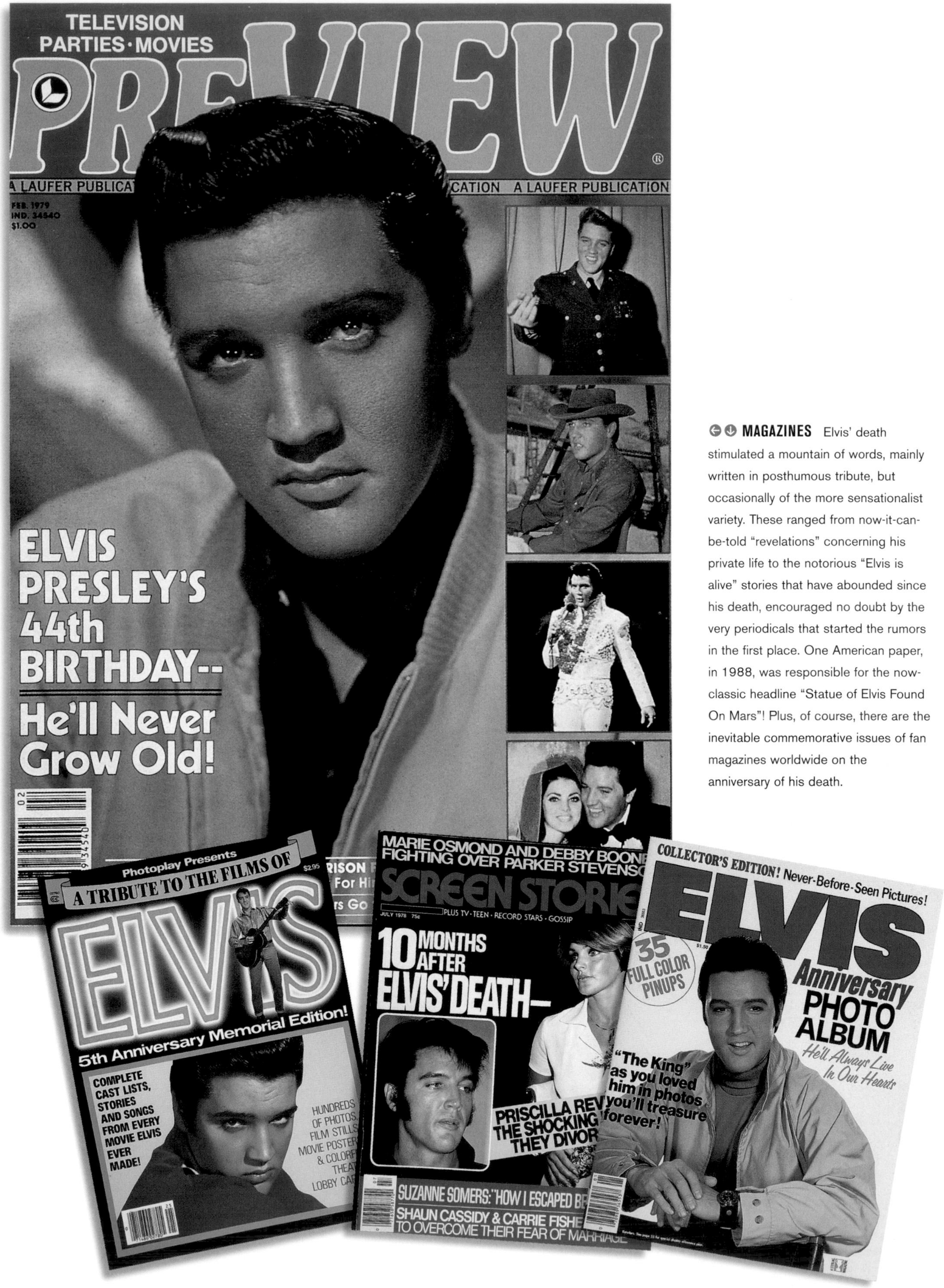

MAGAZINES Elvis' death stimulated a mountain of words, mainly written in posthumous tribute, but occasionally of the more sensationalist variety. These ranged from now-it-can-be-told "revelations" concerning his private life to the notorious "Elvis is alive" stories that have abounded since his death, encouraged no doubt by the very periodicals that started the rumors in the first place. One American paper, in 1988, was responsible for the now-classic headline "Statue of Elvis Found On Mars"! Plus, of course, there are the inevitable commemorative issues of fan magazines worldwide on the anniversary of his death.

1973/1992 PROMOTION AND PACKAGING With the entire Elvis Presley back catalog at their disposal, along with the thousands of pictures and artwork promulgated throughout his career, RCA Records have been able to come up with a huge variety of material in the promotion and packaging of vinyl discs, tapes, and CDs. These two examples which now constitute Elvis memorabilia, are the calendar-cards produced in 1973 (*left*) and the spectacular sheet of souvenir stamps featuring record sleeves from the 1950s which was included in the *King of Rock'n'Roll: Complete 50s Masters* box set of CDs released in 1992.

1981

➲ **1981 THIS IS ELVIS** A row of posters advertising the showing of the drama-documentary film released in 1981 "This Is Elvis," in which authentic footage was spliced in with actors to form a collage picture of Elvis' life, done with the approval of the Elvis Presley Estate. The film starts just before Elvis' death with Johnny Harra acting as Elvis; then a series of flashbacks trace his career with the aid of news film, clips from TV shows and such, as well as more dramatized scenes from his personal life.

THIS IS ELVIS
Selections from the Original Motion Picture Soundtrack

1993

29
USA
ROCK & ROLL SINGER, 1935-1977
ELVIS
INTERNATIONAL COLLECTORS SOCIETY
CERTIFICATE OF AUTHENTICITY
This certifies that the accompanied Elvis Presley Stamps are official, legal tender postage stamps issued by the Government of St. Vincent, recognized by every Postal Authority around the world. The number below has been assigned to these stamps, thus assuring their limited edition status.
ISSUE NUMBER B 3325

1993 ELVIS STAMPS In 1992, the US Postal Service announced that they were planning to use Elvis' image for a commemorative stamp. They narrowed the artwork choices down to two images–one of Elvis in the 1950s as a young rocker, and one of him as a still-svelte concert superstar in his 1973 "Aloha from Hawaii" special. In an unprecedented move, the USPS organized a ballot across America and distributed forms from coast to coast. Over 1.2 million votes were cast, and the image of the younger Elvis won. The stamp was released on January 8, 1993, with first day of issue ceremonies held at Graceland. The Elvis stamp is the top selling commemorative postage stamp of all time. Five hundred million were printed, three times the usual print run for a commemorative stamp. Several countries outside the USA also have issued Elvis stamps over the years, such as those opposite from the Caribbean island of St. Vincent, confirming his continuing status as a truly universal icon.

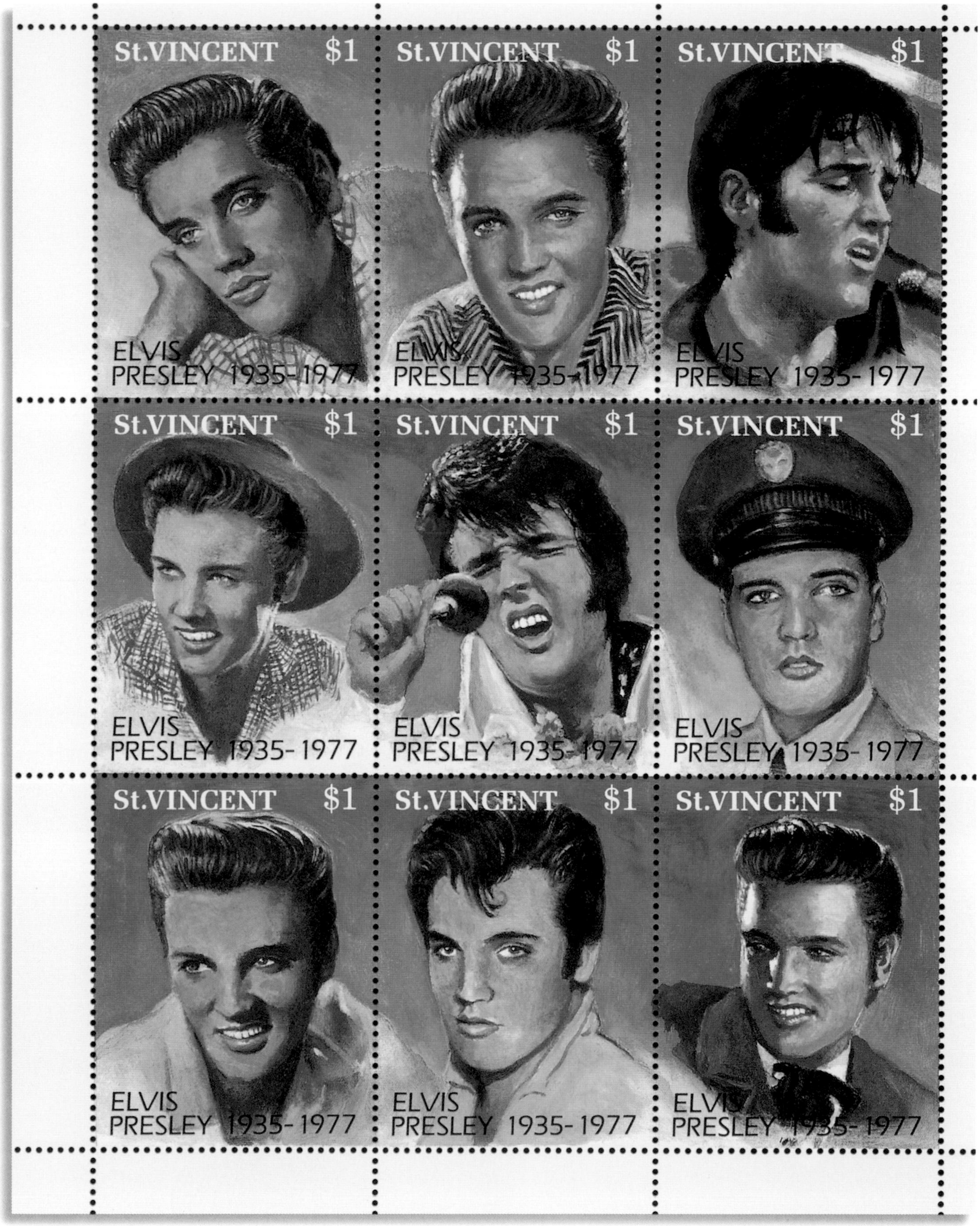
St.VINCENT $1
ELVIS PRESLEY 1935-1977
St.VINCENT $1
ELVIS PRESLEY 1935-1977
St.VINCENT $1
ELVIS PRESLEY 1935-1977
St.VINCENT $1
ELVIS PRESLEY 1935-1977
St.VINCENT $1
ELVIS PRESLEY 1935-1977
St.VINCENT $1
ELVIS PRESLEY 1935-1977
St.VINCENT $1
ELVIS PRESLEY 1935-1977
St.VINCENT $1
ELVIS PRESLEY 1935-1977
St.VINCENT $1
ELVIS PRESLEY 1935-1977

Appendices

1956 LOVE ME TENDER A studio publicity shot used during the promotion of Elvis' first movie *Love Me Tender*. Although only a matter of months into his success as a major recording star, the picture established him as a multi-media entertainer on the concert stage, records, television, and the cinema screen–a pattern that would continue throughout his career.

Facts, figures, and statistics on the life of Elvis

RECORD SALES

It is estimated that Elvis Presley has sold over one billion record units worldwide, more than anyone in record industry history. In the US alone, Elvis has had 131 different albums and singles that have been certified gold, platinum, or multi-platinum by the Recording Industry Association of America (RIAA), with more certifications expected as research into his past record sales continues and as current sales go on. Research is also underway to document his record sales achievements in other countries. It is estimated that 40% of Elvis' total record sales have been outside the United States.

ELVIS' GOLD AND PLATINUM DISC AWARDS

The list below—as of August 1999, when the last presentation was made—is of Elvis albums, singles, and extended-plays the American sales of which had received gold, platinum, or multi-platinum designations from the Recording Industry Association of America (RIAA). Sales required are 500,000 copies for a gold single or album, 1 million copies for a platinum single or album. *(For double or multiple disc albums/CD packages, each disc's sales are counted, so a five-CD box selling 100,000 copies would count as 5x100,000 and go gold.)*

64 ALBUMS

Elvis Presley – GOLD
Elvis – GOLD
Loving You – GOLD
Elvis' Christmas Album (1957 Package) – PLATINUM (x3)
King Creole – GOLD
Elvis' Golden Records Vol. 1 – PLATINUM (x6)
50,000,000 Elvis Fans Can't Be Wrong (Elvis' Gold Records Vol. 2) – PLATINUM
Elvis Is Back – GOLD
G.I. Blues – PLATINUM
His Hand In Mine – PLATINUM
Something For Everybody – GOLD
Blue Hawaii – PLATINUM (x2)
Girls! Girls! Girls! – GOLD
Elvis' Golden Records Vol. 3 – PLATINUM
Roustabout – GOLD
Girl Happy – GOLD
How Great Thou Art – PLATINUM (x2)
Elvis, NBC TV Special – PLATINUM
Elvis' Gold Records, Vol. 4 – GOLD
Elvis Sings Flaming Star – GOLD
From Elvis In Memphis – GOLD
Elvis: From Memphis to Vegas, From Vegas to Memphis – GOLD
On Stage, February 1970 – PLATINUM
Worldwide 50 Gold Award Hits – PLATINUM (x2)
Elvis' Christmas Album (1970 Package) – PLATINUM (x6)
Elvis, That's The Way It Is – GOLD
Elvis In Person At The International Hotel – GOLD
Elvis Country – GOLD
Elvis: The Other Sides; 50 Gold Award Hits, Vol. 2 – GOLD
You'll Never Walk Alone – PLATINUM
Elvis Sings The Wonderful World Of Christmas – PLATINUM (x3)
Elvis Now – GOLD
He Touched Me – PLATINUM
Elvis As Recorded At Madison Square Garden – PLATINUM (x3)
Elvis Sings Burning Love And Hits From His Movies, Vol. 2 – PLATINUM
Separate Ways – GOLD
Aloha From Hawaii – PLATINUM (x3)
Elvis, A Legendary Performer, Vol. 1 – PLATINUM (x2)
Elvis Recorded Live On Stage In Memphis – GOLD
Pure Gold – PLATINUM (x2)
Elvis, A Legendary Performer, Vol. 2 – PLATINUM (x2)
From Elvis Presley Boulevard, Memphis, Tennessee – GOLD
Welcome To My World – PLATINUM
Moody Blue – PLATINUM (x2)
Elvis In Concert – PLATINUM
He Walks Beside Me – GOLD
Elvis, A Legendary Performer, Vol. 3 – GOLD
Memories Of Elvis – GOLD
Elvis Aaron Presley – PLATINUM
Memories Of Christmas – GOLD
The Number One Hits – PLATINUM (x2)
The Top Ten Hits – PLATINUM (x3)
Elvis, The King Of Rock 'n' Roll, The Complete 50's Masters – PLATINUM
Elvis, From Nashville To Memphis, The Essential 60's Masters I – GOLD
Elvis: His Greatest Hits (Reader's Digest Compilation) – GOLD
Blue Christmas – GOLD
Elvis' Golden Records, Vol. 5 – GOLD
Amazing Grace – GOLD
If Everyday Was Like Christmas – GOLD
Walk A Mile In My Shoes, The Essential 70's Masters – GOLD
50 Years – 50 Hits – PLATINUM
Worldwide Gold Award Hits, Vols. 1 & 2 (club version) – PLATINUM
The Elvis Presley Story – PLATINUM (x2)
Elvis Gospel Treasury – GOLD

51 SINGLES

Heartbreak Hotel/I Was the One – PLATINUM (x2)
Blue Suede Shoes/Tutti Frutti – GOLD
I Want You, I Need You, I Love You/My Baby Left Me – PLATINUM
Hound Dog/Don't Be Cruel – PLATINUM (x4)
Love Me Tender/Any Way You Want Me – PLATINUM (x3)
Too Much/Playing For Keeps – PLATINUM
All Shook Up/That's When Your Heartaches Begin – PLATINUM (x2)
(Let Me Be Your) Teddy Bear/Loving You – PLATINUM (x2)

Jailhouse Rock/
Treat Me Nice – PLATINUM (x2)
Don't/I Beg Of You – PLATINUM
Wear My Ring Around Your Neck/
Doncha Think It's Time – PLATINUM
Hard Headed Woman/
Don't Ask Me Why – PLATINUM
I Got Stung/One Night – PLATINUM
(Now and Then There's) A Fool
Such as I/I Need Your
Love Tonight – PLATINUM
A Big Hunk O' Love/
My Wish Came True – GOLD
Stuck on You/Fame and
Fortune – PLATINUM
It's Now Or Never/
A Mess Of Blues – PLATINUM
Are You Lonesome Tonight/
I Gotta Know – PLATINUM (x2)
Surrender/Lonely Man – PLATINUM
I Feel So Bad/Wild In The
Country – GOLD
(Marie's The Name) His Latest
Flame/Little Sister – GOLD
Can't Help Falling In Love/
Rock-a Hula Baby – PLATINUM
Good Luck Charm/Anything That's
Part Of You – PLATINUM
She's Not You/Just Tell Her
Jim Said Hello – GOLD
Return To Sender/Where Do You
Come From? – PLATINUM
One Broken Heart For Sale/
They Remind Me Too Much
Of You – GOLD
(You're The) Devil in Disguise/
Please Don't Drag That String
Around – GOLD
Bossa Nova Baby/
Witchcraft – GOLD
Kissin' Cousins/It Hurts Me – GOLD
Viva Las Vegas/What'd I Say – GOLD
Ain't That Loving You, Baby/
Ask Me – GOLD
Crying In The Chapel/I Believe In
The Man In The Sky – PLATINUM
I'm Yours/Long Lonely
Highway – GOLD
Puppet On A String/Wooden
Heart – GOLD
Blue Christmas/Santa Claus Is
Back In Town – PLATINUM
Tell Me Why/Blue River – GOLD
Frankie And Johnny/Please Don't
Stop Loving Me – GOLD
If I Can Dream/Edge Of
Reality – GOLD
In The Ghetto/Any Day
Now – PLATINUM
Clean Up Your Own Back Yard/
The Fair Is Moving On – GOLD
Suspicious Minds/You'll Think
Of Me – PLATINUM
Don't Cry Daddy/
Rubberneckin' – PLATINUM
Kentucky Rain/My Little
Friend – GOLD
The Wonder Of You/Mama Liked
The Roses – GOLD
I've Lost You/The Next Step
Is Love – GOLD
You Don't Have To Say You Love
Me/Patch It Up – GOLD
I Really Don't Want To Know/
There Goes My Everything – GOLD
Burning Love/It's A Matter
Of Time – PLATINUM
Separate Ways/Always On
My Mind – GOLD
Way Down/Pledging My
Love – PLATINUM
My Way/America – GOLD

16 EXTENDED-PLAY SINGLES

Elvis Presley (including Blue
Suede Shoes) – GOLD
Heartbreak Hotel – GOLD
Elvis Presley (including Shake,
Rattle & Roll) – GOLD
The Real Elvis – PLATINUM
Elvis, Vol. 1 – PLATINUM (x2)
Love Me Tender – PLATINUM
Elvis, Vol. 2 – GOLD
Peace In The Valley – PLATINUM
Loving You, Vol. 1 – GOLD
Loving You, Vol. 2 – PLATINUM
Jailhouse Rock – PLATINUM (x2)
Elvis Sings Christmas
Songs – PLATINUM
King Creole, Vol. 1 – PLATINUM
King Creole, Vol. 2 – PLATINUM
Follow That Dream – PLATINUM
Kid Galahad – GOLD

RECORD CHART STATISTICS

Elvis has had no fewer than 149 songs to appear on *Billboard's* Hot 100 Pop Chart in America. Of these, 114 were in the top 40, 40 were in the top ten, and 18 went to #1. His #1 singles spent a total of 80 weeks at #1. He has also had over 90 charted albums with nine of them reaching #1. These figures are only for the pop charts, and only in America. He was also a leading artist in the American country, R&B, and gospel fields, and his chart success in other countries was substantial.

ELVIS' CHART ALBUMS

Every entry in the *Billboard* Top Twenty US Album chart during his lifetime.

Elvis Presley 1956 – 1
Elvis 1956 – 1
Loving You 1957 – 1
Elvis' Christmas Album 1957 – 1
Elvis' Golden Records 1958 – 3
King Creole 1958 – 2
For LP Fans Only 1959 – 19
Elvis Is Back! 1960 – 2
GI Blues 1960 – 1
His Hand In Mine 1961 – 13
Something For Everybody
1961 – 1
Blue Hawaii 1961 – 1
Pot Luck 1962 – 4
Girls! Girls! Girls! 1962 – 3
It Happened At The
World's Fair 1963 – 4
Elvis' Golden Records,
Vol. 3 1963 – 3
Fun In Acapulco 1963 – 3
Kissin' Cousins 1964 – 6
Roustabout 1964 – 1
Girl Happy 1965 – 8
Elvis For Everyone! 1965 – 10
Harum Scarum 1965 – 8
Frankie And Johnny 1966 – 20
Paradise, Hawaiian
Style 1966 – 15
Spinout 1966 – 18
How Great Thou Art 1967 – 18
Elvis' TV Special 1968 – 8
From Elvis In Memphis 1969 13
From Memphis To Vegas,
From Vegas To Memphis
(2-disc set) 1969 – 12
On Stage 1970 – 13
Elvis Country 1971 – 12
Elvis As Recorded At Madison
Square Garden 1972 – 11
Elvis – Aloha From Hawaii, Via
Satellite (2-disc set) 1973 – 1
Moody Blue 1977 – 3
Elvis In Concert (2-disc set) 1977 – 5

ELVIS' CHART SINGLES

Every entry in the *Billboard* Top Twenty US Singles chart during his lifetime. *(Where two songs are on one entry, it denotes both sides charted as part of the same single, whereas in some cases, such as "Hound Dog" and "Don't Be Cruel", both sides of a single sometimes charted independently.)*

***Heartbreak Hotel** 1956* – 1
***I Was The One** 1956* – 19
***Blue Suede Shoes** 1956* – 20
***I Want You, I Need You, I Love You** 1956* – 1
***Don't Be Cruel** 1956* – 1
***Hound Dog** 1956* – 1
***Love Me Tender** 1956* – 1
***Anyway You Want Me** 1956* – 20
***When My Blue Moon Turns To Gold Again** 1956* – 19
***Love Me** 1957* – 2
***Too Much** 1957* – 1
***All Shook Up** 1957* – 1
***Teddy Bear** 1957* – 1
***Loving You** 1957* – 20
***Jailhouse Rock** 1957* – 1
***Treat Me Nice** 1957* – 18
***Don't** 1957* – 1
***I Beg Of You** 1957* – 8
***Wear My Ring Around Your Neck** 1958* – 2
***Doncha Think It's Time** 1958* – 15
***Hard Headed Woman** 1958* – 1
***One Night** 1958* – 4
***I Got Stung** 1958* – 8
***A Fool Such As I** 1959* – 2
***I Need Your Love Tonight** 1959* – 4
***A Big Hunk O' Love** 1959* – 1
***My Wish Came True** 1959* – 12
***Stuck On You** 1960* – 1
***Fame and Fortune** 1960* – 17
***It's Now or Never** 1960* – 1
***Are You Lonesome Tonight?** 1960* – 1
***I Gotta Know** 1960* – 20
***Surrender** 1961* – 1
***Flaming Star** 1961* – 14
***I Feel So Bad** 1961* – 5
***Little Sister** 1961* – 5
***His Latest Flame** 1961* – 4
***Can't Help Falling In Love** 1961* – 2
***Good Luck Charm** 1962* – 1
***Follow That Dream** 1962* – 15
***She's Not You** 1962* – 5
***Return To Sender** 1962* – 2
***One Broken Heart For Sale** 1963* – 11
***(You're The) Devil In Disguise** 1963* – 3
***Boss Nova Baby** 1963* – 8
***Kissin' Cousins** 1964* – 12
***Such A Night** 1964* – 16
***Ask Me** 1964* – 12
***Ain't That Lovin' You, Baby** 1964* – 16
***Crying In The Chapel** 1965* – 3
***(Such An) Easy Question** 1965* – 11
***I'm Yours** 1965* – 11
***Puppet On A String** 1965* – 14
***Love Letters** 1966* – 19
***If I Can Dream** 1968* – 12
***In The Ghetto** 1969* – 3
***Suspicious Minds** 1969* – 1
***Don't Cry, Daddy/ Rubberneckin'** 1969* – 6
***Kentucky Rain** 1970* – 16
***The Wonder Of You/ Mama Liked The Roses** 1970* – 9
***You Don't Have To Say You Love Me /Patch It Up** 1970* – 11
***Burning Love** 1972* – 2
***Separate Ways** 1972* – 20
***Steamroller Blues/Fool** 1973* – 17
***If You Talk In Your Sleep** 1973* – 17
***Promised Land** 1974* – 14
***My Boy** 1975* – 20
***Way Down** 1977* – 18

GRAMMY AWARDS

Elvis received 14 Grammy nominations from the National Academy of Recording Arts and Sciences (NARAS). The three wins were all for gospel recordings, as follows:

***How Great Thou Art** 1967* (LP)
***He Touched Me** 1972* (LP)
***How Great Thou Art (live Memphis recording)** 1974*

He also received the NARAS Lifetime Achievement Award (known then as the Bing Crosby Award) in 1971. Four of Elvis' recordings have been inducted into the NARAS Hall of Fame:

***Hound Dog** 1956* (inducted 1988)
***Heartbreak Hotel** 1956* (inducted 1995)
***That's All Right** 1954* (inducted 1998)
***Suspicious Minds** 1969* (inducted 1999)

ELVIS ON SCREEN

MOVIES

Title, year of release, director, studio, and length. *(Most movies are available on home video.)*

***Love Me Tender** 1956* (Robert D. Webb) 20th Century Fox (89 mins)
***Loving You** 1957* (Hal Kanter) Paramount (101 mins)
***Jailhouse Rock** 1957* (Richard Thorpe) Metro-Goldwyn-Mayer (96 mins)
***King Creole** 1958* (Michael Curtiz) Paramount (116 mins)
***GI Blues** 1960* (Norman Taurog) Paramount (104 mins)
***Flaming Star** 1960* (Don Siegel) 20th Century Fox (101 mins)
***Wild In The Country** 1961* (Philip Dunne) 20th Century Fox (114 mins)
***Blue Hawaii** 1961* (Norman Taurog) Paramount (101 mins)
***Follow That Dream** 1962* (Gordon Douglas) United Artists (110 mins)
***Kid Galahad** 1962* (Phil Karlson) United Artists (95 mins)
***Girls! Girls! Girls!** 1962* (Norman Taurog) Paramount (106 mins)
***It Happened At The World's Fair** 1963* (Norman Taurog) Metro-Goldwyn-Mayer (105 mins)
***Fun In Acapulco** 1963* (Richard Thorpe) Paramount (97 mins)
***Kissin' Cousins** 1964* (Gene Nelson) Metro-Goldwyn-Mayer (96 mins)
***Viva Las Vegas** 1964* (George Sidney) Metro-Goldwyn-Mayer (86 mins)
***Roustabout** 1964* (John Rich) Paramount (101 mins)
***Girl Happy** 1964* (Boris Sagal) Metro-Goldwyn-Mayer (96 mins)
***Tickle Me** 1965* (Norman Taurog) Allied Artists (90 mins)
***Harum Scarum** 1965* (Gene Nelson) Metro-Goldwyn-Mayer (95 mins)
***Frankie And Johnny** 1966* (Frederick de Cordova) United Artists (87 mins)
***Paradise, Hawaiian Style** 1965* (Michael Moore) Paramount (91 mins)
***Spinout** 1966* (Norman Taurog) Metro-Goldwyn-Mayer (90 mins)
***Easy Come, Easy Go** 1967* (John Rich) Paramount (95 mins)
***Double Trouble** 1967* (Norman Taurog) Metro-Goldwyn-Mayer (90 mins)
***Clambake** 1967* (Arthur H. Nadel) United Artists (97 mins)
***Stay Away Joe** 1968* (Peter Tewksbury) Metro-Goldwyn-Mayer (102 mins)
***Speedway** 1968* (Norman Taurog) Metro-Goldwyn-Mayer (94 mins)
***Live A Little, Love A Little** 1968* (Norman Taurog) Metro-Goldwyn-Mayer (90 mins)
***Charro!** 1969* (Charles Marquis Warren) National General (98 mins)
***The Trouble With Girls** 1969* (Peter Tewksbury) Metro-Goldwyn Mayer (97 mins)

***Change Of Habit** 1969* (Wiliam Graham) Universal (93 mins)

DOCUMENTARY FILMS

***Elvis, That's The Way It Is** 1970* (Denis Sanders) Metro-Goldwyn-Mayer (97 mins)

***Elvis On Tour** 1972* (Pierre Adidge, Robert Abel) Metro-Goldwyn-Mayer (93 mins)

POSTHUMOUS BIOGRAPHICAL MOVIES

***Elvis** 1979* (John Carpenter) Dick Clark Motion Pictures 150 mins (TV movie)

***This Is Elvis** 1981* (Malcolm Leo, Andrew Solt) Warner Bros (101 mins)

TELEVISION SPECIALS

Elvis** 1968 **(AKA The '68 Comeback Special')

***Elvis: Aloha From Hawaii, Via Satellite** 1973*

***Elvis In Concert** 1977*

TV GUEST APPEARANCES

Shows in their entirety have not been put out on home video, but extensive clips appear in various documentaries and specials.

January 28, 1956
Stage Show (The Dorsey Brothers)

February 4, 1956
Stage Show (The Dorsey Brothers)

February 11, 1956
Stage Show (The Dorsey Brothers)

February 18, 1956,
Stage Show (The Dorsey Brothers)

March 17, 1956
Stage Show (The Dorsey Brothers)

March 24, 1956
Stage Show (The Dorsey Brothers)

April 3, 1956
The Milton Berle Show

June 5, 1956
The Milton Berle Show

July 1, 1956
The Steve Allen Show

September 9, 1956
Toast Of The Town (Ed Sullivan)

October 28, 1956
Toast Of The Town (Ed Sullivan)

January 6, 1957
Toast Of The Town (Ed Sullivan)

March 26, 1960
Frank Sinatra Timex Special ("Welcome Home, Elvis")

POSTHUMOUS TV AND VIDEO DOCUMENTARIES

***Elvis '56** 1985*
A television documentary about the first year of Elvis' international fame. Lots of footage from the 1950s' TV appearances.

***Elvis Presley's Graceland** 1984*
A televised tour of Graceland hosted by Priscilla Beaulieu Presley. No longer available on home video.

***Elvis, One Night With You** 1985*
A TV special featuring unseen footage from the 1968 TV special.

***Elvis, The Great Performances** 1991*
(Original Version) A two-volume video collection of some of Elvis' greatest singing performances from movies, TV specials, and TV guest appearances.

***Elvis, The Great Performances** 1992*
(Televised Version). A reedited version of the home video set, created for network television and hosted from Graceland by Priscilla Presley.

***Elvis (TV Series)** 1990*
A short-lived, but highly acclaimed network television series about Elvis' early career. Elvis is portrayed by Michael St. Gerard. Originally aired on ABC-TV in 30-minute episodes in 1990. In the years since, TNT has grouped the episodes together for several long-form broadcasts. No home video release.

***Elvis, The Lost Performances** 1992*
A home video release of unseen footage from the concert films *Elvis, That's The Way It Is* (1970) and *Elvis on Tour* (1972).

***Elvis In Hollywood (The '50s)** 1993*
Video documentary of Elvis' movie career in the 1950s. Footage from his first four films, including some previously unseen outtakes, and interviews with friends and colleagues associated with these films.

***Elvis, His Life And Times** 1987/1993*
A 1987 BBC TV documentary of Elvis' life, reedited in 1993 for a syndicated TV special hosted by Mac Davis and Lisa Hartman Black. A video without Davis and Black hosting was released in 1993.

***America Comes To Graceland** 1993*
A syndicated TV special about Elvis' life and legacy, hosted from Graceland by Mac Davis and Lisa Hartman Black. No home video release.

***Elvis, Touch The Dream, A New Generation** 1995*
A syndicated TV special about Elvis' life and today's new generation of Elvis fans. Hosted by Travis Tritt. No home video release.

***Virtual Graceland** 1995*
The critically acclaimed 2-disc CD-ROM tour of Graceland. Go on a programmed guided tour, or customize the tour for yourself through the main choices of material to access. Includes home movie, newsreel and performance clips, interviews with people from Elvis' personal and professional life, information about Elvis' life and career, and more. No home video version available. Primary production in 1993/94. Released in 1996.

***Elvis Presley, The Alternate Aloha Concert** 1996*
Taped in front of a live audience on January 12, 1973, this is the rehearsal show Elvis did for his January 14 satellite television special *Elvis: Aloha from Hawaii, Via Satellite.* Released on home video in 1996.

***Elvis Presley's Graceland, Official Video** 1997*
The official video tour of Graceland. Shot and released in 1997. Beautiful footage of the full tour of Graceland and its related attractions, plus photography, newsreel footage, and home movies. Highlights of Elvis' life and career and of his years at Graceland. Approximate running time: 50 minutes. (*This video was produced before Elvis' parents' bedroom was added to the tour in 1998. A revised edition sometime in the future will include this room.*)

***Finding Graceland** 1999*
First publicized with the working title "The Road to Graceland." A fictional film shot in 1997 with a few key scenes filmed on location at Graceland. It stars Harvey Keitel as a man of good deeds who thinks he is Elvis Presley and is making his way home to Graceland 20 years after his supposed death. Also stars Johnathon Schaech and Bridget Fonda. Premiered on Cinemax in May 1999 with home video and DVD release the following August.

The Century 1999

ABC News'/Peter Jennings' 12-hour, six-part documentary of the events that shaped the 20th century. Original air dates: March 29, April 1, April 3, April 5, April 8, and April 10, 1999. The rise of Elvis Presley's career is the focus of half the installment that was presented on April 5. This documentary has also run on the History Channel and has been released in a home video set.

***He Touched Me: The Gospel Music Of Elvis Presley** 1999*

A two-part documentary produced by the Gaither Management Group in association with Elvis Presley Enterprises. It was aired as two 45-minute TV specials on TNN (one hour each with commercials). Part I first aired November 1999. Part II first aired January 2000. The home video set is an expanded version—two 90-minute tapes released in November 1999.

KEY DATES

1912 April 25

Gladys Love Smith is born.

1916 April 10

Vernon Elvis Presley is born.

1933 June 17

Gladys Smith and Vernon Presley are married.

1935 January 8

Elvis Aaron Presley is born.

1941 Fall

Elvis enters East Tupelo Consolidated School.

1945 August 18

Elvis sings "Old Shep" in a talent contest at the Mississippi–Alabama Fair and Dairy Show.

1946 January 8

His parents give him a guitar for his 11th birthday.

September

Elvis enters sixth grade at Milam Junior High, Tupelo.

1948 November

Elvis plays his guitar and sings "Leaf on a Tree" for his Milam Junior High class in Tupelo as a farewell.

November 6

The Presley family move to Memphis.

November 8

Elvis enrolls at Humes High School, Memphis.

1953 April 9

"Elvis Prestly" on the bill at the Humes High annual Minstrel Show.

June 3

High school diploma presented to Elvis at Ellis Auditorium, Memphis.

July

Elvis works at Parker Machinists Shop right after graduation.

Summer

He makes an acetate record at his own expense at the Memphis Recording Service (aka Sun).

Fall

Working at the Precision Tool Company, operating a hand drill and drill press.

1954 January

Elvis makes another demo acetate, attracting the attention of Sun boss Sam Phillips.

March 19

Elvis leaves Precision Tools.

April 20

Begins work at Crown Electric.

June 26

Sam Phillips' assistant Marion Kreisker rings Elvis to come in and try out a new song at the studios, though the result is not a success.

July 5

With guitarist Scotty Moore and bass player Bill Black, Elvis cuts "That's All Right" at Sun Studios.

July 8

Local DJ Dewey Phillips plays an acetate of the recording on his radio show.

July 12

Scotty Moore becomes manager and agent of the new group.

July 17

The trio of Elvis, Scotty, and Bill debut with two songs at the Bel Air Club, Memphis.

July 26

Contract signed with Sun Records.

August 28

His Sun single "Blue Moon of Kentucky" enters *Billboard* Country & Western chart for the Mid-South region.

October 2

Debut appearance on the Grand Ole Opry live/radio show.

October 16

Debut appearance on the Louisiana Hayride live/radio show.

November 6

One-year contract for 52 Saturday night Hayride appearances.

1955 January

Elvis signs a contract with Bob Neal, who becomes his manager.

Spring–Summer

Elvis, Scotty, and Bill continue touring on their own and in package shows, including shows with Hank Snow in which Colonel Tom Parker is involved.

August 15

Elvis signs a management contract with Hank Snow Attractions, owned equally by Snow and Parker. Bob Neal remains involved as an advisor.

November 20

Elvis signs his first contract with RCA Records.

1956 January 10

First recording session for RCA, in Nashville. Songs include "Heartbreak Hotel."

January 27

"Heartbreak Hotel"/"I Was the One" is released by RCA and sells over 300,000 copies in its first three weeks on the market.

January 28

Appearance on *Stage Show*, starring Tommy and Jimmy Dorsey on CBS TV, his first network television appearance.

March 3

"Heartbreak Hotel" enters *Billboard* national chart.

March 13

RCA releases *Elvis Presley*, Elvis' first album.

April 1

Screen test for Paramount Studios in Hollywood.

April 3

Elvis appears on *The Milton Berle Show* on ABC TV.

April 6

Elvis signs a seven-year movie contract with Hal Wallis and Paramount Pictures.

April 23–May 9

Two-week engagement at the New Frontier Hotel in Las Vegas.

April 28

"Heartbreak Hotel" hits #1 in the US singles chart.

May 5

Elvis' first LP makes #1 in *Billboard* album chart.

July 1

Appearance on *The Steve Allen Show* on NBC.

August

Elvis begins shooting his first movie, *Love Me Tender*.

September 9

First of three appearances on *The Ed Sullivan Show*, the top television program of the era.

September 26

Triumphant "homecoming" at the Mississippi-Alabama Fair and Dairy Show in Tupelo, Mississippi.

October 28

Elvis makes his second of three appearances with Ed Sullivan.

November 16

Love Me Tender premieres at the Paramount Theater in New York City.

December 31

The front page of *The Wall Street Journal* reports that in the past few months Elvis merchandise has grossed $22 million in sales.

1957 January 6

Third and final appearance on Ed Sullivan's *Toast of the Town Show*, seen only from the waist up.

January 22

Elvis begins production of his second movie, *Loving You*.

March 25

Purchase of Graceland Mansion finalized, for himself, his parents, and his grandmother to live in.

April 2, 3

Elvis performs outside the United States for the first time, during which he plays the Canadian cities of Toronto and Ottawa.

May 6

Work begins on his third motion picture, *Jailhouse Rock* for MGM.

July 9

Loving You premieres and quickly reaches the top 10 at the box office.

August 31

Elvis performs in Vancouver, the last time he will perform in concert outside the United States.

September 27

Elvis returns once more to the town of his birth to perform, at a benefit for the proposed Elvis Presley Youth Recreation Center in Tupelo.

October 17

Jailhouse Rock premieres in Memphis.

November 10, 11

Elvis performs shows in Hawaii for the first time.

December 20

Elvis officially receives his draft notice for service in the US Army.

December 25

First Christmas at Graceland.

1958 January 20

Shooting begins on his fourth motion picture, *King Creole*.

March 15

Two shows in Memphis are to be his last stage performances until after his army release in 1960.

March 24

Elvis Presley is inducted into the US Army at the Memphis Draft Board and is assigned serial number 53310761.

March 25

Elvis gets his famous GI haircut at Fort Chaffee, Arkansas.

March 29

Private Presley arrives at Fort Hood, Texas for basic training and is stationed there for six months.

June 10

After basic training, while on his first leave, Elvis has a recording session, his last until 1960.

July

King Creole, Elvis' fourth motion picture, opens nationally. The reviews are the best he will ever have for his acting.

August 12

Elvis is granted emergency leave to visit his mother who has been hospitalized with acute hepatitis.

August 14

Gladys Presley dies in the early hours of August 14, at age 46.

August 15

Gladys Presley's funeral takes place at Memphis Funeral Home and Forest Hill Cemetery.

August 25

Elvis reports back to Fort Hood.

September 19

Elvis boards a troop train to New York, on his way to service in Germany. He boards the troop ship USS *Randall*.

October 1

Arrival in Germany, where he is stationed at Friedberg.

1959 January 8

Interview off-camera via trans-Atlantic telephone by Dick Clark on his *American Bandstand* show on ABC-TV.

June 13

Start of a two-week leave in which Elvis visits Munich, then goes clubbing in Paris, which includes a visit to the Lido.

September 13

Elvis meets Priscilla Ann Beaulieu, brought to his house in Germany by a mutual friend.

1960 January 20

Promotion to Sergeant.

March 1

Elvis leaves Germany, arriving in New Jersey the next day for a press conference.

March 5

Official discharge from active duty.

March 7

Arrival back in Memphis.

March 8

Press conference at Graceland in his father's office behind the mansion.

March 20

First post-army recording session.

March 21

Elvis receives a first degree black belt in karate, an interest he developed in the army.

March 26

Recording of a special "Welcome Home, Elvis" edition of Frank Sinatra's ABC-TV variety show.

April 21

Filming and recording begin for his first post-army movie, his fifth film, *GI Blues*.

May 8

ABC airs Frank Sinatra's "Welcome Home, Elvis" edition of his variety show, which attracts a 41.5% share of the national television audience.

July 3

Vernon Presley marries divorcee and mother of three sons, Davada (Dee) Stanley, an American whom he met in Germany.

August 1

Work begins on his sixth movie, *Flaming Star*, a drama with limited music.

November 6

Elvis begins recording and filming for his seventh film, *Wild in the Country*.

November 23

GI Blues opens nationally to warm

reviews and big box office sales and is among the 15 top-grossing films of the year.

Late December

Flaming Star opens nationally to good reviews but, unlike *GI Blues*, this dramatic film with little singing does not set the box office on fire.

1961 February 25

"Elvis Presley Day" in Memphis includes a luncheon in his honor, and two shows at Ellis Auditorium to benefit around 38 charities in the Memphis area.

March 25

Elvis arrives in Hawaii for a concert at Pearl Harbor, a benefit to help fund the building of the USS *Arizona* Memorial.

March 27

Elvis remains in Hawaii to start location filming for his eighth motion picture, *Blue Hawaii.*

June 22

Wild in the Country opens nationally to mixed reviews.

July 2

Elvis starts recording and filming for his ninth motion picture, *Follow That Dream.*

October 23

Work commences on his 10th movie, *Kid Galahad,* which he will complete in January.

November 22

Blue Hawaii opens nationally to warm reviews and gets to #2 on the box office charts. It becomes the top-grossing film of Elvis' career thus far.

1962 March 26

Elvis begins filming and recording for his 11th motion picture, *Girls! Girls! Girls!,* working in Hollywood and location shooting in Hawaii.

May 23

Follow That Dream opens nationally and gets to #5 on the box office charts. It is warmly reviewed and does fairly well in sales.

August 28

Elvis reports for pre-production on his 12th motion picture, *It Happened At The World's Fair.* Shooting is in Hollywood and at the World's Fair in Seattle.

August 29

Kid Galahad opens nationally and does reasonably well financially with a brief stay in the top 10 on the box office chart.

November 21

Girls! Girls! Girls! opens nationally and rivals *Blue Hawaii* in box office success.

December 19

Priscilla Beaulieu arrives from West Germany to spend the Christmas holidays with him at Graceland.

1963 January 22

Soundtrack recording begins for Elvis' 13th film, *Fun In Acapulco.*

April 10

It Happened At The World's Fair opens nationally and does relatively well at the box office, though its plot is the most frivolous of any Elvis movie so far.

July 9

Elvis begins work on the music for his 14th motion picture, *Viva Las Vegas*, co-starring Ann-Margret.

October 7

Production begins for Elvis' 15th movie, *Kissin' Cousins.*

November 27

Fun in Acapulco opens nationally and quickly goes to #5 at the box office.

1964 February 13

Elvis presents the former presidential yacht *Potomac,* which he purchased for $55,000, as a gift to St. Jude Children's Research Hospital in Memphis.

March 5

Elvis reports for filming of his 16th motion picture, *Roustabout,* co-starring Hollywood legend Barbara Stanwyck.

March 6

Kissin' Cousins opens nationally.

June 10

Elvis begins recording the music for his next film, *Girl Happy.*

June 17

Viva Las Vegas opens nationally and goes to #8 at the box office. The picture is welcomed as one of the better Elvis movies of this period.

October 12

Elvis begins shooting his 18th motion picture, *Tickle Me.*

November 11

Roustabout opens, and hits #8 at the box office.

1965 March 15

Principal photography begins for *Harum Scarum,* Elvis' 19th motion picture.

April 7

Girl Happy is released nationally and does relatively good business.

May 24

Elvis starts filming for his 20th motion picture, to be released out of chronology as his 21st, *Frankie and Johnny.*

June 24

Elvis donates $50,000 to the Motion Picture Relief Fund, with Barbara Stanwyck and Frank Sinatra accepting for the organization.

July 7

Tickle Me opens nationwide.

August 2

Elvis commences work on the soundtrack music for his 21st motion picture, *Paradise, Hawaiian Style.*

August 27

The Beatles visit with Elvis for several hours at his home in California and have an informal jam session.

November 24

Harum Scarum opens nationally and hits #11 at the box office. The soundtrack album goes to #8.

1966 February 14

Elvis starts recording and filming for his 22nd movie, *Spinout.*

March 30

Frankie and Johnny opens nationally but fails at the box office.

June 27

Elvis reports to MGM studios for his 23rd motion picture (to be the released), *Double Trouble.*

July 6

Paradise, Hawaiian Style is released and doesn't do well. The soundtrack album peaks at #15.

September 27

Preproduction starts filming for Elvis' 24th motion picture (the 23rd to be released), *Easy Come, Easy Go.*

November 23

Spinout is released nationally.

December 24

Elvis formally proposes marriage to Priscilla.

1967 February 8

Elvis buys a 163-acre ranch in Mississippi, renaming it the Circle G.

February 21

Elvis begins soundtrack recording for *Clambake*, his 25th movie.

March 22

Easy Come, Easy Go opens nationally just before Easter.

April 5

Double Trouble opens nationally. Although a better picture than some of his earlier efforts, it too fails at the box office.

May 1

Elvis and Priscilla are married in a private ceremony in front of a small group of family and friends at the Aladdin Hotel in Las Vegas, just after 9:30 AM.

May 29

Elvis and Priscilla dress in their wedding clothes for a second wedding reception at Graceland, for family and friends who were not in Las Vegas for the wedding.

June 19

Elvis begins work on his 26th movie (to be the 27th released), *Speedway.*

July 12

On the movie set, Elvis announces the news of Priscilla's pregnancy.

September 9

Principal photography begins for Elvis' 27th movie (to be the 26th released), *Stay Away, Joe.*

November 22

Clambake is released nationally and goes to #15 at the box office.

1968 February 1

Priscilla gives birth to Lisa Marie Presley at 5.01 PM, at the Baptist Hospital in Memphis.

March 8

Stay Away, Joe opens to mixed reviews.

March 13

Filming begins for Elvis' 28th movie, *Live a Little, Love a Little.* A more adult kind of comedy/melodrama, a real departure from the typical Presley film.

June 12

Speedway is released nationally.

June 25

A press conference is held during rehearsals for his first television special.

June 27, 28, 29, and 30

Videotaping takes place for the TV special, usually known as *The '68 Special* or *The '68 Comeback,* the actual name being simply *Elvis.*

July 22

Principal photography starts for Elvis' 29th movie, *Charro!,* a dramatic western, again a very different kind of role. Elvis grows a beard for this.

October 23

Elvis starts work on the soundtrack for his 30th movie, *The Trouble With Girls (And How To Get Into It).*

October 23

Live A Little, Love A Little opens in the US, doing very well at the box office.

December 3

Elvis, the 1968 TV special, airs on NBC and is one of this biggest television hits of the year, receiving rave reviews from the public and the critics alike.

1969 January 13

Elvis begins recording sessions at American Studios in Memphis, the first time he has recorded in the city since he recorded for Sun in 1955.

March 5

Elvis returns to Hollywood to film his 31st, and final, acting role in a motion picture, in *Change of Habit.*

March 13

Charro! opens in theaters across the nation.

July 31

Elvis commences a four-week, 57-show engagement at the new International Hotel in Las Vegas, the largest showroom in the city.

September 3

The Trouble With Girls (And How To Get Into It) is released nationally.

November 10

Elvis' final fictional movie, *Change of Habit,* opens nationwide.

1970 January 26

Start of a month-long return engagement at the International Hotel. This time he breaks his own attendance records.

February 27

A press conference prior to shows at the Houston Astrodome on the same day, and the next, and March 1. The six shows attracted a record 207,494 people.

June 4

Start of five days of recording sessions in Nashville.

July 14

Back to Las Vegas for rehearsals for another month-long engagement at the International, MGM shooting the documentary *Elvis – That's The Way It Is.*

September 9–14

Elvis takes his show on a nine-city tour, with MGM filming portions of the first show for use in *Elvis – That's The Way It Is.*

November 10–17

Elvis does a successful eight-city concert tour.

November 11

Elvis, That's The Way It Is, his 32nd film, opens in theaters to good reviews and good box office.

December 21

Elvis meets with President Richard Nixon at the White House.

1971 January 16

Elvis is decorated as one of the Ten Outstanding Young Men of the Year by the United States Junior Chamber of Commerce (The Jaycees).

January 26

Another month-long engagement opens at the International Hotel in Las Vegas.

March 15

A recording session in Nashville is cancelled due to pain and inflammation in one eye. Elvis is diagnosed with secondary glaucoma.

May 15

Elvis has recording sessions in Nashville, some of the tracks being for his forthcoming album *Elvis Sings The Wonderful World Of Christmas.*

June 1

The two-room house Elvis was born in opens to the public for tours, having been restored by the East Heights Garden Club in Tupelo.

June 29

Memphis City Council votes to rename a long stretch of Highway 51 South, part of which runs in front of Graceland, Elvis Presley Boulevard.

July 20

Elvis starts a two-week engagement at the Sahara Hotel in Lake Tahoe, Nevada.

August 9–September 6

Elvis plays the second annual "Elvis Summer Festival" at the International Hotel, which has been renamed the Las Vegas Hilton International Hotel.

August 28

Elvis is presented with the Bing Crosby Award from the National

Academy of Recording Arts and Sciences (which also presents the Grammy awards).

November 5

Elvis commences a 12-city concert tour.

December 30

Elvis announces that he and Priscilla are to separate.

1972 January 26–February 23

Elvis plays another successful engagement at the Hilton in Las Vegas.

March 30

Filming begins in a Hollywood recording studio for another documentary, *Elvis on Tour,* which MGM will also film on and off stage during his 15-city concert tour.

June 9, 10, and 11

Elvis' first-ever concert shows in New York, at Madison Square Garden. John Lennon, George Harrison, and Bob Dylan are among the music stars attending.

June 18

Just nine days after it is recorded, RCA rush-releases a live album from one of the New York shows—*Elvis as Recorded at Madison Square Garden*.

July 26

Elvis and Priscilla's separation is formalized. A divorce is to come. Elvis has begun seeing Linda Thompson, his main female companion until late 1976.

August 4–September 4

Elvis plays a month-long engagement at the Hilton in Vegas.

September 5

Elvis holds a press conference in Vegas announcing plans for a TV concert to be broadcast via satellite around the world from Hawaii.

November 1

Elvis on Tour opens to good reviews and good box office, and later its producers receive the Golden Globe Award for Best Documentary of 1972.

November 8–18

A seven-city tour includes Honolulu, where Elvis announces that his upcoming satellite show will be a benefit for the Kui Lee Cancer Fund.

1973 January 14

Elvis makes television and entertainment history with his *Elvis: Aloha from Hawaii, Via Satellite* special, one of the all-time great moments of his career.

January 26–February 23

Elvis plays an engagement at the Las Vegas Hilton.

March 1

Elvis and the Colonel sell RCA the singer's royalty rights on Elvis' entire recording catalog up to that point in time.

April 4

The Aloha special is seen on American television for the first time, having been broadcast live to territories across the Pacific.

April 22

Elvis commences an eight-city concert tour.

May 4–16

An intended 17-day engagement at the Sahara Hotel in Lake Tahoe, Nevada, is cut short due to ill-health.

June 20–July 3

Another cross-country concert tour.

July 21

Elvis records a few songs at the Stax Recording Studio in Memphis—his first time back to record in Memphis since 1969.

August 6–September 3

Back to the Vegas Hilton for another engagement.

October 9

Elvis and Priscilla make a court appearance together and their divorce is granted. They will continue to be close friends.

October 15–November 1

Elvis is hospitalized in Memphis for recurring pneumonia and pleurisy, an enlarged colon, and hepatitis.

December 10

Elvis returns to the Stax Recording Studio in Memphis for a week of sessions.

1974 January 26–February 9

Another season of appearances at the Las Vegas Hilton.

March 1–20

Elvis tours with concert dates throughout the South.

March 3

Elvis returns to the Houston Astrodome and sets a one-day attendance record with his two shows.

March 16

Elvis plays Memphis, the first time since 1961, with four shows in two days. The LP *Elvis Recorded Live On Stage in Memphis* is recorded at one of the shows.

May 16–26

Another short season at the Sahara in Lake Tahoe.

June 15–July 2

Touring concerts dates.

August 19–September 2

Back to the Hilton in Vegas for an engagement.

September 27–October 14

Elvis is on tour again, including the Sahara Hotel, Lake Tahoe, October 11–14.

1975 January 29–February 14

Elvis is hospitalized with health and prescription problems again.

March

Elvis' live recording of "How Great Thou Art" from the *Live On Stage In Memphis* album wins the Grammy for Best Inspirational Performance.

March 18–April 1

Engagement at the Hilton.

April 24–July 24

Elvis tours in concert.

August 18–September 5

Elvis opens in Vegas but ends his engagement on the 20th and is hospitalized in Memphis until September 5.

November 27

The renovation of a Convair 880 jet Elvis bought earlier in the year is complete, and he takes his first flight in the *Lisa Marie*.

December 2–15

Elvis returns to the Hilton in Vegas to make up for the shows that were canceled during his previous engagement.

December 31

Elvis performs a special New Year's Eve concert in Pontiac, Michigan, and sets a single performance attendance record of 62,500.

1976 February 2

During a week of recording in the den at Graceland, RCA bring in mobile equipment, for the album *From Elvis Presley Boulevard, Memphis, Tennessee.*

March 17–22

Elvis tours in concert.

April 21–27

Elvis tours in concert.

April 30–May 9

An engagement at the Sahara Hotel, Lake Tahoe in Nevada.

May 27–June 6

Elvis tours in concert.

June 25–July 5

Elvis tours in concert.

July 23–August 5

Elvis tours in concert.

August 27–September 8

Elvis tours in concert.

October 14–27

Elvis tours in concert.

October 29–30

Continuation of recording in the den at Graceland.

Early November

Elvis and Linda Thompson, his steady girlfriend since 1972, split up.

Late November

Elvis meets Ginger Alden who will be his steady girlfriend until his death.

November 24–30

Elvis tours in concert.

December 2–12

Elvis plays the Hilton in Vegas for what will turn out to be the last time.

December 27–31

Elvis tours in concert, ending with a special New Year's Eve concert in Pittsburgh, Pennsylvania.

1977 February 12–21

Elvis tours in concert.

March 23–30

Elvis tours in concert.

April 1–5

Elvis is hospitalized in Memphis and tour shows scheduled for March 31–April 3 are canceled.

April 2–May 31/June 1–2

Elvis tours in concert.

June 17–26

Elvis tours in concert. Shows on June 19, 20, and 21 are recorded for a live album and are videotaped for an upcoming television special.

June 26

A concert at Indianapolis, Indiana's Market Square Arena. This will turn out to be his very last concert performance.

June 27–August 15

Elvis relaxes in Memphis and prepares for the next leg of touring for 1977.

August 16

Shortly after midnight Elvis returns to Graceland from a late-night visit to the dentist. He retires to his master suite at Graceland around 7:00 AM By late morning, Elvis Presley is dead of heart failure. It is announced by mid-afternoon. In a matter of hours the shock registers around the world.

SELECTED READING

Reel Elvis!
(Pauline Bartel) Elvis' movie information including cast lists, synopsis, and trivia.

Elvis Collectibles: Third Edition
(Rosalind Cranor) Pictorial and value estimates of Elvis memorabilia.

Did Elvis Sing In Your Hometown?
(Lee Cotton) All the available facts covering Elvis on tour in the 1950s.

Did Elvis Sing In Your Hometown, Too?
(Lee Cotton) All the available facts covering Elvis on during the years 1968–1977.

Intimate & Rare
(Joe Esposito and Elena Oumano) Longtime friend and staff member Joe Esposito shares his memories of Elvis from their years together.

The King on the Road
(Robert Gordon) A spectacular account of Elvis' live performances throughout his career.

The Elvis Treasures
(Robert Gordon) Biographicat text and removable facsimiles of documents and memorabilia from the Graceland Archives.

Elvis Presley's Graceland: The Official Guidebook
(Graceland) Photographic journey through the entire Graceland tour includes biographical and historical information.

When Elvis Died
(Neal and Janice Gregory) Chronicles the reaction of the press and the world to Elvis' death. Revised edition in 1992 includes additional chapters on the Elvis phenomenon during the first 15 years following his death.

Last Train to Memphis
(Peter Guralnick) The first volume of the acclaimed biography of Elvis Presley.

Careless Love
(Peter Guralnick) The concluding volume of Guralnick's two-part biography.

Elvis: Day by Day
(Peter Guralnick and Ernst Jorgensen) The definitive record of Elvis' career.

Memphis: Elvis Style
(Cindy Hazen and Mike Freeman) A guide to all the places in Memphis that played a vital role in Elvis' life.

The Official Price Guide to Elvis Presley Records & Memorabilia: Second Edition
(House of Collectibles) Descriptions of and value estimates of Elvis' records. Includes some memorabilia.

Elvis Presley–A Life In Music
(Ernst Jorgensen) Every recording session Elvis held between 1953 and 1977, including home and private sessions as well as live concert recordings.

Elvis: Word for Word
(Jerry Osborne) 43 years of collecting records and tapes of anything Elvis spoke into a microphone.

Elvis & Me
(Priscilla Beaulieu Presley) Priscilla's own recollections of life with, and after, Elvis.

Index

Acknowledgments & Picture Credits

The author wishes to thank the staff at Elvis Presley Enterprises for their invaluable help in researching this book, particularly Pete Davidson, LaVonne Gaw, Kelly Hill, and Todd Morgan.